D1740818

THE EUROPEAN UNION SERIES

General Editors: Neill Nugent, William E. Paterson

The European Union series provides an authoritative library on the European Union, ranging from general introductory texts to definitive assessments of key institutions and actors, issues, policies and policy processes, and the role of member states.

Books in the series are written by leading scholars in their fields and reflect the most up-to-date research and debate. Particular attention is paid to accessibility and clear presentation for a wide audience of students, practitioners and interested general readers.

The series editors are **Neill Nugent**, Emeritus Professor of Politics at Manchester Metropolitan University, UK, and **William E. Paterson**, Honorary Professor in German and European Studies, University of Aston. Their co-editor until his death in July 1999, **Vincent Wright**, was a Fellow of Nuffield College, Oxford University.

Feedback on the series and book proposals are always welcome and should be sent to Andrew Malvern, Palgrave, 4 Crinan Street, London N1 9XW, or by e-mail to **andrew.malvern@palgrave.com**

General textbooks

Published

Laurie Buonanno and Neill Nugent **Policies and Policy Processes of the European Union**

Desmond Dinan **Encyclopedia of the European Union [Rights: Europe only]**

Desmond Dinan **Europe Recast: A History of the European Union (2nd edn) [Rights: Europe only]**

Desmond Dinan **Ever Closer Union: An Introduction to European Integration (4th edn) [Rights: Europe only]**

Mette Eilstrup Sangiovanni (ed.) **Debates on European Integration: A Reader**

Simon Hix and Bjørn Høyland **The Political System of the European Union (3rd edn)**

Dirk Leuffen, Berthold Rittberger and Frank Schimmelfennig **Differentiated Integration**

Paul Magnette **What is the European Union? Nature and Prospects**

John McCormick **Understanding the European Union: A Concise Introduction (6th edn)**

Brent F. Nelsen and Alexander Stubb **The European Union: Readings on the Theory and Practice of European Integration (4th edn) [Rights: Europe only]**

Neill Nugent (ed.) **European Union Enlargement**

Neill Nugent **The Government and Politics of the European Union (8th edn)**

John Peterson and Elizabeth Bomberg **Decision-Making in the European Union**

Ben Rosamond **Theories of European Integration**

Sabine Saurugger **Theoretical Approaches to European Integration**

Ingeborg Tömmel **The European Union: What it is and How it Works**

Esther Versluis, Mendeltje van Keulen and Paul Stephenson **Analyzing the European Union Policy Process**

Hubert Zimmermann and Andreas Dür (eds) **Key Controversies in European Integration (2nd edn)**

Also planned

The European Union and Global Politics

The Political Economy of European Integration

The European Parliament

Ariadna Ripoll Servent

First published 2018 by
RED GLOBE PRESS

Red Globe Press in the UK is an imprint of Springer Nature Limited, registered in England, company number 785998, of 4 Crinan Street, London, N1 9XW.

Red Globe Press® is a registered trademark in the United States, the United Kingdom, Europe and other countries.

ISBN 978–1–137–40708–5 hardback
ISBN 978–1–137–40707–8 paperback

This book is printed on paper suitable for recycling and made from fully managed and sustained forest sources. Logging, pulping and manufacturing processes are expected to conform to the environmental regulations of the country of origin.

A catalogue record for this book is available from the British Library.

A catalog record for this book is available from the Library of Congress.

Summary of Contents

Contents

List of Boxes, Figures and Tables

Boxes

Figures

Tables

Abbreviations and Acronyms

ACP	African, Caribbean and Pacific Group of States
ACTA	Anti-Counterfeiting Trade Agreement
AD	Administrators
AETR	European Agreement on Road Transport
AFCO	Committee on Constitutional Affairs
AfD	Alternative for Germany
AFET	Committee on Foreign Affairs
AGRI	Committee on Agriculture and Rural Development
ALDE	Alliance of Liberals and Democrats for Europe
ASEAN	Association of Southeast Asian Nations
AST	Assistants
AST/SC	Assistants and Secretarial Posts
ATTAC	Association for the Taxation of Financial Transactions and for Citizens' Action
BEUC	European Consumer Organisation
BUDG	Committee on Budgets
BSE	Bovine Spongiform Encephalopathy
CAP	Common Agricultural Policy
CDU	Christian Democratic Party
CETA	Comprehensive Economic and Trade Agreement
CFSP	Common Foreign and Security Policy
CJEU	Court of Justice of the European Union
CLIM	Temporary Committee on Climate Change
CONT	Committee on Budgetary Control
COSAC	Conference of Parliamentary Committees for Union Affairs of Parliaments of the European Union
CRIM	Special Committee on Organised Crime, Corruption and Money Laundering
CRIS	Temporary Committee on Financial, Economic and Social Crisis
CSDP	Common Security and Defence Policy
CSU	Christian Social Union
CULT	Committee on Culture and Education
CWP	Commission's Work Programme
D66	Democraten 66 (Democrats 66)
DEVE	Committee on Development
DG	Directorate-General
DG COMM	Directorate-General for Communication

DROI	Subcommittee on Human Rights
EASO	European Asylum Support Office
EC	European Community
ECB	European Central Bank
ECHE	Temporary Committee on the ECHELON Interception System
ECON	Committee on Economic and Monetary Affairs
ECR	European Conservatives and Reformists
ECSC	European Coal and Steel Community
EDPS	European Data Protection Supervisor
EEA	European Economic Area
EEAS	European External Action Service
EEC	European Economic Community
EFD	European of Freedom and Democracy
EFDD	European of Freedom and Direct Democracy
EFSA	European Food Safety Authority
EFSD	European Fund for Sustainable Development
ELD	European Liberals and Democrats
ELDR	European Liberal, Democrat and Reform Parties
EMAS	European Eco-Management and Audit Scheme
EMIS	Inquiry Committee into Emission Measurements in the Car Industry
EMPL	Committee on Employment and Social Affairs
EMU	Economic Monetary Union
ENF	Europe of Nations and Freedom
ENVI	Committee on Environment, Public Health and Food Safety
EP	European Parliament
EPC	European Political Cooperation
EPP	European People's Party
EPP-ED	European People's Party – European Democrats
EPRS	European Parliament Research Service
EQUI	Temporary Committee of Inquiry into the Crisis of the Equitable Life Assurance Society
ES	European Salience
ESB1	Temporary Committee of Inquiry into BSE
ESB2	Temporary Committee to Monitor Action Taken on BSE Recommendations
ESPAS	European Strategy and Policy Analysis System
ETF	European Training Foundation
EU	European Union
EURATOM	European Atomic Energy Community
EuroLat	Euro-Latin American Parliamentary Assembly
FEMM	Committee on Women's Rights and Gender Equality

FIAP	Temporary Committee on Foot and Mouth Disease
FIC	Food Information to Consumers
FINP	Temporary Committee on Policy Challenges and Budgetary Means of the Enlarged Union
Frontex	European Border and Coast Guard Agency
GATT	General Agreement on Tariffs and Trade
GENE	Temporary Committee on Human Genetics and other New Technologies of Modern Medicine
Greens/EFA	Greens/European Free Alliance
GUE/NGL	European United Left – Nordic Green Left
IGC	Intergovernmental Conference
IMCO	Committee on Internal Market and Consumer Protection
IND/DEM	Independence/Democracy
INTA	Committee on International Trade
IPEX	Interparliamentary EU Information Exchange
ITER	International Thermonuclear Experimental Reactor
ITRE	Committee on Industry, Research and Energy
JHA	Justice and Home Affairs
JPC	Joint Parliamentary Committees
JURI	Committee on Legal Affairs
LGBTI	Lesbian, Gay, Bisexual, Transgender and Intersex
LIBE	Committee on Civil Liberties, Justice and Home Affairs
MARE	Temporary Committee on Improving Safety at Sea
MEP	Member of the European Parliament
MFF	Multiannual Financial Framework
NATO	North Atlantic Treaty Organization
NGO	Non-Governmental Organisation
NPD	National Party Delegation
NSA	National Security Agency
OLAF	European Anti-Fraud Office
OLP	Ordinary Legislative Procedure
ONP	Open Network Provision
PANA	Committee of Inquiry into Money Laundering, Tax Avoidance and Tax Evasion
PCC	Parliamentary Cooperation Committee
PECH	Committee on Fisheries
PES	Party of European Socialists
PETI	Committee on Petitions
PNR	Passenger Name Record
PR	Proportional Representation
QMV	Qualified Majority Voting
RCV	Roll-Call Vote
REGI	Committee on Regional Development

RoP	The European Parliament's Rules of Procedure
S&D	Progressive Alliance of Socialists and Democrats in the European Parliament
SEA	Single European Act
SEDE	Subcommittee on Security and Defense
SMEs	Small and Medium Enterprises
SOE	Second-Order Election
SPD	Sozialdemokratische Partei Deutschlands (Social Democratic Party of Germany)
STOA	Science and Technology Options Assessment
STV	Single Transferable Vote
SURE	Special Committee on Policy Challenges and Budgetary Resources for a Sustainable European Union after 2013
SWIFT	Society for Worldwide Interbank Financial Telecommunication
TAXE 1	Special Committee on Tax Rulings
TAXE 2	Special Committee on Tax Rulings and other Measures Similar in Nature or Effect 2
TDI	Technical Group of Independent Members
TDIP	Temporary Committee on the Alleged Use of European Countries by the CIA for the Transport and Illegal Detention of Prisoners
TEC	Treaty establishing the European Community
TEU	Treaty on European Union
TFEU	Treaty on the Functioning of the European Union
TFTP	Terrorist Finance Tracking Program
TRAN	Committee on Transport and Tourism
TRANSIT	Temporary Committee of Inquiry into the Community Transit System
TSCG	Treaty on Stability, Co-ordination and Governance in the Economic and Monetary Union
TTIP	Transatlantic Trade and Investment Partnership
UEN	Union for Europe of the Nations
UK	United Kingdom
UKIP	United Kingdom Independence Party
UN	United Nations
US	United States
VAT	Value-Added Tax
VVD	People's Party for Freedom and Democracy (Volkspartij voor Vrijheid en Democratie)
WTO	World Trade Organization
WWF	World Wide Fund for Nature

Preface

When Neill Nugent suggested to me that I write a new edition of *The European Parliament*, I was daunted by having to follow in David Judge and David Earnshaw's footsteps. Both of them had played crucial roles in my academic career and their book was a constant companion during my hours of study. It felt somehow strange to rework a book that was solid and whose principal weakness was that it had become largely outdated. For better or for worse, I decided to start from scratch and write a completely new book, which does not mean that there are no legacies from the previous one. Consciously or unconsciously, many of the major themes that Judge and Earnshaw brought to the fore continue to permeate this book. As a student, I particularly appreciated their ability to situate the European Parliament within theoretical debates. That is why this book tries to find a delicate balance between informing readers (that is, providing facts), while keeping in mind analytical frames that help us understand the whys and hows of the European Parliament. I also sought to emphasise the relational aspect of EU politics – the EP is not an isolated institution, but one that is located in a broader environment made up of a complex network that connects it to other EU institutions, European citizens and groups, national actors and even the rest of the world. The previous editions of this book made it clear that we cannot understand the EP without looking at the evolution of the EU and the wider world.

At the same time, the European Parliament has changed considerably since Judge and Earnshaw's book was published in 2008. This book captures the main changes that have driven its evolution since the last edition. It examines the formal changes brought about by the Treaty of Lisbon and the wide range of informal changes that it has triggered. It also looks into the increasing pressure to reconcile the Parliament's role as a co-decider and the demands for more democracy and transparency, especially in a context marked by the rise of Eurosceptic forces. This new edition also reflects a new academic environment – with a new generation that has contributed to studying the European Parliament in a slightly different way. Although EP studies continue to be dominated by rational-choice institutionalism and quantitative methods (with a good dose of formal modelling), there are signs that the field is becoming more diverse. There have been contributions from constructivist (and more qualitative) perspectives – which have particularly helped to open up the 'black box' of Parliament. This means that we now know more about the work of committees and informal negotiations and we have put more emphasis on the role of individual actors. In order to capture these transformations, this new edition seeks to situate the European Parliament into the wider EU political system by focusing on three elements of the policy process – where demands come from, who aggregates the demands and how demands are translated into outputs.

Finally, I would like to express my thanks to Neill Nugent for trusting me with this new edition and offering extremely helpful feedback. Many thanks also to Stephen Wenham, Tuur Driesser and Chloe Osborne for their support, and especially, their patience. I hope that the book will fulfil their expectations. As mentioned above, change is a constant in the European Parliament. As an outsider, it is particularly difficult to capture and keep up to date with the formal and informal changes that occur regularly in the EP. I am, therefore, very grateful for all those insiders (within the EP and outside of it) that have willingly spared some time to share their insights in the many interviews I have conducted over the last eight years and to Jaume Duch for providing very helpful information. I am also thankful to the 'EP crowd', Amy Busby and Maja Kluger Dionigi (formerly Rasmussen) as well as the newly acquired 'trilogue crowd' (Christilla Roederer-Rynning, Gijs Jan Brandsma and Justin Greenwood). A special thanks to my wonderful team at the University of Bamberg, who have provided much needed help with research and editing and who have been extremely supportive in the last stages of production. I hope that Amanda Henson, Vérane Meyer, Lukas Neuhaus, Lara Panning and Franz Wasserhövel know how much a part of this book they are. Finally, I would like to thank my family, and especially Thomas Büttner, for supporting me from beginning to end. I would not have made it without you.

Chapter 1

Introduction: Situating the European Parliament in the EU's Political System

Introduction

With an economic crisis not completely overcome, a new crisis of its migration regime, Brexit and a more uncertain relationship with the United States (US), the European Union (EU) faces a critical turning point in the integration project. A wide array of political and social problems lay at the core of these crises: dissatisfaction with political parties, lack of trust in institutions, a rise in nationalism and protectionism, political apathy and disenfranchisement. These factors all raise questions about representation and legitimacy – questions that affect one EU institution in particular: the European Parliament (EP).

As the only directly elected institution, the EP has become the 'theatre of engagement' where these tensions play out. Its members are elected to serve as a transmission belt between the outside world and the other EU bodies and, as a result, the EP serves as an arena where proponents of different ideological and national views are brought together. There is probably no other EU institution where the cleavages at the core of European integration are more visible: left and right ideologies structure EP politics as much as views for and against integration.

However, does the European Parliament *actually* matter? The purpose of this book is to show that the days of 'talking shop' are clearly over. The EP fulfils the key functions of representation, decision-making and accountability; by sheer force of will, it has carved itself a central place in the life of the EU – one that is not uncontested, but is unlikely to be rolled back. This first chapter situates the EP as a core piece of the EU's political system and considers the main themes of the book: empowerment, representation and normality.

The European Union as a political system

For a long time, the European Parliament was only a marginal object of study. Many considered it a 'unique' parliament that could not be compared to any other international assembly – a problem that mirrored the

1

debate about the nature of the European Union. International relations struggled to find a place for it in its theories and tended to treat it as an institutional 'black box' – that is, it ignored how the EP worked and how it was organised. Over time, however, it became obvious that knowing how things are done is important to understand the nature of the EU and its institutions. Certainly, the EU is not a state, nor a (con)federation of states, but it does display many of the key characteristics of a political system (Hix and Høyland 2011). The idea of a political system was first introduced by Easton (1957: 384), who saw political life as a system of activity:

> The very idea of a system suggests that we can separate political life from the rest of social activity, at least for analytical purposes, and examine it as though for the moment it were a self-contained entity surrounded by, but clearly distinguishable from, the environment or setting in which it operates.

Therefore, although we tend to associate political systems with state systems, this does not need to be the case. Easton identified four conditions intrinsic to any political system: (1) boundaries that distinguish its units from those of other systems; (2) inputs (demands) that are then translated by the political system into outputs (decisions); (3) a division of labour within the system that provides some structure to the translation process; (4) mechanisms to coordinate the work of the different units and allow them to make authoritative decisions. If we apply these four characteristics to the EU, it is not difficult to see that this definition fits well: the EU is recognised as an entity composed of various organs that works independently from its member states; it receives inputs from a range of external actors – citizens, domestic and European interests, international regimes, national governments – and translates those into various types of output (legal instruments like directives and regulations, soft forms of cooperation, networks); it has a division of executive, legislative and judicial power as well as a range of specialised organs, such as agencies or the European Central Bank (ECB); the treaties provide a wide range of legal instruments that allow its organs to make decisions that can be directly applied to member states and individual citizens.

Why is this important for the study of the Parliament? Firstly, if we treat the EU as a political system, we can leave the problem of 'uniqueness' behind and concentrate on comparing it to equivalent organs on the national or international level. Thus, even though the EP as a whole might appear unique, its practices and structures can be compared to those of other legislatures. Secondly, it underlines the relational aspects of the EU and its institutions; the EP is defined not only by its role as representative of EU citizens, but also by its relations with other institutions in charge of translating demands into outputs. This means that we need to consider the actions of the EP within a wider framework of policy-making, where organs like the European Council, the Council of the European Union (hereafter the Council) and the European Commission (hereafter the Commission) act as constraints and opportunities for EP actors. Finally, treating the EU as a political system stresses the importance of processes and change. It allows us to look at how the EP contributes to the political system as part of a wider institutional framework that is in constant evolution. It is, therefore, essential to bear in mind how the EU has changed over time and how the EP has been both a source and a recipient of such changes.

Main themes

The book aims to open the 'black box' of the EU's legislature and examine its functions, key actors and main working structures. To this effect, it combines factual information with conceptual analysis of these different aspects. There are, nevertheless, three main recurring themes that appear – with a varying degree of intensity – in all chapters. They are shortly outlined in the following section.

Empowerment

The EP was not born as a 'parliament', but as an assembly of unelected members representing their national parliaments. The fact that it has been able to transform itself into a fully-fledged legislator enjoying a wide range of decision-making powers is an impressive example of institutional empowerment and a perfect case to study formal and informal institutional changes. Despite its humble origins, the members of the EP (MEPs) have always had a clear vision of the future that has given way to a particular form of institutional 'patriotism'. If there is an area where the EP has shown a stable pattern of behaviour, it is in its defence of stronger parliamentary powers. Its attitude has not just been defensive, but has often gone into the offensive – giving new interpretations to grey areas in the treaties, coming up with informal instruments to tighten the links with other EU institutions or just battling cases in the Court. These initiatives have generally been accepted and formalised over the course of time by national governments keen to fill the democratic gap with more parliamentarism. Somehow, paradoxically, its initial weaknesses could be overcome precisely because it could be compared to national parliaments, which were seen as a major source of legitimacy in domestic political systems.

Chapter 2 examines in depth the process of empowerment, with the various treaty reforms at its core, and shows how the Parliament has managed to expand its powers through a course of formal and informal stages. Chapters 3, 4 and 5 also note the importance of the empowerment process to understand the EP's internal organisation as well as its legislative and non-legislative functions. The issue of empowerment is, however, also important to understand the evolution of the EP's political parties (Chapter 9) as well as the role of the EP as a co-decider (Chapter 11).

Representation

The division of labour among the main EU institutions does not just refer to purely functional matters; it also affects the way demands are represented in the EU's political system. While the Council fulfils a function of territorial representation and the Commission is supposed to represent the 'general interest' of the EU, the EP is seen as the classical channel of democratic (popular) representation. This is, however, a double-edged sword. On the one hand, playing the popular representation card has helped the EP to increase its powers. It is also a very strong legitimising tool – and one employed often by MEPs, claiming to make certain decisions for the good of European citizens. However, the nature of the EU's political system and, in particular, of EP elections makes it difficult for Parliament to relate with voters, since citizens generally do not feel attached to their MEPs and still see the Parliament as something extraneous and far away. This is, of course, closely related to the EU's electoral system: although MEPs are now voted for directly, national parties (and politics) remain the main interfaces between citizens and the EP. EU citizens cannot yet vote for transnational European lists or for MEPs outside of their country of residence. Ironically, this particularity of EP elections is also responsible for the rise of Eurosceptic forces in Europe. European elections have often been a much easier arena for fringe parties to win representation and expand their (financial) resources to strengthen the party back home.

The EP's claims to represent citizens also suffer from the alienation and distance that most citizens experience vis-à-vis the Parliament. This is mostly due to outdated perceptions of the EP as a 'talking shop' incapable of exerting any influence on major decisions concerning EU legislation. This is certainly no longer true, but popular imaginations and media depictions often struggle to keep pace with rapid and periodical institutional changes. In addition, many people have the feeling that the EP does not do anything that actually 'matters'. This is, of course, a more generalised problem related to EU competences, which are generally kept far away from 'bread and butter' issues (for instance, taxation, health or education); however, the EP often faces particular constraints linked to the division of labour across EU organs in different stages of the policy cycle. While the EU has become a key actor in the decision-making stage, it still enjoys very limited competences when it comes to the agenda-setting and implementation stages (Buonanno and Nugent 2013; Versluis et al. 2010). Unlike other parliaments, the EP does not have a right to legislative initiative, so it can only try to exert some indirect influence on the Commission. Equally, implementation is mainly a task left to member states, while the Commission and the Court of Justice of the European Union (CJEU) are charged with overseeing them. Therefore, the EP does not have any formal rights to supervise member states and hold them accountable if implementation fails or is found to be lacking. This might also contribute to the impression of weakness and make Parliament appear less relevant to citizens.

This theme occupies particularly those chapters dedicated to examining the inputs that the EP receives (Chapter 6 on EP elections and Chapter 7 on lobbying and media) as well as those that consider how representation affects the translation of inputs into outputs. To this effect, Chapter 8 looks at the different representative roles exerted by MEPs, while Chapter 9 examines the role of political parties in the aggregation of demands and their translation into outputs with a clear ideological dimension.

Normality

Many aspects of the EP can certainly be compared to national parliaments; indeed, many of the conceptual approaches examined in this book originate in comparative politics and have been used to explain the committee system, the leadership of political parties or the role and behaviour of individual members. Therefore, in many respects, the EP functions like a 'normal' parliament.

In some others, however, it is not yet completely normal. Some of these distinctive features are closely linked to the two other themes. For one, the empowerment of the EP has transformed it into a full legislator and made it comparable to strong parliaments like the US Congress or the German Bundestag. At the same time, the institutional 'patriotism' that emerged during this process of growth remains an important shared norm within the EP. The tendency to put institutional matters before policy is not yet over. It might well be that, with more stability in its institutional environment, the EP loses its appetite for inter-institutional battles, but this moment has not yet arrived.

On the other hand, the presence of Eurosceptic forces within the Parliament questions its 'normality' in that the EP is probably one of the few assemblies to house parties that contest the very existence of the polity in which they work. They do not just contest particular policies (which might be the case of far-right parties) or a certain type of political system (as is the case with republican parties in monarchic systems) – their aim is to abolish the EU *as a polity*, so that the old state-centred regime can be restored. The growing presence of Eurosceptics in the EP also makes it difficult for other 'mainstream' political forces to function normally. The pressure from fringe parties leaves less room for manoeuvre at the centre and reduces the scope for left-right politics. That is why we have seen a persistent use of grand coalitions gathering centre-right, liberal and social-democratic forces in the last legislative terms. Although this is also a reflection of the culture of consensus under which the EP works, grand coalitions show the difficulties in building majorities when too many anti-EU MEPs populate its fringes. This dynamic affects directly the capacity of Parliament to translate inputs into outputs: it makes ideological change more difficult and enhances the tendency to stick to the status quo.

This aspect will be particularly explored in Chapter 9, which looks at the role of political parties and coalition-building, Chapter 10, which deals with the role of expertise in committees and the use of the plenary as a public tribune, and Chapter 11, which focuses on the role of the EP in co-decision negotiations.

Concluding remarks

The book seeks to examine the internal workings of the EP – since knowing who does what matters – while keeping in mind the wider institutional and political environment in which it functions. Parliament cannot be understood if we do not situate it within the EU's political system and consider the shifting balance of power between its organs and levels of policy-making. Therefore, domestic politics, policy-making dynamics as well as the EU's formal and informal constitutional reforms are not separate areas of study, but constitute a complex matrix in which the EP functions and continues to evolve. Change is indeed one of the main challenges for those who wish to understand the EU – and the EP by extension. The book has attempted to capture its major internal and external transformations, but one should not be surprised if some practices and formalities become outdated at some point in the (near) future. In order to capture these changes, the online companion can be used to access updates on the content and data used in this book.

Chapter 2

The Gradual Empowerment of the European Parliament

Introduction: the EP's empowerment – institutional 'patriotism' or institutional opportunism?

It is difficult to imagine that the European Parliament has ever been anything but the self-assured legislator that it is today. However, the active role of the Parliament in the EU's political system is relatively recent. For most of its history, the EP was seen as a 'talking shop': a powerless institution prone to issuing big declarations with no visible impact on the daily business of the EU. It is, therefore, important to understand where the EP comes from and how it has managed to stand on a par with the parliaments of its member states and gain far-reaching powers in the EU's political system.

The history of the EP has been characterised by long periods of slow progress and an exponential empowerment in the last 20 years. These changes have been the product of some epic and ultimately successful battles, notably the fights to have a say in the approval of the budget and to become a co-legislator. Other changes, such as the ability to access the Council building, are the outcome of long-term debates held out of the public limelight. Therefore, we need to consider how the EP managed to become the institution that it is today and why member states have accepted these changes and formalised them in consecutive treaty reforms.

This chapter traces the different steps leading to the empowerment of the EP and examines the wider dynamics of European integration that can help us understand the reasons behind this spectacular change in the EU's institutional set-up (see Box 2.1). It looks at the activism of the Parliament – what has been termed 'institutional patriotism' (Priestley 2008: 9) – and its ability to shape the core norms of the EU's political system by using the initially few opportunities at its disposal: access to the Court of Justice to trigger quasi-constitutional changes, its internal Rules of Procedure (RoP) to set informal precedents for treaty reform and the democratic foundations of the EU to legitimise its empowerment on normative grounds. On the other hand, the chapter also examines why the EP's empowerment has been accepted and supported by even the most reluctant member states. Indeed, the perception

---

Box 2.1   The EP's empowerment at a glance

1951: Establishment of the Assembly by the Treaty of Paris

10 September 1952: First meeting of the European Coal and Steel Community (ECSC) Parliamentary Assembly

1957: Treaty of Rome and expansion of the Assembly to the European Economic Community (EEC) and European Atomic Energy Community (EURATOM)

1962: The Assembly becomes known as the European Parliament

1970/1975: Budgetary power over non-compulsory expenditures

1979: First direct elections

1986: The Single European Act (SEA) introduces the cooperation procedure and the right to give its assent over accession and association agreements

1992: The Treaty of Maastricht introduces co-decision and a vote on the Commission's investiture

1997: The Treaty of Amsterdam enhances co-decision with full veto power over legislation and allows the EP to approve the Commission President

2001: The Treaty of Nice fails to produce wide-ranging changes, though it does give the EP the status of 'privileged litigant', which allows it to challenge other institutions in the Court of Justice

2007: The Treaty of Lisbon changes the name of the co-decision procedure to the ordinary legislative procedure and enlarges its scope; it also widens the right to give its consent over international agreements and gives budgetary powers for compulsory and non-compulsory expenditures

2014: First use of the Spitzenkandidaten in EP elections, which enables the EP to 'choose' the Commission President

---

of the EP as a powerless parliament has presented the perfect opportunity to use new formal powers to a much greater extent than expected (Rittberger 2012).

From the Assembly to the first direct elections

The EP started its life as the Assembly of the European Coal and Steel Community (ECSC) – established on 18 April 1951, but effectively starting work in 1952. The ECSC was the first effort to bridge the conflicts of the early twentieth century that had torn Europe apart. French Foreign Minister Robert Schuman departed from political plans to bring European countries closer together and proposed to start with a technical sector: coal and steel industries. The choice was not neutral, since coal and steel were the main German economic and military engines and had been at the core of the interwar conflicts between France and Germany. The idea, based on Jean Monnet's French Modernisation Plan (1946), was to pre-empt any new episodes of political instability by pooling the control of this industry beyond the reach of particular countries. What made the plan innovative was the intention to create new and independent institutions, which meant moving away from (classic) intergovernmental cooperation and into a new form of supranational integration. However, this was a step too far for the United Kingdom (UK) and ultimately only Italy, Belgium, the Netherlands and Luxembourg joined France and Germany in the project.

Monnet's previous experience with national economic planning led him to realise that integration might come more easily with a mixture of political and technocratic institutions. To this effect, he proposed the creation of a High Authority (now the European Commission) formed by independent experts that could represent the European 'general will', instead of particularistic national interests, working alongside a Court of Justice and an Assembly (Featherstone 1994). His plans were limited by Dutch and Belgian diplomats, who insisted on adding a form of territorial representation in the shape of a Council of Ministers, while the German government supported the idea to create a parliamentary assembly to imbue the project with more democratic accountability (Rittberger 2009). In the end, the Assembly was granted only limited powers, notably the capacity to force the High Authority to resign with a successful motion of censure of its annual report. This did not prevent it from extending its prerogatives further: in addition to the ex post control functions accorded by the Treaty, the Assembly added an ex ante form of control exerted by the newly created committees, which specialised in seven policy areas and could count on the support of an independent secretariat (Guerrieri 2008).

One of the key turning points for the new Assembly was its progressive shift from a house representing national parliaments to a political body organised along ideological lines. As early as 1953, three political groups – Christian Democrats, Socialists and Liberals – were recognised in the internal Rules of Procedure and allocated financial support. The political alignment increased over time and became more organised, to the point that, in March 1958 – when the Common Assembly started to regulate all three European Communities (EC) – it was decided to abandon the alphabetical order of seating and organise members by political groups (Guerrieri 2008; Kreppel 2002).

The new Assembly did not differ much from the original one. The Treaty of Rome (1957) introduced a new legislative procedure, the consultation procedure, which allowed the new Common Assembly to produce a non-binding opinion on the proposals of the High Authority, whose name had been changed to 'European Commission' (see also Chapter 4). In addition, the Treaty extended the possibility to censure the Commission over any issue and at any time, though it still needed a high qualified majority to do so. Finally, a new provision was introduced for direct elections. Most of these new powers proved to be a disappointment. The right to be consulted remained mostly symbolic – especially after the Luxembourg Compromise was introduced in 1966 (see below). As for direct elections, the Assembly drafted various proposals in 1961, 1963 and 1969 but the Council failed to follow up on them. In view of these limitations, the Assembly had to limit itself to more informal and symbolic ways of expanding its power – for example, asking the Council to answer parliamentary questions or the Commission President to seek approval for its annual programme. However, the most notable example is its decision to rename itself the 'European Parliament' in March 1962 (Kreppel 2002).

The end of the 1960s came to underline tensions between supranational and intergovernmental visions of the European Communities, personified in the figure of French President Charles de Gaulle. His main ideas were encapsulated in the 1961 Fouchet Plan, which aimed to eliminate all supranational institutions and strengthen cooperation on foreign policy. According to Moravcsik (2000a), the plan was only a tool to draw attention away from his two main foci of interest: ensuring the establishment of a common agricultural market through the Common Agricultural Policy (CAP) and preventing the UK from accessing the EC. The crisis was restarted in 1965 with the scheduled introduction of qualified majority voting (QMV) for decisions dealing with transport, agriculture and trade. De Gaulle opposed this move by withdrawing from internal Community negotiations (known as the 'empty chair crisis') and insisting on a new (informal) agreement that would see the perpetuation of unanimity if a member state invoked a matter of 'vital interest' (the Luxembourg Compromise). In this way, he ensured the continued control over the financing of the CAP and slowed down the workings of the Community for the next 20 years (Moravcsik 2000b).

With the election of a new French president in 1969, Georges Pompidou, a new era of Europeanisation began. For the EP, this meant an important change: Pompidou advocated the eventual entrance into force of the Treaty of Rome's provision calling for direct elections. Therefore, despite the 'Eurosclerosis' that dominated the EC – a consequence of the oil crises that affected most member states during the early 1970s – the EP witnessed a decade of significant institutional changes that greatly contributed to a qualitative and quantitative empowerment. First, in the Hague Summit (December 1969) member states managed to tackle the ongoing dispute surrounding the financing of the CAP. A new plan was established, which foresaw the creation of a system of 'own resources' for the EC and a new budgetary procedure. The Commission, the EP and most national governments tried to convince the French by arguing that changes in the EU's budgetary system should give more decision-making power to the Parliament. In the end, the 1970 Treaty of Luxembourg (which entered into force in 1975) reflected a compromise: it distinguished between compulsory spending – left to member states – and non-compulsory expenditures – which only covered around 4 to 5 per cent of the budget, but where the EP could have a final say (Rittberger 2003). The EP managed to use its limited budgetary powers to expand its legislative and inter-institutional power by holding the purse strings (see also Chapter 4). Second, the Summit of 1974 in Paris launched the idea of holding regular meetings of the heads of state and government with the aim of facilitating political debates on issues that did not fall under the competences of the EC. The creation of the 'European Council' in 1975 indirectly benefitted the EP, since it was felt that increasing the role and powers of the more supranational Parliament would compensate the push for more intergovernmentalism. Therefore, an agreement was reached to organise direct elections in or after 1978 (Dinan 2014: 159).

Despite raising little interest in the member states, the first direct elections of June 1979 marked a turning point (see also Chapter 6). Even though the EP still lacked significant legislative powers, it enjoyed a new legitimacy for being the only directly elected EU institution. This special relationship was recognised by the European Court of Justice in its 1980 Isoglucose Ruling (cases 138/79 and 139/79), which underlined the authority of the Parliament in the consultation procedure, since it was seen as the only channel through which European citizens could be a part of the legislative process. The ruling gave the EP the power to delay legislation (see also Chapter 4) and encouraged MEPs to use their few powers, such as the capacity to control the Commission and to approve part of the budget, more aggressively.

The accession of Greece in 1981 (and the imminent enlargement to Portugal and Spain) strengthened the calls for more parliamentary powers. In comparison with the more Eurosceptic enlargement of 1973, which saw the accession of Ireland, the UK and Denmark, the Mediterranean enlargement brought with it a new enthusiasm for democracy shaped by the recent experiences of these three members with autocracy. The efforts of the new members to reinforce democratic institutions within the Community were also supported by the German and Italian foreign ministers, who pushed for an enlargement of the Community with their Genscher-Colombo-Plan. The latter aimed also to deepen the effectiveness of the decision-making process and to attribute more power to the EP. The plan was eventually backed by all member states in a watered down version of the Stuttgart Solemn Declaration on European Union of 1983, which also allowed for the EP to be informed about the developments of the European Political Cooperation (EPC) and presented an annual programme by the Commission (Dinan 2014: 189).

The newly elected EP also decided to celebrate the relaunching of the integration project with proposals for a 'European Union'. Led by federalist Altiero Spinelli, a group of MEPs (known as the 'Crocodile Club' after the name of the restaurant where they met) gave themselves the task of reforming the EC's institutional set-up. The meetings resulted in the establishment of a new Committee on Institutional Affairs, which in February 1984 presented the plenary with a Draft Treaty Establishing the European Union (Spinelli Draft, A1-0575/83) with maximalist proposals, such as the creation of a supranational bicameral system that would allow the EP to have a full say on legislative matters. Albeit ignored by most member states, the proposal set the debate for what would ultimately lead to the reforms of the Treaty of Maastricht (Dinan 2014; Lodge 1984).

The Single European Act and the end of the Luxembourg Compromise

Although the Draft Treaty was ignored by member states, the pressure to reform the European Communities increased steadily throughout the 1980s. Contrary to the 1960s and 1970s, France showed greater support for fostering European integration, with French President François Mitterrand pleading for a strengthening of the EP's legislative functions and an end to the Council's veto right. This led to the formation of the inter-institutional Dooge Committee (an ad hoc committee on institutional affairs, named after its chairman, James Dooge, Irish senator and former foreign minister), which presented its report to the European Council in March 1985. The report asked for greater use of QMV and co-decision powers for the Parliament and called for an intergovernmental conference to reform the treaties. While the strengthening of the Parliament was not contested, some member states (such as Denmark, Greece and the UK) disliked the idea of majority voting within the Council. Remaining conflicts were eventually discussed at an Intergovernmental Conference (IGC) that started in September 1985 and culminated with the signature of the Single European Act (SEA) in February 1986.

During the IGC, several member states and the EP emphasised their support for a majority voting system in the Council for a considerable proportion of policy areas, which would signify the demise of the Luxembourg Compromise. Indeed, the call for more QMV was seen as a loss of power for national parliaments, as it might have resulted in an inability to influence the decisions of their governments to the same extent as when unanimity applied. This shift of power from domestic parliaments to national executives was used by some member states and the EP to argue that the loss of parliamentary legitimacy should be compensated by giving more legislative powers to the Parliament (Rittberger 2003). Italy and Germany pleaded for a de facto co-decision responsibility between Council and Parliament and were supported by the Commission and a majority of MEPs. In the end, a compromise was found in the SEA, whereby the EP was given the right to introduce amendments to the Commission's proposal, but without gaining full veto powers. The new cooperation procedure proved an important step towards co-decision and the gradual empowerment of the EP (see also Chapter 4). The SEA also made the name of 'European Parliament' official and attributed the EP with the assent procedure – the right to veto the accession of new member states and the ratification of association agreements (see Chapter 4).

Despite the major advancements in the SEA, MEPs were still not satisfied and pushed for further formal and informal reforms that would expand their powers. Notably, British Conservative Sir Christopher Prout defied the position of his government by rewriting the Rules of Procedure so that Parliament could exploit and magnify the SEA reforms (see Box 2.2).

In the years following the SEA, the EP produced a series of reports that called for new treaty reforms, which were not well received by the national governments and the Commission, since they had little interest in modifying the treaties so shortly after the implementation of the SEA. Nonetheless, the development of the Single Market raised the need for further revisions, especially when it came to the establishment of a monetary union. Therefore, the EP took advantage of the planned IGC on the Economic and Monetary Union (EMU) and political union (started in December 1990) to raise the issue of the need for further political integration and other reforms to strengthen the democratic character of the EC. Notably, the Martin Reports (A3-47/90; A3-166/90; A3-210/90) prepared specific amendments that sought to increase the powers of the EP through a new co-decision procedure and the involvement of the EP in the appointment of the Commission; they also advocated for wider EC competences and the extension of QMV voting in the Council. Although the EP could not participate in the Intergovernmental Conference, it managed to influence the outcomes by setting the agenda and gaining the support of national parliaments. To this effect, in November 1990, it organised a Conference of Parliaments (or 'Assizes') in Rome, which concluded in a declaration supporting the main demands of the EP (Corbett 1999). Most of these demands were effectively incorporated into the Treaty of Maastricht, which was signed in 1991 but ratified

---

Box 2.2   The EP's Rules of Procedure: Formalising informal norms

Parliament has traditionally taken the Treaties and tried to stretch them like a piece of elastic, in order to enhance the efficiency and democratic accountability of the Union. Of course Parliament cannot contravene the treaties in its Rules of procedure but the Treaties inevitably leave scope for interpretation and room for imagination (Corbett Report A4-0070/99).

When Article 25 of the Treaty of Paris (1951) declared that 'the Assembly shall fix its own rules of procedure, by vote of a majority of its total membership', it could not have predicted the impact this article would have on the EP's empowerment (now Article 232 of the Treaty on the Functioning of the European Union [TFEU]). And yet, the power of a legislature to organise itself is one of the major paths towards its institutionalisation and crystallisation, since 'chamber rules begin as informal practices, are incorporated into precedent as the practice continues, and eventually are codified into the standing rules [of the parliament]'; therefore, 'seemingly minor decisions about rules made early in a legislature's existence ... can have profound consequences for institutional development' (Evans 1999: 606, 632). The EP's Rules of

→

---

only in 1992 due to an initial negative vote in the Danish national ratification referendum.

Maastricht: a turning point

By the time the Treaty of Maastricht entered into force in 1993, the EP's legislative power had been significantly strengthened. The Treaty introduced the first version of the co-decision procedure, which gave Parliament the chance to reject legislative proposals and foresaw the possibility to establish a conciliation committee if the Council did not accept the amendments introduced by the EP in the second reading (see also Chapter 4). The new procedure gave the EP almost full veto power over large parts of Community legislation. Furthermore, the EP also increased its powers vis-à-vis the Commission, with it now being able to cast a vote on the nomination of the European Council for Commission President and give a vote of confidence also on the Commission as a whole. In addition, the term of office of the Commission was aligned with the EP's elections, strengthening the link between the two institutions.

→ Procedure have done exactly that: they have turned informal practices into codified behaviour and helped MEPs navigate the growing complexity of its internal organisation.

The RoP have thus become a significant tool in the institutional evolution of the EP, especially when it comes to enlarging its powers and competences after major treaty reforms (see, for instance, the reforms of 1999, 2002, 2009 and 2016: 1997/2286/REG; 2001/2040/REG; 2007/2124/REG; 2016/2114/REG). The EP has modified its RoP to 'keep up' with treaty changes so that it does not become marginalised, but it has also used them to 'stretch' the treaties by placing new obligations on other EU institutional actors (especially when unsatisfied with the outcomes of the treaty reforms) or by streamlining and centralising its internal structures (Kreppel 2002). For instance, after Maastricht, the EP decided to introduce a new rule (Rule 78), which asked MEPs to reject any attempt to reintroduce the Council's common position if the two legislators had failed to find an agreement at the conciliation committee. This effectively gave full veto power to the EP, which was then formally incorporated in the Treaty of Amsterdam (Hix 2002). Therefore, as will be shown throughout this book, the RoP have shaped the life of the EP and its position within the EU's political system and should not be dismissed as unimportant technical details.

In addition to the procedural rules that closely altered the inter-institutional balance of power, the Treaty of Maastricht also marked a turning point in the wider process of European integration. On the one hand, it supposed the formalisation of a European Union that went beyond purely economic matters to embrace political areas, including the introduction of a European citizenship that allowed EU nationals residing in other member states to vote and be voted into the EP and local elections. On the other hand, the inclusion of more sensitive competences meant a departure from the Community method. The Treaty established a three-pillared structure: the first pillar comprised the traditional EC policies linked to the Single Market as well as the new EMU; the second pillar initiated the Common Foreign and Security Policy (CFSP); and the third pillar incorporated in the new field of Justice and Home Affairs (JHA) the initiatives that had been started outside the Community structures under the Schengen Agreement (1985/1990). While the first pillar was mostly regulated by QMV and co-decision, the second and third pillars were mostly intergovernmental. There, the EP had (almost) no say and the Council had to decide under unanimity. It was also the start of differentiated integration, since not all member states participated in all policies: the EMU, JHA, defence and social policies included opt-outs by various member states – notably, the UK and Denmark.

The period after Maastricht was also characterised by efforts to informally modify the rules and expand the powers of the EP. Once again, Parliament used the Rules of Procedure to empower its main political groups and consolidate the EP's position in the inter-institutional triangle. As we have seen in Box 2.2., one of the major changes was the introduction of then-Rule 78, according to which MEPs were requested to reject the Council's text if the latter tried to reintroduce its common position. The Rules of Procedure were also changed to provide a tighter relationship with the Commission, which was asked to seek the agreement of the EP over its working programme and pay attention to Parliament's request for new legislative initiatives (Nicoll 1994). These internal changes accompanied other structural evolutions, notably the German reunification of 1990 and the 1995 enlargement that welcomed Finland, Austria and Sweden, which led to an increase in the number of seats and the incorporation of two new official languages.

The Treaty of Maastricht had already foreseen another IGC in 1996, with the intention of revising the Treaty and expanding co-decision to more policy areas. The EP could, therefore, prepare in advance and seek to set the agenda from an early stage. Contrary to the SEA and Maastricht, Parliament managed to be more closely involved in the preparation of the conference. In 1994, the European Council set up a 'Reflection Group' composed of foreign ministers and two MEPs (French Socialist Elisabeth Guigou and German Christian-Democrat Elmar Brok). There, the EP representatives received widespread support for their main ideas: co-decision and QMV as a norm, greater involvement in the nomination of the Commission President and an extension of EU competences. More importantly, the EP managed this time to sit in some of the preparatory meetings of the IGC, which gave it full access to documents and the chance to draft amendments on the ongoing discussions. (Corbett 1999)

Amsterdam: from talking shop to full co-legislator

After almost one and a half years of negotiations, the Treaty of Amsterdam was finally signed on 2 October 1997 and entered into force in 1999. The Treaty might appear as having been less significant than its predecessor but, for the EP, it marked an important stepping stone that confirmed it as a full co-legislator (Moravcsik and Nicolaïdis 1999). The main institutional advance for the Parliament was the formalisation of those changes that it had striven to introduce through informal means. Basically, the Treaty changed the co-decision procedure to reflect informal institutional practices and, accordingly, eliminated the possibility for the Council to reintroduce its common position if the conciliation committee failed to reach an agreement. It also recognised the possibility of ending the procedure at the first reading stage – a modification that led to much wider consequences for the functioning of the EU's political system than anyone might have expected, with this small change gradually leading to an increase of early agreements between the institutions and the creation of new structures that facilitated inter-institutional compromise (see Chapters 4 and 11). The Treaty also confirmed other informal changes developed in the EP's Rules of Procedure, notably its right to approve the candidate for Commission President, and in addition gave it a role in the procedure of appointing Commissioners.

However, the EP did not manage to get all that it had wished for. On the one hand, the ongoing request that Parliament should be allowed to decide on the location of its own seat was rejected and the three different seats (Strasbourg, Brussels and Luxembourg) were confirmed. Similarly, it did not manage to gain access to the European Court of Justice. On the other hand, the EP continued to be excluded from the CFSP and the JHA pillars, although the changes introduced by the Treaty to internal security matters ended in a particularly complicated architecture: parts of the former third pillar were shifted to the first pillar but they were made subject to a five-year transitional period during which the old decision-making rules (consultation and unanimity) remained largely in place; the rest (police and judicial cooperation in criminal matters and regular migration) formed the core of the third pillar and, thereby, maintained their intergovernmental nature.

The Treaty of Amsterdam also failed to address some of the key structural questions that were already expected to arise with the upcoming enlargement to Central and Eastern Europe, Cyprus and Malta in 2004. These 'Amsterdam leftovers' led to another IGC in early 2000, which resulted in the signature of the Treaty of Nice in January 2001. Contrary to previous occasions, the EP was deemed to have been less successful at setting the Nice agenda. This was due to its attempts to delay the start of negotiations and then only coming up with a resolution late into the process in April 2000 (Gray and Stubb 2001: 19). The Parliament's resolution was based on a report drafted by Giorgos Dimitrakopoulos and Jo Leinen (A5-0086/2000), which contained two major requests: more democracy and more efficiency in the EU's policy process. This meant enlarging the scope of QMV in areas where co-decision applied, new weighting of votes in the Council and adjusting the composition of the Commission to fit 25 member states – and 27 when Romania and Bulgaria would join. The EP's resolution foreshadowed some of the changes that were to play a central role in the Constitutional Treaty (and Lisbon). For instance, it asked for the incorporation of the Charter of

Fundamental Rights – drafted between 1999 and 2000 by the European Convention made up of representatives of the EP, the Commission and national governments and parliaments – into the Treaty to give it binding force. It also asked for legal personality for the Union to strengthen its external relations, the EP's election of the Commission President from a pool of candidates proposed by the Council as well as the right of the EP to bring an action to the European Court of Justice. In relation to its internal structure, the EP asked to maintain the cap at 700 MEPs, as had been decided in Amsterdam, and even proposed to change the electoral system, so that 10 per cent of seats would be directly elected by citizens on the basis of a single European constituency and European party lists. This would also require the establishment of a statute and funding for European political parties (Resolution A5-0086/2000 of 13 April 2000).

From Nice to Lisbon: the constitutional Convention and the eastern enlargement

The Treaty of Nice was seen as a disappointment for the EP. The Parliament did gain the status of 'privileged litigant', which gave it the power to challenge the acts of the other institutions before the European Court of Justice. However, none of its other requests were met: co-decision was only extended to uncontentious matters and, notably, it was not linked to the use of QMV. That meant that key areas such as agriculture continued to exclude the EP from decision-making. The request to maintain the number of seats at 700 was disregarded and increased to 732; in addition, the distribution of MEPs across old and new member states appeared to have been decided at random – Hungary and the Czech Republic received fewer seats than Belgium despite having a similar size. Finally, the Charter of Fundamental Rights was solemnly declared but did not become binding (Shaw 2001). The Parliament was also not satisfied with the major issue in Nice, namely the reallocation of votes in the Council and the change of threshold for obtaining a qualified majority. The original threshold, which was already very high at 71 per cent, was raised to 74 per cent. Such a high threshold was intended to ensure that decisions taken in the EU would always reflect the will both of the majority of member states and of the EU population. The EP tried to ensure that the outcome would reflect a more proportional distribution of votes in the Council but was unsuccessful (Corbett et al. 2016: 443–444).

The EP was not the only one disappointed with Nice; the aftermath of the IGC was one of frustration, particularly the inability to deal with the challenges of enlargement. As a result, the Treaty incorporated a

'Declaration on the Future of Europe' that foresaw a new IGC for 2004 and asked member states to define the process of treaty reform in the Laeken European Council of December 2001. The EP's Committee on Constitutional Affairs and an informal group, the 'Friends of Laeken', advocated in a resolution on 31 May 2001 (A5-0168/2001) the use of a convention similar to the one used to draft the Charter of Fundamental Rights to prepare the next IGC. That meant including members of national parliaments and governments as well as representatives of the Commission and the EP. The proposal was certainly to the advantage of the EP, which could now sit at the table and participate fully in drafting and amending the new treaty proposal. Parliament, however, was not alone; smaller member states in favour of more integration also supported this format, especially Finland, Belgium and the Netherlands. Indeed, the Belgian Presidency managed to play a very skilled game to convince Eurosceptic and larger member states to accept the idea of a convention in the Laeken declaration: it offered them a series of 'safeguards' (for instance the choice of former French President Valéry Giscard d'Estaing as Chair), while presenting the option of a convention as a way to render treaty reforms more open and democratic, which even the most reluctant of governments could not be seen to oppose – especially after the Irish voted in a referendum against the Treaty of Nice in June 2001. However, despite the innovative character of the Convention and its potential for far-reaching reforms, neither its new components (especially national parliaments and the EP) nor the presence of transnational political parties managed to develop alternative visions and the traditional cleavages of supranationalists vs. intergovernmentalists and small vs. big member states dominated the debates (Magnette and Nicolaïdis 2004). These cleavages showed the difficulty of the EP to act as a unitary actor – especially when it came to policy issues – and the emergent competition between the EP and national parliaments. The latter failed to coordinate among them and acted rather as supporters of their governments, which brought national issues increasingly to the forefront (Dinan 2004).

The Convention lasted for a year and a half (February 2002–July 2003) and ended with a Draft Treaty establishing a Constitution for Europe. Of the 105 members of the Convention, 16 represented the EP and two of them (Klaus Hänsch and Íñigo Méndez de Vigo) were also part of the Praesidium – a collective organ in charge of providing impetus and compromises. The influence of the EP on the text is contested, but Beach (2007) convincingly traced the 'fingerprints' left by Parliament in the draft and even the final Constitutional Treaty that emerged out of the 2004 IGC. He showed, for instance, how the idea to call it a 'constitution' was persistently advocated by MEPs and became more compelling after British MEP Andrew Duff produced in September 2002 a draft for a constitution with a short institutional section. MEPs were also crucial in claiming the end of the pillar structure, making co-decision and QMV the general rule or giving the EP powers to decide over the entire budget.

The final draft was presented to national governments as a *fait accompli*: the Italian Presidency, with the support of France (and the EP), attempted to push the text without opening it for changes; this led to the failure of the IGC organised in Brussels at the end of 2003. Once more, the main controversies revolved around institutional issues, notably the proposal for a double majority to calculate QMV in the Council, the composition of the Commission and the distribution of seats in the EP (Beach 2007: 1281; Dinan 2004). The EP was involved in informal discussions at the start of 2004 and its Constitutional Affairs Committee organised a hearing in mid-February that brought together members of the Convention and served to resume negotiations. The lead was then taken by the Irish Presidency, which saw the need to reopen certain chapters to ensure the conclusion of a Constitutional Treaty.

In the end, the Constitutional Treaty settled for a double majority in the Council of 55 per cent of member states and 65 per cent of the EU population. However, as a concession to Poland, it included a provision similar to the Ioannina Compromise – namely, until 2014, if a group of member states fell short of forming a blocking minority, an attempt would be made to continue negotiating until a consensus was reached that would satisfy the members in the minority. The Commission continued to be composed of one Commissioner per member state until 2014, when it would be reduced to two-thirds of member states. Finally, the EP's number of seats was raised to 750, ranging from a minimum of six for the smallest member states to a maximum of 96, which meant Germany would have to cut its number of MEPs. Therefore, although most of the main achievements of the Convention were maintained (the name, the end of the pillars, a bigger role for national parliaments, a new president for the European Council and a Foreign Affairs 'Minister'), those that affected the EU institutions were 'retrograde steps' (Dinan 2005). Despite its potential shortcomings, the EP 'wholeheartedly' supported the Constitutional Treaty with a majority of over two-thirds. In its resolution voted on 12 January 2005 (P6_TA(2005)0004), the EP underlined, among its main achievements, the fact that 'the European Parliament will as a rule decide on an equal footing with the Council on the Union's legislation' (that is, the extension of co-decision); that 'the President of the Commission will be elected by the European Parliament, thereby establishing a link to the results of European elections'; that 'a new budgetary procedure will require the approval of both the Council and the European Parliament for all European Union expenditure, without exception'; and that 'the exercise of delegated legislative powers [comitology] by the Commission will be brought under a new system of supervision by the European Parliament and the Council'.

However, the success of the Constitutional Treaty would prove to be short-lived. On 29 May 2005, France voted in a referendum against the Treaty, followed almost immediately by a negative vote in the Netherlands on 1 June 2005. The failure to ratify the EU Constitution in two of the founding members led to a generalised feeling of uncertainty followed by a two-year 'period of reflection'. Despite this setback, the EP continued to advocate for an EU Constitution and called for further dialogue with national parliaments and citizens to facilitate an end to the impasse (see reports 2005/2146/INI; 2006/2576/RSP). Andrew Duff (liberal British MEP) even produced a plan on how to save the Constitution, which called for improving the social aspects and the financial system of the Union (Duff 2006). Not everyone in the EP shared his views, though; Timothy Kirkhope (a conservative British MEP), for instance, considered that 'the constitution is a non-starter. All this talk of resuscitating it is a huge waste of effort, time and money' (in Euractiv 2006). Member states seemed to share his opinion and in 2007 reopened treaty reforms with two objectives in view: first, frame the output as a 'Reform Treaty' to avoid opening Pandora's box; second, eliminate from the new treaty any reference to the 'constitutional' aspects – in particular, the name, symbols such as the flag and the anthem – and rename the 'Foreign Minister' back into a 'High Representative' (Dinan 2008). This did not sit well with a majority of the EP, which continued to declare its support for the Constitution and expressed its regret that the mandate for the new IGC 'allows for various drafting changes to the Constitutional Treaty, which give an impression of distrust vis-à-vis the Union and its institutions' and that it showed 'the decreasing European goodwill and political courage of Member State representatives' (2007/0808/CNS).

The IGC opened in July 2007 under the Portuguese Presidency (but after intense preparations by the German Presidency). One of the specificities of this treaty reform was the inclusion of EP representatives who had already participated in the Convention – Elmar Brok (European People's Party-European Democrats [EPP-ED]), Klaus Hänsch (Party of European Socialists [PES]) and Andrew Duff (Alliance of Liberals and Democrats for Europe [ALDE]) – and the importance of legal experts, who examined the proposed draft in detail to make sure that any issues had been sorted out. During the Lisbon Summit of 18–19 October 2007, the allocation of seats in the EP became again a major political dispute. The EP had issued a report in which it reallocated the 750 seats foreseen by the Constitutional Treaty on the basis of 'degressive proportionality' (2007/2169/INI). Italy did not agree with the number of MEPs it had been allocated, which forced member states to raise the total number to 751. In the end, when signed in Lisbon on 13 December 2007, the Reform Treaty did not incorporate any major changes compared to the Constitutional Treaty. It extended the period in which national parliaments could examine drafts and incorporated into the text of the Treaty the declaration regarding the use of the Ioannina Compromise until 2017. It was also the first time that co-decision and QMV were designated as the 'ordinary legislative procedure', but it kept the existing terminology to designate EU laws. It also maintained and even enlarged some of the opt-outs, opt-ins and derogations regarding Economic and Monetary Union (EMU), Schengen and the Charter of Fundamental Rights. Finally, the new text also contemplated a simplified treaty amendment process and confirmed the provision introduced in the Draft Constitutional Treaty that allowed member states to voluntarily withdraw from the EU (the now notorious Article 50).

The Treaty had to be modified once more due to the failed ratification by Ireland in June 2008. The solution 'would involve a series of carefully choreographed steps' (Dinan 2009: 118); notably, the assurance that, after successful ratification, all member states would keep a Commissioner, which addressed the fear of smaller countries that they would lose their voice in the EU's executive branch. In addition, the Eurosceptic Czech President Václav Klaus threatened with refusing to sign the ratification instrument, which led to adding a new Czech opt-out from the Charter of Fundamental Rights. Eventually, he agreed to ratify the treaty in November 2009, which meant it could enter into force by 1 December 2009.

Post-Lisbon the EP as an ordinary legislature

The Treaty of Lisbon inaugurated a new era in the EU's political system, with new 'input' channels like the European Citizens' Initiative and improved chances for national parliaments to participate in EU policy-making by introducing a subsidiarity control mechanism (see Box 2.3). When it comes to the composition of the Commission, the Treaty of Lisbon also led to unexpected developments. Formally, the EP now elects the Commission President by a majority of its members. The European Council is still in charge of selecting the candidate, but this has to be done while taking into account the results of the EP elections. Although this last proposition seemed relatively innocuous, it has turned into one of the major developments of the post-Lisbon period. The EP used this relatively bland statement to propose 'Spitzenkandidaten' (top candidates) for most political groups in the 2014 elections. Although member states were not formally forced to accept the EP candidates, it proved difficult to bypass them since it looked highly undemocratic. As a result, Jean-Claude Juncker became the first Commission President

Box 2.3   A Europe of Parliaments? Enhancing the role of national parliaments

The empowerment of national parliaments in the Treaty of Lisbon mirrors the logic behind the increase in powers of the European Parliament, namely, the belief that the EU's democratic deficit should be addressed by giving a stronger voice to those institutions that represent EU citizens (Rittberger 2005). Following this logic, the Treaty of Lisbon introduced a new Early Warning Mechanism, which allows national parliaments to issue 'yellow' or 'orange' cards if they believe the EU is encroaching on their rights in areas where it shares competences with member states. As of now, three 'yellow cards' have been issued: in 2012 on a Council regulation on the exertion of the right to take collective action (Monti II); in 2013 on a Council regulation on the establishment of the European Public Prosecutor's Office; and in 2016 on the Posted Workers Directive. The scarcity of 'yellow cards' shows the difficulty in reaching the threshold in the space of only eight weeks. It requires a speed and a level of coordination across national parliaments that are difficult to achieve, especially among those parliaments that are weakly organised or cannot rely on specialised European affairs committees.

The enhanced role of national parliaments has led to new dynamics of cooperation and competition in the EU (Neuhold et al. 2015). Formally, the relationship between the two parliamentary levels has been reinforced with the establishment of two EP Vice-Presidents and a new directorate in charge of relations with national parliaments. The Conference of Parliamentary Committees for Union Affairs of Parliaments of the European Union (COSAC, active since 1989) continues to form the central contact point, while the former Conference of Speakers has been integrated into a new platform for EU Interparliamentary Exchange (IPEX). In specific areas, contacts between national and European parliamentarians have been further institutionalised in the shape of new bodies such as the Article 13 Conference in the area of economic governance or the Interparliamentary Conference for the Common Foreign and Security Policy (CFSP) and the Common Security and Defence Policy (CSDP). Informally, contacts between elected members and parliamentary staff have increased substantially, especially among those national parliaments showing a greater interest and/or having greater resources to get involved in EU affairs (Auel and Christiansen 2015). However, despite the assumption that the EP and national parliaments should be natural allies, 'the EP and national chambers are also competitors in the marketplace for the provision of democratic legitimacy and rivals in the search for voters' (Auel and Christiansen 2015: 276). Indeed, national parliaments and the EP have 'co-evolved', adapting their respective powers and functions to the new balance of power brought about by European integration; however, whether this translates into cooperation or competition is often a matter of domestic politics: generally, more conservative parliaments feel more threatened by the EP and develop stronger oversight measures (Winzen et al. 2015).

that had been nominated by the EP political group with the highest electoral support. His election, albeit highly contested, has turned the Commission into a more politicised body that enjoys a new source of legitimacy (see also Box 5.3).

When it comes to the functioning of the EU as a political system, the Treaty of Lisbon did affect some of the main instruments of policy-making as well as the inter-institutional balance of power. First, it transformed co-decision into the 'ordinary legislative procedure' and brought the EP on par with member states in the allocation of the annual budget. It also gave it the power to give its consent over most international agreements. This means that the EP now has the power of both the purse and the pen for a large number of policy fields – including agriculture and trade, two of the EU's core competences (see also Chapter 4). These changes have transformed (or at least accelerated) the working methods of the EP in the legislative arena. The dialogue between the main EU institutions has intensified and, thereby, strengthened the informal aspects of co-decision. This trend is particularly noticeable in the exponential rise of informal meetings between the EP, the Council and the Commission (trilogues) used to further compromises and achieve early agreements in co-decision (see Chapters 4 and 11). In addition, the Treaty of Lisbon has brought other changes in the distribution of roles and the functioning of institutions. Since 1 November 2014, the Council has been voting under the new double majority rules; this has helped to strengthen larger member states and is slowly eroding its traditional norms of consensus. For instance, in what became a highly salient episode, Slovakia, Hungary, Romania and the Czech Republic were overruled in September 2015 by all other member states in a decision on whether to relocate 120,000 asylum-seekers across the EU (Politico 2015b). New positions such as the President of the European Council or the double-hatted High Representative of the Union for Foreign Affairs and Security Policy have had to forge new roles for themselves. This has often led to the sidelining of long-established roles, such as the Council Presidency, or to an increased competition between bodies, as is the case of the Commission and the European External Action Service (EEAS). The presence of more EU presidents and representatives has also increased the number of voices speaking for the Union, which has not always contributed to transparency and better communication with its citizens.

These new positions have also contributed to a different style of policy-making – one that has had a clear impact on the EU's policy outputs. If we look particularly at the management of the Euro crisis and of the rise in the number of asylum-seekers, we can see some common trends. First, solutions have been events-driven and highly intergovernmental. Second, the voice of supranational institutions – and the EP in particular – has been almost non-existent. This evolution is more evident in the financial crisis, since it has been longer in the making. Some consider that the crisis led to furthering European integration, but that it was done in an intergovernmental manner that bypassed any efforts at supranationalisation (Fabbrini and Puetter 2016). Indeed, the leadership of the crisis was provided mostly by the European Council – which paved the way towards a new Treaty on Stability, Co-ordination and Governance in the Economic and Monetary Union (TSCG or 'fiscal compact') and the necessary legislative measures to ensure financial stability in the Euro area (the so-called 'six-pack' and 'two-pack'). While in the case of the fiscal compact the EP did not have the prerogative to participate in decision-making, in the other two legislative packages it had the possibility to have a say as a co-decider. There seems to be agreement that, although the EP managed to obtain some improvements and enhanced its own role compared to the regime under the Stability and Growth Pact, it could not effectuate major changes and accepted outcomes that had been decided elsewhere (Bressanelli and Chelotti 2016; Fasone 2014). One of the major changes introduced by the new rules on economic governance was the requirement to keep Parliament informed about economic and budgetary surveillance and its capacity to foster a dialogue with the major decision-makers. Therefore, while weak in terms of actually enforcing policy change, Parliament did prove one of the major spaces for debating and legitimising the new economic and fiscal policies. It exerted normative pressure, especially when it came to questions of democratic oversight and the general chains of accountability leading from citizens to the ECB (Fasone 2014; Rittberger 2014).

Conclusion

With this historical overview, we have seen the European Parliament evolve from a 'talking shop' to a mature parliamentary body with full legislative powers and a strong position in the EU's political system. The EP is now able to make itself heard. It has become a major motor of integration, fighting for its own empowerment and (generally) for closer European integration. Its efforts have been helped by a shared belief that the principle of representative democracy should take roots in the EU polity as much as it has done in most of its member states. Therefore, the EP has often been the beneficiary of attempts to fill the democratic gap thought to exist in the EU. Many of the successes enjoyed by the EP are due to the presence of strong personalities, who have not hesitated to use Parliament's formal powers to go beyond the limits of the treaties. The emergence of strong political groups and a European political class has helped the EP find the agency necessary to develop informal institutions and new rules that have contributed to increasing its reputation and influence.

This, however, is a historical interpretation that has been mostly put forward by those that favour a stronger role of the EP. Indeed, despite its substantial empowerment, the EP remains a contested institution – with national parliaments often resenting its tendency to encroach on their own field of action and citizens seeing it as a faraway institution that does not inspire any real attachment. More importantly, the EP is also becoming a field of contestation and a new arena for those opposed to the EU project. The rise of Eurosceptic MEPs in the last 2014 elections poses new challenges to the internal workings and external status of a Parliament that has always been seen as favouring 'an ever closer union'. With the slow awakening of the European Council as a key policy-maker, its place in the EU's political system is also disputed. If the European Union is indeed facing the dawn of a new intergovernmental period, the EP might face the challenge of reinstating itself in the EU's balance of power.

Chapter 3

Internal Organisation

Introduction: organisation as a form of institutionalisation

> For a political system to be viable, for it to succeed in performing tasks of authoritative resource allocation, problem solving, conflict settlement, and so on ... it must be institutionalized. That is to say, organizations must be created and sustained that are specialized to political activity (Polsby 1968: 144)

Although concentrating on the US House of Representatives, Polsby underlined the necessity to organise legislative life in a political system for it to be stable. Indeed, legislatures need to develop internal rules that allow them to make decisions on, for example, the allocation of resources such as time, money and staff as well as to assign parliamentary rights – such as the right to propose amendments or negotiate compromises (Krehbiel 1991: 2). Therefore, the internal organisation of a legislature reveals its capacity to perform in a political system as well as its independence from other institutional actors. Formal and informal rules can decide on the levels of expertise, the capacity of different actors to influence political outputs as well as the loci of power and decision-making.

This chapter describes how the EP is organised and who are the main actors working within the institution. The objective is to set the fundaments for the subsequent chapters, which will explore in more depth its organisational structure and the role of the various institutional actors. Before we explore the functions and role of the EP within the EU's political system, we need first to understand how it controls its various resources and uses its internal rules to organise the legislative life of the institution. Therefore, the chapter examines the different levels of deliberation that contribute to the EP's decision-making process – namely, committees, intergroups and delegations, as well as the plenary. Second, it looks at political structures, focusing on the composition and character of the EP's political groups. It then looks at other ancillary structures, such as the Conference of Presidents, the Conferences of Committee and Delegation Chairs and the Bureau; less well-known bodies that are essential in the daily organisation of the EP. Finally, the chapter turns to the key actors shaping the way the EP translates citizens' demands into outputs. It examines the profile and functions of the MEPs, the EP

President and Vice-Presidents, the Quaestors, committee chairs, political group leaders and coordinators as well as the staff supporting the work of parliamentarians. The aim of the chapter is to provide the necessary knowledge of the main structures and actors in order to better understand how the EP exerts the functions explained in Chapter 4.

Policy-making structures

Various bodies comprise the main policy-making fora of the Parliament. The plenary is certainly the most visible since it regroups all MEPs and is the ultimate decision-making body. However, actual policies and decisions are generally made elsewhere – principally in standing committees

---

Box 3.1   The battle for a single seat

Few parliaments can boast of having three seats, each with its own hemicycle. According to the Treaty of Amsterdam, Strasbourg is the EP's official seat but most work takes place in Brussels, while Luxembourg continues to house the Secretariat. This complicated arrangement is the result of historical developments and the reason why they cannot be undone is easy: the decision on where the EP should seat is in the hands of member states and some of them – particularly France – are unwilling to unravel the status quo.

In the early days of the ECSC, Luxembourg emerged as the headquarters of the High Authority but did not have a place to host the Assembly. It was then decided to use the Council of Europe hemicycle in Strasbourg, at least until 1973, when Luxembourg inaugurated a new hemicycle in the Schuman building and MEPs started to commute between the two cities. The hemicycle in Schuman became too small after the first direct elections in 1979 and was abandoned after 1981. By that time, Strasbourg had built a new seat that became the preferred space to hold plenary sessions, at least until the end of the 1980s, when the EP decided to erect a new seat in Brussels in what is known as the Espace Léopold.

Calls for a single seat started in the early 1980s and have only become louder over time. Already in 1981, the Zagari Report (Doc. 1-333/81) requested the establishment of one single seat. This led to the EP limiting plenary sessions to Strasbourg and committee meetings to Brussels, which was then contested by the Luxembourgish government in the Court of Justice (Case 230/81). As a result, the EP was allowed to abandon plenaries in Luxembourg, but had to keep its Secretariat there. Several resolutions of the EP to narrow its location were hindered by the authorities in both Luxembourg and Strasbourg throughout the 1980s. When the new parliamentary building in Brussels was opened in 1992, Strasbourg and Luxembourg feared becoming marginalised, which led to a deal that ensured plenary sessions would still take place in   →

but also in specialised bodies, such as delegations and intergroups. This section offers an overview of these different fora and their functions in the daily life of the EP.

Plenary

The plenary session is where the 751 MEPs sit to debate and vote. It is the most symbolic body in the EP (see Chapter 10): all decisions must be voted on there and it is also the site where the EP holds the Council, Commission and other EU bodies accountable. Since the Treaty of Amsterdam, the EP is obliged to hold at least 12 plenary sessions per year in Strasbourg and to schedule additional sessions in Brussels (see Box 3.1).

→
Strasbourg on a regular basis – namely 12 sessions per year. At the same time, the Constitutional Affairs Committee requested an amendment to the Treaty of Nice so as to give the EP the right to decide on its own seat by an absolute majority of its members (A5-0086/2000, point 7). The complications that come with navigating three seats became even more problematic after the 2004 enlargement, since Strasbourg was difficult to reach for many new MEPs. This led to a series of initiatives, such as the 'One Seat' online petition (630/2006) launched by the Campaign for Parliament Reform, which took inspiration from the Constitutional Treaty's New Citizens' Initiative and managed to gather over one million signatures (Kaufmann 2006). The EP's Petitions Committee examined the issue in February 2008, which continues to appear regularly in each decision regarding the EU budget (see for instance Resolution P8_TA(2016)0411. On 20 November 2013, the EP gave overwhelming support to a new resolution on the issue with 483 votes to 141 and 34 abstentions, where it committed itself to launch 'an ordinary treaty revision procedure under Article 48 TEU [Treaty on European Union]' since 'the European Parliament would be more effective, cost-efficient and respectful of the environment if it were located in a single place. ... [T]he continuation of the monthly migration between Brussels and Strasbourg has amongst most EU citizens become a symbolic, negative issue detrimental to the European Union's reputation' (P7_TA(2013)0498, points 4 and 2). The 'Single Seat' campaign (http://www.singleseat.eu/), supported by three-quarters of MEPs, has calculated that the running of three seats amounts to the spending of an extra €180 million per year. Catherine Trautmann, Vice-President of Strasbourg Eurometropole and former MEP, has launched an alternative campaign (http://www.theseat.info) to make Strasbourg the only seat of the EP. Therefore, the discussion continues and it will be difficult to solve as long as the decision has to be made under unanimity in the Council, which means that France will continue to block any attempts to move the seat away from Strasbourg, unless a solid counter-offer is presented at the negotiating table.

This means that Parliament meets in Strasbourg one week per month (except in August). There it holds 'part-sessions' lasting four days (from Monday to Thursday). In addition, it also meets in Brussels for two days (Wednesday and Thursday) six times every year. Plenary sittings are usually divided into a tight schedule: Monday evening is dedicated to miscellaneous issues such as announcements from the President or declarations about recent events organised in 'one-minute speeches'; Tuesday, Wednesday and Thursday are dedicated to debating legislative, non-legislative and budgetary reports, interrupted by the midday voting sessions. Voting takes place by a show of hands or roll-call vote – depending on how tight or salient a vote proves to be (see Chapter 10) – and is the time when most MEPs are present in the hemicycle. Tuesday afternoon houses the debates with the Commission, the Council or the High Representative. It may also accommodate a 'key debate' or a formal sitting with important guests, during which no other activities are programmed, so that all MEPs can be present in the plenary.

Debates are chaired by the EP President or one of the 14 Vice-Presidents, who are in charge of ensuring that the rules are respected and speakers limit themselves to the (short) time provided for interventions. MEPs usually communicate in their native language, although some might opt for English to make communication easier and more direct (see Box 3.2).

Box 3.2   Speaking in tongues: Multilingualism in the EP

Multilingualism in legislative bodies is not infrequent; however, few parliaments can boast having 24 official languages that are actively used in the daily work of the institution. India with its 22 languages is probably the closest example, and even there, English and Hindi predominate as working languages. Multilingualism is certainly an asset of the EP – it allows MEPs to communicate directly with their voters, which enhances transparency and accountability. All official languages are considered equal by the Treaties and by the EP's Rule 158, which establishes that all documents of the EP have to be translated into the 24 official languages and that MEPs have the right to interpretation of their own language during debates. In committees and delegations, interpretation is provided as requested by its members or substitutes. On more informal occasions, rules might be relaxed and only a smaller number of combinations provided. →

Committees

Parliamentary committees have been a characteristic of the EP since the early days of the Common Assembly. Despite their limited functions, it was recognised that committees would be essential to coordinate work in a legislature that met in plenary only a few times a year. The importance of committees became particularly apparent after the first direct elections in 1979, when they were significantly expanded (from seven to 16) and turned into the 'backbone' of the Parliament (Westlake 1994: 191). Indeed, most of the work in the EP takes place inside committees: they are responsible for drafting amendments to legislation, scrutinising the work of other EU bodies and organising public hearings and other debates on pressing issues. They enjoy a high level of autonomy, which has led to differentiated norms of conduct, but also recurrent questions about their transparency and accountability (see Chapter 10).

Since 1999, there have been 20 parliamentary committees with a membership ranging from 25 to 71 MEPs (see Table 3.1). Committees should reflect the composition of Parliament as a whole (Rule 199), but it is up to the political groups to nominate members and their substitutes. Most MEPs serve as a member in one committee and as a substitute in a second one. Substitutes have full voting and speaking rights if they are replacing another member and can also serve as rapporteurs. In cases where MEPs act as members of 'neutralised committees' (since 2009, the

---

→ The equality of official languages means that the EP has to ensure up to 552 potential language combinations, which leaves little room for improvisation and has led the EP to employ 330 interpreters and make occasional use of 1,800 external accredited interpreters (European Parliament 2016c). This policy favouring multilingualism has not, however, solved the issue of regional languages such as Catalan or Welsh. This has led to curious situations, where Catalan MEPs prefer to speak French or English rather than addressing the Chamber in Spanish (Clark and Priestley 2012: 172–174). In practice, however, the number of working languages is much more reduced, with English being the most commonly used (The *Guardian* 2014a). Indeed, most EP members and staff are more likely to communicate in 'globish' (also known as 'Eurenglish' or 'EU-speak') than proper English (Busby 2014: 117). And in any case, one should not forget that 'in the European Parliament, decisions are taken in German, communicated in English and applied in French' (Clark and Priestley 2012: 175).

Table 3.1   *Standing committees in the 8th parliamentary term (July 2017)*

	Chair	Full members
Policy-oriented committees		
Agriculture and Rural Development (AGRI)	Czesław Adam Siekierski (EPP, Poland)	45
Civil Liberties, Justice and Home Affairs (LIBE)	Claude Moraes (S&D, UK)	60
Culture and Education (CULT)	Petra Kammerevert (S&D, Germany)	31
Development (DEVE)	Linda McAvan (S&D, UK)	28
Economic and Monetary Affairs (ECON)	Roberto Gualtieri (S&D, Italy)	61
Employment and Social Affairs (EMPL)	Thomas Händel (GUE/NGL, Germany)	55
Environment, Public Health and Food Safety (ENVI)	Adina-Ioana Vălean (EPP, Romania)	69
Fisheries (PECH)	Alain Cadec (EPP, France)	25
Foreign Affairs (AFET)	David McAllister (EPP, Germany)	71
Human Rights (DROI, sub-committee)	Pier Antonio Panzeri (S&D, Italy)	30
Security and Defence (SEDE, sub-committee)	Anna Fotyga (ECR, Poland)	30
Industry, Research and Energy (ITRE)	Jerzy Buzek (EPP, Poland)	67
Internal Market and Consumer Protection (IMCO)	Anneleen van Bossuyt	40
International Trade (INTA)	Bernd Lange (S&D, Germany)	41
Legal Affairs (JURI)	Pavel Svoboda (EPP, Czech Republic)	25
Regional Development (REGI)	Iskra Mihaylova (ALDE, Bulgaria)	43
Transport and Tourism (TRAN)	Karima Delli (Greens/EFA, France)	49

→

→

Thematic committees

Budgets (BUDG)	Jean Arthuis (ALDE, France)	41
Budgetary Control (CONT)	Ingeborg Gräßle (EPP, Germany)	30
Constitutional Affairs (AFCO)	Danuta Maria Hübner (EPP, Poland)	25
Petitions (PETI)	Cecilia Wikström (ALDE, Sweden)	35
Women's Rights and Gender Equality (FEMM)	Vilija Blinkevičiūtė (S&D, Lithuania)	35

Source: European Parliament.

Budgetary Control as well as the Women's Rights and Gender Equality Committees), they can still act as full members of another committee. Once the composition of a committee has been set, a chair, and up to four vice-chairs (which compose the Committee Bureau) are elected for two and a half years (although most stay for the full five-year term). In addition, each committee is supported by a secretariat that gives policy and legal advice and lends support in daily organisation. Committee sittings take place once or twice a month in Brussels, and it is there that legislative, budgetary and own-initiative reports are drafted, amended or adopted. Most standing committees are organised around policy issues, such as environment, trade or agriculture. Some specialise in specific themes, such as drafting or controlling the budget, or examining questions of gender equality. Two of them focus on institutional matters, namely the Constitutional Affairs Committee (AFCO), in charge of regulating the internal organisation of the EP, and the Petitions Committee (PETI), which examines problems and questions brought to the Parliament by EU citizens.

Apart from the standing committees, the EP can set up two other types of temporary committee: special committees (Rule 197) and committees of inquiry (Rule 198 and Decision 95/167/EC). Special committees are set up for up to one year (which might be extended) and examine specific issues; at the moment of setting them up, Parliament can decide on their powers and composition. Special committees have dealt with many different issues and have often had widespread political impact (see Box 3.3). For instance, in July 2000, a special committee on the Echelon Interception System investigated the existence of 'a global system for intercepting communications' (A5-0264/2001, point A) and started a

---

Box 3.3   Special committees in the European Parliament

1997: ESB2 – Monitoring the action taken after the 'mad cow' (BSE) disease crisis

2000–2001: ECHE – Assessing the impact of global interception systems

2001–2002: GENE – Examining new developments in the field of human genetics and the use of new technologies in medicine

2002: FIAP – Following up on the 2001 food-and-mouth disease crisis

2003–2004: MARE – Improving safety at sea after notorious accidents such as those that affected the ships Prestige and Erika

2004–2005: FINP – Defining the EP's priorities for the financial perspectives 2007–2013

2006–2007: TDIP – Investigating the use of EU countries by the CIA to transport and illegally detain prisoners

2007–2009: CLIM – Proposing new EU policies on climate change

2009–2011: CRIS – Evaluating the extent and impact of the financial, economic and social crisis

2010–2011: SURE – Defining the EP's priorities for the post-2013 Multiannual Financial Framework

2012–2013: CRIM – Developing an integrated strategy on organised crime, corruption and money laundering

2015: TAXE 1 – Examining allegations that some EU countries use special tax regimes to favour large corporations

2015–2016: TAXE 2 – Recommending ways of making corporate taxation fairer and clearer

---

still ongoing debate on the use of personal data for surveillance purposes (see also the 2014 Moraes Report on the US National Security Agency [NSA] mass surveillance programme 2013/2188/INI).

Committees of inquiry are generally set up when there are suspicions that EU law has been breached or maladministered (see Box 3.4). It should not investigate issues currently being dealt with in a national or EU court, but otherwise, the EP has the power to set its remit and rules. They can be proposed by one-quarter of MEPs (that is, 187 out of 751 MEPs), but need to be supported by a majority in plenary. Usually, they should not last longer than one year, although their duration can be extended twice by three months. These committees are dependent on external contributions to do their work: they can invite witnesses, hold hearings and request documents, but they cannot force anyone to appear in front of the committee (what is also known as the power to 'subpoena' witnesses). Therefore, if member states or other EU bodies consider the inquiries to affect public security, they can refuse to provide information

> ## Box 3.4   Committees of inquiry in the European Parliament
>
> 1995: TRANSIT – Inquiry into the Community Transit Regime
> 1996: ESB1 – Inquiry into BSE (bovine spongiform encephalopathy)
> 2006–2007: EQUI – Inquiry into the failure of the Equitable Life
>   Assurance Society
> 2016–2017: PANA – Inquiry into money laundering, tax avoidance and
>   tax evasion
> 2016–2017: EMIS – Inquiry into emission measurements in the
>   automotive sector

or ask to hold meetings 'in camera' (not open to the public). Although the EP cannot impose sanctions if it finds fault, it can nevertheless recommend the Commission to initiate infringement proceedings. Equally, the recommendations in its final report are not binding, but standing committees can be asked to monitor the actions taken in its aftermath (European Parliamentary Research Service 2016c).

The idea of these committees dates back to the Rules of Procedure developed after the 1979 direct elections, when the EP organised nine committees to investigate a variety of issues, such as the rise in racism or the handling of nuclear materials. It was not until the Treaty of Maastricht that these instruments were formalised in Article 138c TEU (now Article 226 TFEU). Since then, there have been notable disagreements between the EP and the Council concerning the remit and 'teeth' of these committees (Shackleton 1998). A first compromise was found in the 1995 Inter-Institutional Agreement (Decision 95/167/EC), but since then, the EP has extended some provisions, for instance establishing the practice of going on fact-finding visits in member states or third countries. In 2009, the Constitutional Affairs Committee proposed to substitute the Inter-Institutional Agreement with a new EP regulation, binding on member states, which would have increased the investigative powers of the EP (P7_TA(2014)0429). The resolution was adopted in April 2014, but, since then, the EP has not managed to reach an agreement with the Council and the Commission. Member states are especially concerned about the potential provision of sanctions and investigative means (European Parliamentary Research Service 2016c).

Delegations

The main function of delegations is the external representation of the EU and the promotion of its values; namely, liberty, democracy, human rights, fundamental freedoms and the rule of law. In early 2017, there were 44 delegations with between 12 and 70 members, proposed by political groups. The composition of each delegation should 'ensure as far as possible that Member States and political views are fairly represented' (Rule 212). There are four different types of delegation: joint parliamentary committees, parliamentary cooperation committees, delegations to multilateral parliamentary assemblies and, lastly, inter-parliamentary delegations. The first type, joint parliamentary committees (JPCs), are organised with parliaments of other countries that have signed association agreements with the EU or have already been declared as accession countries. For instance, the EU has established JPCs with Chile and Mexico – with which it has association agreements – Albania and Serbia – candidate countries – and with other international organisations – such as the Arab Maghreb Union and the European Economic Area (EEA). JPCs normally meet once or twice a year and are charged with developing policy priorities and, as appropriate, scrutinising the implementation of association agreements or the progress made in candidate countries. The second type, parliamentary cooperation committees (PCCs), are set up with countries part of the European Neighbourhood Policy that have signed a strategic partnership agreement with the EU. In 2017, there were PCCs with Armenia, Azerbaijan and Georgia; Moldova; Russia; Ukraine and a joint delegation for Kazakhstan, Kyrgyzstan, Uzbekistan, Tajikistan, Turkmenistan and Mongolia. The third group contains delegations to parliamentary assemblies, such as the North Atlantic Treaty Organization (NATO), the Euro-Latin American Parliamentary Assembly (EuroLat) and the African, Caribbean and Pacific Group of States (ACP)-EU Joint Parliamentary Assembly. Each parliamentary assembly has different functions, but the EP delegation often sits there as a representative of the EU as a whole. Finally, there are other inter-parliamentary delegations, which aim to promote relations with third countries that do not fall under any of the other categories. Some of these delegations aim to establish contacts with parliaments of a single country (for instance with South Africa, the US or India), while others work with regional groups, like the Arab Peninsula or the Association of Southeast Asian Nations (ASEAN). The EP can also set up ad hoc delegations or organise election observation teams. Some of these ad hoc delegations have become permanent, such as the one for relations with Iraq. Others might investigate crises that emerge during the legislature, as with the 2014 visit to assess the conditions of Palestinian inmates in Israeli prisons, which became highly controversial when the Israeli government denied them access to prisons (European Parliament 2014d). Ad hoc delegations can serve a more functional service, such as attending specific events like the annual session of the Parliamentary Conference on the World Trade

Organization (WTO). The Foreign Affairs Committee coordinates the work of the delegations, but also cooperates with the Committees on Development and on International Trade.

The widespread activities of these different delegations show that the EP has acted as an activist for parliamentarism and multilateralism. It has been a keen promoter of parliaments as channels for popular representation, especially among developing or newly democratised countries. The EP has sometimes acted as a proselytiser of parliamentarism, forcing dialogue with largely sceptical organisations like the WTO or the United Nations (UN). It has also favoured multilateralism with regional organisations like the ACP or with the Union for the Mediterranean, set up in the framework of the 1995 Barcelona Summit. There is now extensive overlap between bilateral and multilateral forms of cooperation, which does nothing to alleviate the increasing workload and media criticism of 'MEPs' jaunts'. The reasons for this high level of activity are complex, going back to the EP's attempt to have a bigger say in foreign policy (especially before it had any say in international agreements), the cultural links of some MEPs with specific world regions, and the presence of MEPs with past careers in foreign policy. Despite the problems associated with this form of parliamentary activism and the potential overlap with other EU bodies – particularly the High Representative – the work of delegations has proved useful to raise and maintain attention on human rights breaches. In the case of the US, the EP delegation has shifted from acting as a slightly overenthusiastic counterpart to becoming an established partner with a permanent office in Washington and an institutionalised 'transatlantic legislative dialogue' (Clark and Priestley 2012: 346–354; Stavridis and Irrera 2015).

Intergroups

Intergroups are consortia formed by MEPs with the intention of exchanging views on specific topics in which they have a common interest and to maintain close contact with civil society. These groups are not official bodies and, therefore, cannot reflect the EP's official position. However, they can receive the logistical support of political and external groups, with any external assistance having to be declared and published on the EP's website (Rule 34). At the beginning of the 2014 legislature, 28 groups were recognised by the EP, ranging in both interests and number of members. For instance, the intergroup on 'anti-racism and diversity' has only 28 members, while the 'lesbian, gay, bisexual, transgender and intersex rights (LGBTI)' intergroup has a whopping 139 members. There are also groups for small and medium-sized enterprises, for minority communities and languages, for those interested in sports, one on the Western Sahara and the appealingly named 'Wine, Spirits and Quality Foodstuffs'.

Apart from official intergroups, Corbett et al. (2016: 246) make reference to a parallel world of non-registered intergroups, too small or irregular to become official. Nedergaard and Jensen (2014) mapped these intergroups and confirmed a great variance in the amount of institutionalisation and resources. This variation is generally dependent on whether intergroups have been formally recognised by and receive logistical support from the EP. Intergroups can become a point of access for interest groups and lobbyists (see Chapter 7), but they also foment networks beyond political groups or committees, improve information flows and develop into specialised fora in which to nurture new policy proposals (Bouwen 2004b: 484; Dutoit 2016; Nedergaard and Jensen 2014). Participation in intergroups can also send a signal to voters and might even improve the chances of being re-elected (Wilson et al. 2016).

Political structures

Apart from the policy-making structures that act as central fora for deliberation, over time, the EP has developed a set of political structures that organise the daily life of MEPs and help to resolve internal conflicts.

Political groups

Central among the EU's political structures are political groups. If committees are said to be the backbone of the EP, then political groups are its life force. Indeed, they have made of it a true parliament organised along ideological lines and not just a house representing territorial interests (see also Chapter 9). This is a direct legacy of the ECSC Assembly, which decided early on to recognise the formation of three political groups: Christian Democrats, Socialists and Liberals (see Chapter 2). Indeed, these three groups still constitute the core of the Parliament, but other formations have now been added along the political spectrum. In 2017, there were eight political groups in the EP (see Table 3.2) ranging from extreme left to extreme right, with most Eurosceptics situated at both ideological poles. Political groups can be formed by at least 25 MEPs sharing the same political affinity and representing at least one-quarter of member states (seven out of 28) (Rule 32). MEPs cannot belong to more than one political group and those that decide not to be part of a political group are labelled as 'non-attached'.

The requirement that MEPs share a 'political affinity' seeks to avoid the formation of purely technical groups. In 1999, several small parties (among them the French Front National and the Italian Radicals of the Emma Bonino List) attempted to create a Technical Group of Independent Members (TDI) but it was rejected by the EP plenary and

Table 3.2   *Political groups at the European Parliament (July 2017)*

Political group	Size	Number of MS represented	Political orientation
European People's Party (EPP)	215	27	Centre-right/ right-wing
Progressive Alliance of Socialists and Democrats in the European Parliament (S&D)	189	28	Centre-left
European Conservatives and Reformists (ECR)	73	18	Conservative/ Eurosceptic
Alliance of Liberals and Democrats for Europe (ALDE)	68	21	Centrist
European United Left Nordic Green Left (GUE/NGL)	52	14	Far-left
Greens/European Free Alliance (Greens/EFA)	51	18	Left-wing
Europe of Freedom and Direct Democracy (EFDD)	42	8	Eurosceptic
Europe of Nations and Freedom (ENF)	40	9	Far-right/ Eurosceptic

Source: European Parliament.

dissolved in 2001. They brought the case to the Court of First Instance and then to the European Court of Justice, which dictated that the EP could indeed dissolve groups without political affinity to ensure its proper functioning (Joined Cases T-222/99, T-327/99, T-329/99; Case C-486/01 P). Meanwhile, the Constitutional Affairs Committee revised the Rules of Procedure and decided to add an interpretation to make it more explicit that if the members that want to form a group denied having any political affinity, then the EP may evaluate whether they are following the rules (1999/2181/REG).

This case raises the question: why would MEPs want to be part of a political group – even when they hold radically opposed ideologies? The main reason is that political groups possess formal and informal resources that are not available to individual MEPs. Crucially, political groups control the appointment of leadership positions, such as vice-presidencies or committee chairmanships, and the allocation of reports. They also enjoy more speaking time in plenary, a bigger budget and more support in terms of secretariat and staff. Therefore, it is difficult to function outside the structures and resources of political groups. That is why parties at the fringes, especially those on the far right of the political spectrum, have tried repeatedly to form stable political groups.

Usually, political groups are organised around a Bureau composed of the chair and vice-chairs as well as the leaders of each national party delegation (NPD). They also have treasurers in charge of the group's finances as well as 'whips', who ensure that MEPs stick to the voting lists and attend the plenary sessions. However, as we will examine in more depth in Chapter 9, whips have hardly any tools to ensure the discipline of members and often have to compete with alternative voting lists drafted by national delegations. Vice-chairs or other collaborators of the group's leader often act as 'floor leaders', which might comprise a high diversity of tasks, such as chairing meetings with political coordinators (see below) or allocating speaking time. The rest of the vice-chairs might also be allocated other responsibilities, like liaising with the media (Clark and Priestley 2012: 201–202).

Conference of Presidents

The Conference of Presidents is the political body composed of the EP's President and the leader of each political group. One representative of the non-attached group can also attend, but does not have the right to vote. The Conference of Presidents is in charge of organising the daily business and legislative planning of the EP. To this effect, Rule 27 defines its duties, which consist in preparing the EP's timetable and the agenda for the plenary sittings; deciding on the responsibilities and composition of committees and delegations as well as on the allocation of plenary seats; deciding on matters concerning the EP's relations with other EU bodies, national parliaments, third countries and international bodies; and consulting civil society on major topics by organising public debates.

The idea of a Conference of Presidents emerged during the Treaty of Rome negotiations as a coordination mechanism inspired by the workings of the French National Assembly (European Parliament 2007b: 33; Teasdale 2012). Since then, the Conference of Presidents has gradually concentrated more powers and grown into the strongest political body of the EP (see also Box 3.5). It usually takes place twice a month and its decisions are made either by consensus or by weighting the votes according to the political groups' size. Some have remarked that the Conference of Presidents has developed a working culture where consensus and dialogue prevail, which means that smaller groups are rarely outvoted; rather, they tend to punch above their weight when it comes to seeing proposals or initiatives voted through (Clark and Priestley 2012: 84–85). At the same time, these decisions might hide power struggles

---

Box 3.5 The 'G5' is dead – long life to the 'G6'?

Since Juncker became Commission President in 2014, a new form of informal dialogue emerged between the leaders of the EP and the Commission. About twice a month, Commission President Jean-Claude Juncker, Commission Vice-President Frans Timmermans, EP President Martin Schulz, European People's Party (EPP) group leader Manfred Weber and Socialist and Democrats (S&D) group leader Gianni Pittella met for a so-called 'G5' dinner. It is said that Timmermans came up with the idea to help the EP get Juncker's agenda through in an increasingly Eurosceptic plenary. It also reflected the 'grand coalition' that the EPP and the S&D struck at the beginning of the legislative term. The meetings served to agree on the agenda of the EP, broker deals between the two largest groups and ensure a stable legislative coalition. Not everyone in the EP welcomed the 'G5' meetings. Smaller groups resented the power of the two largest groups and were reluctant to rubber-stamp a largely 'pre-cooked' agenda. Some, like liberal leader Guy Verhofstadt, tried to convince the 'G5' members to turn it into a 'G7', which would include him and Commission Vice-President Andrus Ansip (also a Liberal). On the other hand, the S&D became increasingly sceptical of these meetings, which served to implement a largely EPP agenda. The 'G5' claimed some successes, such as the support of the Commission's 2015 budget plans or the defeat of a motion of censure against Juncker presented by the far-right groups in November 2015. However, after the election of Antonio Tajani (EPP) as EP President and the break-up of the 'grand coalition' in January 2017, the 'G5' ceased to exist. In its aftermath, some MEPs have promoted a 'G6', which would sit the chairs of all EP political groups around the table – except those of the Eurosceptic and far-right parties (Politico 2015e, 2017f). Therefore, even if the membership changes radically, the original idea (to isolate Eurosceptics) remains in place.

---

between groups, especially between large and small groups. That is why the content of minutes is carefully controlled before it goes to other MEPs: the Conference of Presidents is unwilling to let out any hints of inter-party disagreement and always tries to prevent 'the political fall-out likely to result from divergent interpretations of conference deliberations' (Judge and Earnshaw 2008: 164).

The Bureau

The Bureau is the administrative and governing body of the Parliament. It is composed of the EP's President, 14 Vice-Presidents and five Quaestors (although only in a consultative capacity, see below) elected for a period of two and a half years and renewable for the same length of time. According to Rule 25, the Bureau administers the internal functioning of the EP, especially when it comes to drafting the EP's budget and deciding on extraordinary meetings or the formation of ad hoc delegations (see above). It is also in charge of appointing the Secretary General – who has become an increasingly powerful figure inside the EP – and establishes the organisation of the EP's Secretariat. More importantly, since 2004, it decides on funding for European political parties, which has not been without controversy. Despite the manifold rules for obtaining a grant, in April 2016, the alarm bells sounded when it was discovered that the EP had been funding an EU-wide neo-Nazi political party. As a result, the EP launched the rarely used Rule 225 procedure (modified by Rule 223a), which allowed the Constitutional Affairs Committee to ascertain 'whether or not a political party at European level is continuing (particularly in its programme and in its activities) to observe the principles upon which the European Union is founded' (European Parliament 2016d). Shortly after, the Bureau also asked Eurosceptic MEP Morten Messerschmidt to repay a €400,000 grant deemed to have been used to promote his national party (Danish People's Party), which is not allowed by the EP's rules (Euobserver 2016a, see also Chapter 9).

College of Quaestors

The College of Quaestors is composed of five MEPs elected by a majority secret ballot after the President and Vice-Presidents have been selected. As with Vice-Presidents, candidates can be proposed by political groups or at least five per cent of MEPs (Rules 15 and 18). That gives the opportunity to offer leadership positions to smaller delegations (although in the 2014–2019 parliamentary term most members came from large or medium-sized countries). In some cases, such as with the election of Astrid Lulling in 1999 or Bill Newton Dunn in 2009, Quaestors have been elected among candidates who had not been proposed by their political groups, but enjoyed a good reputation or promised to protect the interests of members.

The role of the College of Quaestors is to regulate administrative and financial issues that affect directly the working conditions of MEPs. In this sense, it has a more limited function than the bodies of the French and Italian assemblies on which it was modelled, which leads to a certain overlap or competition with the Bureau. Usually, the tasks are relatively menial, such as distributing office space or ensuring the quality of the EP's canteen; they can also act as the voice of members, especially when there are attempts at limiting their rights or burdening them with complex rules. However, given their extensive knowledge of administrative matters, they have often slowed down reform processes, such as the introduction of a Member's Statute. As a result, the Quaestors have enjoyed a complicated relationship with the Bureau – which has at times tried to abolish them – and with the Budget and Budgetary Control committees, often reluctant to implement the College's decisions (Clark and Priestley 2012: 210–211). When it comes to regulating lobbying (see also Chapter 7), the Quaestors in charge of security could potentially act as gatekeepers in the admittance of interest groups' representatives, since they are in charge of granting and withdrawing badges (the access cards to enter the EP buildings, see Rule 116a). However, since badges are hardly ever denied and almost never revoked, in reality they rarely play an active role as gatekeepers (Bouwen 2003).

The Conference of Committee Chairs

Once a month, usually during the Strasbourg session, the chairs of all standing and temporary committees meet in order to coordinate their work and resolve conflicts. At the beginning of a new legislative term, they elect a chair among their members – Cecilia Wikström (ALDE) for the 2014–2019 term – who is also present at the meetings of the Conference of Presidents. The Conference of Committee Chairs was formerly part of the Conference of Presidents, but with the increasing workload and growing membership, it was decided to set up a separate body, eventually institutionalised when the Rules of Procedure were modified in 1993 (now Rule 29). The tasks of the Conference have also become more substantial, especially with the heavier legislative agenda that has come as a result of co-decision. It is now responsible for programming the inter-institutional legislative work and contributes to drafting the EP agenda. It also scrutinises the Commission's annual programme and maintains a regular dialogue with the Council Presidency. However, one of the major roles of the Conference is its function as mediator, since it decides on the allocation of reports and can thus settle conflicts of competences or decide whether a report should be shared among various committees (see also Chapter 10). In general, it has become a forum for deliberation where chairs can exchange best practices and information regarding the internal work of committees or their role in inter-institutional activities (European Parliament 2012: 37–38).

The Conference of Delegation Chairs

As with committees, the growing number of delegations has led to the creation of an independent body in charge of coordinating their activities and potential overlaps (Rule 30). It functions in a similar manner to the other conferences; namely, it gathers the chairs of all standing inter-parliamentary delegations and elects its chair. It is in charge of drafting the annual calendar, coordinating with the Foreign Affairs and Development Committees and making recommendations to the Conference of Presidents.

Key actors

These different bodies would not signify much without the actors that constitute them. The personality, background and reputation of specific persons can make or break an institutional role. That is why this last section reviews the key actors that institute the actual machinery and power of the EP and examines their main profile and functions. One should not forget that MEPs also receive the support of lesser-known actors, such as assistants and the Secretariat, but these will be examined in more depth in Chapter 8.

The EP has concentrated its governing and political powers in the hands of several leadership positions that reinforce the institutionalisation provided by structures such as committees and political groups. The most renowned roles are those of the President and the 14 Vice-Presidents. Together with the Quaestors, they are nominated by political groups or at least five per cent of MEPs and elected for a period of two and a half years renewable for another term (Rule 15). Formally, all leadership positions are distributed proportionally, using the D'Hondt method, first among the political groups and then among national party

---

Box 3.6   A week in the agenda of the EP President (20/06/2016–26/06/2016)

Monday, June 20, 2016: Berlin

13:30 Participating in discussion 'Don't ask what Europe can do for you, but what you can do for Europe!' at event 'Europe calling #Berlin: What is keeping Europe together?'
17:00 Meeting with Angela Merkel, Chancellor of Germany

Tuesday, June 21, 2016: Brussels

15:00 The European Eco-Management and Audit Scheme (EMAS) and Environmental Policy signing ceremony

Wednesday, June 22, 2016: Brussels

10:30 Meeting with Michael Bloomberg, UN Secretary General Special Envoy for Cities and Climate Change
14:30 Meeting with Reuven Rivlin, President of the State of Israel
15:00 Chairing of the Plenary: Address by Reuven Rivlin, President of the State of Israel   →

delegations. There is, however, room for negotiation about the exact distribution and the names attached to each position. These negotiations are then translated into a list of candidates that is submitted to the EP plenary for a vote. Therefore, leadership positions are a way to reward MEPs that have contributed to advancing the interests of their political group or the EP as a whole.

President of the EP

The role of President is the highest position that can be reached within the EP. The President has manifold responsibilities: as we have seen above, (s)he chairs the plenary sittings as well as the Conference of the Presidents and the Bureau. (S)he is also in charge of implementing the Rules of Procedure and overseeing all activities of the assembly, including representing it in legal matters. When it comes to the EP's legislative and budgetary functions, (s)he signs the final acts and may chair the conciliation meetings. However, the President also has an external representative function. At the inter-institutional level, (s)he is allowed to express the views of the EP before the start of a European Council meeting and during treaty reforms; (s)he also sits at the ministerial meetings of the Intergovernmental Conference. Finally, the President also acts as the EP's voice outside of the Union, for instance going on official visits to third countries. This list makes for a very busy agenda and requires a lot of travelling within and outside of the EU (see Box 3.6).

→

Thursday, June 23, 2016: Brussels

11:00 Chairing of the Plenary: Address by Mahmoud Abbas, President of the Palestinian National Authority
11:30 Meeting with Mahmoud Abbas, President of the Palestinian National Authority
12:00 Press statement with Mahmoud Abbas, President of the Palestinian National Authority

Friday, June 24, 2016: Brussels

08:00 Extraordinary Conference of Presidents, followed by press point (press conference)
10:30 Meeting with Donald Tusk, President of the European Council, Jean-Claude Juncker, President of the European Commission and Mark Rutte, Prime-Minister of the Netherlands

Saturday, June 25, 2016: Constituency
Sunday, June 26, 2016: Constituency

Source: European Parliament (2016a).

Until the re-election of Martin Schulz in 2014, no other President had managed to stay longer than 30 months in the job. This was mostly due to the unofficial rule used since the 1979 direct elections that limited the mandate of each President to a term of two and a half years. This trend became even more marked after 1989, as an even more informal rule saw the EPP and the S&D taking turns at the presidency, with the party receiving more votes in the elections holding the office in the first half-term and passing it to the other in the second half. Only in 1999 was the rule broken due to disagreements about which political group should go first; as a result, the EPP made a deal with the Liberals, which voted in Nicole Fontaine in return for a run at the presidency in 2002 by Pat Cox (Kreppel and Hix 2003). Subsequently, the normal rhythm was re-established, with Josep Borrell (Socialist) occupying the first half of the sixth parliamentary term (2004–2007) and passing it to Hans-Gert Pöttering (Christian Democrat), who acted as President from 2007 to 2009. He was followed by Jerzy Buzek (EPP, 2009–2012) and Martin Schulz (S&D, 2012–2017). Many former Presidents have stayed in the EP and, although some have become leaders of their groups or committee chairs, they have often found it difficult to return back to their life as a 'normal' parliamentarian (Clark and Priestley 2012: 228–234).

Schulz's re-election turned him into the longest-serving President, even though an EPP candidate should have been elected in 2014, since they had won the largest number of seats. His nomination, however, should be understood in the context of the Spitzenkandidaten campaign and his support for Jean-Claude Juncker as Commission President (see Box 5.2). These 'backroom deals', however, have been increasingly contested by smaller political groups, which denounce the lack of transparency and democracy in the procedure. This did not stop the EPP and ALDE from signing a new deal to replace Schulz in January 2017. The election of Antonio Tajani (Italian Christian-democrat and former spokesman of Prime Minister Silvio Berlusconi) was viewed mostly as a victory for the Liberals, which managed to break up the 'grand coalition' between the EPP and the S&D and became once again the Parliament's 'kingmaker' (Crombez 2017). Indeed, the election of the EP President has become increasingly contested, which reflects the gradual acquisition of 'imperial powers' (Clark and Priestley 2012: 227). Rule 22 states that the President 'shall enjoy all the powers necessary to preside over the proceedings of Parliament and to ensure that they are properly conducted'. However, the rule leaves wide room for interpretation and for very different forms of leadership. Over the years, we have seen a range of presidential styles that have reflected the personality of the different Presidents and their personal agendas. Among those with an activist agenda, some have adopted a more institutional profile – Klaus Hänsch (1994–1997), for instance, introduced new procedures such as the hearings of Commissioners-Designates – while others have preferred to focus on specific issues, as was the case with Pat Cox's pro-enlargement activities. Others, like José Maria Gil-Robles (1997–1999), have seen themselves as *primus inter pares* – speaking on behalf of the EP's majority.

Josep Borrell (2004–2007) was probably the first case of presidential activism, which led him to adopt a higher profile and more active role in dealing with the other institutions. The brief length of his mandate and the efforts of the EPP group to stop his initiatives stifled his ambitions for change. Indeed, the fact that most Presidents only stay for two and a half years has made it more difficult to implement larger institutional changes. The election of Martin Schulz, however, supposed a qualitative leap in terms of powers and visibility. Schulz took presidential activism to the extreme and was lauded and criticised in equal parts for it. In 2012, when he replaced Buzek, Schulz adopted a more confrontational style with member states and 'sought to fashion a new, overtly political model for the EP Presidency, in contrast to the more reserved, ceremonial model followed by his predecessors' (Dinan 2013: 79). His initial thrust was clearly an attempt to make a successful bid for the position of socialist Spitzenkandidat. Although he did not manage to become Commission President, the post-electoral bargaining among member states and EU institutions helped him to be re-elected to the EP presidency. Thereafter, he continued on his ambitious path to become the face and voice of the EP. Indeed, he openly expressed his goals by declaring: 'I told myself, the moment I become president of the European Parliament, I will try to make the institution more audible, more visible' (cited in Politico 2015d). In an EP less charged with legislative work (due to the Commission's 'less but better' motto), Schulz attempted to turn Parliament into the EU's main debating arena – turning the 'State of the European Union' speech of Jean-Claude Juncker into a high profile event and hosting debates with Greek Prime Minister Alexis Tsipras at the height of the bailout crisis (Politico 2015d). These ambitions were accompanied by a strengthening of the President's office and his closest allies, which was not well received by other MEPs and political leaders. Many saw his efforts as an attempt to strengthen his own position and that of the major political groups and some were concerned that a great part of the top jobs in the EP had landed in German hands (Politico 2016d). His gamble seems to have paid off: despite much incertitude, on 24 January 2017, he was named Spitzenkandidat for the role of German Chancellor by the German Social-Democrats (SPD).

Vice-Presidents

The main task of the 14 Vice-Presidents involves representing the President in case of his or her absence. Vice-Presidents are also responsible for chairing plenary sessions, supporting the Bureau's work and representing the EP in international relationships. The order of precedence is established by the number of votes they receive in a secret ballot election, which leaves some space for running individual campaigns and playing political games. However, candidates still need the support of their political group; the only MEP who managed to get himself elected running an 'independent' candidature (Edward McMillan-Scott) was eventually forced out of the British Conservatives and the European Conservatives and Reformists (ECR) group (Clark and Priestley 2012: 212). Normally, each Vice-President will be allocated a 'portfolio', such as security, relations with the press, buildings, budget or multilingualism, among others. A group of Vice-Presidents are in charge of representing the EP in conciliation committees (though there are now very few of these) and another is in control of relations with national parliaments. Vice-Presidents have interpreted the responsibility of a portfolio differently – some treat it as a ministerial post, others prefer to delegate their duties to the Secretariat in charge of their area, while most take a middle course and expect to have an input on the proposals made by EP officials (Clark and Priestley 2012: 215–216).

The nomination of Vice-Presidents in 2014 showed a larger presence of MEPs from new member states (seven, compared to five in the previous legislature), which seemed to indicate the growing experience and influence of these MEPs as well as the rise in Eurosceptic and radical parties in old member states. However, the mid-term reshuffle in early 2017 brought the number back to five. When it comes to the distribution across party lines, the election of Tajani as President changed the balance across the largest groups: while the EPP went from six to four Vice-Presidents, the S&D managed to secure two more positions (from three to five). The Liberals kept their two Vice-Presidents, as did the Greens/European Free Alliance (Greens/EFA), European United Left – Nordic Green Left (GUE-NGL) and ECR, which had one each. This means that the far-right and Eurosceptic groups were not represented in the Bureau.

Political group leaders

At the top of the EP's political hierarchy sit the chairs of the political groups. They are in charge of providing political leadership, dealing with the other groups and contributing to collective agreements and legislative decision-making. Acting as a political group leader is often seen as a necessary step to becoming EP President; therefore, they need to deliver a good performance and build their reputation across party lines. Each group has a different tradition in terms of selection procedures and types of chairmanship but, as Table 3.3 shows, candidates from the largest

Table 3.3 *Chairs of the EP political groups 2014–2019 (July 2017)*

Group	*Chair*	*Nationality*	*National Party*
European People's Party (EPP)	Manfred Weber	German	Christlich-Soziale Union (CSU)
Progressive Alliance of Socialists and Democrats in the European Parliament (S&D)	Gianni Pittella	Italian	Partito Democratico
European Conservatives and Reformists Group (ECR)	Syed Kamall	British	Conservative Party
	Ryszard Legutko	Polish	Prawo i Sprawiedliwość
Alliance of Liberals and Democrats for Europe (ALDE)	Guy Verhofstadt	Belgian	Open Vlaamse Liberalen en Democraten
Confederal Group of the European United Left – Nordic Green Left (GUE-NGL)	Gabriele Zimmer	German	Die Linke
Greens/European Free Alliance (Greens/EFA)	Ska Keller	German	Bündnis 90/Die Grünen
	Philippe Lamberts	Belgian	Ecologistes Confédérés pour l'Organisation de Luttes Originales
Europe of Freedom and Direct Democracy Group (EFDD)	Nigel Farage	British	United Kingdom Independence Party
Europe of Nations and Freedom Group (ENF)	Marcel de Graaff	Dutch	Partij voor de Vrijheid

Source: European Parliament.

national party groups tend to have better chances of becoming political group leaders. As can be seen, groups occasionally decide to elect two members to act as co-chairs. This might have different grounds based on the group's culture or history. In the case of the Greens, it reflects the values of a party that has traditionally tried to avoid hierarchical structures and concentrating leadership in one person. The statutes of the group also underline that at least one of the co-chairs has to be a woman. In comparison, until January 2017, the Europe of Freedom and Direct Democracy (EFDD) group had two chairs that reflected the two ideological wings of the group, with Farage representing the right-wing Eurosceptic line and Borrelli representing the left. These two ideological lines often made it difficult for the chairs to work together and find some sort of cohesion inside the group, which explains the attempts of Borrelli to defect to ALDE – and the need to give up the leadership of the EFDD group when his strategy failed (Politico 2017a). The presence of co-chairs in the far-right Europe of Nations and Freedom (ENF) group used to reflect the character of their founders – Marine Le Pen (Front National) and Geert Wilders (Party for Freedom) – who were keen to maintain their strong leadership inside the group. This has become increasingly complicated, since Wilders, who was never an MEP, had to appoint a member of his party (Marcel de Graaff) to act as co-chair in his place. De Graaff was left as the sole chair of the group after Marine Le Pen won a seat in the French Assembly in the elections of June 2017. Finally, Brexit opened new challenges for the ECR, since the British Conservatives were its largest national delegation. Therefore, the group decided to create a joint chairmanship in July 2017 to assist the transitional period leading to the UK's exit from the EU.

The usual path to become group chair is to climb the leadership steps and give a strong performance that can convince the other party members. In a way, Schulz's ascendancy owed much to Silvio Berlusconi, who during Italy's 2003 Presidency addressed him in plenary and declared: 'Mr Schulz, I know there is in Italy a man producing a film on the Nazi concentration camps. I would like to suggest you for the role of leader. You'd be perfect' (in The *Guardian* 2003). The incident served to make Schulz better known to the European public and to convince his colleagues of his adequacy to become first vice-chair and then chair of the socialist group (Clark and Priestley 2012: 205). Albeit receiving less attention from the media, Manfred Weber, EPP chair for the 2014–2019 legislative term, followed a similar career path. After acting as political group coordinator in the Civil Liberties Committee from 2006 to 2009, he became vice-chair of the group in 2009 and stood as the only candidate in the election of the chair in 2014. Others have had to overcome higher hurdles to become chairs. Gianni Pittella, a former Vice-President of the S&D group, stood to substitute Hannes

Swoboda (Austria) as group leader. He had points in his favour, such as his parliamentary experience and the fact that, after the 2014 EP elections, the Italian Partito Democratico had superseded the German SPD and become the largest party inside the S&D. However, his election as EPP leader in July 2014 was not straightforward – he was not only perceived as not very charismatic and lacking language skills, but also had to stand against a candidate (Pina Picierno) handpicked by former Italian Prime Minister Matteo Renzi. Despite these challenges, Pittella managed to gather enough support, although some have pointed out his difficulties to keep up with the 'G5' dinners (see Box 3.5 above) due to his poor English and lack of proficiency in German (European Voice 2014a; Politico 2015e).

Committee chairs

The role of committee chairs in the EP is similar to that of their national counterparts: they are in charge of presiding over committee sessions, facilitating coordination among the members and representing the committee in the outside world. They are also increasingly associated with inter-institutional negotiations, since they are part of the team representing the EP in trilogues (see Chapter 11). Chairs have very different working styles and personalities; some adopt more 'presidential' styles and become recognised figures by committee members and outsiders, while others prefer to adopt a lower profile and more technocratic type of management. Some of them have become fixtures of a committee and shaped its role and image. For instance, Elmar Brok (German EPP member) chaired the Foreign Affairs Committee between 1999 and 2017; despite not having legislative powers, the committee has gained such a reputation that it is now considered a reward for high profile members, like former Prime or Foreign Ministers. Ken Collins was chair of the environmental committee for 15 years (and was succeeded by two long-standing members of the committee), which greatly helped to shape the reputation of the EP as an environmental champion (Burns et al. 2012: 66).

Although chairs are theoretically elected by committees, in reality positions are allocated by political groups. This means that, in practice, the number of committees allocated to each political group is based on their size. The D'Hondt system also sees that chairs are allocated proportionally in an alternate fashion. Therefore, the system does not allow the largest group to select its preferred committees all at once. Instead, if we take the example of the elections in 2014, the EPP could choose its preferred committee, then the S&D had a chance to do the same, then again the EPP could go on to select its second choice among what was left, then the same for the S&D, and so on. Smaller groups such as the ECR and

ALDE would only appear in the sixth or seventh round, while the Greens would need to wait until the 11th round. Therefore, the two largest groups have a bigger choice and more opportunities to be allocated their preferred committees. In the end, in 2014, the EPP received eight chairs, the S&D seven, ALDE three, and the ECR two, while the GUE/NGL and the Greens received one each. Although the EFDD should have received the chair of the Petitions committee, its members decided to 'revolt' and voted instead for ALDE's Cecilia Wikström. The vote managed to kill two birds with the same stone: it allowed mainstream parties to ostracise the Eurosceptics and deny them any leadership positions and it rewarded the liberal group for supporting the 'grand coalition' of the EPP and the S&D (Politico 2014).

Once the chairs have been distributed among the political groups, it is up to their leaders to decide which national delegation and specific member is going to occupy the position. Usually, they are allocated either to those nationalities that have been left out of other jobs or to the biggest national delegations inside the political group. Therefore, the distribution follows a complex process that tries to maintain some proportionality in terms of political affiliation and nationality. Indeed, political groups need to ensure a delicate balance among their national party delegations, which means that those countries that have missed out on another leadership position, such as Vice-President or political group leader, might then be allocated a committee chairmanship. For instance, in 2014, a Bulgarian Liberal (and newcomer to the EP) was nominated as chair of the Committee on Regional Development; Iskra Mihaylova's party (Movement for Rights and Freedoms) is the second largest in ALDE. Since political groups are in charge of appointments, it is often difficult to ensure a balance among nationalities. For instance, at the beginning of the 2014–2019 term, there was a slight increase in the number of chairs from the new member states, which held eight out of 22 chairmanships (compared to only one in the previous term), but after the mid-term reshuffle in early 2017, the big member states maintained their numerical advantage – with Germany, Poland, France and the UK leading the number of appointments (see also Box 10.3).

However, other matters such as expertise and reputation often influence the selection of individual members. For instance, in 2014, Danuta Hübner (Polish EPP member) was elected as chair of the Committee on Constitutional Affairs, which did not come as a surprise given her long-term engagement with parliamentary reform. At the same time, Jean Arthuis (ALDE French MEP) received the chairmanship of the Budgets Committee (BUDG), a big prize for a newcomer to the EP. It was, however, appreciated that Arthuis had a thorough knowledge of such technical matters and had acted as the French Finance Minister and chair of the Finance Committee of the French Senate before coming to the EP (European Voice 2014b). In general, chairs are often former political coordinators or active members of the committee, as was the case with Claude Moraes (UK), elected chair of the Civil Liberties (LIBE) committee in 2014 after acting as the S&D political coordinator in the previous legislature and being a very engaged member since 2004.

Political group coordinators

Political groups have made increasing use of committee members charged with coordinating the positions of their colleagues and working closely with rapporteurs and shadow rapporteurs. Coordinators are elected by their peers and usually are long-serving members of the committee with high levels of expertise. They act as an information channel and play a mediating role between individual members, the wider political group and national delegations. According to Rule 205, political group coordinators are in charge of appointing rapporteurs and shadow rapporteurs and organising the hearings of Commissioners-Designates. They also ensure the coherence of the group in committee and plenary by drafting voting instructions and ensuring attendance. Since they have become more involved with the day-to-day organisation of the committee and its legislative agenda, they may be perceived as competitors of the committee Bureau and the chair, although this depends largely on each committee and the personalities of coordinators and committee leaders (Kaeding and Obholzer 2012; Ringe 2010: 59).

Table 3.4 offers an overview of the distribution of political coordinators across groups and nationalities. As can be seen, the number of coordinators was relatively similar for both mainstream and Eurosceptic groups. As for nationalities, the dispersion was more accentuated, with Germany leading with a whopping number of 36 coordinators – far ahead of the other larger countries (for instance, France with 22 and Italy with only 17). It is interesting to note that Brits were the second biggest collective – which shows their ability to occupy key positions of influence in the EP, a fact that could prove interesting when the UK leaves the EU.

Conclusion

This overview of the EP's internal workings has shown how complex the EP has become; it has grown in terms of both size – with more members and political parties – as well as functions. The response of the EP has been to institutionalise increasingly refined structures to help

Table 3.4 Political coordinators per nationality and political group (August 2016)

	EPP	S&D	ECR	ALDE	GUE/NGL	Greens/EFA	EFDD	ENF	Total per country
Austria	0	1	0	1	0	1	0	1	4
Belgium	0	1	1	1	0	1	0	1	5
Bulgaria	0	0	0	0	0	0	0	0	0
Croatia	1	0	0	1	0	0	0	0	2
Cyprus	0	0	0	0	1	0	0	0	1
Czech Republic	0	0	0	1	1	0	1	0	3
Denmark	0	0	1	1	1	1	0	0	4
Estonia	0	0	0	1	0	1	0	0	2
Finland	1	0	0	0	1	1	0	0	3
France	1	1	0	2	2	3	1	12	22
Germany	9	10	3	2	4	7	0	1	36
Greece	0	0	1	0	1	0	0	0	2
Hungary	1	0	0	0	0	1	0	0	2
Ireland	1	0	0	1	1	0	0	0	3
Italy	0	3	0	0	2	0	11	1	17

↑

									Total
Latvia	1	0	0	0	0	0	0	0	1
Lithuania	0	0	0	1	0	0	0	0	1
Luxembourg	0	0	0	1	0	1	0	0	2
Malta	1	0	0	0	0	0	0	0	1
Netherlands	2	1	1	3	1	2	0	0	10
Poland	3	2	0	0	0	0	0	1	6
Portugal	1	0	0	1	3	0	0	0	5
Romania	1	2	0	0	0	0	0	0	3
Slovakia	0	0	0	0	0	0	0	0	0
Slovenia	0	0	0	0	0	0	0	0	0
Spain	1	3	0	2	3	1	0	0	10
Sweden	0	0	0	2	1	2	1	0	6
United Kingdom	0	3	13	0	0	0	7	1	24
Total per group	24	24	22	21	22	22	21	19	175

Source: Gathered from the political groups' websites and internal EP sources.

with policy-making and political decisions. Therefore, we see somewhat contradictory trends, since the EP has both multiplied the fora in which inputs are translated into outputs and given MEPs the opportunity to participate in a widening range of activities. At the same time, it has developed new forms of governance that have helped to manage complexity by gradually concentrating powers in the hands of a few political and administrative bodies. Old and new bodies continue to coexist – sometimes as a well-functioning engine, sometimes developing into competitors for power and influence and making the internal workings evolve and adapt to new political realities. The chapter has also shown that these structures are of little importance without the actors that constitute them. Leadership is not just given by a label but is shaped by individual people, which might strengthen or weaken their position depending on their ability to play political games, gain the trust of their peers and have a clear vision of their tasks and of the institution they represent.

Chapter 4

Legislative and Budgetary Functions

Introduction: a 'normal' parliament?

As seen in Chapter 2, the European Parliament has witnessed an astonishing increase in its formal and informal powers. As a result, it has become a full partner in the EU's institutional triangle and can now exert its influence in both legislative and budgetary matters. This chapter analyses the formal procedures in which the EP can have a say and thereby shape the outputs of the EU's political system. It examines how the legislative powers of the EP have emerged over time through formal and informal revisions of the treaties as well as the EP's shifting position in budgetary matters. The aim is to reflect on whether the EP is a 'unique' parliament or whether it can be compared to other forms of parliamentarism.

Legislative functions

The chapter starts by reviewing the three main legislative procedures (consultation, co-decision and consent). It looks at the formal powers allocated by the treaties to the procedure and how the EP has managed to push the boundaries over time, enabling it to expand its influence in most internal and external areas of EU policy-making.

Consultation

Until the Treaty of Lisbon entered into force, consultation was the oldest and one of the most frequent legislative procedures of EU decision-making. The Treaty of Rome (1957) established that the governments of the member states would be responsible for making legislative decisions and gave the EP only a consultative role. In this sense, the system is based on a very simple procedure, where the Commission proposes and the Council decides after receiving a non-binding opinion of the EP (now Art. 289 TFEU).

As can be seen in Figure 4.1, under consultation, power is concentrated in the hands of the Commission and the Council. Typically, the Commission is in charge of drafting a proposal, which is then transmitted to the Council. Before making any decisions, the EP has the right to submit

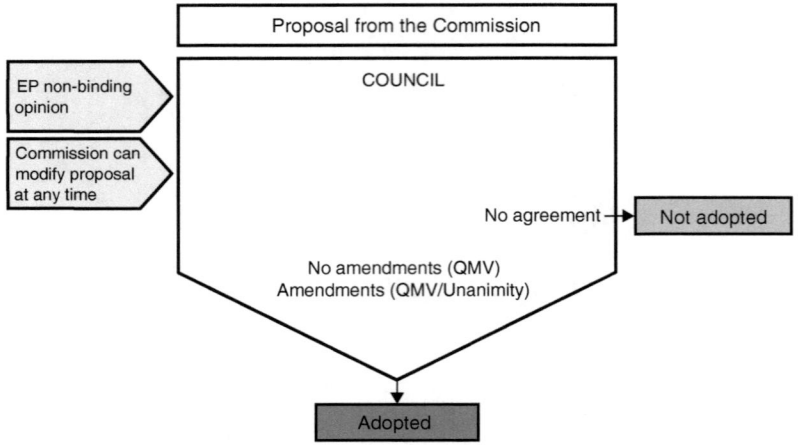

Figure 4.1   *The consultation procedure*

a report offering an opinion on the Commission's proposal. The Council, however, is not constrained by any amendments or proposals included in the EP report. Afterwards, the Council decides under qualified majority voting (QMV), but only if the Commission agrees to any changes introduced in the initial proposal. If it refuses, the national governments have to reach unanimity to overrule the Commission. This gives an important leverage to the Commission, which can keep its proposal under tight control, either by forcing the national governments to take its views into account if they wish to avoid unanimity or by withdrawing its proposal, which can be done at any time (Steunenberg 1994). It should be remembered that the use of QMV was absent from EU decision-making for a long time. In some cases, this is due to Treaty provisions, which foresee the use of unanimity in some sensitive areas such as taxation, but it was more commonly due to the continued use of the Luxembourg Compromise between 1966 and the entry into force of the SEA in 1987 (Garrett 1995; see also Chapter 2).

Given the central role of the Council, the consultation procedure was seen as a 'unicameral solution' (Costello 2011: 124), which led most authors to concentrate on the powers of the Commission and the Council (e.g. Crombez 1996; Tsebelis and Garrett 2000). However, more recent studies have come to recognise that the EP does exercise some, albeit limited, influence under this procedure (Kardasheva 2009; Varela 2009; Yordanova 2009b). This influence stems largely from the EP having been very effective in using the CJEU to extend and solidify its leverage through its 'power to delay' and a right to re-consultation (McCown 2003). The power of delay was introduced in the *Isoglucose* case, where the Court declared that a Council regulation on production quotas was invalid because the Council had failed to wait for the EP's opinion before adopting the text (Cases 138/79 and 139/79). After the ruling, the EP made active use of its power to delay, especially in those cases where member states were impatient and wanted to reach a decision quickly. It also used this power to put pressure on the Commission; if the latter did not accept the amendments proposed by the EP, the plenary threatened to reject the Commission's text and ask for a new proposal or to refer the text back to the leading committee for re-examination, which would effectively postpone the decision (Kardasheva 2009). A second group of rulings resulted in the right to be re-consulted when the Council introduced modifications to the Commission's text that departed substantially from the original proposal (Cases 1253/79 and 21/94). Interestingly, McCown (2003: 988) has noted that the failure of the Council to re-consult the EP was often a direct consequence of the power to delay: when the Council was under pressure to reach an outcome, it often failed to ask the EP for a new opinion. The necessity to re-consult the EP was slowly accepted and codified into inter-institutional agreements (see point 40 of the 2010 Framework Agreement on Relations between the European Parliament and the European Commission). Therefore, the consultation procedure does not render the EP completely powerless.

Figure 4.2 shows how, despite the growing importance of co-decision, consultation remained the main decision-making procedure until recently

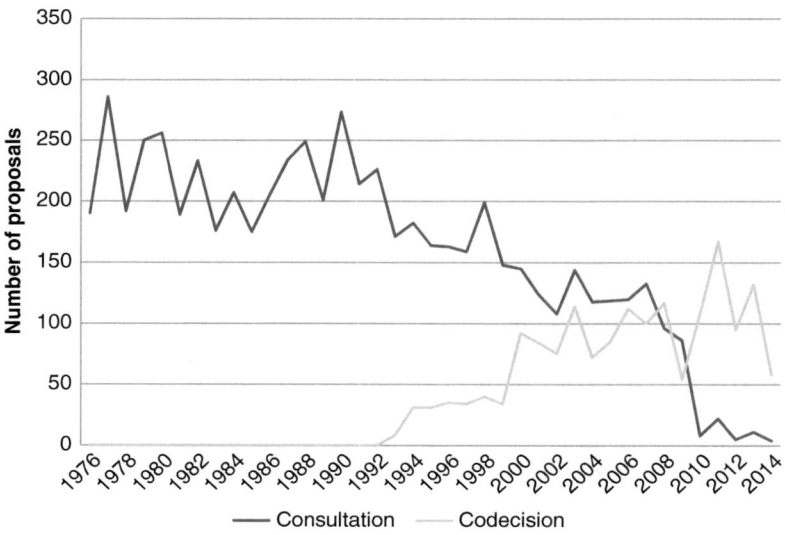

Figure 4.2 *Number of consultation and co-decision proposals 1976–2014*

Source: Häge (2011).

Note: Data for 2013 and 2014 are incomplete (http://frankhaege.eu/data/eupol).

(Varela 2009: 10). The Treaty of Lisbon has considerably changed this picture, bringing some of the most prolific areas such as trade, agriculture, and police and judicial cooperation in criminal matters under co-decision.

Table 4.1 *Areas covered by the consultation procedure*

Consultation from EP and unanimity in Council

Social security or social protection (Art. 21.3 TFEU)

Right to vote and to stand as a candidate at municipal and European Parliament elections (Art. 22 TFEU)

Measures constituting a step backwards in Union law as regards the liberalisation of the movement of capital to or from third countries (Art. 64 TFEU)

Passports, identity cards, residence permits or any other such document (Art. 77.3 TFEU)

Family law with cross-border implications and passerelle clause to OLP (Art. 81.3 TFEU)

Minimum rules with regard to the definition of criminal offences and sanctions for areas that fall under consultation (Art. 83.2 TFEU)

Operational cooperation between police authorities (Art. 87.3 TFEU)

Joint operations in the area of judicial and police cooperation (Art. 89 TFEU)

Taxes, excise duties and other forms of indirect taxation (Art. 113 TFEU)

Approximation of laws directly affecting the establishment or functioning of the internal market not covered by Art. 114 (Art. 115 TFEU)

Language arrangements for the European intellectual property rights (Art. 118 TFEU)

Replacement of the Protocol on the excessive deficit procedure (Art. 126.14 TFEU)

Delegate tasks to the ECB for the prudential supervision of credit institutions and other financial institution (Art. 127.6 TFEU)

Social security and social protection of workers; protection of workers where their employment contract is terminated; representation and collective defence of the interests of workers and employers; conditions of employment for third-country nationals legally residing in Union territory and passerelle clause to shift to OLP (except for first category) (Art. 153.2 TFEU)

Environmental measures of a fiscal nature (and potential passerelle clause) and related to water or energy resources (Art. 192.2 TFEU)

Fiscal measures related to energy policies (Art. 194.3 TFEU)

Association of the overseas countries and territories – rules and procedure for issues falling under consultation (Art. 203 TFEU) →

There are, however, some important matters that remain under consultation, such as internal market exemptions and competition law, which means that the procedure is still relevant for EU decision-making (see Table 4.1).

Conclusion of formal agreements on an exchange-rate system for the euro in relation to the currencies of third states (Art. 219.1 TFEU)

Jurisdiction to the CJEU on European intellectual property rights (Art. 262 TFEU)

Statute of the European Investment Bank (Art. 308 TFEU)

Provisions relating to the system of the Union's own resources (requires national ratification) (Art. 311 TFEU)

Enhanced cooperation outside CFSP – passerelle clause to shift Council decisions from special procedure to OLP (Art. 333.2 TFEU)

Consultation from EP and QMV in Council

Protection by the diplomatic or consular authorities of any member state (Art. 23 TFEU)

Administrative cooperation in the area of Freedom, Security and Justice (Art. 74 TFEU)

Emergency measures in the event of a sudden inflow of nationals of third countries (Art. 78.3 TFEU)

Implementing measures on transport (Art. 95.3 TFEU)

Implementation of competition policy (Art. 103.1 TFEU)

Implementation of state aid policy (Art. 109 TFEU)

Definitions for overdraft, credits and debt within the EMU (Art. 125.2 TFEU)

Implementation of the Protocol on the excessive deficit procedure (Art. 126.14 TFEU)

Harmonisation of the denominations and technical specifications of euro coins (Art. 128.2 TFEU)

Partial provisions on the Statute of the European System of Central Banks and of the ECB (Art. 129.4 TFEU)

Admission of new Eurozone members (Art. 140.2 TFEU)

Adoption of the specific programmes to implement the research framework programme (Art. 182.4)

Provisions to set up joint undertakings in the area of research (Art. 188 TFEU)

Methods and procedure to make budget revenue from the Union's own resources available to the Commission (Art. 322.2 TFEU)

Special measures for outermost regions (e.g. Canary and Caribbean Islands) (Art. 349 TFEU)

Note: OLP – ordinary legislative procedure.

The structure of consultation and the only limited powers offered to the EP have often led to rather confrontational relationships between the two main legislative bodies. While Parliament has tried to make the most of the consultation procedure, the Council has traditionally perceived the need to consult the EP as a nuisance. Parliament must be heard, but not necessarily listened to; which means that the Council has tended to ignore the opinion of the EP (Jupille 2004: 48). However, Varela (2009) has pointed out that, on those occasions when the EP has a good idea, the Council has been willing to incorporate its amendments into the legislative proposal. The EP has tended to perceive consultation as a process where it is safe to foster conflicts and confrontations, since the EP will not be held accountable for the decisions that come out of the Council. As a result, MEPs pay less attention to issues discussed under consultation than in co-decision and participate less actively, which offers greater opportunities to individual members (especially rapporteurs) to push for more extreme positions (Costello and Thomson 2010: 223; Roger 2016; Scully 1997).

Yordanova (2011) has also shown that those MEPs who are perceived as being further away from the middle of the political spectrum tend to secure consultation rather than co-decision reports. Therefore, it is often easier for smaller and more extreme political groups to influence the content of consultation reports, especially given the fact that these reports are considered to raise lower political and electoral stakes (Farrell and Héritier 2004: 1201; Scully 1997: 239). In addition, because the EP can only marginally affect the outcomes of legislative exchanges between the Council and the Commission, members treat each proposal in an issue-by-issue manner – except on those occasions when it might help to expand the powers of the EP (Hix et al. 2003: 310). As a result, consultation reports have been characterised by a wider range of opinions and policy alternatives and a more varied support from political parties.

Co-decision (ordinary legislative procedure)

Co-decision, in its current Amsterdam form (also known as co-decision II), reflects a long process of formal treaty changes and informal rule interpretation, which has resulted in equal rights for the Council and the EP over legislative decisions (Hix 2002; Rittberger 2005; Rittberger 2012). Renamed as the 'ordinary legislative procedure' (OLP) by the Treaty of Lisbon (Art. 294 TFEU), it is now the default legislative procedure. Therefore, we need to understand how we came from consultation – which gave only a very marginal role to the EP – to the current situation, where the EP has become the Council's equal.

Box 4.1 The birth and death of the cooperation procedure

Although it does not exist anymore, the first opportunity for the EP to test its legislative powers came with the introduction of the cooperation procedure in the SEA. The EP had already had some experience with drafting amendments in the budgetary procedure, but, for the first time, the cooperation procedure gave it a chance to introduce formal amendments (Corbett et al. 2007: 214; Priestley 2008). The procedure essentially added a second reading to consultation, which meant that the EP could either (1) accept the Council's common position (which had to then be adopted by the Council) or (2) propose amendments by absolute majority. The Commission could then incorporate the amendments into a modified proposal, which was sent again to the Council. The latter had a period of up to four months to either accept it by QMV or modify it by unanimity. If nothing happened, the proposal was deemed not adopted. A third option was for the EP to reject the Council common position by absolute majority. In this case, the text was not adopted, although the Council had three months to overrule the EP's rejection, for which it needed a unanimous decision of its members *and* the Commission. Although the EP proved reluctant to reject the Council's common position under cooperation, its involvement in the procedure taught Parliament the importance of shaping first-reading positions, rather than waiting for the second reading. It also showed a change in the strategies of the Commission, which learnt to make use of the EP as an ally in order to combine their efforts when negotiating with the Council (Earnshaw and Judge 1993; Fitzmaurice 1988; Judge 1992). The new procedure sparked a lengthy academic debate on the EP's success (or lack of it), though it died quickly after the introduction of co-decision I in Maastricht, which superseded and led to the disappearance of the cooperation procedure (Moser 1997; Tsebelis 1995; Tsebelis and Garrett 2000).

The first version of co-decision (also known as co-decision I) was the outcome of difficult negotiations among member states in the forerun to the Treaty of Maastricht. Although there was a majority supporting the claims for more involvement of the EP in decision-making, the final agreement was not as generous as expected (see Chapter 2). On the positive side, the new co-decision procedure introduced proper veto power for the EP, since it could reject legislative proposals even if the Council reached unanimity for its common position. In addition, it institutionalised a third reading, the new conciliation procedure, which effectively required an inter-institutional agreement in the form of a joint text if the Council and the EP failed to agree at the second reading. To this effect, a conciliation committee was convened from a team of Council representatives (one per member state) and the same number of EP representatives. If there was no agreement on a joint text, the Council could reconfirm its common position, which could only be stopped if the EP managed to reach an absolute majority against it. Finally, if the EP declared that it planned to reject the common position, a period of re-consultation with the Council known as the 'petite' conciliation would lead to a reconfirmation of the EP's wish to reject the common position or to the introduction of amendments (Boyron 1996; Crombez 1997; Earnshaw and Judge 1995).

The procedure was indeed rather obscure and some considered that it only gave 'negative' powers to the EP, since its veto power was difficult to put into practice in the second reading and potentially disappeared if it did not manage to reach an agreement in conciliation (Boyron 1996). The first years of the procedure also raised questions about the status of the EP's first-reading opinion and whether the conciliation procedure could reopen any issues or only those introduced in EP amendments. More generally, this first version already pointed to the trade-off between efficiency (due to rather vague time limits and an extra reading) and transparency. The Council and the EP managed to find new channels of negotiation and dialogue, in the form of trilogues and informal bargaining. Trilogues are secluded settings in which representatives of the EP, the Council and the Commission can meet to sort out differences as early as possible in the procedure. Therefore, under co-decision I, we already saw a tendency towards early agreements and in-camera decision-making (see Chapter 11). In fact, many remarked that, even if still around half of the decisions went on until conciliation, this supposed a much lower number of cases than had been expected when co-decision was introduced (Boyron 1996; Earnshaw and Judge 1995).

Co-decision I also announced two important features for inter-institutional relations. First, the EP showed a taste for using informal interpretations of the rules to widen its influence (Nicoll 1994). For instance, it introduced a new provision in its Rules of Procedure (at the time, Rule 78), which made it more difficult for the Council to reconfirm its common position if a joint text was not found in conciliation. This informal provision was effectively used in the Open Network Provision (ONP) to Voice Telephony Directive (98/10/EC) and, after that, the Council did not try to reconfirm its common position ever again (Hix 2002). The second feature concerned the new position of the Commission in the inter-institutional triangle, which had a more limited role under co-decision, especially since it was not clear whether it could still amend or withdraw its proposal after the Council reached a common position. This led to a new dynamic of reinforced bilateral contacts between the EP and the Council (Boyron 1996; Crombez 1997; Earnshaw and Judge 1995). In general, co-decision I was considered very successful. Between November 1993 and May 1999 (when co-decision II entered into force), 165 dossiers were completed under co-decision (around 30 per year), 66 of which entered conciliation (40 per cent), and only three cases ended in failure (see Box 4.2 below).

The Treaty of Amsterdam (Art. 251 TEC) introduced three important changes to co-decision I. First, it made conciliation the last formal stage of the procedure; if the EP and the Council failed to produce a joint text, the legislative act was deemed not adopted and the Council could not fall back to its common position. This change was only a formalisation of the practices that had developed informally between Maastricht and Amsterdam (Crombez et al. 2000; Hix 2002). Second, co-decision II also eliminated the 'petite' conciliation, which had been hardly used. Third, co-decision II made it possible to conclude the legislative procedure at the first reading. Although probably unexpected, this change proved to be the most important one, since it made it possible to 'fast-track' legislation and gave way to an increase in early agreements (see Chapter 11). The Treaty of Lisbon (Art. 294 TFEU) only changed some aspects of the procedure's terminology, such as replacing the name of co-decision with the 'ordinary legislative procedure' and dropping the 'common' from the Council common position. In addition, it extended the remit of the procedure to most policy-making fields (see Table 4.2).

Figure 4.3 delineates the main steps of the co-decision procedure after the changes introduced in Amsterdam.

First reading
The process starts with a proposal of the Commission sent to the EP and the Council. Generally, the right of initiative is reserved for the Commission, although the EP and the Council may ask the Commission to submit legislative proposals. In a few scenarios, the right of initiative is shared with other actors. For instance, a quarter of member states can propose legislation in police and judicial cooperation in criminal matters (what used to be the third pillar until Lisbon, Art. 76 TFEU) and the European Central Bank can issue recommendations on certain matters related to the Statute of the European System of Central Banks and of the European Central Bank (Art. 129 TFEU). The CJEU can also request the establishment of specialised courts and changes in its statute (Art. 281 TFEU).

The first task of the EP after receiving the proposal (usually known as a 'file' or 'dossier') from the Commission is to appoint a committee responsible for discussing and negotiating it. In turn, the committee will appoint an MEP (a rapporteur) to write a report giving an 'opinion' on the Commission's proposal (see Chapters 10 and 11). Once the

Table 4.2   *Areas covered by the ordinary legislative procedure (co-decision)*

Services of general economic interest (Art. 14 TFEU)

Right of access to documents (Art. 15.3 TFEU)

Processing of personal data (Art. 16.2 TFEU)

Prohibition of discrimination on grounds of nationality (Art. 18 TFEU)

Support actions to combat discrimination based on sex, racial or ethnic origin, religion or belief, disability, age or sexual orientation (Art. 19.2 TFEU)

Right to move and reside freely within the territory of the member states (Art. 21.2 TFEU)

Procedures and conditions required for a citizens' initiative (Art. 24 TFEU)

Customs cooperation (Art. 33 TFEU)

Competition rules for the production of and trade in agricultural products (Art. 42 TFEU)

Common organisation of agricultural markets in the common agricultural and fisheries policy (Art. 43.2 TFEU)

Freedom of movement for workers (Art. 46 TFEU)

Social security as necessary to provide freedom of movement for workers (Art. 48 TFEU)

Freedom of establishment (Art. 50.1 TFEU)

Exceptions to freedom of establishment (Art. 51 TFEU)

Coordination of special treatment for foreign nationals on grounds of public policy, public security or public health (Art. 52.2 TFEU)

Mutual recognition of diplomas, certificates and other evidence of formal qualifications (Art. 53.1 TFEU)

Extension to nationals of a third country of the provisions on freedom to provide services (Art. 56 TFEU)

Liberalisation of services (Art. 59.1 TFEU)

Measures on the movement of capital to or from third countries involving direct investment establishment, the provision of financial services or the admission of securities to capital markets (Art. 64.2 TFEU)

Capital movements and payments in relation to preventing and combating terrorism and related activities (Art. 75 TFEU)

External borders order and visa policies (Art. 77.2 TFEU)

Common European asylum system (Art. 78.2 TFEU)

Common immigration policy and combating trafficking in persons (Art. 79.2 TFEU)

Supporting measures on integration of third-country nationals residing legally (Art. 79.4)

Judicial cooperation in civil matters having cross-border implications (Art. 81.2 TFEU)

→

→

Judicial cooperation in criminal matters (Art. 82.1 and 2 TFEU)

Definition of criminal offences and sanctions in cross-border serious crime and approximation of criminal laws and regulations in areas falling under the OLP (Art. 83.1 and 2 TFEU)

Supporting measures in crime prevention (Art. 84 TFEU)

Eurojust's structure, operation, field of action and tasks (Art. 85.1 TFEU)

Police cooperation (Art. 87.2 TFEU)

Europol's structure, operation, field of action and tasks (Art. 88.2 TFEU)

Implementation of common transport policy (Art. 91.1 TFEU)

Sea and air transport (Art. 100.2 TFEU)

Approximation of laws for the establishment and functioning of the internal market (Art. 114.1 TFEU)

Measures to eliminate distortions in the conditions of competition in the internal market (Art. 116 TFEU)

European intellectual property rights, except for language arrangements (Art. 118 TFEU)

Multilateral surveillance procedure for economic policies (Art. 121.6 TFEU)

Partial provisions on the Statute of the European System of Central Banks and of the ECB (Art. 129.3 TFEU)

Measures necessary for the use of the euro as the single currency (Art. 133 TFEU)

Supporting measures in the field of employment (Art. 149 TFEU)

Improvement in particular of the working environment to protect workers' health and safety; working conditions; the information and consultation of workers; the integration of persons excluded from the labour market; equality between men and women with regard to labour market opportunities and treatment at work (Art. 153.2 TFEU)

Equal opportunities and equal treatment of men and women in matters of employment and occupation (Art. 157.3 TFEU)

European Social Fund (Art. 164 TFEU)

Supporting measures in the field of education and sport (Art. 165.4 TFEU)

Supporting measures in the field of vocational training (Art. 166.4 TFEU)

Supporting measures in the field of culture (Art. 167.5 TFEU)

Common safety concerns in public health and supporting measures in major cross-border health scourges (Art. 168.4 and 5 TFEU)

Supporting measures in the field of consumer protection (Art. 169.3 TFEU)

Guidelines on trans-European networks (Art. 172 TFEU)

Supporting measures in the field of industry (Art. 173.3 TFEU)

→

→
Economic, social and territorial cohesion (Art. 175 TFEU)

Tasks, priority objectives and the organisation of the Structural and Cohesion Funds (Art. 177 TFEU)

Implementation of European Regional Development Fund (Art. 178 TFEU)

Multiannual framework programme for research and implementation of the European research area (Art. 182.1 and 5 TFEU)

Implementation of the multiannual framework programme on research (Art. 188 TFEU)

Space policy (Art. 189.2 TFEU)

Environmental policy and general action programmes (Art. 192.1 and 3 TFEU)

Energy policy (Art. 194.2 TFEU)

Tourism policy (Art. 195.2 TFEU)

Civil protection policy (Art. 196.2 TFEU)

Supporting measures in the field of administrative cooperation (Art. 197.2 TFEU)

Common commercial policy (Art. 207.2 TFEU)

Implementation of development cooperation policy (Art. 209.1 TFEU)

Economic, financial and technical cooperation with third countries other than developing countries (Art. 212.2 TFEU)

Humanitarian aid operations and establishment of the European Voluntary Humanitarian Aid Corps (Art. 214.3 and 5 TFEU)

Regulations governing political parties at the European level and their funding (Art. 224 TFEU)

Establishment of specialised courts attached to the General Court (Art. 257 TFEU)

Amendment of the statute of the Court of Justice of the European Union except Title I and Article 64 (Art. 281 TFEU)

Rules and general principles concerning mechanisms for monitoring the exercise of implementing powers (Art. 291.3 TFEU)

Staff Regulations and the Conditions of Employment (Art. 298.2 and 336 TFEU)

Financial rules (Art. 322.1 TFEU)

Measures in the fields of the prevention of and fight against fraud (Art. 325.4 TFEU)

Measures for the production of statistics (Art. 338.1 TFEU)

committee responsible has sent its report to the plenary, the EP can vote by simple majority (that is, a majority of votes cast) on whether it should (1) approve the proposal without any changes, (2) approve the proposal with amendments or (3) reject the proposal. The last option

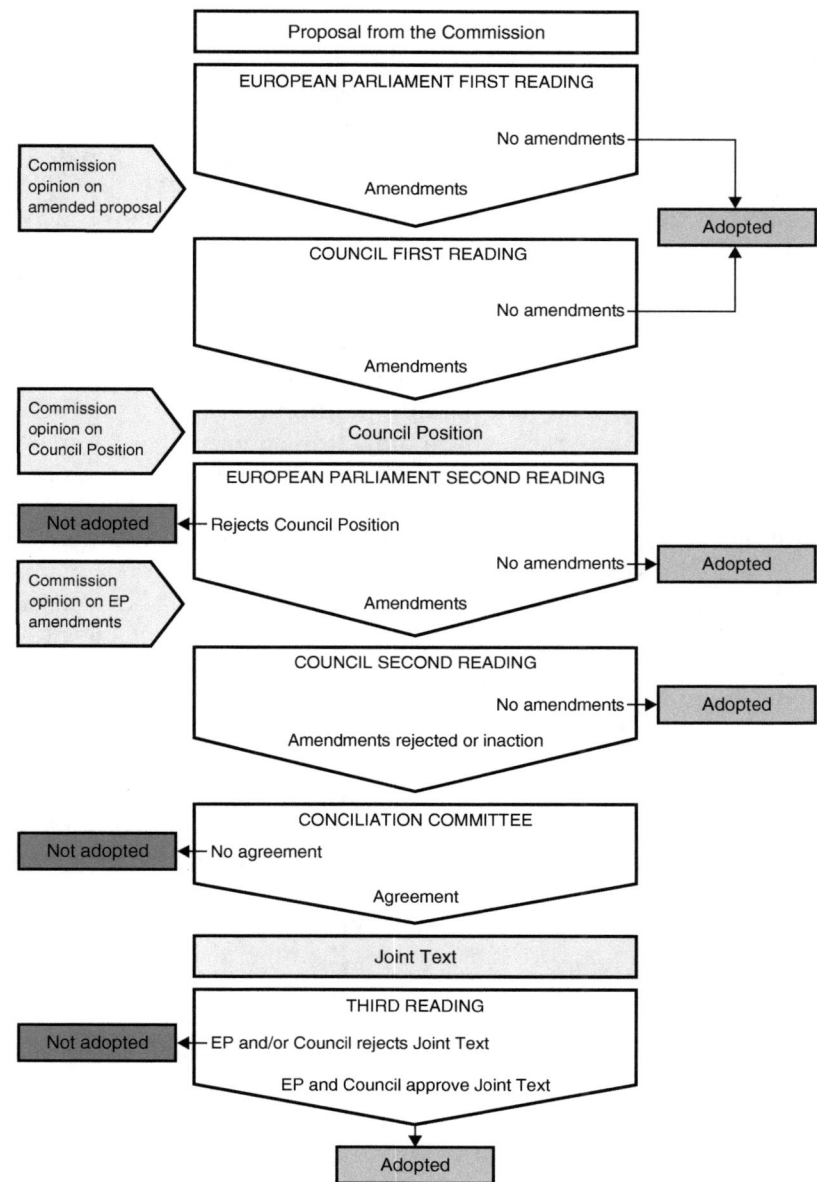

Figure 4.3 *The ordinary legislative procedure*

is not actually foreseen in the Treaty, but the EP can informally ask the Commission to withdraw its proposal or, if it refuses to do so, it can send it back to the responsible committee for further consideration. Once the EP has cast its first-reading vote, it sends its position to the Commission (which can give an opinion or modify its proposal to incorporate the EP's opinion) and then to the Council, which will have already considered matters internally. The Council's next moves depend on the EP's position. If the EP has decided to accept the proposal as it is, the Council can do the same, in which case the legislative act is adopted. The same happens if the EP has proposed amendments and the Council accepts all of them. These two scenarios are then considered first-reading agreements. If the Council decides to propose amendments, then it adopts a first-reading position either by QMV (if the Commission has agreed to incorporate the amendments) or by unanimity (if the Commission has not agreed to incorporate them or in the areas of taxation, social security, foreign policy, defence and operational police cooperation). It is important to remember that the Commission remains in control of its proposal until the Council has reached a first-reading position, which means that it can decide to amend or withdraw it at any time. Although not foreseen in the Treaty, the Council may reject the Commission proposal as a whole; however, generally, the Council has preferred to just discontinue or not even start work on a proposal, so that it informally blocks it instead of rejecting it.

One of the most relevant characteristics of the first-reading stage is that it is not subjected to time limits. This offers ample opportunities to the EP, the Council and the Commission to engage in informal negotiations in the form of trilogues. It has become relatively normal to see an agreement between the EP and the Council either before the EP has reached its first-reading position (known as a 'general approach') or before the Council's first-reading vote (the more frequent 'political agreements').

Second reading
The procedure for the second reading is similar to that of the first reading. The responsible committee drafts a 'recommendation' (a second-reading report) and transmits it to the plenary. The plenary can then decide to (1) accept the amendments proposed in the Council's position (known as an early second reading), (2) reject the Council's position, in which case the legislative act is not adopted or (3) table amendments to the Council's position. If it fails to decide within the time limits, the result is the same as in an early second reading. If it decides to amend the text, the Commission has to decide whether it accepts or rejects the amendments. If the Commission accepts them, the Council has three (or a maximum of four) months to vote with QMV on the EP amendments and, if accepted, the act is adopted. If the Commission does not agree

with the amendments, then the Council needs unanimity to adopt the act. As in the first reading, the Council and the EP hold informal talks in trilogues to try to find an agreement. If the Council decides to reject the EP amendments, then the text is referred to the conciliation committee. Therefore, the second reading sets strict time limits for both legislators; in addition, the EP has to achieve an absolute majority of its members to either amend or reject the Council's first-reading position. That is why we have seen an increasing number of 'early second readings', where the EP can accept by simple majority all the amendments introduced by the Council in its first-reading position.

Conciliation and 'third reading'

If there is no agreement after the second reading, the conciliation committee has to be convened within six weeks (or a maximum of eight in some specific cases) and then has again six weeks (or a maximum of eight) to produce a joint text. Usually, before the conciliation committee officially starts, the Council and the EP are already meeting in trilogues that gather a smaller number of representatives rather than the official 'conciliation team'. The Council team is composed of a representative of each member state (either ministers or, normally, the permanent representative). It can vote on a joint text by QMV, except for those legal bases requiring unanimity (see above). The Parliament team is composed of an equal number of representatives (28 in 2017, plus 28 substitutes). Three vice-presidents are permanent members of the conciliation committee and the other 25 are drawn from political groups in proportion to their size (see also Box 10.2). The EP team votes on the joint text by an absolute majority (that is, a majority of its members, 15 votes at the time of writing). A vice-president of the EP and the Council's Presidency are responsible for chairing the committee. The Commission also sits in the conciliation committee, usually represented by a Commissioner, who is in charge of moderating and facilitating an agreement. If the EP and the Council fail to produce a joint text, the legal act is deemed not adopted. However, even if they manage to produce a compromise, the latter still needs to be confirmed within six weeks (maximum eight) in what is often called a 'third reading'. There, the EP plenary decides by a simple majority of votes cast and the Council by QMV. If any of the two chambers fails to confirm the joint text, the legal act is not adopted.

Although the procedure looks very convoluted, Figure 4.4 shows that, since 2004, most decisions are made at an early stage (either at the first reading or an early second reading). This means that, in practice, the EU institutions face a much less harrowing process than is required if the procedure runs its full course (see also Chapter 11). In the seventh legislature (2009–2014), only nine files reached the conciliation stage and only one could not be agreed upon (see Box 4.2). As was the case

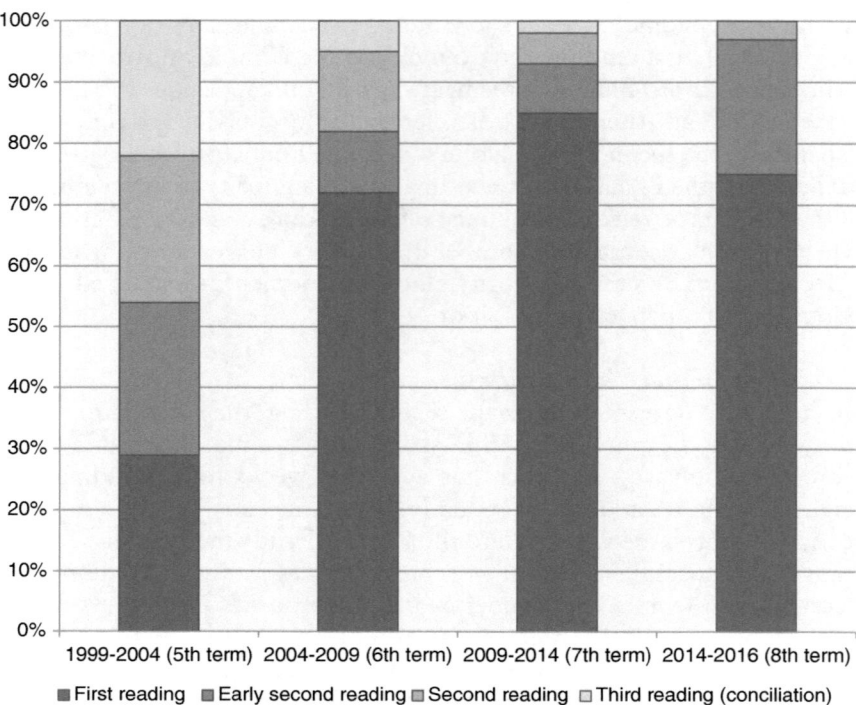

Figure 4.4   *Changes in the percentage of co-decision files and early agreements*

Source: European Parliament (2017, p. 10)

also in co-decision I, the majority of files that reached the conciliation stage concerned inter-institutional disagreements on the definition of implementing and delegated acts (what used to be known as 'comitology'; see also Box 11.3). This trend seems to have intensified in the last years: in the first half of the eighth legislative term (2014–2016), conciliation was never used and the full second reading was only used in four out of 124 co-decision files.

The co-decision procedure can thus be considered a very efficient decision-making procedure. It has formally situated the Council and the EP on an equal footing and transformed the way in which the EU political system works (see Chapter 11).

Consent (formerly known as 'assent')

The consent procedure is a simple mechanism used mostly for the ratification of international agreements and for those internal adjustments that have some sort of 'constitutional' or symbolic character. In essence,

Box 4.2 Rare occurrences: Rejection of co-decision files

Contrary to what many imagined at its outset, co-decision has proved relatively effective and there have been few cases of inter-institutional gridlock. Since its inception in Maastricht, only seven files have failed the conciliation test and in most cases this was due to a limited number of grounds – namely, comitology, ethics or social affairs (workers' rights). Four of these files have failed to reach an agreement at the conciliation committee. That means that the EP team did not reach the simple majority of its members to approve the joint text. The two first occasions were the abovementioned ONP in Voice Telephony (rejected in 1994 and agreed upon later in 1998 in Directive 98/10/EC) and the Securities Committee (95/0188/COD rejected in 1998), which failed due to disagreements on the workings of technical committees (comitology). The other two cases were the Working Time Directive (2004/0209/COD in 2009) and the Novel Foods Regulation (2008/0002/COD in 2011). In the former case, the Council and the EP were so far away from each other that it resulted in an impossibility to reconcile their views, while the latter touched on very sensitive ethical issues such as cloning.

In other cases, the conciliation committee managed to produce a joint text, but the EP as a whole rejected it at the third reading. This was the case in the Biotechnology Patenting Directive, rejected in 1995 and eventually agreed upon in 1998 (Directive 98/44/EC), which also dealt with difficult ethical issues. The Takeover Directive failed in 2001 after a vigorous effort by the German government to block the decision successfully split the EP's political groups along national lines and was only adopted in 2004 (Directive 2004/25/EC); the Port Services Directive was rejected in 2003 (2001/0047/COD) and 2006 (2004/0240/COD) again due to diverging views on workers' rights and only accepted as a Regulation in 2017 (2017/352/EU).

There have also been some cases where the EP has rejected files at the first reading, such as the European Statistics on Safety from Crime Regulation in 2012 (2011/0146/COD) – where the EP was not convinced of the methodology and financing proposed by the Commission. Also some second-reading files have failed to go forward, such as the Software Patents Directive (2002/0047/COD), which failed in 2005 due to disagreements on the principles underpinning the proposal. However, even if rejections remain rare, most observers concede that the EP often uses them to make a point on institutional rather than policy matters. It is often an instrument to show disagreement on how the other institutions have handled negotiations or to indicate that the EP should not be ignored (Judge and Earnshaw 2008).

it requires Parliament to say 'yes' or 'no' to a decision without any formal opportunity to introduce amendments.

As with the other procedures, the EP's right of consent is the result of long-term processes of institutional change. Already in the 1960s, some member states in the Council aimed to involve the EP in association agreements. To this effect, the 'Luns procedure' introduced the practice of informing the EP's responsible committee about the content of these agreements. In the 1970s, it was expanded under the Luns-Westerterp procedure so as to cover commercial and other types of international agreement. In addition, in 1971, the European Court of Justice reinforced the role of the Parliament in its AETR ruling (Case 22/70), which established parallel competences between the EU's internal and external domains. This meant that, if the EC had already made use of its competences in the internal domain, it had a right to act outside as well. In practice, the ruling required the consultation of the EP for some international agreements, such as decisions falling under the field of transport

Table 4.3   *Areas covered by the consent procedure*

Consent of the EP with simple majority
Composition of the EP (Art. 14.2 TEU)
(Non-)establishment of a convention for treaty revision (Art. 48 TEU)
Withdrawal of a member state (Art. 50 TEU)
Action to combat discrimination (Art. 19.1 TFEU)
Extension of EU citizenship rights (Art. 25 TFEU)
Extension of mutual recognition for criminal procedures (Art. 82.2 TFEU)
Extension of definition of criminal offences and sanctions (Art. 83.1 TFEU)
Establishment of the European Public Prosecutor's Office (Art. 86.1 TFEU) and extension of powers (Art. 86.4 TFEU)
Agreements relating to the common commercial policy (Art. 207.3 TFEU)
Association agreements (Art. 218.6 TFEU)
Agreement on Union accession to the European Convention for the Protection of Human Rights and Fundamental Freedoms (national ratification required) (Art. 218.6 TFEU)
International agreements establishing a specific institutional framework by organising cooperation procedures (Art. 218.6 TFEU)
International agreements with important budgetary implications for the Union (Art. 218.6 TFEU)
International agreements covering fields to which either the ordinary legislative procedure applies, or the special legislative procedure where consent by the European Parliament is required (Art. 218.6 TFEU)
→

or agriculture, but it left out crucial areas such as the common commercial policy (Corbett et al. 2016: 296–297).

In order to strengthen and clarify the role of the EP, the SEA introduced the consent procedure, then known as 'assent' (Arts 8 and 9). At that moment, it only applied to association agreements with third countries and the accession of new member states. This remit was gradually extended by the subsequent treaties, to the point that, under the Treaty of Lisbon, the EP has a right to give its consent to most international agreements (except those in CFSP), accession decisions, association agreements as well as sanctions for violations of the EU's values (see Table 4.1 for a full list). In most cases, the EP decides by simple majority (that is, a majority of those present during the vote), although in some cases an absolute majority of its members, occasionally even a two-thirds majority, is required.

As can be seen in Table 4.3, the matters covered by the consent procedure are highly diverse and cover both internal and external

→

Implementation of the Union's own resources (Art. 311 TFEU)

Enhanced cooperation outside CFSP (Art. 329.1 TFEU)

Implied competences (action necessary to achieve treaty objectives not provided elsewhere) (Art. 352.1 TFEU)

Consent of the EP with absolute majority

Passerelle clauses to shift Council decisions from unanimity to QMV or from special procedure to OLP (Art. 48.7 TEU)

Accession of new member states (Art. 49 TEU)

Uniform electoral procedure (Art. 223.1 TFEU and national ratification)

Multiannual Financial Framework (Art. 312.2 TFEU)

Consent of the EP with two-thirds majority constituting a majority of members

Determine risk of serious breach by a member state of EU values (Art. 7.1 TEU)

Sanctions for serious and persistent breach of EU values (Art. 7.2 TEU)

Consent of the Council

MEPs statute (Art. 223.2 TFEU)

Exercise of the EP's right of inquiry (Art. 226 TFEU)

Duties of the ombudsman (Art. 228.4 TFEU)

Note: OLP – ordinary legislative procedure.

competences. Despite their differences, most matters can be considered highly symbolic, so the consent procedure can become a double-edged sword. On the one hand, a positive vote is a highly significant gesture showing the support of the EP; this explains why, in the case of enlargement or association agreements, the EP has never made use of a negative vote (Judge and Earnshaw 2008: 235–236). On the other hand, negative votes have been equated to a 'nuclear' power (Smith 1999: 76), since they can abruptly derail the decision-making process. In comparison to co-decision, the act of withdrawing consent represents a more potent, but also a much riskier veto power; if it is perceived to be 'unconstructive' it can affect not only inter-institutional relations, but also the EU's international position (Krauss 2000: 219). This was evident in 1992, when the EP refused to give its consent to the fourth generation of financial protocols with Morocco and Syria on human rights grounds. In retaliation, Morocco decided to delay negotiations with the Commission on the renewal of a fisheries agreement (Haddadi 2002). It is, therefore, a highly symbolic *negative* power, which explains why the EP has been very reluctant to use it.

Figure 4.5 illustrates the formal procedure leading to the ratification of an international treaty in a non-CFSP matter. When analysing an international agreement, decision-making can be divided into three stages: agenda setting, negotiation and ratification. The Council is the institution in charge of setting the agenda by drafting a negotiation mandate and deciding who will act as EU negotiator (either the Commission or the Council Presidency). If the EU is represented by the Commission, the Council can oversee its activities through directives (used, for instance, to change the mandate) or by way of a special committee foreseen in Article 218.4 TFEU. Once finalised, the Council is in charge of signing and deciding on a provisional application. However, it can only ratify the agreement if the EP gives its consent; whichever the result of the EP's vote, the Council cannot bypass this decision and is bound to either ratify or reject the agreement. Mixed agreements have to be ratified by the EU and member states (Delreux 2008; Meunier and Nicolaïdis 1999).

Formally, the EP only plays a role in the last stages of the procedure, even if the Treaty contemplates that the EP has the right to be informed *at all stages* of the procedure (Art. 218.10 TFEU). The vagueness of the formulation has opened a door for an informal re-interpretation of the rules, to the point that the consent procedure has been reshaped into a *quasi-co-decision* (Ripoll Servent 2014). The use of the EP's 'nuclear' power to empower the EP and widen its influence through informal channels is, however, not new. After the Single European Act, the EP refused to ratify a set of three protocols to the EEC-Israel Association Agreement. The grounds for the negative votes were based on very diverse political and

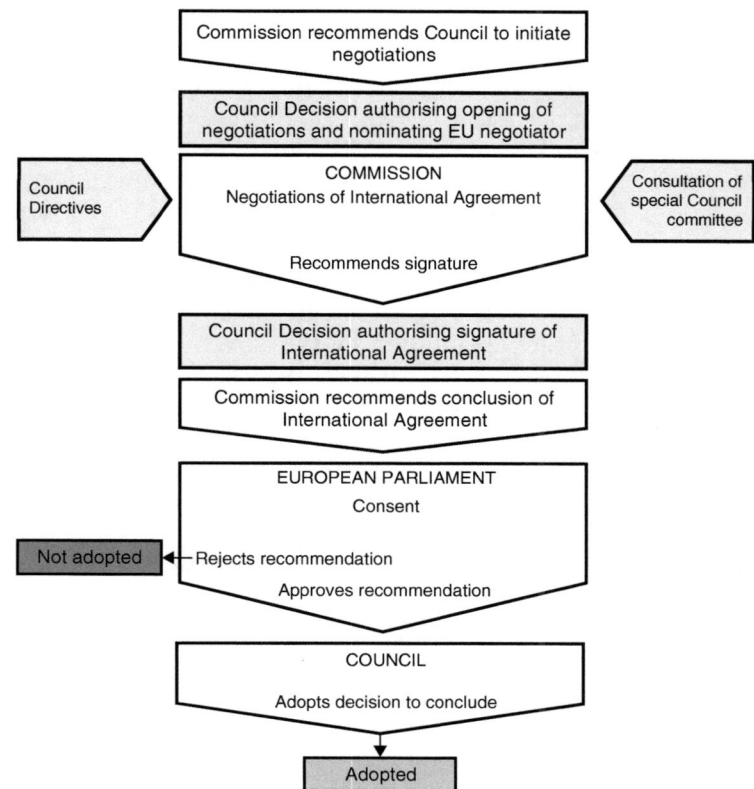

Figure 4.5 *Consent procedure (non-CFSP international agreements)*

economic motivations, but they were also interpreted as a show of parliamentary strength (Greilsammer 1991). A similar episode took place after the entry into force of the Treaty of Lisbon, when the EP refused to give its consent to an EU-US Agreement on bank data transfers (TFTP, also known as the SWIFT Agreement). Although there were concerns about data protection, what made most MEPs vote against the agreement was the feeling that the EP was being asked to rubber-stamp the Council's decision. The renegotiation of the agreement showed that institutional rather than substantive concerns had indeed triggered the rejection, since the second deal still left considerable gaps and grey areas when it came to data protection. With the SWIFT episode, the EP managed to transform its right to be informed into a 'right to be involved' (Ripoll Servent 2014; Ripoll Servent and MacKenzie 2012).

This informal shift was semi-formalised in the 2010 Framework Agreement between the EP and the Commission on Relations between the European Parliament and the European Commission, which dedicates section ii and annex III to spelling out the rights and duties of both institutions in international negotiations and even foresees the possibility of including a 'delegation of Members of the European Parliament as observers' in negotiations (point 25). There are, however, disagreements over the extent to which the EP should be involved. The latter understands its right to be informed (or rather involved) in a way that includes not only the agenda-setting and negotiation stage, but also the 'signature, possible provisional application, conclusion, suspension of the agreement, modifications to the agreement ... and the positions to be adopted in bodies established by the agreement' (Corbett et al. 2016: 301), which goes too far for the Council. Similarly, the role of EP delegations as observers remains unclear. Since the 1990s, the EP has pushed to have a role in international settings, but the meaning of a 'negotiating role' is still open for debate, and in this respect, the 2010 Framework Agreement did not provide any further clarification (Corbett et al. 2016: 301).

Since the SWIFT Agreement, there has been mixed behaviour from the EP when it comes to ratifying international agreements. Some, like the 2012 EU-US Passenger Name Record (PNR) Agreement, went without a hitch, despite the fact that the EP had shown strong opposition towards similar agreements in the past (cf. Kaunert et al. 2012). Others, however, have been voted down, notably the multilateral 'counterfeiting' agreement (ACTA), which in 2012 managed to gather an 'overwhelming' majority against it (The *Guardian* 2012). Matthews and Žikovská (2013) noted that one of the reasons for the EP to withdraw its consent to ACTA was the need to exercise its new veto power, although it also raised concerns related to the transparency of negotiations. A similar development was observed in the EU–South Korea trade agreement of 2011, where the EP used its newly acquired ratification power to force the Commission to renegotiate certain clauses of the agreement and set a clear path for implementation. On that occasion, 'the EP ... ascended as a key player during the ratification game ... For the EP, the treaty with South Korea provided the possibility for it to flex its muscles and set a precedent' (Elsig and Dupont 2012: 502). The EP has also cast a shadow on some of the biggest negotiations in the last years – the EU–US Transatlantic Trade and Investment Partnership (TTIP) and the EU–Canada Comprehensive Economic and Trade Agreement (CETA). In both cases, the EP has had to be persuaded of the necessity to conclude these free trade agreements – especially in the face of mounting popular opposition. Parliament ultimately gave its consent to CETA on 15 February 2017; at the time of writing, due to Donald Trump's election to the US presidency, a deal on TTIP seems far from completion (Frantescu 2016; The *Guardian* 2017). These past experiences have proved useful to the EP, which has not hesitated to ask for an early involvement in Brexit negotiations. To this effect, it nominated Guy Verhofstadt (liberal Belgian MEP) as the EP's representative in negotiations and passed with a very high majority (516 votes in favour, 133 against and 50 abstentions) a resolution fixing the conditions for Parliament's ratification of the UK's withdrawal agreement (P8_TA(2017)0102). Therefore, the EP is once again using its power to consent to (international) agreements to influence the priorities and red lines of the EU's negotiating team and thereby set the agenda of Brexit negotiations from an early stage.

We have thus seen a tendency towards a growing influence of the EP in all stages of international negotiations. It has effectively used its 'nuclear' power in the ratification stage to cast a shadow over the agenda-setting and negotiation stages. As a result, the Commission and the Council are now aware that the EP will not be satisfied with rubber-stamping their decisions, but will try to have a say over the content of the agreements. This new inter-institutional dynamic is still not settled and we need to wait for further developments, but in the areas of internal security and trade, we have already witnessed an increase in the politicisation of negotiations, both within the EU and towards its international partners (Hoffmeister 2014; Ripoll Servent 2014; Van den Putte et al. 2014).

Budgetary functions

One of the most underestimated powers of the EP is its capacity to set and control the budget. In fact, the acquisition of budgetary powers in the 1970s was one of the main steps towards its empowerment. It gave Parliament a chance to steer the political priorities of the EU by directing more money towards those areas it wanted to promote. Indeed, it is still an important way to control the actions of the other EU institutions, especially in policy areas where it does not enjoy any real legislative powers. During the 1980s, the EP fought several battles to expand its budgetary powers and have a say over the level of expenditure not only for the following year, but also with a long-term perspective; to this effect, it refused to pass the 1980 and 1985 budgets (Benedetto 2013: 349; see Chapter 2). This led to the introduction in 1988 of the first multiannual financial perspective (Delors I), which aimed to establish some predictability and stability in the budget. The Treaty of Lisbon changed the rules considerably. It formalised the long-term financial perspectives, now called the 'Multiannual

Financial Framework' (MFF). These are regulations decided by the Council under unanimity upon the consent of the EP. The MFFs are now set for five years and determine the priorities and overall ceilings for spending. Therefore, annual budgets are decided within the framework of the MFF, which means that they might have some leeway to shift priorities between different types of spending, but cannot decide to increase the overall ceilings. The 2017 budget, for instance, tried to invest more on instruments that aimed to tackle the migration crisis, but that came at the expense of other areas of spending, such as regional policy or research.

This is, however, a significant development compared to the rights that the EP had before the Treaty of Lisbon. For, at that time, the EP could only have a say over non-compulsory spending, which left out core parts of the EU annual budget, such as agriculture or foreign policy. The Lisbon reforms were seen as a new form of parliamentary empowerment, since the distinction between compulsory and non-compulsory expenditures was abolished and the EP could now decide on both. However, the last few years have seen repeated breakdowns in budget negotiations, for both the MFF and the annual budget. This questions the idea that the EP was one of the big winners on budgetary matters in the Treaty of Lisbon. This section, therefore, looks at where money comes from, how the MFF is decided and how it affects annual budgetary politics as well as the definition of specific spending programmes.

Budgetary income

The EU budget is mostly financed through various types of 'own resources'. Historically, most of its income came from custom duties on imports, but this source of money has steadily decreased over time due to the shifting trade regime since the General Agreement on Tariffs and Trade (GATT) and the creation of the World Trade Organization (WTO). Therefore, most of the revenue comes now from a percentage of each country's value added tax and contributions from member states based on their gross national income. Given the sensitive nature of these contributions, member states have sought to keep control over decisions on the EU's own resources and have involved the EP only marginally (Art. 311 TFEU): the Council – deciding by unanimity and requiring national ratification – can decide on the system of own resources after consultation with the EP. It can implement these measures with a regulation, which needs the consent of the EP. The last reform of the system of own resources was agreed in May 2014 (2014/335/EU). It reduced the payments of traditional net contributors, such as Germany, the Netherlands and Sweden. Given the growing difficulties of the EU to pay its bills, the EP has been pushing since 2006 for a reform of the system (Euractiv 2014c). It made it one of its central points in the 2014–2020 MFF negotiations, where it was agreed that a 'high level group' would be set up composed of EP, Council and Commission representatives and chaired by the former Italian Prime Minister and EU Commissioner Mario Monti. The high level group's final report was rather cautious about the possibility of introducing substantial changes to the current system of own resources, but proposed some potential new sources of income, such as environment-related taxes on carbon fuel or other types of energy, a common corporate income tax, a reformed value-added tax (VAT) or a tax on the financial sector (High Level Group on Own Resources 2016).

Budgetary expenditure

If deciding on how much each member state should contribute to the EU budget is difficult, allocating the money is not any easier. Negotiations on budgetary contributions and spending are fraught with conflicts and have become some of the most politicised decisions in EU policy-making. The periodic battles surrounding each new MFF have now stolen the political limelight, but one should not overlook the linkage between these 'history-making' decisions and the more routinized contests between the EP and the Council that decide on the annual spending of the EU. Indeed, the increasing number of conflicts on budgetary matters has helped to underline the lack of synchronicity between long-term financial plans and the legislative cycle. Despite the Commission's efforts to introduce a 5+5 financial framework (five years and then a revised plan for five more years), member states still prefer the usual seven-year plan. The EP, however, is calling for five-year plans so that each newly elected parliament can have a say on long-term budgetary matters (Sapala 2013).

Multiannual Financial Framework
Article 312 TFEU establishes that, for the MFF, the EP has the right to give its consent, but, to do so, an absolute majority (that is, a majority of all its component members) is required. This is, in itself, not so different from the pre-Lisbon system, which also foresaw a Council decision and then the EP's consent; the current system has eliminated the need for national ratification, which reduces the potential number of veto actors. Benedetto (2013), however, underlines that the post-Lisbon arrangement is less flexible and tends to reinforce the status quo. He points out that the MFF has now become 'constitutionalised' in the treaty, which means that the current rules need to undergo a process of treaty reform

in order to be changed. The previous system was based on an inter-institutional agreement, which could be more easily modified or even cancelled by any of the participant institutions. In addition, the new rules have introduced an expenditure ceiling, which leaves fewer opportunities for reform during the period of implementation of the MFF and fewer chances for the EP to call for a change in the ceilings of spending. This means that, since the limits are fixed, the EP and the Council have less room for manoeuvre when they negotiate the annual budget.

The EP was quick to realise these limitations and used the first MFF negotiations after the entry into force of the Treaty of Lisbon to settle some formal uncertainties, such as the exact use of the consent procedure and whether the European Council should play a role in negotiations. This explains the tumultuous negotiations for the 2014–2020 Multiannual Financial Framework. The EP was aggravated when member states closed a deal early in February 2013 during a European Council meeting, since it raised concerns on the leading role of the European Council and its President (at that point Herman Van Rompuy) in budgetary matters. The EP refused to take the deal as a *fait accompli* and preferred to treat it as a 'draft', which led to its rejection in March 2013.

Part of the problem resided also in the attempt of the European Council to set the spending for specific funding programmes, for which the EP enjoys co-decision rights. Indeed, one should not forget that the MFF is only a general guideline, which needs to be complemented with funds for a wide range of programmes. The power to co-decide in this area gives Parliament an important leverage in setting the direction of core distributive policies, such as agriculture, cohesion, research or migration. These programmes and funds allow more flexibility than the annual budget and can be used as an instrument to re-orient the priorities of the EU (Núñez Ferrer and Katarivas 2014). The EP realised the importance to preserve its right of co-decision while negotiating the 2014–2020 MFF, especially when the deal reached in the European Council in February 2013 included not only specifications on financial headings and ceilings, but also aspects that concerned 65 additional files that had to be decided under co-decision. The EP saw the deal as an attempt by the Council to mix up procedures and legislate without any democratic control. The EPP, the S&D and ALDE declared that 'the (European Council) heads of state and government legislating alone, behind closed doors, simply goes against the EU Treaty and good democratic practices' (Socialists & Democrats 2013).

A final political agreement was reached on 27 June 2013, although the EP did not vote on it until November 2013. In the end, the EP could not convince member states to depart from an 'economic crisis' mindset and was, therefore, unable to make them think about the policies behind the budget. However, it did manage to include a clause that makes it possible to carry over unspent money from one year to the next, instead of returning it to national budgets, and it foresaw a mid-term review to evaluate the need to adjust the spending ceilings of the MFF. The mid-term review became a bargaining chip for the EP in the negotiations of the 2017 budget, accepting it only on the condition that the MFF would be reformed substantially for the 2017–2020 period (Euractiv 2016a).

Annual budget
While the EP is only involved to a limited extent in the MFF negotiations, it is one of the two main decision-makers in charge of the annual budgetary procedure, which has been considerably modified by the Treaty of Lisbon in Article 314 TFEU. The procedure, introduced in 1975, made a distinction between compulsory and non-compulsory spending. Compulsory spending affected intergovernmental areas such as agriculture, fisheries and foreign policy. Non-compulsory expenses covered the rest and grew significantly in time, providing more (unanticipated) powers to the EP (see Chapter 2). The main difference between the two types of spending resided in the capacity of the EP to introduce amendments. For compulsory expenditures, the EP could easily propose a shift or reduction in the types of spending, but if it proposed to increase the ceiling, then it needed the support of a qualified majority in the Council. For non-compulsory spending, the budget procedure was organised in two readings and, due to the very high majorities needed to introduce amendments or reject the text, it was very difficult for the EP to introduce any raises to compulsory expenditures. For the non-compulsory half, it proved easier to accept than to amend the Council's first-reading amendments (Benedetto and Høyland 2007).

The Treaty of Lisbon introduced two main changes to the budgetary procedure. First, it eliminated the distinction between compulsory and non-compulsory spending, which formally gives the EP a bigger say in crucial matters such as agriculture or foreign policy. Informally, however, the difference between these two types of spending had become irrelevant, since the EP used the areas where it had control as a bargaining chip to exert influence on those where it did not have much of a say (Laffan and Lindner 2015: 235). Second, the Treaty of Lisbon has reduced the procedure to one reading, complemented by a conciliation committee (instead of a second reading). The procedure is characterised by very rigid time limits, which should ensure that a budget is agreed upon before the end of the financial year. Figure 4.6 provides an overview of the different steps of the budgetary procedure.

Although the Commission has until 1 September to present a draft budget, the procedure generally starts earlier than that. The EP publishes

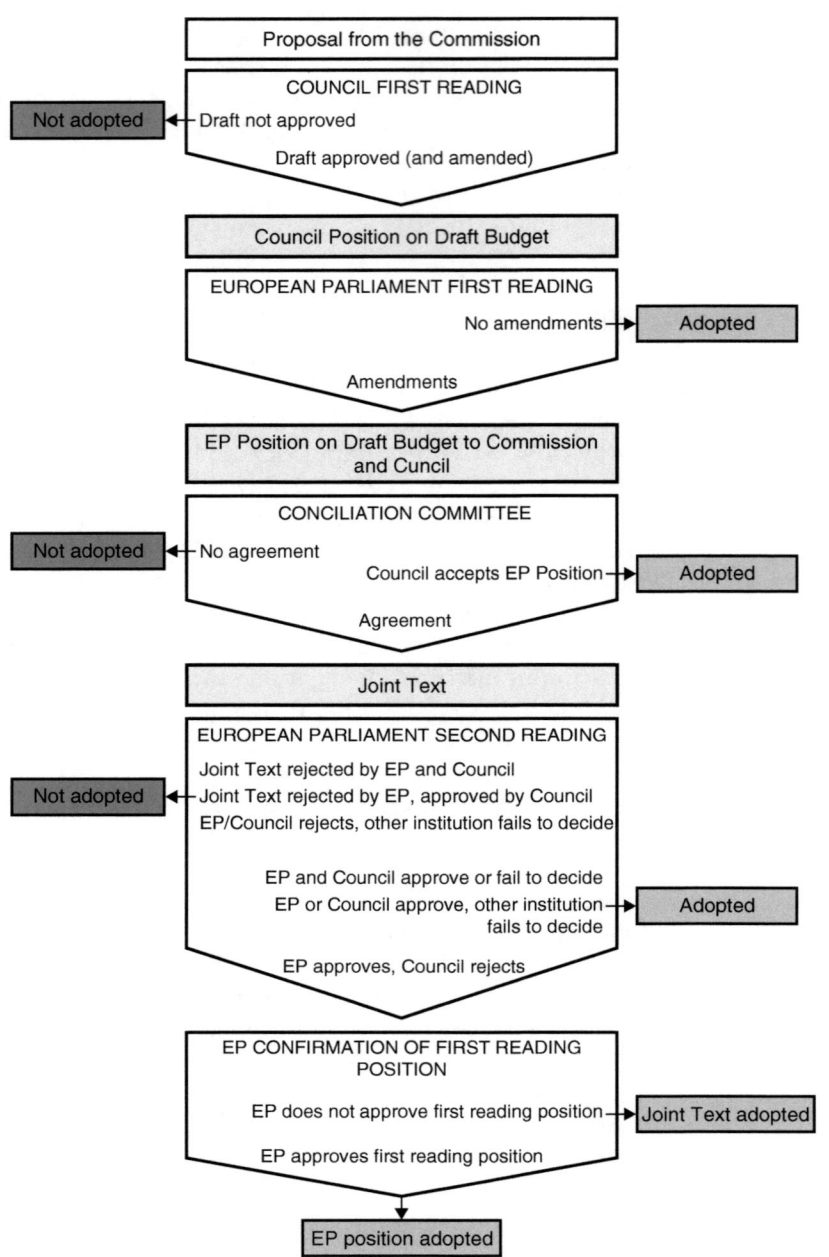

Figure 4.6   *Budgetary procedure*

its guidelines on the general budget in March, which serves as an orientation for the Commission. The draft budget is then normally presented in April and examined by both the EP and the Council. Formally, the Council has time until 1 October to issue its position. If it cannot support the Commission's proposal, it sends it back for a new draft budget to be produced. Otherwise, it sends its position to the Budgets committee, which is in charge of drafting the EP's position. Within a maximum of 42 days, the EP has to decide whether it approves the Council position (with a simple majority) or whether it introduces amendments (with an absolute majority). If it approves the Council position or fails to act, the budget is deemed approved. Otherwise, it issues its opinion on the draft budget, and if within ten days the Council gathers a qualified majority that supports the EP position, the budget is adopted.

In the event that the Council does not accept the changes proposed by the EP, a conciliation committee is convened 'immediately' by the presidents of the Council and the EP. As in co-decision, the committee gathers 28 delegates of member states and 28 MEPs representing the EP's political composition generally led by the EP rapporteur and the chair of the Budgets committee. It has a maximum of 21 days to produce a joint text, which has to be approved within 14 days. If the conciliation committee fails to produce a joint text, the budget is deemed not adopted and it goes back to the Commission, which is tasked with producing a new draft budget.

If the EP and the Council manage to produce a joint text, a complex procedure follows. The steps that follow the production of a joint text reflect the complicated compromise reached during the intergovernmental conferences that led to the Treaty of Lisbon (cf. Benedetto and Høyland 2007). The easiest scenario is the situation where the EP with a simple majority and the Council with QMV approve the joint text (or fail to decide) or where one of the EU institutions approves it and the other fails to act. In these cases, the joint text is deemed adopted and becomes the new budget. A more complicated scenario is presented in the situation where the Council rejects the joint text, but the EP approves it. In that case, the EP has 14 days to decide whether it wants to reintroduce all or some of its first-reading amendments. This new version needs the support of three-fifths of votes cast to become the final budget. Otherwise, the joint text is deemed adopted. Finally, after the agreement on a joint text, the budget may also fail in three different situations. First, the EP voting by absolute majority and the Council with QMV reject the joint text – this is, of course, highly improbable, since it has just been passed in the conciliation committee. Second, it may be that the Council approves the joint text but the EP rejects it, or third, one of the EU institutions rejects it and the other fails to act.

If the budgetary procedure fails to lead to an agreement, the Commission is asked to produce a new draft budget. If this has not happened before the start of the new financial year, the expenditure is frozen and the system of 'provisional twelfths' enters into force. This system foresees a provisional budget calculated on the basis of one-twelfth of the previous year's budget or the draft budget – whichever is lower. While before the Treaty of Lisbon the EP could decide with a three-fifths majority to increase non-compulsory expenditure (within the ceilings agreed in the financial framework), now it can decide on the entire budget, but only if it wants to block any increases or propose cutbacks in the provisional twelfths (Art. 315 TFEU).

The budgetary procedure is, therefore, a shortened version of the co-decision procedure. It diverges mostly in the last steps of the procedure, where in theory the EP can overrule the Council and impose its own version of the budget. However, the procedure has been judged 'not well designed' (Crombez and Høyland 2015: 83). It is indeed conducive to breakdowns, given that it is generally easier to reject the whole budget than to pass amendments. For instance, if the Council is afraid that the EP will ultimately overrule it, it might prefer to send the text back to the Commission already during the first-reading stage. Similarly, negotiations may falter at the conciliation stage if member states are not sure whether they can gather a qualified majority. They will prefer not to reach an agreement on a joint text rather than risk the scenario where the joint text is rejected in the Council. Therefore, the procedure is now biased towards maintaining the status quo and reducing spending (Benedetto 2013; Benedetto and Høyland 2007; Crombez and Høyland 2015). The 'ease of mutual veto' has become a shadow over annual budget negotiations and has led to a change in the behaviour of the EP and the Council. Since 2011, the fear of non-agreement and the need to fall back to the status quo has led to more moderate positions and has narrowed the gap between the two co-deciders (Benedetto 2017). In general, this favours the Council, since it is in a better position to control the pace of budgetary expenditures; therefore, 'the power of the purse resides with the Council' and, in most cases, the EP has lost budgetary power after the last treaty reforms (Benedetto 2017: 649).

Budgetary control

After the annual budget is passed, the EP remains in control of its implementation. With the entry into force of the Treaty of Lisbon (Article 322 TFEU), it gained the power to co-decide how the budget should be spent and managed through the Financial Regulation (966/2012/EU), which was previously decided under consultation. The Financial Regulation sets the rules and principles of implementing the budget, indicating, for instance, how grants should be allocated and the funds managed. It also provides for procedures to allow the Commission to transfer money between chapters or draw from the reserve. Generally, the Commission only needs to notify the EP and the Council, except if the sums exceed a given limit, in which case it would need to be expressly approved by the budgetary authorities.

Apart from this control over the current budget, since 1975, the EP is the only EU institution responsible for the discharge of the Commission's management of the budget. Article 319 TFEU indicates that the EP can grant discharge of the budget after a recommendation by the Council. The discharge procedure is a rather lengthy affair (see Box 4.3). By the end of the year, the Commission sends its audited accounts to the Court of Auditors, which examines them and forwards its annual report and a statement of assurances 'as to the reliability of the accounts and the legality and regularity of the underlying transactions' (Article 287.1 TFEU) by November of the following year. The Budgetary Control (CONT) committee is in charge of examining the Court of Auditor's report and drafting a recommendation to the EP's plenary on whether discharge should be granted, postponed or refused as well as indications for the Commission on how to improve certain practices or to which matters it should pay more attention. In order to elaborate these recommendations, the committee has developed a system of oral discharge hearings, which complements the information received by OLAF (the anti-fraud agency) and the annual reports of each director general.

In addition, the committee has taken it into its stride to grant discharge for the implementation of the budget not only to the Commission, as is foreseen in the Treaty, but also to all other EU institutions, agencies and joint undertakings (public–private partnerships, such as 'Fusion for Energy', which manages ITER, the international fusion energy project). This informal development has been incorporated into the EP's Rules of Procedure (Rule 93, 94 and Annex IV) and is also mentioned in Article 208 of the Financial Regulation, but only in regard to agencies and joint undertakings. In general, the other EU institutions have accepted these efforts at widening the interpretation of the Treaty rules, except for the Council, which does not look kindly upon the EP's examination of its budget. This has become a matter of inter-institutional friction, with the EP refusing to grant discharge of the Council's budget since the 2009 financial year. The Council has appealed to a 'Gentlemen's Agreement' of 1970, interpreting it as a promise to not scrutinise each other's budget; however, the EP understands it to cover only the preparation of the budget, not its scrutiny. It accuses the Council of not cooperating

---

Box 4.3   A typical calendar for the discharge procedure

To ensure the discharge of the 2013 budget, the Commission sent its audited accounts to the Court of Auditors by the end of 2013. In October 2014, the EP had hearings with the most relevant director generals of the Commission (those in charge of agriculture, regional and development policies, research and taxation) to discuss their annual reports. By mid-November, the Court of Auditors presented its annual report to the Budgetary Control committee and the EP plenary. From early December until the end of January 2015, the different director generals of the Commission, as well as the secretary generals of all the other institutions (the EP and the Council included) and those in charge of agencies and joint undertakings had to appear in front of the Budgetary Control committee, which then discussed the draft reports until the end of February. At the beginning of March, the time for amendments was closed and before the end of the month the committee voted on a recommendation. By April 2015 (and no later than 15 May), the 2013 budget was to be discharged. In case of a postponement, a new recommendation and vote would have taken place in October 2015.

---

with the EP and impeding its right of discharge and budgetary control by not providing sufficient information (Corbett et al. 2016: 334–335; European Parliamentary Research Service 2014b).

The issue of information has always been high on the EP's agenda. Indeed, the discharge procedure is not only a matter of ensuring the proper management of the budget; it is also an important source of information about the activities and political priorities of the other institutions and a powerful tool to make them reconsider these priorities. To this effect, the EP can decide to postpone the discharge of an institution, so as to extract more information or commitments during the six-month interlude between the two votes (April and October). In the past, the EP has also used the threat of refusing to grant discharge to put pressure on the Commission and investigate any hints of mismanagement or fraud. It occurred in 1984, when the EP did not grant discharge just before the Commission ended its term, and again in 1999, which set off the crisis and resignation of the Santer Commission (Judge and Earnshaw 2002; Laffan 2003). However, it is not yet clear what the formal consequences of refusing to grant discharge might be beyond the political scandal it would probably occasion.

Conclusion

The chapter has offered an overview of the EP's legislative and budgetary powers. As can be seen, the EP can now be considered a 'normal' parliament in many respects. Over time, it has gained the capacity to decide over almost all outputs of EU legislation. Like many national parliaments, it participates in the ratification of constitutional decisions and international agreements. It can also control the budget and scrutinise its implementation. In many other respects, however, the EP is certainly not yet a 'normal' parliament. Many of its powers stem from its own efforts to push the formal boundaries, leaving these powers in an uncertain position. Recent history has shown that the EP has generally been successful in formalising these changes and transforming them into official rules and procedures. However, the EP's push for influence has sometimes backfired. The budgetary reforms contained in the Treaty of Lisbon are probably the best example of this in that even though the changes were presented as being advantageous for the EP, they have proved less so in practice and left parliamentarians unsatisfied.

Chapter 5

Non-Legislative Functions

Introduction: accountability and control

Apart from the classic formal powers, the EP can make use of a wide range of less well-known instruments. Most of these are symbolic functions: they are used to scrutinise and control other EU institutions, enhance the link between the EP and EU citizens or raise awareness of current political debates. Some of these functions have become increasingly relevant over time and served to enhance the powers and legitimacy of the EP.

Although the original treaties already foresaw some of these functions, the majority have evolved through processes of informal interpretation and formal incorporation into the treaties. As we have seen in Chapter 2, the EP has proved very skilled at enlarging its own powers and used them to shift the EP's political system into one where Parliament is in charge of appointing and holding other EU institutions accountable. This has particularly been the case with the nomination of the Commission's President and the College of Commissioners, where the EP has used the rules to expand the linkage between its political composition and that of the Commission. These different non-legislative functions are overviewed in this chapter, ranging from the purely symbolic to strong control and accountability mechanisms over external actors.

Parliamentary questions

One of the oldest symbolic functions of the EP is parliamentary questions, in either oral or written form. The right to ask questions of the Commission was already included in the Treaty of Rome (Art. 140, now 230 TFEU), but after 1973 the EP extended this prerogative to the Council. The practice was partially formalised in the Stuttgart Solemn Declaration on European Union of 1983 and it is now part of Article 36 TEU, which establishes that 'the European Parliament may address questions or make recommendations to the Council or the High Representative'. However, it has always proved difficult to receive a comprehensive reply from the Council, since the Presidency can only offer an answer that reflects the views of all member states. All questions are published in the Official Journal, including those that are left unanswered. There are, formally, three types of parliamentary question: written questions, questions for oral answer with debate, and Question Time. Informally, however, MEPs hold a regular correspondence with the Commission, since it is often a quicker way to obtain information (Corbett et al. 2016: 372).

Written questions

Formal written questions are regulated by Rule 130, which establishes that any MEP can request clarification or further information from the Commission, the President of the European Council, the Council or the High Representative. The last reform of the rules has limited the amount of written questions to 20 over a rolling period of three months. The questions have to be transmitted electronically to the EP President, who settles their admissibility and transfers them to the pertinent institution. Written questions are sub-divided into 'priority' questions, which should be answered within three weeks; MEPs can only submit one priority question per month. 'Non-priority' questions can be answered within six weeks. If the deadlines are not observed, an MEP may request to raise the issue in committee, although the practice is not often used.

There have been two further changes to written questions. Rule 130a contemplates the possibility that a committee, a political group or at least 5 per cent of MEPs refer 'minor interpellations' on specific issues, to be answered within two weeks by the abovementioned institutions. In addition, Rule 130b introduces a new modality of 'major interpellations for written answer with debate', which function similarly to the minor interpellations but can be accompanied by a brief explanatory statement. The answer should come within three weeks but, even if the other institutions fail to respond, the major interpellation will be put on the plenary agenda and can be accompanied by a debate. In addition, MEPs can draft a maximum of six written questions about matters related to the European Central Bank or to the Single Supervisory and Single Resolution Mechanisms (Rules 131 and 131a).

The changes introduced in the Rules of Procedure responded to criticism of the Commission, which saw its workload increase substantially due to the extensive use of written questions by some MEPs. To this effect, the 2008 and 2016 Corbett Reports (2007/2272/REG; 2016/2114/REG) have given more discretion to the EP President and introduced some guidelines in Annex II: written questions should not exceed 200 words, they should refrain from asking about strictly personal matters and they should not contain more than three sub-questions. In addition, the EP Secretariat is allowed to bundle similar questions and use answers from similar questions referred within the last six months as well as requests for purely factual or statistical information. The 2016 reforms have added a new point to the annex, which specifies that MEPs are not allowed to ask the Council questions dealing with ongoing co-decision negotiations or with its budgetary functions.

Oral questions

Since 1973, the EP has organised a 'Question Time' session with the Commission. The idea was imported from the British House of Commons to allow for more dynamic debates between the EP and the other institutions. It introduced the possibility for any MEP to table questions one week in advance so that representatives of the Commission could answer them in a 90-minute debate. MEPs were limited to ask one question to each institution per session and the EP President could decide on the admissibility of questions and supplementary questions as well as their order. Those questions left unanswered for lack of time could then be answered in writing or raised for debate in committee. This system proved a good source of scrutiny and information, but was not completely satisfactory, since it was quite stale and devoid of emotion. The 2008 Working Party on Parliamentary Reform considered that 'the current system of prefabricated questions and answers is hardly satisfactory' (European Parliament 2008: 58). In June 2011, the Conference of Presidents introduced some changes to the procedure with the aim of making it more dynamic. It decided to focus each Question Time session on one specific horizontal topic during which MEPs questions would alternate with answers from the other institutions. It also eliminated the need to submit questions in advance and allowed for three or more Commissioners to be present for the debate. After a trial period, the EP reformed the system in 2014: it limited the number of Commissioners to a maximum of two (allowing the presence of three Commissioners only in exceptional occasions) and decided to change the system of interventions for a 'ballot' system. The latter consisted of a box left outside the chamber before Question Time. Any MEP could fill in a form and deposit it into the ballot box. The EP President then proceeded to draw one ballot form from the box and read out the name of the MEP. The procedure has not been used since January 2013 and the latest reform of the Rules of Procedure has again modified Question Time, turning it into a 'ping-pong-style' debate, where MEPs can ask one-minute questions and then follow it up with a 30-second question. The choice of MEPs is left to the President, who should ensure a fair representation of all political views.

Similarly lapsed is the modality of questions for oral answer with debate, defined in Rule 128. Theoretically, a committee, a political group or at least 5 per cent of MEPs can table them. The same criteria apply to proposals for a resolution containing a conclusion to the debate, which should see a vote on the same day. Oral questions are addressed in writing to the EP President, who discusses them with the Conference of Presidents. The latter decides whether to place a question on the agenda and in which order. Questions to the Commission and to the High Representative have to be transmitted one week in advance, while those to the Council need three weeks advanced notice. The Rules of Procedure make an exception for matters dealing with common security and defence policy, where it is only said that 'the reply must be given promptly to keep Parliament properly informed'.

A 'Question Hour' introduced through the 2010 Framework Agreement between the European Parliament and the Commission has replaced these two modalities. Rule 129.3 now makes only a passing reference to the possibility that 'specific question hours may be held with the Council, with the President of the Commission, with the [High Representative] and with the President of the Eurogroup'. The hour is divided into two types of debate. The first half-hour is dedicated to spontaneous questions from the political groups' leaders or their representatives. The second half is spent discussing a specific theme; the questions can come from any MEP, who can also ask questions spontaneously. This format can also be used with the Council, the High Representative and the president of the Eurogroup; in this case, there is no debate with the groups' leaders. The format is seen as more flexible and, therefore, it has come to replace the two traditional models of oral questions.

Parliamentary questions are still relatively under-researched, which makes it difficult to assess their impact. Raunio (1996) examined them in the mid-1990s and established that they were a useful technique to force the Commission to produce a reply, which, in turn, MEPs could exploit for their own purposes. He also considered them a valuable channel of communication between the EU institutions and the electorate, through which members could raise grievances or point to overlooked issues. This logic seems to apply to parliamentary questions addressed to EU agencies, which concentrate only on the most visible agencies – such as the European Food Safety Authority (EFSA) or the European Border and Coast Guard Agency (Frontex) – since they generate more public debate (Font and Pérez Durán 2016). Recent research has also shown that members who are in the opposition at the national level often use questions to warn the Commission about failures in the implementation of European legislation or to get information from other EU institutions to better oversee their national governments (Jensen et al. 2013; Proksch and Slapin 2011).

Since drafting questions does not require a lot of work, it can be a useful tool for smaller political groups or backbenchers. Votewatch (2015b: 8) has shown that fringe parties use parliamentary questions more often than centrist ones. Their tendency to use parliamentary questions may show the inability of fringe parties to employ other

Table 5.1　*Parliamentary questions per addressed institution*

	Commission	Council
7th parliamentary term (2009–2014)		
Written questions	53,262	2,469
Oral questions	787	269
Question Time (until 2011)	715	384
8th parliamentary term (2014–2016)		
Written questions	29,009	968
Oral questions	291	64

Source: European Parliament.

instruments, like amendments and votes, to exert influence, although it could also correspond to the fact that they can be used without limitations and can offer an alternative way to communicate with the public. This second explanation might help in understanding why in the seventh legislative period (2009–2014) southern MEPs from Portugal, Spain, Italy and Greece – all countries that have suffered an economic crisis – were amongst those highest in the rankings (Votewatch 2014a: 6). Indeed, these rankings seem to be one of the causes behind the implosion of parliamentary questions (see Table 5.1), since they consider questions as a way to measure the performance and level of activity of MEPs (see, for instance, http://www.mepranking.eu/).

Of course, this hides a lot of variation across MEPs – in terms of both quantity and quality. For instance, Marlene Mizzi (Malta, S&D) was at the top of the ranking with 564 between 2014 and early 2017 – with most questions concentrating on human rights issues. Evidently, asking questions on this topic is a worthy pursuit but, if we consider that the Commission calculated that each question might 'cost' 490 euros to its directorate generals, one wonders whether all of them are necessary and it explains the efforts by the EP leadership to cut down on the number of parliamentary questions (Politico 2015a).

Agenda-setting powers

With the changes introduced by the Treaty of Lisbon, the EP has gained almost full legislative power. However, in contrast with some national parliaments, it still does not enjoy a formal right of initiative. The European Council is the EU institution in charge of setting the general political directions and the Commission is the one responsible for putting them into place in the form of specific legislative proposals. That is why, in the last legislatures, one of the main tasks that the EP has given itself is that of broadening its influence in the agenda-setting stage. The main instruments used to steer the Commission's Work Programme are own-initiative reports and written declarations. Often the information necessary to write a recommendation to the Commission comes from previous commissioned studies or hearings organised by the responsible committee (see Box 7.1).

The EP can now draft five different types of own-initiative report: legislative-initiative procedures, strategic reports dealing with the Commission's Work Programme, non-legislative reports, annual activity or monitoring reports and implementation reports. While the first three are oriented towards setting the EU's agenda, the last two are used for evaluating the effects of legislation and will, therefore, be considered in the next section.

Legislative-initiative procedure

This type of own-initiative report is based on Article 225 TFEU, which gives the EP a right to 'request the Commission to submit any appropriate proposal on matters on which it considers that a Union act is required for the purpose of implementing the Treaties'. Rule 46 specifies that a proposal can be written by an individual MEP or a group of a maximum of ten members; their request has to indicate an adequate legal basis and add an explanatory statement. They are often complemented by an annex that sets precise recommendations to the Commission on what the proposal should include, and since 2012 also contain a 'European Added Value Assessment' that justifies the need for the proposal (see also Box 5.1). If the proposal is declared admissible by the EP President, it is referred to the responsible committee, which is in charge of drafting an own-initiative report, and later voted on in the plenary under absolute majority. The EP may also set a deadline for the Commission to act upon its recommendations.

Since the Treaty of Lisbon, if the Commission refuses to adopt the EP's recommendations, it needs to justify its decision. The Inter-Institutional Framework Agreement of 2010 specified that an answer should come within three months, and that in case of a positive reaction, any proposal should be included in the Commission's Work Programme within a year (see also Box 5.2). The EP considers that the Commission has not always complied with the rules of the game, since it has often refused to present a new proposal or it has failed to include all of the EP's recommendations (European Parliament 2014f: 17). In practice, the Commission does tend to reply to the requests, but only

---

Box 5.1   Better regulation: Assessing the potential impact of EU laws

Since the Barroso I Commission, a new mantra has guided the proposal of new legislation: the EU should produce fewer but also better laws. This attempt at 'better' or 'smart' regulation strengthened the use of impact assessments as an ex ante evaluation tool during the agenda-setting stage. Impact assessments estimate the expected costs and examine the benefits of an intervention as well as the costs of a non-intervention, while the Commission's aim is to assess the need for EU action and the potential economic, social and environmental impact of alternative policy options. Impact assessments are also carried out three years into the implementation stage, so as to evaluate ex post how well laws have been executed in member states and whether there are any gaps that call for (legislative) revisions.

In 2011, the Niebler Report (2010/2016/INI) underlined the necessity to engage with the concept of impact assessment and use it through the policy cycle. As a result, the EP installed the Directorate for Impact Assessment and European Added Value in January 2012, which today accommodates seven different units dealing with both ex ante and ex post evaluation. These units are tasked with scrutinising the impact assessments provided by the Commission and potentially publishing alternative studies. This is often considered necessary in order to evaluate whether the Commission has disregarded other available options. The unit also provides 'European Implementation Assessments', in which it assesses how successful policies operate in the field. These resources provide legislators with more expertise generated independently from the Commission, which helps them better evaluate the necessity and adequacy of new legislative proposals and take the initiative if they see a gap in the implementation of EU laws (European Parliamentary Research Service 2015b, 2016a, 2016b).

---

a few recommendations end up as new legislative proposals (European Parliamentary Research Service 2017).

Between 1994 and 2009, the EP submitted only 29 such initiatives; while in the seventh parliamentary term (2009–2014) this number rose to 22. In the first half of the eighth parliamentary term (2014–2016) only five proposals were submitted to the Commission – ranging from a proposal to reform the EU's electoral law (P8_TA(2015)0395) to one on civil law rules regarding robotics (P8_TA-PROV(2017)0051). A reason for the limited use of formal legislative initiatives is that Parliament reserves them for highly symbolic occasions or to give them more weight (Corbett et al. 2016: 311).

Non-legislative reports and written declarations

Compared to the low number of legislative initiatives, the EP adopted 576 non-legislative own-initiative reports in the 2009–2014 period, and by February 2017 it had adopted 245 reports in the 2014–2019 period. Rule 52 establishes that a committee can draft non-legislative reports, usually after the Conference of Presidents has granted authorisation. The aim is to reduce the workload and avoid clogging up the EP's agenda with unsuitable proposals. Reasons for refusal might be that it does not fall under the Commission's competences or that the topic has already been dealt with by Parliament in the last 12 months. To this effect, own-initiative reports are capped at six per committee for the first half of the legislative period and three for the second half. Those committees with sub-committees (such as Human Rights, which is part of the Foreign Affairs committee) have three extra reports for the first half and two more for the second half – but the extra reports have to be written by the sub-committee (Corbett et al. 2016: 181).

The content of non-legislative reports is extremely broad: they cover such diverse issues as the prospects of e-democracy for the Union and the role of whistle-blowers in the protection of the EU's financial interests. This form of report has become one of the main sources of agenda-setting power in the hands of the EP and an important channel of inter-institutional communication. As Herzog and Rasmussen (2015) note, non-legislative reports often hide similar aims to legislative initiatives and are also used to influence the EU's agenda-setting process by calling for new legislative proposals. Some of the most well-known initiatives, such as the ban on tobacco advertising, stem from this type of report (European Parliament 2013: 5).

Written declarations – a text of a maximum 200 words focusing on a specific issue proposed by a group of MEPs – used to be a similar route of influence. They had to be proposed by at least ten MEPs from at least three different political groups and, after authorisation by the EP's President, they were then opened for signature by other parliamentarians in a public electronic register. In the seventh term (2009–2014), 40 written declarations were adopted, while 200 lapsed because they could not reach the necessary number of signatures. Those adopted covered a wide array of issues, for instance on fish as a common good or on the establishment of European Artisanal Gelato Day. However, written declarations have been considered for a while as a relic of the past, used when the EP did not have much legislative influence. Now, they have 'very limited impact, in terms of both agenda-setting and influencing decisions taken by the institutions' (P7_TA(2012)0502, para. I). As a result, the 2016 reform of the Rules of Procedure (2016/2114/REG) considered them to steal time away from more relevant activities and decided to abolish them.

Strategic reports and the Commission's Work Programme

The Conference of Committee Chairs can turn the final type of own-initiative report into 'strategic reports' if they deal with non-legislative strategic and priority initiatives included in the Commission's Work Programme (see Box 5.2). However, they remain a residual instrument, given that none were tabled after the sixth parliamentary term (2004–2009). Another untapped potential to influence the agenda-setting stage lies in the wording of Article 17.1 TEU, which determines that the Commission 'shall initiate the Union's annual and multiannual programming *with a view to achieving interinstitutional agreements*' (emphasis added). The latter is now increasingly seen as a call for a new consultative process, which should deepen the dialogue and participation of the EP and the Council during the elaboration of the Commission's annual Work Programme and any multiannual programming activities (European Parliament 2013: 4). To this effect, Parliament uses various instruments with a view to influencing upcoming inter-institutional programming exercises. For instance, the EP's Secretariat now produces 'Long Term Trends Reports' through the European Strategy and Policy Analysis System (ESPAS) and 'Cost of Non-Europe' maps, which aim to put in a graphical form the cost of not introducing EU legislation. In effect, the new 'ten-point programme' presented in the EP by Juncker in July 2014 just before his nomination as Commission President (and expanded upon in November 2014) is clearly influenced by the 'Cost

---

Box 5.2   The Commission's Work Programme

The annual Commission's Work Programme (CWP) sets the priorities and objectives for the upcoming year and delineates the steps to achieve them. It is one of the main instruments of the 'Strategic Planning and Programming' process, a measure introduced by Prodi to check progress in the Commission's work and create new feedback loops. The CWP provides specific details on how to achieve the five-year policy objectives set by each new Commission. The CWP is drafted by the Commission's Secretary-General and the President's cabinet and generally adopted by the College in autumn of the year preceding its implementation (for instance, the 2017 CWP was adopted in October 2016). Although the CWP offers the Commission an opportunity to give precedence to certain initiatives and set the work schedule of the institutions, it is largely constrained by the priorities of other EU institutions. Therefore, the CWP often incorporates the concerns expressed by the European Council's conclusions, the work programmes of the Council Presidencies as well as the requests made by the EP in July in response to the plans reported by each Commissioner to their respective EP committee (Nugent and Rhinard 2015).

of Non-Europe' maps and further demands of the EP's political parties (European Parliament 2014f: 19).

Annex 4 of the 2010 Inter-institutional Agreement sets a timetable for completing the Commission's Work Programme, which includes all legislative and non-legislative proposals for the following years. During the first half of the year, the next programme is discussed with the responsible EP committees, which then report the outcome of this dialogue to the EP's Conference of Committee Chairs. The latter drafts a report in June for the Conference of Presidents that serves as a basis for the EP's resolution, voted on in July, which can also include any legislative initiative report. The President of the Commission should then respond to the EP's priorities in the annual State of the Union debate, held in the first part-session of September. This should be followed by a new round of contacts between the Commission and the responsible EP committees to further define the priorities of each policy area. This process finishes in October, when the Commission formally adopts its Work Programme and presents it to the EP, which then holds a debate in December (Corbett et al. 2016: 314).

Ex post evaluation

Apart from trying to influence EU policy-making during the agenda-setting stage, the EP is increasingly looking at the implementation stage to monitor the practical impact of EU legislation. It has several instruments at its disposal. First of all, it can table two types of own-initiative report: annual activity and monitoring reports as well as implementation reports. The former are now equated to strategic reports and are used to scrutinise specific policy areas or EU organs. Some of them – for instance, an annual report on access to documents or on the European Ombudsman – are explicitly mentioned in the Rules of Procedure, and therefore excluded from the quota of own-initiative reports. Others, such as a report on human rights or on the ECB, are a matter of tradition and do not need authorisation from the Conference of Presidents.

Implementation reports have seen an increase in the last years, especially since the Conference of Presidents decided in March 2014 to eliminate the cap of one report per year for each committee. These reports serve to scrutinise the transposition of EU law in member states, thereby offering a general overview of the entire policy cycle which may result in a new legislative initiative if the EP detects any gaps or deficiencies during the implementation process. The tabling of implementation reports is overseen by a responsible committee and is often accompanied by other scrutiny activities, such as hearings, expert studies or public debates (European Parliament 2014f: 42).

In recent years, the EP has also launched several mechanisms that serve to monitor the activities of the EU's main agenda-setters. For instance, since 2013, the 'Political Work Programme' offers a compilation of all of the EP's calls for legislative initiative and their progress (European Parliament 2014f: 15). In addition, there are also two new 'rolling checklists'. The first aims to compile all information that member states are requested to provide on the transposition of EU legislation in order to fulfil the 'review clauses'; these clauses are mentioned at the end of almost all legislative acts and serve to evaluate the need for further legislative action. The rolling checklist for review clauses should put EP committees in a better position to evaluate the outcomes of legislation that they have adopted in the past. The second rolling checklist serves a similar purpose, but is aimed at checking the European Council's commitments and whether (and to what extent) they have been implemented (European Parliamentary Research Service 2017). The objective is to be in a better position to influence the long-term legislative agenda of the EU by aligning the work of the EP and the European Council.

'Theatre of engagement'

Apart from influencing the general legislative agenda and scrutinising the implementation of EU laws, the EP uses a variety of tools at its disposal in order to raise awareness of political issues that operate outside the legislative agenda. Non-legislative own-initiative reports are often used for this purpose, since they generally deal with non-legislative matters and serve to publicise the interests and positions of the EP as an institution or of some of its members. Often, they are based on motions for resolution tabled by one or several MEPs (Rule 133). Motions for resolution can be tabled by individual members, but have been limited to one motion per month. They cannot act as a substitute for other procedures; for instance, they cannot propose new legislation or raise a matter that is already being dealt with in legislative negotiations. Admissible motions are then sent to committee, which may adopt them in the form of an opinion, a letter or an own-initiative report.

As an example, a recent own-initiative report on 'green growth opportunities for Small and Medium Enterprises (SMEs)'(2014/2209/ INI) tabled by the Committee on Industry, Research and Energy, was based on various motions for resolution that aimed to raise awareness on improving access of SMEs to finance and reindustrialising Europe to promote competitiveness and sustainability. Herzog and Rasmussen (2015) have shown that there is still a high correlation between those committees that have a 'light' legislative workload and the number of 'genuine' own-initiative reports (that is, those initiated by the EP and not coming as a response to the Commission's communications such as white and green papers) they produce. That means that this type of report is still largely used as a 'theatre of engagement' – that is, to feign high levels of influence or legislative activity – by those committees that are not very involved in the 'ordinary' legislative process (for the symbolic use of plenary, see Chapter 10).

Appointments and accountability

One of the most important powers of the Parliament is that of appointing and scrutinising other EU bodies – particularly the Commission and its President. This role was not foreseen by the original treaties and is another example of hard-won powers through informal means.

Appointing the Commission and its President

With its first direct election in 1979, the EP strove to strengthen its role in the appointment of the Commission's team. On its own initiative, it decided to organise a debate and a vote of confidence on the work programme of the incoming Commission. The practice was formally recognised in the Stuttgart Solemn Declaration on the European Union of 1983, which also accepted that the EP's enlarged Bureau should be consulted on the choice of Commission President. The EP's efforts were endorsed by the Commission's acquiescence to the rules: the three Delors Commissions waited for the EP's vote of confidence on the proposed college before taking the oath of office.

The Treaty of Maastricht formalised and enlarged the EP's involvement in the appointment of the Commission. The EP gained the right to be consulted on the choice of President and the Commission's mandate was aligned to the Parliament's five-year term, which strengthened the link between EP elections and the choice of the Commission's President and College. It was also at this moment that the EP developed various informal practices in its Rules of Procedure, which gave it a bigger say in their appointment. First, it foresaw a vote by simple majority on the choice of candidate for President, requesting from the European Council to withdraw the candidate and propose a new one if the vote was negative. Therefore, its interpretation went further than just giving an opinion on the candidate; the decision was transformed into a proper vote of investiture (Hix 2002: 276–277). Second, the Rules of Procedure also incorporated the practice of holding parliamentary hearings before the vote on the President-designate. Since Jacques Santer was not the preferred candidate for a large section of the Parliament, he was willing to accept the idea of hearings if it could win him the EP's vote of confidence (Corbett et al. 2016: 342). With the subsequent treaties, the EP gradually confirmed and expanded its involvement in the appointment of the President and Commissioners. This has led to closer links between the EP and the Commission and has transformed the balance between the executive and legislative powers of the EU's political system. Since Maastricht, there has been a gradual process of presidentialisation and politicisation of the Commission, which is now more dependent on (and accountable to) the EP.

Since the entry into force of the Treaty of Nice in 2003, the appointment of the Commission has moved away from its intergovernmental origins. The increasing involvement of the EP and the possibility to use QMV in the European Council means that there is now a higher potential to choose a Commission that is situated farther away from the status quo. This could lead to Commissions with a more marked political profile, although any initiative will always have to convince the Council and the EP, which have now a strengthened role in controlling the Commission during the legislative process (Crombez and Hix 2011). Already in the aftermath of the 2004 elections, Barroso's vote of investiture was highly contested due to the opposition of the left-wing groups in the EP (Socialists, Greens and the radical left); however, by claiming that Barroso represented the largest political group in the chamber, the EPP-ED anticipated a rule that would become a part of the failed Constitutional Treaty and ultimately one of Lisbon's main innovations (Corbett et al. 2016: 344; Judge and Earnshaw 2008: 206).

Barroso's re-election in 2009 was a clear confirmation of the gradual politicisation of the Commission. As in 2004, there was a clear ideological divide during the vote of investiture. Even though the Lisbon Treaty had not yet entered into force, the EPP-ED insisted once again that Barroso should have priority, since he was a member of the political party that had received the most votes in the elections. The left wing of the EP was not happy with the choice and claimed that the European Council had not consulted Parliament on Barroso's candidacy (Dinan 2010). In addition, the election of Barroso in 2009 also marked a change in the expectations of the EP towards the Commission President. It was the first occasion that the candidate for the presidency offered concrete commitments in the form of written political guidelines before his investiture. The EP threatened not to invest him if he did not effectuate certain changes to the work programme, which led to a much stronger control over the Commission's political direction (Wille 2010).

The Treaty of Lisbon formalised the necessity to take into account the results of the EP's elections when nominating a candidate for the role of Commission President; EP political groups made use of this provision to its full extent and came up with a new method to designate 'Spitzenkandidaten' (candidates-designate) during the electoral campaigns (see Box 5.3). The Treaty also raised the threshold for the election

Box 5.3   How Jean-Claude Juncker came to be the Commission President

With the introduction of the Treaty of Lisbon, the Commission President came to be elected from a group of 'Spitzenkandidaten' (candidates-designate) for the first time. The Treaty of Lisbon emphasises that the European Council should take 'into account the elections to the European Parliament' when proposing 'to the European Parliament a candidate for President of the Commission' (Art. 17.7 TEU). The national governments were rather mute on how they would interpret these changes, so the EP political groups boldly promised that the European public would decide through their vote who would become the head of the EU's executive (Hobolt 2014). The solution for most political groups in the EP (all except the ECR and the Europe of Freedom and Democracy [EFD]) was to propose their own candidate for the role of Commission President. For the EPP, the nominated 'Spitzenkandidat' was Jean-Claude Juncker. The former Luxembourgish Prime Minister was elected as the party's candidate during the party's congress in Dublin on 6–7 March 2014, where he defeated his competitor, French Michel Barnier (later appointed as head EU negotiator in Brexit). His main opponent as 'Spitzenkandidat' was Martin Schulz (acting EP President), who had already been nominated as candidate of the S&D on 1 March 2014 in Rome.

After the EP elections on 22–25 May, the EPP won most of the seats, but not enough to have a majority in its own right. However, on 27 May, five of the seven parties in the Parliament agreed that Juncker should be given the first chance to form a majority (only the ECR and the EFD disagreed). During negotiations, the EPP and the S&D agreed on a compromise where the Socialists would support the candidacy of Juncker but in return the Commission would shift the focus away from austerity so as to propitiate more growth and job creation. Furthermore, some of the top jobs in the European institutions – like the presidency of the European Parliament and the post of High Representative – should go to the Socialists (Euobserver 2014a; Euractiv 2014e). After this compromise, the European Council officially proposed Juncker to the EP for President of the Commission on 27 June 2014. What is interesting is that, for the first time, the Council did not act in consensus but only 26 out of 28 member states voted in favour of Juncker. This is, however, higher than might have been expected, since not only the UK and Hungary had opposed Juncker's nomination during the election campaign – Angela Merkel had also expressed strong doubts before he became 'Spitzenkandidat' and after the EP elections (Der Spiegel 2013; *Financial Times* 2014). On 15 July, the Parliament elected Juncker as President of the Commission with 422 votes in favour and 250 votes against – that is, with 50 votes more than was required for an absolute majority.

of the Commission President, which now requires an absolute majority rather than the previous simple majority. This is significant, since it means that the candidate to the Commission's presidency needs broader support than in the past; as Corbett et al. (2016: 346) note, Santer would not have managed to reach an absolute majority in 1994 and in 2009 Barroso would have just made it. Rule 117 states that after the European Council proposes a candidate, the EP should hold a debate on his (and maybe in the future her) political guidelines, followed by a vote by secret ballot. If the candidate gathers the support of a majority of component members, the Council is informed and then the European Council and the elected President can go on to propose the Commissioners. If the EP rejects the candidate, it invites the European Council to propose a new one within one month.

Hearings are now a largely formalised affair, regulated by Rule 118 and Annex VI. Corbett (2014) has remarked that the three-hour-long hearings are 'rigorous and often dramatic'. Before the hearing, each Commissioner-designate has to answer a written questionnaire with seven questions – a practice introduced with the Prodi Commission in 1999 and gradually refined. Two of the questions are asked by the Conference of Committee Chairs and cover the general competence of the candidates, their European commitment and personal independence as well as their knowledge of the portfolio and how they see their relationship with the EP. The other five questions come from the responsible committee. The answers to the questionnaire are followed up by an oral statement of 15 minutes in front of those committee members that are associated with their portfolio; the latter then have the opportunity to ask a maximum of 25 questions. The session is closed with a brief statement by the candidate and an 'in-camera' evaluation by the committee chairs and political coordinators of each group. They should take into consideration the general suitability of the candidate as well as more general principles like gender balance and make their decision public within 24 hours of the hearing. Once the EP has gathered all the committees' opinions, it organises a debate where the Commission-designate can present its programme, which is followed by a vote of investiture with simple majority.

The EP has used the threat to reject the whole Commission if some individual Commissioner candidates did not pass muster, which has given it an informal right to force the Commission President to ask for new nominees or to reshuffle their portfolios. The first (successful) incident came in 2004 with the Buttiglione affair, which captured the attention of the media and underlined the importance of hearings (Beukers 2006). The Italian candidate was appointed to the Home Affairs portfolio; however, his comments on women's and gays' rights raised questions about his adequacy to deal with issues of discrimination and civil rights. The Italian government was put under extreme pressure and finally capitulated and sent its foreign minister (Franco Frattini) in his place. The 2004 election also saw a change in the Latvian candidate (Ingrīda Ūdre, replaced by Andris Piebalgs) and the Hungarian Commissioner (László Kovács) reappointed to another portfolio. In 2009, all eyes turned to the Bulgarian candidate Rumiana Jeleva's financial affairs. Pressure from the EP forced the Bulgarian government to seek a substitute (Kristalina Georgieva).

Similar incidents were repeated in the 2014 confirmation of the Commissioners' candidates. Alenka Bratušek was seen as a poor candidate – some even accused her of having nominated herself in the last hours of her role as Slovenian Prime Minister – and was rejected by a majority of 13 in favour and 112 against. Violeta Bulc was presented as a replacement, and although she only had four days to prepare for her hearing, she was generally seen as a fast learner with better language skills and more personality, which was enough to convince most MEPs (Euractiv 2014a, 2014b). Similar to the Buttiglione affair, the EP raised doubts about the adequacy of the Hungarian candidate, Tibor Navracsics, to deal with matters of education and culture – which also included citizenship – given his participation in the Orbán government and its attacks on civil rights (Euractiv 2014d). The portfolio of citizenship was ultimately shifted to Migration and Home Affairs, led by Greek Commissioner Dimitris Avramopoulos. The EP also secured an important shift in portfolios, bringing back the issue related to pharmaceuticals – which had been moved to Internal Market, Industry, Entrepreneurship and SMEs – to the Health portfolio. More interesting was the Arias Cañete affair: the Spanish candidate was widely seen as unsuitable to lead the Climate Action and Energy portfolio due to his involvement with oil companies. His potential conflict of interests even triggered a popular petition to reject his nomination. However, he eventually secured the post thanks to a deal struck between the two largest EP political groups, which traded Arias Cañete (an EPP member) for Pierre Moscovici, the French candidate (a Socialist). The EP, however, received reassurances: in order to avoid potential problems, Frans Timmermans, new First Vice-President and 'super-Commissioner' for Better Regulation, Interinstitutional Affairs, Rule of Law and Charter of Fundamental Rights, would supervise Arias Cañete in matters of sustainable development (Euractiv 2014f). In the end, the EP approved the Juncker Commission with a very large majority of 423 votes in favour, 209 against and 67 abstentions by a coalition formed by the EPP, the S&D and ALDE. The radical left and the Greens voted against, together with the Eurosceptics (EFDD). The conservative ECR group advised its

MEPs to abstain, and in the end was split between a large majority of abstentions and some votes against and in favour (Votewatch 2014b).

The last appointment procedure shows how, although theoretically the EP has no role in the nomination of individual Commissioners, there has been an increase in horse trading inside the EP, leading to a more politicised investiture procedure and also a more active role in the supervision of the Commission (Corbett 2014). This reflects the growing importance of the Commission offices and explains why member states have started sending candidates with a high political profile and long (domestic and international) political careers (Wille 2012). Compared to the low profile of previous Commissioners, the current College is composed of candidates who had previously acted as ministers (19), (deputy) prime ministers (9), Commissioners (7) and MEPs (8). This has also contributed to strengthening the partisan dimension of the EU's political system; since the Prodi Commission, members of the College have cultivated much closer relationships with MEPs from the same political family (Wille 2013).

Censuring the Commission

Apart from appointing the Commission, the Treaty of Lisbon also contemplates the possibility that the EP censures and dismisses the Commission (Article 234 TFEU). Rule 119 foresees that one-tenth of MEPs can submit a motion of censure – which is a relatively low threshold and explains the high number of attempts that the EP has put to the vote. That is why the Rules of Procedure now also include a clause that raises the threshold to one-fifth of MEPs if a motion of censure has already been put to the vote in the last two months. However, even if a proposal for censure gathers the necessary support, its success is doubtful, since the treaty requires a 'two-thirds majority of the votes cast, representing a majority of the component Members of the European Parliament' (that is, 376 votes out of 751). This double majority sets a very high hurdle, which explains why there have not been any successful motions of censure. For instance, 76 Eurosceptic and non-attached MEPs tabled a motion of censure soon after the Juncker's Commission started work due to the 'Lux leaks' scandal concerning tax evasion in Luxembourg. The motion was defeated in November 2014 by a large majority of 461 votes against, 101 in favour and 88 abstentions (European Parliament 2014e).

In addition, this modality of censure means that the EP cannot formally ask for the resignation of an individual Commissioner. Despite these formal restrictions, the EP managed to strengthen its role in the cessation of Commissioners through the 2005 Inter-institutional Agreement, where it was agreed that individual members of the College would take responsibility for their personal actions and those of their Directorate-Generals (DGs). At the same time, if the EP lost confidence in a Commissioner, it could ask the Commission President to ask for their resignation (Wille 2010). As Judge and Earnshaw (2008: 211–212) remarked, the EP can thus use this informal tool as a 'smart bomb' to signal its disagreement before deploying the full 'nuclear option' of censuring and dismissing the Commission as a whole.

Appointing other EU bodies

The EP is also involved in appointing other EU bodies, although its involvement varies in depth and formalisation. These appointments all share certain characteristics and are not that different from the confirmation of new commissioners. In most cases, the EP has institutionalised the system of confirmation hearings in the responsible committees, which then provide a recommendation for a vote to the EP plenary. What does diverge is the right to propose a candidate and the consequences in case of a negative vote.

For instance, the EP has almost complete control over the appointment of the ombudsman, who is elected after each EP election and sits in the Parliament building in Strasbourg. The candidates are interviewed by the Petitions committee; the latter transmits a list to the plenary, which then votes by simple majority (but with the presence of at least half of its members). The EP can also hold a vote so that the CJEU can dismiss the ombudsman in cases of serious misconduct (Rule 221). Irish Emily O'Reilly was elected on 1 October 2013 as ombudsman after the previous one, Nikiforos Diamandouros, decided to retire. She was confirmed in her role after the 2014 elections. Article 228 TFEU and Rule 229 determine that nominations for the position of ombudsman can come from at least 40 MEPs representing at least two different member states.

In contrast, the European Data Protection Supervisor (EDPS) is proposed by the Commission. The potential candidates are examined and interviewed by an inter-institutional selection board, which proposes a final list to the Council and the EP. Although the final decision has to be made in consensus, the EP asks candidates to appear before the Civil Liberties, Justice and Home Affairs committee (LIBE) for a public hearing. Similarly to the ombudsman, in cases of grave misconduct, the EDPS can be dismissed by the CJEU after a request by the EP, the Council or the Commission. The current supervisor, Giovanni Buttarelli, and his assistant, Wojciech Wiewiórowski, were elected on 4 December 2014 for a period of five years.

In other cases, nominations are proposed by member states and the EP has only a right of consultation. However, even in those cases,

Parliament has used its informal powers to expand its influence over the final solution by introducing confirmation hearings. The success of these hearings has been, however, uneven. In the case of the European Central Bank, Article 283(2) TFEU states that the Council proposes the candidates for the roles of President, Vice-President and members of the executive board and the European Council decides after consultation with the EP and the Governing Council of the ECB. However, since the selection in 1993 of the first ECB President, Alexandre Lamfalussy, the EP has used hearings in its Economic and Monetary Affairs Committee (ECON) to vote for the candidates to the ECB executive board (Rule 122). Interestingly, it was the candidates themselves who embraced the procedure early on; in 1997, Wim Duisenberg promised that he would withdraw his candidacy if the EP voted against him. The EP has also gained a role in the selection of executive offices of the Single Supervisory and Resolution Mechanisms, the European Supervisory Authority as well as the European Fund for Strategic Investments (Rule 122a).

This form of influence has not come without contestation. The appointment of members of the Court of Auditors shows the limits to the system of parliamentary hearings. As in the case of the ECB, Article 286 TFEU establishes only a consultative role for the EP. Nominations come from individual member states and the final decision is in the hands of the Council. The EP introduced the practice of hearings after the Merger Treaty in 1975 formally created the Court of Auditors. In 1981, it asked candidates to appear before its Budgetary Control Committee (CONT) to answer questions in a hearing for the first time. The practice is now included in Rule 121, but remains controversial. In most cases where the EP has voted negatively, the Council has gone ahead and confirmed the candidate. Some examples include Neven Mates, from Croatia, who was considered unsuitable for the role in 2013, and Janusz Wojciechowski, a Polish MEP, who was rejected by the EP's budgetary control committee in April 2016 given its concerns around his 'independent judgement'. Both were confirmed by the Council and became members of the Court of Auditors. However, the most challenging nomination has been that of the Maltese candidate: Toni Abela was rejected by the EP in March 2016 due to a drug scandal in a social club of his national political party; he ended up resigning from the candidature and was replaced by Leo Brincat, a senior member of the ruling party. Brincat was also rejected by the EP due to his links with the 'Panama Papers' scandal, but the Maltese government decided to confirm him to the position (Politico 2016c). The appointment of new members remains, thus, a source of inter-institutional conflicts between the EP and the Council. In 2014, the EP voted on a resolution on the future role of the Court of

Auditors and its appointment procedure, where it stressed 'the need for a Treaty change putting the Council and Parliament on an equal footing when appointing Members of the Court of Auditors, in order to ensure [their] democratic legitimacy, transparency and complete independence' (P7_TA(2014)0060, para. 35).

Finally, the EP also has a say in the appointment of European regulatory agencies, although it is a highly complex and diverse system. The major differences concern whether the EP can appoint its own representatives to an agency's executive board and whether it has a say over the selection of the director or members of the scientific committee – although in some cases it has the power to do neither. Indeed, if we exclude the six executive agencies that depend directly on the Commission, as of 2017, the EU has 36 regulatory agencies, but the EP is only represented in nine, generally with one or two representatives. Only in the case of the European Training Foundation (ETF) can the EP appoint three members of the management board.

Lord (2011) looked at how the growing budgetary and legislative powers of the EP have given it an increasing say over the design of new agencies. During negotiations on new regulatory agencies, the EP has used a stock of ready-made amendments that have strengthened its control over them by requesting higher reporting duties to parliament committees, more representation in the management boards and increased participation in the appointment of directors. For instance, the EP included clauses asking for a 'cooperation' procedure between Parliament and the Council in the selection of candidates. This evolution has been particularly noticeable in the Area of Freedom, Security and Justice, where many new agencies have been created in a short period of time. Trauner (2012) compared the creation of Europol (established originally through a Convention), Frontex (decided under consultation) and the European Asylum Support Office (EASO, created under co-decision) showing how the gradual empowerment of the EP has translated into a bigger say in ex ante control mechanisms, especially with regards to the appointment of the EASO's director.

The regulation of agencies is still a matter for open discussion. In the early 2000s, there were calls for a more unified structure, which led the Commission to propose in 2005 an Inter-institutional Agreement on the Operating Framework for the European Regulatory Agencies. Despite a warm welcome from the EP, the draft agreement was blocked in the Council and eventually withdrawn by the Commission in 2008, which replaced it with a legally non-binding Common Approach on Regulatory Agencies in 2012. This new tool gives general guidelines on the structures of new agencies, their accountability duties and the evaluation of their performance.

Conclusion

Although the increase in legislative powers has been the focus of attention, one should not overlook the increase in non-legislative powers that the EP has experienced in the last decades. It has pushed formal rules to the limit by interpreting them in the most favourable way possible in order to increase its own powers. It has also had enough resolve to engineer new institutional practices and force them upon other actors. As was shown in Chapter 2, the EP's capacity to draw on institutional norms of democratic representativeness and its position as the only directly elected institution have helped to empower it in crucial areas such as the appointment and scrutiny of other EU bodies. Therefore, although the EP's empowerment has been most noticeable in the area of legislative decision-making, it has also recognised the need to expand its activities to ex ante and ex post control functions. Its competences are still relatively marginal in the agenda-setting and implementation stage, but they are more substantial than a decade ago. As a result, the EP has managed to have a much greater influence on the choice of the Commission and its overall political agenda. This process of formalising informal changes has led to major transformations in the relationship between executive and legislative powers and has broken down some of the walls separating these two branches of the EU's political system.

Chapter 6

Elections and Electoral Support

Introduction: what determines the outcome of EP elections?

This chapter looks at the Parliament as part of a political community that raises demands and provides enough support to legitimise the eventual (policy) outputs. In the end, the Parliament is the only directly elected EU institution, and, therefore, is supposed to be the main representative of EU citizens. It examines to what extent EP elections are representative by looking at how they are organised in different member states and how citizens make use of them. The objective is to determine whether institutional elements, such as differences in the national electoral systems, or individual explanations on citizens' voting behaviour, affect the quality of representation – that is, the capacity of MEPs to filter inputs from EU citizens into the EU's political system.

An examination of EP elections shows that they are rarely fought on European issues, but are rather seen as secondary national elections revolving around domestic concerns. Already in the aftermath of the first direct elections in 1979, Reif and Schmitt (1980) pointed out that EP elections should not be analysed as an EU-wide phenomenon, but rather treated as (at the time) nine simultaneous national second-order elections. Since then, the second-order elections (SOE) model has dominated most explanations of EP elections. The model poses five main theses: first, second-order elections are characterised by lower levels of turnout than national first-order elections; second, electoral campaigns tend to focus on national rather than EU-related issues, with a prominent presence of national politicians; third, government parties are often defeated, especially when, fourth, the timing of the elections takes place in the middle of a national electoral cycle (when citizens tend to be most tired of or disappointed with parties in government), and finally, larger parties – whether in government or part of the opposition – tend to suffer losses in favour of smaller and more extreme political parties. Underlying these five theses is the assumption that citizens see less at stake in EP elections. Given that the results of their votes will not lead to the instauration of a government, citizens find it more difficult to evaluate the importance of their decision and this leads them to abstain or vote for smaller parties. Therefore, the 'less at stake' assumption explains individual voting behaviour by supposing that instead of choosing their candidate strategically (that is, 'with the head'), they can afford to vote for the party or candidate that they sincerely support, choosing rather 'with their heart'. In some cases, their vote will turn into a protest against (generally) the government, which is understood as voting 'with the boot' (Viola 2015: 42).

However, these explanations are not satisfactory for everybody. Some point out that the 'less at stake' assumption has become less relevant with the evolution of the EU and the growing powers of the EP and that the European dimension is now a determinant of EU and national elections (e.g. de Vries et al. 2011; Hobolt and Spoon 2012; Tillman 2004; van der Eijk and Franklin 1996). This line of research has been named the 'Europe Salience' (ES) model and its central assertions are: Green parties tend to perform better in EP than in national elections because voters sensitive to the environment think that Green parties might have more chances to influence policy outputs at the EU level; extreme parties perform better in EU elections; and anti-EU parties have more chances of success than in national elections because EU issues are more salient in EP electoral contests (Viola 2015: 44).

The theses of these two models are not necessarily contradictory – for instance, they both predict that smaller (and more extreme) parties will do better than larger parties in EP elections. However, their explanations depart from very different sets of assumptions: while the SOE model considers that voters do not care about EP elections because they do not recognise their implications, the 'Europe Salience' model considers that the different outcomes in EP elections can be explained by looking at the dimensions of electoral debates, especially the pro- and anti-EU dimension.

This chapter, therefore, considers which of these two models holds more explanatory value when examining the last eight EP elections (from 1979 until 2014). It also looks, however, at other explanations that focus on institutional choices (that is, structural differences across national electoral systems) in order to consider whether they might complement and nuance some of the expectations raised by the SOE and ES models. For instance, can different institutional choices explain the proportion of women in the Parliament or whether citizens feel close to their representatives? In order to examine these different aspects, the chapter starts by exploring the normative debates around the issue of representation in the EU: does the EP act as representative of one single (EU) demos? It then turns to the institutional dimensions of elections, examining how differences in the organisation can have important implications for the type and quality of representation, affecting also the way candidates are selected and how close they are to the views of EU citizens. The latter part considers the main aspects of the SOE and ES theses, focusing in particular on the issues of turnout and changes in voting behaviour. The chapter concludes by looking at various initiatives seeking to put an end to the second-order nature of EP elections and assessing their chances of success.

One demos or several?

According to its etymological origins, the notion of democracy implies the governance of a demos, designating 'a political community of citizens who reliably identify with the polity and possess a strong sense of solidarity towards its other members' (Hurrelmann 2015: 19; cf. Cheneval et al. 2015). Therefore, Weiler (1999) considers that there is a necessary link between citizenship and democracy, which would imply that the existence of a demos is a necessary condition for democracy. In his words:

> [A] parliament without a demos is conceptually impossible, practically despotic. If the European Parliament is not the representative of *a* people, if the territorial boundaries of the EU do not correspond to its political boundaries, then the writ of such a parliament has only slightly more legitimacy than the writ of an emperor (Weiler 1995: 231).

For Weiler, the problem is not whether there is a link between citizens and the EP or whether the EP elections remain predominantly of a national character. Indeed, even though European institutions experienced an empowerment and the overall competencies of the EU increased, the European demos still has its groundings on national (or even regional) political parties, public spheres and identities. Therefore, the main problem is the absence of a common identity that recognises the EU as a single political community. This absence is due to the inherent diversity within the EU and the absence of 'the necessary common public culture' (Bellamy and Castiglione 2013: 218).

To remedy this issue, the EU has attempted to foster a sense of shared EU identity by introducing the principle of European citizenship in the Treaty of Maastricht. EU citizenship cannot be acquired independently from national citizenship, but it does provide additional rights, such as the right to vote (and be voted for) in EP and local elections when residing in another EU country. Article 10 TEU explicitly refers to democracy as a core principle of the EU's political system. It states:

1 The functioning of the Union shall be founded on representative democracy.
2 Citizens are directly represented at Union level in the European Parliament. Member States are represented in the European Council

by their Heads of State or Government and in the Council by their governments, themselves democratically accountable either to their national Parliaments, or to their citizens.

3   Every citizen shall have the right to participate in the democratic life of the Union. Decisions shall be taken as openly and as closely as possible to the citizen.

4   Political parties at European level contribute to forming European political awareness and to expressing the will of citizens of the Union.

Therefore, there has been an active attempt to foster a sense of shared identity and representation from the top. In addition to a formal EU citizenship, other elements, such as the direct EP elections or the creation of state-like symbols such as the flag and anthem, have constituted an effort to foster a common EU identity – whether they have been successful remains debatable. Most authors looking into the EU's democratic character conceptualise it as a system composed of many different 'demoi' rather than a single 'demos' (Bellamy 2013; Cheneval et al. 2015; Jiménez Lobeira 2012). In this sense, the EU could then be defined as a 'demoi-cracy', which captures the 'dual character of the EU as a community of both states (peoples) and individuals in a common supranational polity' (Cheneval et al. 2015: 2). Some even argue that the EU as a 'demoi-cracy' could be seen as something positive, in the sense that the EU is actively building its identity and legitimacy upon this notion of demoi. Instead of seeing it as an inherent problem, it could be seen as an opportunity for a third way, between national and supranational modes of legitimisation. For Nicolaïdis, 'the EU can be democratically legitimated by a *plural pouvoir constituant* (if the topic is constitutional) or by *multiple but connected national politics*' (2013: 352). This requires a transnational conception of democracy that goes beyond the need to share a common identity and emphasises instead the will to work and govern together.

If that is the case, then the accent should be put on the quality of representation in the EU, rather than whether citizens share a common identity. Indeed, many have raised questions on the quality of representation and how it could be improved (Hix et al. 2007; Hix 2008b; Hix and Bartolini 2006; Magnette and Papadopoulos 2008). How is it related to the quality of representation in EP elections? Recent research notes that, despite the big part that national parties play in European elections, voters are still presented with clear options and can make meaningful choices (Bressanelli 2013). National parties generally offer both ideological alternatives along the left-right divide, as well as a choice for and against the EU (Wüst 2009). In addition, even if citizens follow national rather than European cues when they vote in EP elections, the congruence between national parties and their European counterparts ensures that citizens' positions are still well represented at the EU level (Lefkofridi and Katsanidou 2014). However, one should not forget that the quality of representation cannot be assumed equal for all kinds of voters: those who do not vote, who switch parties between national and European elections or who have low political knowledge are not as well represented as the better educated, middle-class citizens with previous political knowledge (McEvoy 2012; Walczak and van der Brug 2013).

How are elections organised?

Since 1979, the EP has been directly elected. The Treaty of Maastricht stipulated in what is now Article 223.1 TFEU that 'the European Parliament shall draw up a proposal to lay down the provisions necessary for the election of its Members by direct universal suffrage in accordance with a *uniform procedure* in all Member States or in accordance with principles common to all Member States' (emphasis added). However, since a uniform procedure would have to be approved by unanimity in the Council, this objective has remained unfulfilled. In order to fill the gap, the Treaty of Amsterdam introduced in 1997 the possibility to agree on 'common principles', which were then defined by the Council in Decision 2002/772/EC. The latter established that all member states would have to follow the principles of proportional representation (PR) and introduced rules dealing with incompatibility between national and European mandates. The rules were tested for the first time in 2004 and showed that, despite the introduction of 'common principles', national electoral systems were still widely divergent (see below).

EP elections are held every five years, between Thursday and Sunday of the same week, to accommodate different national traditions. However, no polls or provisional results can be published until the last polling station has closed, so as to avoid any potential bias in the final results (in 2014, Italy closed its polling stations on Sunday 25 May at 10 p.m.). The 2014 elections were advanced from June to the end of May, so as to give more time to prepare for the election of the Commission President. Apart from these common features, electoral systems diverge greatly across the EU.

Voting and standing for candidate

In four member states (Belgium, Cyprus, Greece and Luxembourg), both national voters and registered EU citizens are legally obliged to go to the polls. This has clear consequences for the rate of participation in European elections, which tends to be much higher than in other member states (see below) – although there are also differences between these four countries. For instance, in the 2014 elections, the turnout in Greece was just below 60 per cent, while in Cyprus it only reached 44 per cent, which shows that, even if compulsory voting exists on paper, the law is not enforced in practice. In comparison, Luxembourg reached over 85 per cent and Belgium achieved almost a 90 per cent turnout.

According to Article 4 of the Directive on Voting Rights and Eligibility (93/109/EC), European citizens have the right to vote either in their country of residence or from abroad in their home country (not both). Nonetheless, there are a few exceptions, namely the Czech Republic, Ireland, Malta and Slovakia, in which voting from abroad is not possible. In the other member states, different rules apply; in some cases, voters have to register with the electoral authorities in their home countries in order to be able to vote by post or in embassies or consulates. In Estonia, it is possible to vote electronically. In some cases, like Denmark, those who vote in an embassy or consulate might be able to do it some days before the election takes place (European Parliamentary Research Service 2014a).

National law regulates the minimum age for voting and standing as a candidate for the European elections. These regulations differ across member states: whereas the minimum age for voting lies at 18 in all member states (except for Austria, which allows voting at the age of 16), the minimum age required to become a candidate lies generally at 18 or 21. The only exceptions are Romania, where candidates have to be at least 23 years old, and Italy and Greece, where they must be over 25. Furthermore, in a few member states, candidates are also required to be a member of a political party or political organisation in order to be nominated (Lehmann 2014: 17).

Table 6.1 summarises the electoral rules used for the EP elections in the 28 member states. As can be seen, even though national electoral systems have to respect the common provisions set by the Council Decision – proportional representation, direct universal suffrage and the free and secret ballot – the interpretation of these rules varies substantially across national systems. For instance, when it comes to the voting system, some citizens may be able to choose a party, but not their preferred candidate (closed lists), while others may be allowed to express their preferences by moving individual candidates up or down the list or giving them a higher number of votes (open lists). However, only in Luxembourg can voters express their preferences by choosing individual candidates among the different political parties (a system known as 'panachage'). Finally, some member states have chosen the 'single transferable vote' (STV) system, where voters are able to rank individual candidates according to their preferences. There, political parties are less visible, since the election of the candidates depends on the number of

Table 6.1 *Electoral systems in the 28 member states*

	Voting system	Constituency	Calculation method	Threshold	Compulsory voting
Austria	Preferential voting: open list	One district	D'Hondt	4%	No
Belgium	Preferential voting: open list	Three districts	D'Hondt	None	Yes
Bulgaria	Preferential voting: open list	One district	Hare-Niemeyer	5% (valid votes)	No
Croatia	Preferential voting: open list	One district	D'Hondt	5%	No
Cyprus	Preferential voting: open list	One district	D'Hondt/Droop	1.80%	Yes
Czech Republic	Preferential voting: open list	One district	D'Hondt	5%	No
Denmark	Preferential voting: open list	One district	D'Hondt	None	No
Estonia	Closed list	One district	D'Hondt	None	No
Finland	Preferential voting: open list	One district	D'Hondt	None	No
France	Closed list	Eight districts	D'Hondt	5% (per district)	No
Germany	Closed list	One district (regional lists)	Sainte-Laguë	None	No
Greece	Preferential voting: open list	One district	Droop	3%	Yes
Hungary	Closed list	One district	D'Hondt	5%	No
Ireland	STV	Three districts	STV-Droop	None	No
Italy	Preferential voting: open list	Five districts	Hare-Niemeyer	4%	No

Latvia	Preferential voting: open list	One district	Sainte-Laguë	5%	No
Lithuania	Preferential voting: open list	One district	Hare-Niemeyer	5%	No
Luxembourg	Preferential voting: open list and panachage	One district	Hagenbach-Bischoff	None	Yes
Malta	STV	One district	STV-Droop	None	No
Netherlands	Preferential voting: open list	One district (regional lists)	D'Hondt + Hare-Niemeyer	None	No
Poland	Preferential voting: open list	13 districts	D'Hondt/Hare	5%	No
Portugal	Closed list	One district	D'Hondt	None	No
Romania	Closed list	One district	D'Hondt	5% (valid votes)	No
Slovakia	Preferential voting: open list	One district	Droop/Hagenbach-Bischoff	5%	No
Slovenia	Preferential voting: open list	One district	D'Hondt	None	No
Spain	Closed list	One district	D'Hondt	None	No
Sweden	Preferential voting: open list	One district	modified Sainte-Laguë	4%	No
UK (GB)	Closed list	12 districts	D'Hondt	None	No
UK (NI)	STV	One district	STV	None	No

Source: Corbett et al. (2016); European Parliamentary Research Service (2014a); Lehmann (2014).

votes that each one receives individually. Currently, this system is only used in Ireland, Malta and Northern Ireland.

National electoral systems also diverge widely in how they translate votes into seats. Generally, there are two types of formula used to adjudicate seats: 'highest average' systems, like D'Hondt, Sainte-Laguë or modified Sainte-Laguë, are based on a formula that divides by a given quotient the number of votes obtained by a political party (1, 2, 3, 4 for D'Hondt; 1, 3, 5, 7 for Sainte- Laguë). In comparison, 'largest remainder' formulas, such as Hare-Niemeyer and Droop, establish quotas for each seat; they then allocate 'integral' seats and distribute the remaining seats based on the proportion of the quota left to each party (cf. Farrell 2011). It is interesting to see that a majority of member states have adopted the D'Hondt system to translate votes into seats, especially since this formula is considered the least proportional (Farrell and Scully 2005: 971).

District magnitude and electoral thresholds

Generally, EP elections are based on one single electoral district, although in some cases (such as Germany and the Netherlands) parties might propose different lists at the regional level. Six member states have multiple constituencies, namely Belgium, France, Ireland, Italy, Poland and the UK. Although in November 2012, the EP called on member states to introduce electoral thresholds, arguing that this measure ensures the effective functioning of the EP (P7_TA(2012)0462), half of them have no threshold. The rest have thresholds that vary between 1.8 and 5 per cent. In France, the 5 per cent threshold applies to each constituency (that is, its eight regions). Electoral thresholds are more disputed in large member states, where there is more competition for every single seat; in smaller member states, party lists usually require more votes than the formal threshold to obtain a seat – what is known as the 'natural threshold'. In some cases, the threshold level has become a political and legal battle. In Germany, for example, electoral thresholds have been accused of being unconstitutional and have, therefore, been decreased from 5 to 3 per cent in 2013 and eventually abolished by the German Constitutional Court in 2014 (case 2 BvE 2/13 - Rn. [1-116]).

Differences in national electoral systems and their implications

Despite efforts to move towards a uniform electoral system (see Box 6.1), the European electoral system differs widely among member states. Do these differences matter? Most research shows that they do – either

---

Box 6.1   The attempts to introduce wide-ranging electoral reform

The European Electoral Act of 1976 (76/787/EEC) was amended in 2002 (2002/772/EC) mostly to emphasise the use of proportional representation and STV; it also set 5 per cent as a maximum threshold. However, the electoral system remained widely diverse across the EU. For this reason, there have been several attempts to reform the Electoral Act with only limited success (Duff et al. 2015). The Constitutional Affairs committee charged Andrew Duff in 2009 with an own-initiative report on electoral reform, which was not taken up by the plenary (2009/2134/INI). An amended version had equally little success – Duff (2012) considered that most MEPs were 'intimidated by the prospect of making a radical proposal for electoral reform'. Eventually, he was successful in passing another own-initiative report (P7_TA(2013)0323) that introduced some practical improvements for the 2014 elections (European Parliamentary Research Service 2015c).

The matter was taken up by the new Parliament in 2014, whose Constitutional Affairs committee asked Danuta Hübner (EPP) and Jo Leinen (S&D) to draft a new report on electoral reform (2015/2035/INL). The proposal has some interesting innovations that should be considered for the 2019 elections. For instance, it formalises the idea of the 'Spitzenkandidaten' and sets a common deadline of 12 weeks before the elections to nominate them and set the electoral lists. It also proposes to add the symbols of the different European political parties next to the national parties affiliated with them and fosters the possibility of voting from abroad through postal or electronic voting. The report was supported by a majority of 315 votes in favour, 234 against and 55 abstentions. Interestingly, the report was solely supported by the EPP, the S&D and ALDE groups, with those at the extremes mostly voting against it (Votewatch 2015a). However, Parliament's decision is of little importance if the Council does not agree to these measures unanimously, which, at the time of writing, does not look promising (Votewatch 2015a).

---

when it comes to the formal effects that different electoral systems have on the link between citizens and their elected members or more generally on the democratic quality of EP elections.

Geographical representation

One of the main effects expected from different electoral systems concerns the link between MEPs and their constituents. Farrell and Scully defined geographical representation as '... [the] representation of individual voters on the ground ..., as opposed to thematic or functional representation (which tends, on the whole, to privilege organized interests)' (Farrell and Scully 2010: 38). Their analysis showed that MEPs from 'open' electoral systems – that is, candidate-based, especially STV systems – tend to focus more on constituency issues than those from 'closed' (list-based) systems. This finding resonates with past studies, which already indicated that domestic electoral systems had an impact on the different roles adopted by MEPs (Bowler and Farrell 1993; Farrell and Scully 2005). Hix (2004) also showed that national parties are better able to 'control' their MEPs if they are elected in countries with closed lists decided by central organs and organised in small districts, while those from countries with open PR systems, formed by large districts or with decentralised selection processes, are usually in a better position to vote against their national party and vote according to their constituency or the EP political group's wishes.

Selection of candidates and electoral campaigns

The link can also work in the other direction; depending on how MEPs are selected at the national level and especially how campaigns are fought, European citizens may develop different levels of interest for and attitudes towards EP elections.

A recent comparative study has shown that the selection of candidates varies according to three dimensions (Pilet et al. 2015): first, national parties diverge in level of inclusiveness during the selection processes, which may range from the whole electorate being involved in proposing and/or approving candidates to only allowing the party leadership to decide – most national parties tend to be more exclusive than in national elections. Second, selection procedures tend to be classified along a centralised-decentralised axis depending on whether local branches of each political party can decide on their own candidates. The comparison shows that most candidates are selected by national organs without any formal inclusion of European party federations in the process (see also Chapter 9). Finally, the third dimension concerns selection criteria for individual members, with the rules generally being similar to national elections, and selection depending on personal characteristics – such as age, party membership or expertise – and party criteria, such as gender balance or other types of quota. To give just some examples: Gherghina and Chiru (2010) found that in Romania (which has a closed PR system) wealthier candidates with longer political experience were placed higher on the lists. In Finland, Arter (2015) noted how the preferential-voting system created incentives for candidates to pursue a more active campaign and enhanced intra-party competition. As a result, one could see more national parliamentarians deciding to stand for the EP elections – a step generally welcomed by parties given their expertise and ability to mobilise voters.

The proportion of women elected to the EP (37 per cent in 2014) is consistently higher than in most national parliaments, where the average is 27 per cent (Lühiste and Kenny 2016: 2). Many have explained this trend by noting that PR systems with large district magnitude are expected to assist the election of female candidates. However, recent research has showed that this theory does not hold for the EP (Fortin-Rittberger and Rittberger 2014); neither does the existence of quotas. What does seem to matter is whether the pool of candidates proposed during the early stages of the selection procedure contains a large number of female nominations (Fortin-Rittberger and Rittberger 2015). Generally, the career paths of both men and women are strikingly similar, although there is still a traditional left-right cleavage in old member states, with more women being elected from left-wing parties, and a new pro-/anti-EU cleavage in new member states, with those supporting EU norms more willing to include female candidates (Chiva 2014; Lühiste and Kenny 2016).

What about those MEPs who want to continue in the EP? Do they have higher or lower chances of being re-selected as candidates and then re-elected? This is certainly an interesting question, since the EP has been characterised by high levels of turnover, with only half of the MEPs staying over for the next legislature (51 per cent of MEPs in 2014 were newly elected). When it comes to the selection of incumbents, Pemstein et al. (2015) show that national parties that emphasise the EU in their electoral programme tend to favour incumbents over other candidates, since they consider that incumbents will be better at influencing EP policy-making. This is especially noticeable for parties that are part of the EPP, the S&D and ALDE groups and those that have only minimal representation at the national level (see also Daniel 2016). This, however, does not explain the chances for individual MEPs to be re-elected. In domestic electoral systems, seniority and party loyalties are extremely important to ensure re-appointment and re-selection. However, this is generally not the case for EP candidates. In a parliament where policies are shaped by policy experts rather than political parties (see Chapter 10), building a good reputation, attending regularly, acting as rapporteur and participating in intergroups is more relevant for national parties and voters than any of the usual factors at the domestic level (Frech 2016; Sigalas 2011; van Thomme et al. 2015).

Once on the field, the type of electoral system does play a role in the way MEPs run their campaigns. Although candidates might exert the same effort to become elected, the way they do so differs depending on their country's electoral system. Those running in member states with open PR systems and/or with low district magnitude tend to pursue more personal goals and emphasise contact with voters, employing both classic techniques such as door-to-door canvassing, but also more modern ones, like blogging. In comparison, those in countries with closed lists and/or high district magnitude tend to put more emphasis on getting votes for their party rather than for themselves, which means that they prioritise their participation in collective events, such as public meetings and media events (Bowler and Farrell 2011).

However, there are other differences among member states that are not directly linked to their electoral system. Generally, campaigns tend to focus on national topics and political figures, while political parties spend fewer resources on European than on general elections (de Vreese et al. 2006; Maier et al. 2011; van der Eijk and Franklin 1996). This is significant, since a less politicised domestic debate might affect the extent to which citizens vote on national considerations rather than EU ones; this assumes that, if voters are provided with more information about the EU, they are more likely to vote on European considerations (Hobolt and Spoon 2012; Hobolt and Wittrock 2011). Therefore, the amount of information and the ability to process it seem to be important elements in EP campaigns. For instance, one can see how more politically sophisticated citizens have disproportionate influence on their surroundings and that citizens from decentralised (federal) political systems are better able to grasp the complexity of a multilevel system and actively engage with it (Clark 2015; de Vries et al. 2011). That ultimately affects the quality of electoral campaigns as well as the types of debate that dominate at the national level, which is particularly important given the rise of Euroscepticism (see Box 6.2).

Electoral turnout

The most distinctive issue in EP elections is the low turnouts, which have been a matter of discussion for the last couple of decades. It is indeed interesting to observe that, even if the EP has gradually gained more power, this does not translate into more interest on the part of voters (Rozenberg 2009). As can be seen in Table 6.2, turnout has gone from almost 62 per cent in 1979 down to 42.61 per cent in 2014. Why is that the case? There are two predominant answers – one that focuses on institutional factors and another that looks into socioeconomic explanations, such as the affection people feel for the EU.

The first set of explanations looks at institutional factors that affect not only EP elections, but also other types of election: turnout is higher in countries where voting is compulsory, in countries with multiple constituencies, among people that have adopted a habit of voting and if the election takes place on a Sunday rather than a Thursday. On the other

Box 6.2   How voters and parties adapt to Euroscepticism in EP elections

Not all publicity is good publicity: although European issues are often more visible in the new member states, it is often due to a wider range of pro-/anti-EU attitudes offered by national parties and a negative framing of the EU in the media (de Vreese et al. 2006; Wüst 2009). Therefore, the effects of campaigns on citizens' attitudes depend largely on how they are framed – if positive, they are likely to encourage supportive views on the EU; if negative, they may foster higher levels of Euroscepticism (Maier et al. 2011). Whether these 'European effects' have an impact on electoral results is still an open question; some consider that political parties need to adopt a clear (positive or negative) position on Europe if they want to do well in EP elections (Ferrara and Weishaupt 2004), while others consider that positions on European integration matters do not have a substantive impact on electoral results (Hix and Marsh 2007).

What is clear is that the 2014 elections have seen a steep rise in the number of Eurosceptic parties being elected to the Parliament. This seems to be the result not merely of protest votes against incumbent governments, but also of a wider shift of the electorate, which shows more critical stances towards the effects of EU policies and what they perceive as the EU's 'democratic deficit' (van Spanje and de Vreese 2011; Treib 2014). Political parties have reacted very differently to this change in attitudes. On the one hand, Mattila and Raunio (2012) observe that large parties have gradually converged and now share a clearly pro-EU stance; as a result many voters do not feel well represented by mainstream parties and have turned to smaller and more extreme parties that openly criticise the EU. On the other hand, more recent research shows that, in countries where public opinion has become more Eurosceptic, larger parties have reacted swiftly and adopted manifestos with more anti-EU stances (Williams and Spoon 2015). Therefore, Eurosceptic parties have revitalised politics in what was seen as a largely depoliticised arena. Although they do not always conform to the traditional left-right dimension, they have managed to open up new spaces of contestation and mobilise disaffected citizens. In this sense, Eurosceptic parties have used their opposition towards the EU to restructure domestic party competition and forced the other parties to move away from their focus on EU policies towards a focus on the nature of the EU as a polity. At the same time, in a more politicised electoral context, pro-EU parties can also be more assertive in their support towards the EU (Adam et al. 2013; Braun et al. 2016; Hernández and Kriesi 2016).

Table 6.2 *Electoral turnout in EP elections 1979–2014 (in percentages)*

	1979	1984	1989	1994	1999	2004	2009	2014	Difference between 2009/2013 and 2014	Last national election	Difference between last national election and 2014 EP election
Overall result	61.99 (EU9)	58.98 (EU10)	58.41 (EU12)	56.67 (EU12)	49.51 (EU15)	45.47 (EU25)	42.97 (EU27)	42.61 (EU28)			
Austria				67.73 (1996)	49.4	42.43	45.97	45.39	−0.58	74.9 (2013)	−29.51
Belgium	91.36	92.09	90.73	90.66	91.05	90.81	90.39	89.64	−0.75	89.68 (2014)	−0.04
Bulgaria						29.22 (2007)	38.99	35.84	−3.15	39.20 (2014)	−3.36
Czech Republic						28.32	28.22	18.2	−10.20	59.48 (2013)	−41.28
Croatia							20.84 (2013)	25.24	4.40	60.82 (2015)	−35.58
Cyprus						72.5	59.4	43.97	−15.43	78.7 (2011)	34.73
Denmark	47.82	52.38	46.17	52.92	50.46	47.89	59.54	56.32	−3.22	87.70 (2011)	−31.38

Estonia						26.83	43.9	36.52	−7.38	63.50 (2011)	−26.98
Finland	60.71	56.72		57.6 (1996)	30.14	39.43	38.6	39.1	−0.50	70.50 (2011)	−31.40
France			48.8	52.71	46.76	42.76	40.63	42.43	1.80	55.40 (2nd round) (2012)	−12.97
Germany	65.73	56.76	62.28	60.02	45.19	43.00	43.27	48.1	4.83	71.50 (2013)	−23.40
Greece	81.48 (1981)	80.59	80.03	73.18	70.25	63.22	52.61	59.97	7.36	56.6 (2015)	−2.53
Hungary						38.5	36.31	28.97	−7.34	61.24 (2014)	−32.27
Ireland	63.61	47.56	68.28	43.98	50.21	58.58	58.64	52.44	−6.20	69.19 (2011)	−16.75
Italy	85.65	82.47	81.07	73.6	69.76	71.72	65.05	57.22	−7.83	75.19 (2013)	−17.97
Latvia						41.34	53.7	30.24	−23.46	58.85 (2014)	−28.61
Lithuania						48.38	20.98	47.35	26.37	35.91 (2nd round) (2012)	−11.44

↑

Luxembourg	88.91	88.79	87.39	88.55	87.27	91.35	90.76	85.55	-5.21	91.40 (2013)	-5.85
Malta						82.39	78.79	74.8	-3.99	92.90 (2013)	-18.10
Netherlands	58.12	50.88	47.48	35.69	30.02	39.26	36.75	37.32	0.57	74.57 (2012)	-43.25
Poland						20.87	24.53	23.83	-0.70	48.92 (2011)	-25.09
Portugal		72.42 (1987)	51.1	35.54	39.93	38.6	36.77	33.67	-3.10	58.07 (2011)	-24.40
Romania						29.47 (2007)	27.67	32.44	4.77	41.76 (2012)	-9.32
Slovakia						16.97	19.64	13.05	-6.59	59.11 (2012)	-46.06
Slovenia						28.35	28.37	24.55	-3.82	51.73 (2014)	-27.18
Spain		68.52 (1987)	54.71	59.14	63.05	45.14	44.87	43.81	-1.06	71.69 (2011)	-27.88
Sweden				41.63 (1995)	38.84	37.85	45.53	51.07	5.54	85.81 (2014)	-34.74
United Kingdom	32.35	32.57	36.37	36.43	24.00	38.52	34.7	35.6	0.90	66.1 (2015)	-30.50

Source: European Parliamentary Research Service (2015a, 2015b).

127

hand, the general decline in cleavage politics – which enhances the loyalty of voters towards a party – can explain to a large extent the general decrease in turnout across Europe. In the case of EP elections, the electoral cycle can also be an important aspect – turnout tends to be higher when EP elections are close to a national general election or taking place on the same day (Mattila 2003; van der Eijk et al. 1996; Wessels and Franklin 2009).

If we look at how these factors have evolved over time, we might be able to better understand why turnout has steadily decreased. One factor, as Franklin (2001) noted, is that the proportion of countries with compulsory voting has declined; another factor is that the 'first-election-after-enlargement effect' that boosted turnout in earlier elections has faded. In the last elections, turnout seemed to be determined by whether someone had acquired the habit of voting. For those who are not used to voting, especially among young people, EP elections can actually inculcate habits of non-voting (Franklin and Hobolt 2011). These factors can help us understand why Eastern European countries have lower levels of turnout. There, the transition to democracy has made it more difficult for citizens, especially younger ones, to develop loyalties towards particular parties and acquire a habit of voting (Franklin 2014; Kostadinova 2003).

However, institutional factors are not the only possible explanation for the low and steadily decreasing turnout. There might also be socioeconomic aspects that contribute to the variation among member states and explain changes over time. It is often argued that people do not vote in EP elections either because they do not care for or do not trust the EU; indeed, it seems that in those member states where there is generally more support for the EU (for instance, those that receive economic subsidies), turnout tends to be higher (Blondel et al. 1997; Clark 2014; Mattila 2003; Stockemer 2012). In addition, while EU-level issues affect attitudes in older member states, national-level concerns are more important in Eastern European countries, where lack of trust in their own government or high unemployment contributes to lower turnout (Fauvelle-Aymar and Stegmaier 2008; Flickinger and Studlar 2007).

Vote switching

Therefore, we see that the explanations for the low levels of turnout can support both the 'second-order' and the 'Europe salience' theses. One can understand the reluctance of voters to go to the polls as either a lack of interest or a form of protest against the EU. However, does this actually matter for the outcome of the elections? It actually does: low turnout is good for right-wing parties, while higher turnout tends to benefit left-wing groups (Pacek and Radcliff 2003; van der Eijk and Egmond 2007). In addition, EP elections show a much higher volatility in voters' behaviour than other national elections. This means that, when voting for the EP, citizens are more ready to switch their vote and support a different party than the one they supported in the last general election.

We can use the SOE and ES theses to derive some potential explanations for this type of behaviour: The SOE would assume that EP elections are seen as less important than national ones due to a focus on national rather than European issues. They are, therefore, an occasion for citizens to cast a punishment vote ('vote with the boot') against incumbent governments. In comparison, the ES thesis would consider that vote switching is the result of 'voting with their heart': Europe matters – whether in a positive or a negative way. In that case, people may be more ready to follow their heart and vote for smaller and more extremist parties. In some cases, the decision to switch is related to the electoral system: in countries that do not employ PR systems for general elections, citizens may have the feeling that in EP elections they have the freedom to vote for their preferred party without 'wasting their vote'. However, in other cases the heart might lead them to express their doubts about the EU and give their support to Eurosceptic parties (cf. Hix and Marsh 2007; Kousser 2004).

The studies that have been undertaken over time seem to confirm the SOE hypothesis: people switch their vote mostly as a form of punishment, especially when EP elections fall mid-term in the national electoral cycle and governments are unable to mobilise their voters effectively and produce distinct proposals. The chances for governments to lose votes to other parties (and particularly opposition parties) increase when the economy is doing badly. This effect is amplified in single-party governments; in the case of coalition governments, citizens find it more difficult to attribute blame and, therefore, parties that are part of a governing coalition tend to suffer less in comparison (Bartkowska and Tiemann 2015; Hix and Marsh 2011; Kousser 2004; Marsh 2009; Schmitt and Toygür 2016; Tilley et al. 2008; Weber 2007). Carrubba and Timpone (2005), however, remark quite rightly that a 'vote with the boot' might indicate that people do actually care about who gets to be in the EP. Therefore, voters do not think that casting a protest vote against parties that are perceived to have performed badly will have no effects. Indeed, this could explain why Eastern Europeans do not use protest votes: in their case, EP elections are seen as 'throw-away' elections and, therefore, people prefer to vote sincerely for the party they prefer rather than attempt to convey a message to the incumbent government (Koepke and Ringe 2006).

The SOE thesis seems to hold less explanatory value when it comes to accounting for vote switching to niche parties, particularly Eurosceptic parties, because citizens who switch from a large to a niche party are driven by protest voting *and* anti-EU attitudes (Boomgaarden et al. 2016; Hong 2015). As seen above, when campaigns focus on European issues – especially if they do so in a negative light – voters tend to feel more disconnected from larger governing parties, which tend to be more in favour of the EU than most citizens (Hobolt et al. 2009). This has led some parties to anticipate demands for more critical positions on the EU, prompting them to shift their positions in order to win more votes in EP elections (Tillman 2004).

Still second-order elections?

The SOE thesis has dominated the debate on EP elections for decades. Despite some challenges from the ES school, which has tried to situate the European dimension at the centre of explanations, it is still generally agreed that EP elections continue to fit the expectations of the SOE thesis better (Schmitt and Toygür 2016; Viola 2015). However, the distinction between first and second order is becoming less clear-cut and does not remain constant across time and space; it is particularly unsuitable to explain the results of EP elections in Eastern European countries (Schmitt 2005; Viola 2015; Weber 2009). We do see, however, that the low levels of turnout and the presence of high levels of vote switching from large to small and niche parties are caused by a complex set of factors that range from the effects of institutional rules and divergent electoral systems to a general lack of interest in European matters that is increasingly turning into mistrust and dissatisfaction.

Does it matter whether EP elections are second-order elections? In many ways, it does, since EP elections have been mostly seen as a source of democratic representativeness for the EU's institutional structure. If elections do not matter to citizens and they are fought on national issues, it raises questions about the representativeness of the EP and whether it can legitimately claim to be the only EU institution that speaks for EU citizens (cf. Blondel et al. 1998; Kaniovski and Mueller 2011; Marsh and Norris 1997; Mattila and Raunio 2012). Others, however, remain more cautious on casting the second-order nature of EP elections in a negative light. Certainly, larger parties have converged on the European dimension, exacerbating the feeling of alienation in parts of the electorate. At the same time, EP elections have offered an opportunity to vote sincerely for parties that might not have a chance to govern. This has often put new energy in national party systems, serving as a launching board for smaller parties that present a wider ideological range and ensure a more critical contest during both EP elections and national polls (Prosser 2016; Schmitt and Teperoglou 2015).

Conclusion

The 2014 EP elections were in many respects different from past ones, especially as the presence of 'Spitzenkandidaten' attempted to change the nature and organisation of the campaign in order to raise its European dimension and improve the link between the citizens and those elected to the EP. It seems to have had only a modest success: while it raised awareness of the impact elections have on the choice of the Commission, campaigns remained anchored at the national level and many voters remained unaware of the Spitzenkandidaten and their role (Hobolt 2014, 2015; Schmitt et al. 2015). At the same time, the increase in Eurosceptic parties elected to the EP has had a smaller impact than expected as the centrist groups have continued to dominate policy-making both inside the EP and in the Commission, not leaving much room for manoeuvre for extreme and Eurosceptic parties (Kroh 2014).

As we have seen, the 2014 elections opened new debates on the necessity to move towards a uniform electoral system for EP elections. The changes proposed by the Constitutional Affairs committee attempt to improve some of the current shortcomings – such as the difficulties that some citizens face when voting from abroad. However, they might not be enough to address some of the essential problems highlighted by the 'second-order' and 'Europe salience' theses. To address issues of turnout and dissatisfaction, the EU might need to develop a single electorate with common European lists and more involvement of European party federations. At the same time, changes to the electoral rules, such as smaller districts and open lists, might also improve the link between citizens and the EP and the quality of representation (Hix and Hagemann 2009; van der Brug et al. 2008).

Chapter 7

Lobbying, Interest Representation and the Media

Introduction: representing which and whose interests?

In the previous chapter, we saw how citizens express their demands through their votes in EP elections. However, demands can also come from other channels, notably interest groups and the media. The Treaty understands the EU as a pluralist political system; for instance, Article 11 TEU considers:

> The institutions shall, by appropriate means, give citizens and representative associations the opportunity to make known and publicly exchange their views in all areas of Union action; the institutions shall maintain an open, transparent and regular dialogue with representative associations and civil society.

Indeed, anyone who has spent some time in Brussels will have noticed the high amount of offices dedicated to representing a myriad of interests – from corporate business, to religious faiths, civil society as well as regions and international organisations. Despite the high density in interest representation, we still do not know much about how lobbyists and other representatives interact with the EP. As Dionigi (2017) has remarked, this is surprising, since now that the EP is a co-legislator in almost all policy fields, interest groups should recognise an additional channel to exert influence on the decision-making process – one that is more open and accessible than the Council and even the Commission.

Indeed, the number of interest representatives present in the EP has increased steeply in recent years. For instance, while in 2012 the EP gave around 2,000 personal accreditations to people representing organised interests, in 2016 the number had gone over the 6,000 mark (LobbyFacts 2016). The presence of a higher number of lobbyists raises the question of transparency and oversight. After various scandals and the increasing pressure from external organisations, the EP has sought to regulate access to MEPs and render the process more open to scrutiny. Despite these efforts, to what extent do lobbies and interest groups exert influence over the policy process? The lengthy decision-making process offers various opportunities to input demands and shape outputs; not only at the agenda-setting stage, but also later when amendments are drafted and negotiated inter-institutionally. Therefore, this chapter looks at alternative input channels and focuses on lobbying and interest representation, examining the different types of group that seek access to the EP. Is there any relationship between the type of group and a given policy area? Or is it rather linked to the political orientation of MEPs?

While lobbying has become an intrinsic part of Brussels life, the role of the media is still far from reaching a Europeanised status. Media have retained their national lenses and the reporting is still framed by and for domestic audiences. And yet, traditional and new communication channels are essential to transmitting demands and publicising outputs. We see, indeed, that they have developed a symbiotic relationship with MEPs: in order to fulfil their representative function, parliamentarians need the media to be aware of citizens' concerns and to disseminate their own activities and opinions; at the same time, the media play an active role in framing demands and political issues – which requires close contacts with insiders in order to know what is actually going on at the Parliament. Therefore, the last section of this chapter examines the growing importance of these different communication channels and examines the claims of transparency and accountability put across by the EP.

Whom are interest groups representing?

At the time of writing, there were over 10,000 groups inscribed in the Transparency Register shared by the Commission and the EP – a similar number to those working in Washington DC. Of course, it is difficult to know with certainty how many people actually act as representatives of interest groups in Brussels (or Strasbourg), but Transparency International (2016) has estimated this number to be over 37,000 – out of which, some 26,500 would have a regular presence in Brussels. However, the number of people from registered organisations with an accreditation to access the EP is just below 6,500. Therefore, the question is: who are these groups, what do they represent and do they exert any sort of influence over policy outputs? These questions have occupied researchers for some decades, but only a small number of them have concentrated on the EP. This section, therefore, draws on a wider literature on lobbying and interest representation to examine the types of group and their ability to influence the EU institutions (cf. Greenwood 2011). The question of influence has raised long-lasting debates on how to evaluate the success of these groups and how to measure and observe their impact on policy outputs. Therefore, this chapter uses these various contributions to assess the extent to which interest groups can use – and are used by – the EP to channel demands and translate them into policy outputs.

Types of interest group

The first question is, of course, who are these 10,000 groups trying to convince EU institutions to incorporate their interests during the policy-making process. There are multiple ways of defining and categorising interest groups. Binderkrantz et al. (2017: 312) define them as 'membership organisations seeking political influence without running for elections'. In general, we can differentiate between business or professional groups, on the one hand, and diffuse interest groups, on the other. The former regroup a variety of actors and interests, such as (business) companies with representatives in Brussels or professional associations (for instance, medical associations or chambers of commerce). The second group is much more diverse and can comprise citizen, territorial or labour interests – for instance, trade unions, regional governments or churches – as well as civil society organisations – namely, non-governmental organisations (NGOs). In addition, two other categories of representatives are also present in Brussels, but are more difficult to classify. First, think tanks and research institutions are also part of the Transparency Register, but do not act as representatives of specific interests – they use this channel to access the institutions and their members more easily and to maintain a fluid dialogue with policy-makers. Second, professional consultants and law firms do not represent just one interest but can be engaged by any group to represent them and help them hone their lobbying strategies. They are some of the biggest players in Brussels: 70 professional consultancy firms hold over 600 EP passes. The three biggest firms – Fleishman-Hillard, Burson-Marsteller and Interel European Affairs – have between 20 and 45 passes to access the EP and spend between €4.75 and €6.5 million per year on lobbying activities. In comparison, over 200 registered NGOs share almost 900 passes; among them, the biggest organisation – the Bureau Européen des Unions de Consommateurs (BEUC, the European Consumer Organisation) – has 28 passes and spends over €1.75 million per year, while the European unit of Greenpeace has 10 passes and spends just under €1 million (LobbyFacts 2016).

Table 7.1 shows that the distribution of interest groups is overall biased towards business and corporatist interests. The preponderance of business interests has been a constant feature of EU lobbying since the 1990s, when the relaunch of the Single Market and the shift in

Table 7.1   *Number and type of registered organisations (February 2017)*

Type of organisation	Number	Percentage	EP passes	Percentage
Professional consultancies/law firms/self-employed consultants	1,310	11.7	1,044	16.2
In-house lobbyists and trade/business/ professional associations	5,602	49.9	3,290	51.0
Non-governmental organisations	2,894	25.8	1,659	25.7
Think tanks, research and academic institutions	828	7.4	276	4.3
Organisations representing churches and religious communities	49	0.4	54	0.8
Organisations representing local, regional and municipal authorities, other public or mixed entities, etc.	543	4.8	129	2.0
Total	11,226	100	6,452	100

Source: European Commission (2016); LobbyFacts (2016).

competences introduced by the Treaty of Maastricht led interest groups to take the EU level more seriously (Coen 2007). At the same time, the economic logic that characterises the core principles of the EU – namely, the four freedoms that make up the Single Market – privileges the presence of business groups and encourages the use of their practical expertise. However, as we will explore below, this bias does not automatically translate into more influence: diffuse interests might possess other types of resource that make them more attractive for the EU institutions (Dür et al. 2015).

What Table 7.1 does not show is the number of 'institutional' lobbyists present in Brussels and Strasbourg. It is not only big corporations or

NGOs that lobby the EP, but also other EU institutional actors, member states' governments, other international organisations as well as non-EU governments. It is well known that MEPs receive policy briefs from their own governments, which can make a difference when it comes to deciding whether their loyalty should go to their political grouping or their national government (see also Chapter 9). Their activities have become more coordinated and many permanent representations have attachés in charge of following up on the work of the EP (Judge and Earnshaw 2008: 107–108). This, of course, is particularly important in the framework of co-decision, where negotiations have become increasingly informal and shifted to very early stages of the policy-making process (see also Chapter 11).

Why does the EP listen to interest groups?

Briefings, draft amendments and tailored information are the main currency of those who want to lobby the EP – although some go to greater lengths and propose to write the entire report for the rapporteur (Clark and Priestley 2012: 247). In some cases, the amount of information provided might become overwhelming. For instance, the reform of the Data Protection Directive (now the General Data Protection Regulation, 2016/679/EU) became notorious for the unprecedented amount of lobbying, which ended up with 3,999 amendments submitted to the LIBE draft report. Lobbying came from every possible side – from the US government, to tech firms such as Google and Facebook to NGOs specialised in data protection and privacy (Euractiv 2012, 2016c).

There are generally two different types of lobbying technique: formal (short-term) contacts and informal (long-term) contacts. The former may include a wide range of services, like writing position papers, parliamentary questions or offering input for own-initiative reports. Many lobby groups, however, concentrate on writing amendments for MEPs, which is why one sees identical amendments tabled by different political groups. In order to be successful, amendments have to follow the format of the EP template and speak the language of MEPs. These formal strategies are, however, rarely successful if they are not backed up by long-term strategies that can foster trust between lobbyists and EP actors. That is why lobbying groups often seek frequent contacts, share information on other (institutional) actors and participate in intergroups (Dionigi 2017). This last aspect has become all the more important with the growth of digital instruments, which are substituting some of the main income-earners of many consultancy firms. Tracking apps based on the use of algorithms allow for tracing and gathering information more efficiently than the traditional way of digging information by going to places and asking for documents. However, what these 'digital disruptors' cannot do is provide the kind of personal insights and long-term contacts on which success often depends (Politico 2017d).

Why has the EP become such an attractive forum for lobbyists? The main reason is that MEPs need interest groups and often welcome their inputs. As we have seen in previous chapters, EU legislation is highly technical and MEPs generally lack the necessary expertise to evaluate the policy solutions proposed by the Commission – not just in technical terms, but also for their potential impact on their constituencies – and make relevant changes in the form of amendments. One should remember that the EP's total staff levels are 3.5 times smaller than those of the Commission (Dionigi 2017: 14). Therefore, interest groups act as a transmission belt and help to translate complex information into data that are accessible and can be directly used by MEPs. They can also help them monitor the progress made in the Commission or the Council and provide information on their positions or those of other EP committees. Their input is undeniably attractive in an environment where time is scarce and personal staff limited (Judge and Earnshaw 2008: 103–104; Kohler-Koch 1997: 6).

The relationship between lobbyists and EP actors is symbiotic – lobbyists need to get access to the policy process and MEPs need technical information as well as a connection with wider societal interests that can help legitimise their positions (Bouwen 2004a). In this sense, the EP presents both an opportunity and a challenge for lobbyists. On the one hand, MEPs tend to be 'exceptionally accessible to interest groups'(Dür 2008: 1216) and those lobbyists who can demonstrate high expertise, good reputation and information tailored to the needs of the EP will have better chances of accessing the institution and demonstrating their value (Coen 2007: 334). As a result, lobbying the EP might be a good opportunity to get concerns addressed in a later stage of policy-making. Even groups that have successfully lobbied the Commission try to convince the EP as well, so that the changes they have introduced in the proposal stay there and are not diluted or even removed during negotiations. Those who are unsuccessful in lobbying the Commission see the EP as a last resort to seek influence (Dionigi 2017: 2). Nonetheless, interest groups need to be aware of the limitations that the function as citizens' representatives can put on MEPs, who are unlikely to endorse the demands of an interest group if they fear it might backfire and damage their chances of being re-elected (Dür 2008: 1216). Therefore, the success of interest groups depends to a great extent on their ability to supply essential goods, such as citizen support, policy-relevant information and the backing of economically powerful actors. This means that MEPs will be particularly open to those groups that represent a large number of voters or that voice major economic interests (Klüver 2013).

Analysing the influence of interest groups over the policy process

When lobbying the EP, interest group representatives often go by the following mantra:

> Lobby at the earliest available point in the legislative process (framing the debate); lobby those with the most influence over the policy outcome; and lobby legislators who are likely to be sympathetic to your position (friends/allies), as opposed to the possibly counterproductive action of lobbying legislative foes (Marshall 2010: 560).

This 'operating logic' shows that being there or spending money on lobbying does not automatically translate into influence. Lobbying success depends on a variety of factors, such as the degree of counter-lobbying, the importance attached to an issue or the receptiveness of key actors like rapporteurs or shadow rapporteurs (Dionigi 2017). To understand why some groups are more effective than others, this section examines the most important factors attached to interest groups' influence.

Resources

As we have seen, some of the most prized resources that interest groups can offer EP actors are legitimacy, expertise, information on other institutional actors and political support. To provide these goods, interest groups need material resources – most notably money and a certain size – but also more diffuse ones. For instance, they may benefit from a solid internal organisation that allows them to use their internal membership effectively or a geographic concentration of members which makes communication easier (Dür 2008). To put it simply, if a business interest acts in a united way, it will make it easier for this group to start lobbying early and address EP actors with one single message. That, in turn, will make it more likely that they are successful in putting issues on the agenda and convincing MEPs that their way of seeing things and the solutions they propose are the right ones (Rasmussen 2015: 376). Carroll and Rasmussen (2017) have also noted that other diffuse resources, such as cultural aspects in their country of origin, might explain different levels of interest group density in Brussels. Therefore, the absence of civil society engagement in some countries, especially in Central and Eastern Europe, may explain why they have a smaller presence in Brussels than groups from older member states.

If having more of these different resources is important to be successful, it is then logical that sharing them with other groups can prove a beneficial strategy, especially for those with limited budgets or no permanent base in Brussels. To this effect, lobbying groups often enter into partnerships to maximise their resources. Such coalitions might be issue-specific and not last once a solution has been found – often due to their inability to reconcile their views beyond the lowest common denominator (Dionigi 2017: 109), but some might survive and become semi-permanent umbrella associations. For instance, the ten biggest European environmental NGOs have formed a platform – the Green 10 – that includes Greenpeace, the World Wide Fund for Nature (WWF) and Friends of the Earth; they try to coordinate their responses and recommendations to policy-makers and claim to represent 20 million people (http://www.green10.org/). Lobbying in coalitions might help divide labour – with European umbrella associations focusing on lobbying key MEPs and relais actors, while national members concentrate on lobbying their national MEPs – and it can also provide more legitimacy to the groups' positions and convince MEPs that they represent a wide section of society or economic interests (Coen 2007: 339; Dionigi 2017: 142; Klüver 2013).

Policy cycle and salience

However, while possessing resources is important, it is not enough to ensure success. Influence often comes from choosing the right time to put an idea on the table – to the point where 'timing is considered to be most essential for successful performance' (Kohler-Koch 1997: 9). One of the problems that most interest groups had when accessing the EP in the early days of co-decision was that they were often too late. Once the draft report is ready and open to debate in committee, the time has passed and there is a reduced chance of shaping the proposal. Therefore, interest groups have had to learn the hard way and they start now contacting MEPs from the earliest possible stages – for instance, while amendments are being tabled to the Commission proposal in committee.

Marshall (2010) has shown that interest groups start lobbying while rapporteurs are drafting the report, since it is then when they have more control over the content and it proves easier to influence the parliamentary agenda. Even if rapporteurs are unsympathetic to the positions of an interest group, its contributions might still be welcome if they are needed to find an intra-institutional compromise and make other political groups happy and ready to agree to the amendments proposed by the rapporteur. When the report is open to all committee members, interest groups generally adapt their strategies to the level of involvement of different MEPs. Key members (for instance shadow rapporteurs) are likely to have more expertise; that means they seek more targeted information and are also better at discerning the quality of the information on offer. Committee members that do not participate actively in negotiations can prove a better channel to introduce more friendly amendments. In the last stage, when political groups are busy trying to find a compromise, interest groups tend to focus their efforts on friendly committee members who have a say in negotiations. In the case of business interests, their success also depends on how salient an issue becomes. If member states start lobbying MEPs and the media shows interest in a file under negotiation, it is a sign that it has become contested and that lobbyists representing businesses will have a harder time trying to access EP committees (Dür et al. 2015: 958–959; Rasmussen 2015: 377).

Access

Access can be defined 'as the frequency of contacts between interest organizations and EU institutions' (Eising 2007: 386), which includes a range of activities: from informal contacts over the phone or via email to formally institutionalised meetings. Access, therefore, is highly dependent on the resources mentioned above but also on the opportunities offered by the EU institutions to establish contacts with different actors. In the case of the EP, access is sought mostly by EU associations and large business groups, rather than national associations, and once they manage to get in, it is relatively easy to obtain information from MEPs and other staff members (Eising 2007). This is not surprising, since interest groups based in Brussels have more opportunities to get in contact with EP actors and build up their reputation (Coen 2007: 335). This strategy is particularly important for diffuse interests, which might find it more difficult to find an audience in the Commission and especially the Council. In their case, the EP is easier to access and allows diffuse interests to spread their contacts and try to set their ideas on the policy-making agenda (Beyers 2004).

However, getting into the EP might not always be synonymous with influence or success. Gaining access might not be enough if one does not know the key players and cannot get across the main gatekeepers. For instance, sending a draft amendment to all MEPs might not be as successful as getting to talk to one political advisor or the assistant of the rapporteur (see also Chapter 8). Similarly, discussing a proposal by the Commission with key actors might not be enough if they are not willing to listen to the lobbyist or change their opinion on that issue. Access might not even be the best route to success: First, it is perfectly possible that some groups are powerful enough not to need access to exert influence. They might opt for other strategies like influencing the media and framing the political arena. Second, those who face difficulties in entering the policy-making institutions might opt to voice their concerns from the outside. This is particularly the case with diffuse interests, which might find it easier to organise protests or coordinate media appearances

(Beyers 2004; Binderkrantz et al. 2017). Many probably remember the various campaigns involving blockades and protests organised by European farmer associations. In the first half of 2016, an organised action targeted dropping milk prices and saw farmers spraying milk outside official buildings in Brussels (Reuters 2016).

The most important lobby targets

With limited resources and a myriad of potential targets, whose contact should interest groups prioritise? The most obvious answer is: legislative committees. As we have seen in previous chapters, committees are a particularly good target for lobbyists: they have almost full control of the EP report, negotiate in relative isolation and are highly specialised (see also Box 7.1). Therefore, although it might prove difficult to access them, once the gatekeepers have been negotiated, there are high chances of success. On the contrary, those who wait until the plenary vote might face disappointment, since the thresholds for introducing amendments there are much higher than in committees and it is, therefore, a relatively rare occurrence (Bouwen 2004b; see also Chapter 10). Committees, on the other hand, offer multiple access points that range from the most obvious (rapporteur, shadow rapporteurs and committee chairs) to those, such as assistants and committee officials, who exert influence and frame the agenda behind the scenes (see also Chapter 8).

Lobbyists have an ideal audience in legislative committees, since interest representatives are often the most immediate source of information. Therefore, lobby groups can try to diversify their strategies by contacting rapporteurs – who tend to write the first draft report in relative isolation and often welcome external inputs – as well as other members of the committee. Indeed, in most cases, an informal subcommittee composed of policy specialists is formed to scrutinise the work of the rapporteur and make sure that all points of view are treated fairly. They also look for technical problems and seek to improve the drafting of amendments (Marshall 2010). Apart from these two types of committee member, lobbyists can also try to influence negotiations through committee officials, who generally act as policy experts and advise rapporteurs during the drafting process (Marshall 2012).

When it comes to lobbying political groups, the clearest strategy is to contact members of the three main groups, the EPP, the S&D and ALDE, since they are generally part of the winning coalition, and, therefore, have more chances to steer the final outcome. These three groups might, however, not be enough to ensure success and lobbyists might also need to exert influence on those that are less sympathetic to their ideas, especially if some of their members are key actors in the policy process. It might be more effective to try to

---

Box 7.1   Hearings: An institutionalised lobbying channel?

The EP – or better said its committees – organises frequent meetings with experts and civil society in the form of hearings, workshops or conferences. The objective of these events is to facilitate parliamentary work and allow MEPs to enter into contact with a diverse range of views on a certain issue. In comparison to hearings, workshops are not necessarily made public, although they are often held during committee meetings. Most of these events serve to prepare for negotiations on a legislative file or debate pressing societal issues. For instance, in the aftermath of Julian King's nomination as Commissioner for Internal Security, the LIBE Committee held a public hearing in November 2016 on 'Preventing and countering radicalisation and violent extremism' to discuss potential new initiatives in the field. At the same time, the Committee on Agriculture and Rural Development (AGRI) held a workshop to prepare the next reform of the Common Agricultural Policy (CAP), which exposed the views of experts on potential policy solutions.

Hearings are, therefore, a useful tool for keeping in touch with experts and civil society. They also allow MEPs to gain expertise quickly and in a more representative way – since they encourage a broader dialogue than one-to-one meetings with selected groups. At the same time, they can also provide a cheaper and easier point of access for lobbyists, since they only have to get an invitation or simply attend the event. The practice, however, has not been without controversy; in June 2015, the Special Committee on Tax Rulings invited several multinationals to discuss issues of tax avoidance in a workshop. Most of the companies refused and the EP threatened to withdraw their access passes (Euobserver 2015b) – a practice that has now been included in the 2016 revision of the Rules of Procedure (Rule 116a).

---

convince rapporteurs, even if they are members of a political group that does not share the same positions as the lobbyist, than talking to those who are easy to convince but have no say in negotiations (Marshall 2015). For instance, in the example given earlier in this chapter, Jan Albrecht (Greens, Germany), rapporteur for the General Data Protection Regulation, was expected to be more sympathetic towards data protection organisations than towards big businesses, but that did not stop the latter from exerting an enormous amount of pressure on him and the members of his team.

Finally, one should not forget that interest groups also have other potential targets in the EP, for instance leadership structures like the College of Quaestors or delegations, especially when issues are linked to particular world regions. As we have seen in Chapter 3, intergroups are a perfect setting for lobbying, since they regroup members interested in specific issues, who are thus naturally more inclined to hear from groups that can provide expertise and external inputs.

Is the European Parliament biased towards business groups?

The question is, thus, to what extent do issues of access and resources make it easier for certain groups to lobby the EP? Traditionally, the EP has been considered a lobbying venue for weak interests, since MEPs tend to be more open to civil society issues (Dionigi 2017). In the late 1990s, Kohler-Koch (1997: 6) already identified the EP as a supporter of 'weak' interest groups, especially those dealing with environmental, social and consumer matters, because they attracted the attention of the public and allowed the EP to portray itself as the 'real' representative of EU citizens.

The evidence, however, is at odds with this idea. For instance, Dür et al. (2015) argue that business groups tend to have less success when trying to lobby the EP because they are more attached to the status quo, while diffuse interest groups tend to seek changes in legislation – which is much more to the taste of MEPs. At the same time, this means that business groups will be more successful in cases where the consultation or consent procedures are used, since there the EP has only a limited role in decision-making. In comparison, Rasmussen (2015) has observed that business groups are more successful in committees working under co-decision than those working under consultation – since the latter tend to adopt more extreme points of view and favour more biased positions as they have not adapted to the norms and working methods of the co-decision procedure. Therefore, business interests are often more successful when trying to influence committees working under co-decision, while diffuse interests have better chances of being heard in committees that usually work under consultation. Andlovic and Lehmann (2014) also note that this bias might be the result of the resources that interest groups can invest in following informal negotiations; those with more resources (usually business interests) are better able to adapt to the quicker pace of decision-making under co-decision than those with fewer staff and less money.

If we examine specific examples, the findings are also similarly disputed. For instance, in the case of the Food Information to Consumers (FIC) Regulation, Kurzer and Cooper (2013) have claimed that the rapporteur produced a report biased towards business interests and left consumer protection to the side. They have argued that NGOs were at a disadvantage because they were not part of a larger lobbying coalition, and, therefore, the solutions they proposed were not able to survive the decision-making process. These findings have been contested by Hoff et al. (2016) who noted the importance of examining the role not just of the rapporteur, but also of all other actors involved in negotiations in order to evaluate more accurately the extent of bias in the EP. This divergence in evaluating influence and the ability to shape policy outputs – and whether business or diffuse interest groups are more successful – reveals the difficulty in observing and measuring influence and success. Finding the right balance between examining a large number of cases in order to determine general trends in the amount and direction of bias while, at the same time, evaluating specific cases in all their depth is still one of the main challenges left to researchers willing to dig deeper into this question.

Regulating access to MEPs

The question of bias has revealed itself as politically and socially relevant after several lobbying scandals affecting MEPs. For instance, some years ago, the *Sunday Times* (2011) revealed in a covert investigation that four (out of 60 contacted) MEPs had accepted to table amendments in exchange for money. Although some of the MEPs involved argued that they had done nothing illegal, the 'cash for laws' scandal led President Jerzy Buzek to organise a working group charged with developing a stricter code of conduct (Dionigi 2017: 18). As a result, a new Code of Conduct entered into force on 1 January 2012 (Annex I of the Rules of Procedure) and was supplemented with an Advisory Committee on the Conduct of Members responsible for helping other parliamentarians interpret the Code of Conduct and advise the President in cases of (alleged) breaches. Since then, MEPs have been asked to declare their financial interests online, as well as any events they attend if they get some of the expenses reimbursed by third parties. The EP also keeps a register of gifts received in an official capacity, which include a wide variety of treasures – from a tea service offered by the Vietnamese government to a phone charger given by a pharmaceutical lobby. The 2016 revisions to the Rules of Procedure have strengthened these provisions by mentioning explicitly that MEPs should 'not solicit, accept or receive any direct or indirect benefit or other reward, whether in cash or in kind, in exchange for specific behaviour in the scope of the Member's parliamentary work, and shall consciously seek to avoid any situation which might imply bribery, corruption, or undue influence' (Annex I, Article 2b).

This was not the first attempt to regulate lobbying in the EP. In 1996, the EP's Rules of Procedure required interest groups' representatives to sign a code of conduct if they wished to receive an entry badge (access pass) that would allow them to enter the buildings freely. This attempt at self-regulation of interest groups was a pioneer at both the EU and the domestic level – with the Commission introducing a voluntary register only in 2008. In 2011, the Commission and the EP signed an Inter-institutional Agreement that set up a common Transparency Register – online since 2012. The register is still voluntary, but as we have seen in the previous section, it has made it easier to appreciate the sizes and types of group seeking to influence the EU's policy process. The new Rules of Procedure specify that MEPs should avoid meeting interest representatives who do not appear on the Transparency Register and that anyone falling under its scope has to sign a Code of Conduct in order to get a long-term badge (Rule 11.2 and 116a).

Enhancing transparency in relation to interest groups is, however, not unproblematic. The stricter regulation of lobbying activities is a relatively recent trend that contravenes traditional pluralist understandings of politics. In the past, lobbying was seen as a necessary condition to ensure that economic interests were tied into the policy-making process, thereby providing their support and legitimacy of new governmental measures. Slowly, concerns about corruption and undue bias have led to new ideas about transparency and accountability. Paradoxically, resistance to open up the process has come first and foremost from the side of the EU institutions; lobbyists, on the other hand, have expressed a preference for mandatory regulation, since they believe it is a way to show that their activities do not need to be pursued in an underhanded manner to be legitimate (Holman and Luneburg 2012).

In September 2016, the Commission attempted to introduce a mandatory Transparency Register that would also apply to the Council. The Commission proposal reveals several weak points: for instance, it is not yet clear whether there should be any sanctions for those violating the codes of conduct other than being taken off the register. The proposal also limits the mandatory aspect of the register to senior officials, while desk officers (who are often in closer contact with interest groups) are still free to meet with non-registered lobbyists. Therefore, while the Transparency Register has gone a long way to improve our knowledge about lobbying actors in the EU, it is not a foolproof solution (Dionigi and Martens 2016). More telling is the conflict emerging across the EU institutions; even if the Commission has only proposed very limited reforms, as of 2017, sides are already being drawn and a speedy solution is not foreseeable in the near future (Politico 2017g).

In the EP, the EPP, the S&D and ALDE immediately blocked the attempts made by the rapporteur on lobbying reform and transparency (Sven Giegold, German Green MEP) to rein in the external professional activities of MEPs and the consequences of 'revolving doors', which involves MEPs starting to work for lobbying groups after leaving the EP

(Euractiv 2016b). In his draft report (2015/2041/INI), he also proposed tighter transparency measures, such as the introduction of a legislative footprint – which would force MEPs to draw a list of interest groups who had participated in policy-making and which amendments they had proposed. The reaction to his proposal was thunderous and received 385 amendments, most of them trying to dilute the most radical suggestions (Politico 2016a). As a result, Giegold decided to move most of his key proposals to another report dealing with a general overhaul of the EP's Rules of Procedure (the Corbett Report 2016/2114/REG). The latter incorporated a relatively weak provision asking MEPs to 'not engage in paid professional lobbying directly linked to the Union decision-making process' (Annex I, Article two) – which leaves Verhofstadt free to continue in his secondary job (see Box 7.2).

The media: framing demands and disseminating outputs

Who better to communicate demands to the institutional actors composing the EU's political system than the media? Indeed, MEPs need to work with both traditional modes of communication, such as newspapers and television, as well as new social media to evaluate the 'moods' of EU citizens and to disseminate their activities and contributions. However, the EP faces a challenging arena when it comes to gathering demands and communicating outputs, since the European media landscape is still extremely compartmentalised and based on national coverage.

Second-order reporting?

The role of the media in EU policy-making is undeniable – they are vital in framing political debates and setting the agenda. They signal whether an issue is salient, which can be both positive or negative for decision-makers: on the one hand, it might underline the added value of EU institutions and their contribution to citizens' lives; on the other, it might bring issues to the attention of the public that decision-makers might have preferred to treat out of the public limelight (Semetko et al. 2000). At the same time, the media is also responsible for confining EU politics to 'history-making' events, underlining stories about the process of European integration (and its crises) rather than reporting on day-to-day policy-making. This means that media attention concentrates on European Council meetings, leaving the activities of the Commission and, particularly, the Parliament largely unreported. There is, therefore, a discrepancy between the actual influence of the EP (and the EU more

Box 7.2   Of side jobs and revolving doors

The EP has always been quick to criticise the Commission when cases relating to conflict of interests emerged. One of the latest examples of 'revolving doors' is the senior executive post that Goldman Sachs offered José Manuel Barroso two years after he left the post of Commission President, which spurred the EP to issue a resolution calling for a longer 'cooling off' period and a more detailed declaration of interests (P8_TA-PROV(2016)0477). Such practices are, however, not reserved to the other institutions. Side jobs (also known as 'moonlighting') and 'revolving doors' are also widespread in the EP (Transparency International 2017), which explains why some groups might be unwilling to accept some of the far-reaching reforms proposed by Sven Giegold. His report also included a 'cooling off' period during which former MEPs should not be allowed to take new jobs as lobbyists. He also wanted to preclude MEPs from working as 'consultants' on the side. His remarks reflect a growing concern about conflict of interests inside the EP: despite their obligation to declare their professional activities and remunerated functions, they do not need to do that with exact numbers. For instance, Guy Verhofstadt – leader of the liberal group – declares getting 'more than €10,000 monthly' acting as a board member of Sofina, a Belgian investment holding company. These activities might end up raising eyebrows, as was the case of the two German co-rapporteurs (Petra Kammerevert and Sabine Verheyen) in charge of the Audio-Visual Media Services Directive, who were both simultaneously sitting on the board of a German public broadcaster (Politico 2016e). There have also been various examples of MEPs becoming lobbyists, with a long list of former members of the ECON committee now working in the financial industry – sometimes for interest groups that are not even listed in the Transparency Register (see, for instance, the cases of Olle Schmidt, Arlene McCarthy or Sharon Bowles in https://corporateeurope.org/).

Recent research has looked into the practice of moonlighting and determined that it might be more conducive to lower presence in the chamber – especially for those with a highly remunerated regular side job. It is less clear, however, whether this practice also affects the pro- duction of reports. Variance may be linked to the type of job or even the electoral system in their country of origin. It seems, however, that receiving an additional income might not always be a bad thing: for one, it can encourage some people who would otherwise be reticent to lose their previous income to take up office; it might also be an indicator of expertise in a specific area and, even, a necessary stimu- lus for workaholic MEPs (Hurka et al. 2017; Staat and Kuehnhanss 2017).

generally) and how much media attention it receives. This is mostly due to the fact that the media landscape is still dominated by national outlets, which are generally not interested in (or not aware of) EU topics. Although the quality and amount of reporting have improved over the years, their attention focuses on a limited range of issues, such as agriculture or economic news, and is tinted by their specific national frames (Trenz 2004; van Noije 2010).

Gattermann (2013) examined articles in various national newspapers in order to assess how visible the EP is on the national level. Contrary to other studies, she deems the EP to be generally newsworthy – coverage of its activities usually follows the parliamentary calendar, with more attention paid during the winter months (when the EP is at its most active), and in particular, during its plenary sessions in Strasbourg. This, of course, hides a large variation in the visibility of individual MEPs, which often depends on how interesting journalists find them for national audiences. Therefore, media focus on specific MEPs might depend on a wide range of factors, for instance whether they were already known in national politics, whether they might be opting for a leadership position or whether they have been involved in scandals. Also, MEPs who spend more time back home and are good at delivering speeches have better chances of building a reputation among journalists and getting more attention (Gattermann and Vasilopoulou 2015).

Reporting on the EU (and hence the EP) is, therefore, largely a matter of style, with national cultures influencing the way journalists are formed and how they report. For instance, why would MEPs be more present in French than in British media? The answer may lay in their different journalistic cultures: French journalists are well known for their attachment to EU institutions, which means they often become insiders and, thus, are less critical than British journalists. The latter have been trained in a media landscape that emphasises the use of journalism to investigate and scrutinise EU activities, which probably explains the negative reporting of EU institutions in the UK. Therefore, since reports on EU politics suffer from the similar second-order effects as EP elections, it is not surprising that citizens know as much or as little about the EU as their national media considers it is (news)worthy to cover (Gattermann and Vasilopoulou 2015; Semetko et al. 2000; van Noije 2010).

Modern technologies as a new way to connect with EU citizens

Given the absence of a European-wide media landscape, European institutions have always been keen to fill in the gap. However, putting these ideas into practice has not always been straightforward. Until the advent of the internet, EU communications were characterised by rivalry between the Commission, the EP and member states, wishing to appropriate any success story. The EP in particular was perceived as having a communication deficit: neither the press service nor individual MEPs had the necessary skills to produce effective messages and were lacking the necessary (budgetary and human) resources (Anderson and McLeod 2004).

In response to these criticisms, by the mid-2000s, the EP decided to reform its internal organisation by extending its Directorate-General for Communication (DG COMM) and investing it with more resources and autonomy. By 2009, 15 per cent of EP officials (excluding those in the area of translation and interpretation) were working for the various communication services and they had been mostly recruited among professionals with previous experience in this area. This proportion has remained stable; by the end of 2016, 723 officials (out of a total of around 5,000) were working for DG COMM. They enjoyed a budget of €92,559,100 – that is, around 5 per cent of the total Parliament annual budget. The high number of resources (in terms of both staff and budget) can be explained by functions exerted by the DG, which is not only facilitating access to the institution, but also acting as an intermediary between the EP and the press corps. To provide these different services, the EP has heavily invested in media facilities in Brussels and Strasbourg – making material such as cameras, satellite links and TV and radio studios available to journalists. In addition, the EP also produces raw visual and textual material (e.g. videos of the plenary) that can then be used by media outlets as well as briefings and press conferences (Clark and Priestley 2012: 391–393).

The efforts to act as a provider of impartial information have been highly successful and DG COMM is now regarded as an asset for journalists, since it can provide the necessary expertise in the language and standards used by media professionals. The EP's press services are often sought-after in order to confirm sources seen as less reliable. The credibility accumulated over the years can be very useful to publicise more effectively the work of the Parliament and spin messages that manage to transmit the main perspectives and priorities of the institution. In order to mediate better with national media, the press services need to constantly adapt their message to the interests and particularities of each country or region in Europe (Laursen and Valentini 2015). These efforts show a clear political will from the EP's leadership to improve the communication of the EP and develop channels that allow it to speak directly to citizens. To this effect, DG COMM created a new Web Communications Unit in 2008 composed of a multilingual team of editors that help to keep the various social media sites running. The Bureau also adopted a Web Strategy in 2010 (PE 447.025/BUR), in which it decided to revamp its webpage. The new version was made more interactive and integrated other online media like EuroparlTV more effectively (cf. Leston-Bandeira 2014; see also Box 7.3). The EP is now on Facebook, Twitter, Flickr, LinkedIn and YouTube and has even developed a 'News Hub' (http://www.epnewshub.eu), which shows the latest news, videos and pictures published on social media by MEPs and official EP services. It also lists the latest digital content on a tumblr blog (http://epnetwork. tumblr.com) ready to be downloaded in all 24 official languages.

Box 7.3   EuroparlTV: Bringing Parliament near you

One of the first measures that the EP undertook to bridge its communication gap was to develop a parliamentary TV channel comparable to those that already existed in other countries, like the US or France. However, setting up a traditional broadcasting channel was very expensive, so a study in 2005 proposed to develop an internet-based system. This solution killed two birds with one stone: it made the project economically and technically manageable and solved the issue of languages, since videos could be easily subtitled in all official languages. EuroparlTV was born and started functioning officially in February 2008 (find it under http://www.europarltv.europa.eu).

The launch of the broadcasting system raised several criticisms: some were concerned about the cost, especially when it did not manage to attract a high number of viewers; others were more concerned that transmitting only via the internet might lead to 'digital exclusion' or that it would turn into a tool for propaganda. To this effect, the project received a thorough facelift in 2010, when it ran the risk of being cancelled. Since then, EuroparlTV has diversified its contents and tried to capture younger audiences. Aside from broadcasting the plenary and committee meetings live and on demand, the video service also includes three distinct channels: Parliament News, which includes overviews of topical issues as well as interviews and documentaries; Young Parliament, featuring 'Blink' the animated TV character that explains the EU in a more vivacious manner; and Discover Parliament, which concentrates on the internal functioning and history of the EP.

EuroparlTV has to strike a difficult balance between providing entertaining and high-quality inputs while keeping the necessary objectivity and ensuring that all political groups are represented fairly. To this effect, the broadcasting service developed an editorial charter and set up an internal committee composed of representatives from all political groups to check its implementation. EuroparlTV has managed to balance these different objectives and has been rewarded with a steady increase in viewers. However, in an age of rapid technological change, the media consumption habits of citizens shift very quickly and this opens up the question as to whether EuroparlTV will be able to maintain the current format or whether it will need to adapt to the times (Clark and Priestley 2012: 403–407; Corbett et al. 2016: 404–405).

The investment in social media has changed how the EP communicates with citizens and has provided an array of activities that seek to engage the public and facilitate a dialogue with the institution and its MEPs. The EP Facebook page started organising regular chats with MEPs in 2011; since then, it has expanded its range of activities so that citizens can also express their opinions and share their experiences. For instance, on 29 November 2016, there was a live chat with Manfred Weber (EPP leader) on Facebook, with the title: 'What direction should the EU take? What challenges lie ahead?' Shortly after, the EP asked citizens to post 'what your plans are for this festive month'. Albeit these activities might seem superfluous, the EP has managed to gather a solid number of followers on social media. By the end of 2016, the Facebook page had over 2 million likes, which was around the same amount as Angela Merkel's page. On Twitter, it had almost 280,000 followers. In comparison, the UK Parliament had over 1 million, but the Bundestag only over 26,500 followers on Twitter – neither of them has an official presence on Facebook. It is, however, difficult to appreciate the impact of the EP through Twitter, since the number of followers is often spread over the 'Twitteropolis', which comprises various languages (the EP tweets in the 24 official languages); various bodies (for instance, most committees have their own account); as well as a multitude of personal accounts, both from official sources (such as the EP's spokesperson, Jaume Duch) or from individual MEPs (for a full overview, see European Parliament 2016e).

The EP has managed to rise from its ashes and has become an example of a highly successful institutional communicator. By taking a proactive role, the EP's press services have become more than a mediator and built themselves a role as an agenda-setter and a producer of news. This raises clear challenges for Parliament's institutional integrity and legitimacy. In the first place, officials in the press services have to strike a fine balance between appearing as impartial and credible sources, while still trying to push a specific institutional agenda. This is made more difficult by the inherent difficulty that the EP often does not have one single unified agenda, but a multitude of voices representing national and partisan interests. It is, therefore, a highly delicate exercise to publicise the EP, while keeping an unbiased message about its daily business. This challenge has become even more pressing in the 'Web 2.0' environment, which is based on interaction and immediate reactions. As a consequence, the EP's press services now face the added difficulty of maintaining their official voice, while trying to engage with citizens in social media that call for a more open and forthright style of communication. In this environment, media officials cannot present themselves as faceless civil servants, but need to become more personable – all the while maintaining the neutrality and credibility of the institution.

Therefore, while Facebook chats and 'tweeting' offer the potential to engage new sectors of society and make citizens feel closer to the EP, they also present serious challenges in their efforts to build (and control) a unique institutional voice (Clark and Priestley 2012; Laursen and Valentini 2015; Leston-Bandeira 2014).

The last question is, of course, how many people actually listen to this voice? Despite the efforts made by DG COMM to provide its material in all official languages and maintain close contacts with national media, the feeling remains that it is mostly speaking to a 'bubble'; it is probably only a small group of citizens already engaged in European affairs who get involved in the EP's activities, while the majority of people still depend on how much interest their national media pay to EU affairs – and the quality of their reporting – to be kept informed about what is going on in Brussels and Strasbourg (Clark and Priestley 2012; Leston-Bandeira 2014).

MEPs 2.0? Online communication as a new form of representation

The introduction of the internet and social media has also supposed a revolution for MEPs and how they communicate with EU citizens. While in 2009 only 33 per cent of MEPs used social networks, now 88 per cent of them are on Facebook and 76 per cent on Twitter. This trend is significant, since it means that parliamentarians have become increasingly aware of the need to communicate through the internet and to do it in a more interactive manner. Indeed, one-way forms of communication, such as email newsletters or online videos, have lost importance; Twitter and Facebook are now seen to be an equally efficient way to communicate with constituents and stakeholders and may even substitute personal meetings. The confidence in social media has increased rapidly– in 2015 Facebook was seen as an effective tool by 95 per cent of MEPs, while Twitter was trusted by 88 per cent of members, up from 61 per cent and 31 per cent respectively in 2009. Even the use of networking platforms like LinkedIn is slowly growing, with 28 per cent of MEPs using it to listen to their networks and expand their contacts. Finally, even those who might not actively use social media to promote their work accept that it is a great source to follow events and keep in touch with both national and European media (Fleischman Hillard 2011, 2015).

Therefore, the way to communicate and campaign has changed rapidly since the 2009 elections and has had to adapt to the shifting habits of EU citizens, who are now more often engaged in social media than conventional sources like TV or printed news (see Box 7.4). MEPs have slowly realised that social media can provide an added value compared

---

Box 7.4   Spitzenkandidaten and the use of social media in the 2014 elections

As we have seen, the 2014 EP elections introduced a new form of partisan competition with the election of Spitzenkandidaten. Did this innovation have any impact on the debates going on in social media? Nulty et al. (2016) examined this question and determined that the presence of Spitzenkandidaten and their televised debates fostered more communications on social media and helped to target a Europe-wide audience. However, these communications were dominated by a pro-/anti-EU discourse, rather than the traditional left-right competition. Therefore, those anti-EU candidates who had a Twitter account used it disproportionately in comparison to pro-EU politicians and used social media to promote an anti-EU rhetoric that was much less present in other media channels. Indeed, their findings were confirmed in April 2014 by a ranking of followers' statistics on Twitter, which showed Marine Le Pen (Front National) sharing the top positions with two other Eurosceptics, Jean-Luc Mélenchon (Front de Gauche) and Nigel Farage (United Kingdom Independence Party [UKIP]) (Euobserver 2014b).

---

to traditional modes of communication. They allow them to reach new audiences and maintain links with their constituents without too many costs. These wide trends, however, hide very different levels of adoption and active use of social media and the internet. There is still a big gap between those who use new technologies as a one-way form of communication (for instance, writing blogs) and those who see them as a form of interaction that should allow for a permanent dialogue with voters (what is known as Web 2.0 communication). Therefore, having a Twitter account does not always translate into an active use of it. Indeed, there are studies showing that most MEPs only tweet from time to time and still use their account to 'broadcast' rather than to 'chat' (Scherpereel et al. 2017).

Based on their use of personal webpages, Lilleker and Koc-Michalska (2013) have defined three different styles of communication: home style, impression management and participatory. The home style predominates, since it allows MEPs to inform constituents about their activities and to present themselves as active, hardworking representatives. The impression management style follows and allows them to appeal to voters on the basis of their personal characteristics, such as lifestyles and qualifications. Finally, the participatory style is based on the Web 2.0 communication model, that is, an attempt to keep the information flow going and to involve citizens in chats and discussions. Although this style is still infrequent among MEPs, it seems to provide more political capital and earn more followers; it also generates more input that can help parliamentarians build their positions and arguments.

The adoption of different styles does not come out of the blue; it is conditioned by personal characteristics as well as contextual factors like the type of electoral rules in their country of origin. First, among the personal characteristics, gender does not seem to make a big difference, while education does seem to be correlated with a more dynamic use of new technologies. The most defining feature is age: younger MEPs tend to adopt a more participatory style and to provide personal news feeds on Facebook or Twitter. Indeed, if they have a Twitter account they use it not just to tweet, but also to retweet and post @-replies. In general, those MEPs who represent a constituency with many young voters have higher incentives to be familiar with more participatory tools and to use social networking. Second, there is also a link between the levels of technological development in different countries and the use of these tools. In general, there seems to be a diagonal cleavage crossing from the north-west to the south-east, with countries like Spain and Italy being very active on Twitter, while Greece, Hungary and Lithuania are lagging behind. At the same time, some have indicated that former communist countries, despite having lower levels of internet penetration, have been better at adapting to the Web 2.0 style than older EU members. Finally, there seems to be a difference between political groups that is related to ideology and size. The Greens and the radical left speak to an electorate that is keen on new technologies, while more traditional parties might find it difficult to convince their electorate of the need to engage with social media. This trend could also be linked to the size of the parties, but there the evidence is mixed, since smaller parties do not seem to engage beyond the home style and are often concerned that experimenting might steal them the few votes they can secure. At the same time, there are indications that those MEPs who are unsure of their prospects of being (re-)elected tend to adopt a more participatory style in order to increase their followers and convince them of their commitment towards their constituency (Braghiroli 2010; Larsson 2015; Lilleker and Koc-Michalska 2013; Lorenzo Rodríguez and Garmendia Madariaga 2016; Scherpereel et al. 2017).

The adoption of new technologies is not without challenges. As many European politicians do not yet know how to use these tools properly, the use of social media is not always entirely effective. For instance, it is important to understand that, while Facebook might allow for more casual and relaxed interactions, Twitter requires speed and immediacy. It implies a constant presence and using the opportunity of delivering a scoop, which makes it extremely time-consuming. If one wants to take social media seriously and do a good job of it, it requires a level of interaction that is often difficult to keep up with on a daily basis, even if MEPs get help from assistants. Therefore, Facebook and, especially, Twitter might not be as compatible with the routines of politicians as one might think: it might be a good idea for politicians to contemplate whether it is worth engaging with them, especially in particularly busy times like during electoral campaigns. Finally, the use of the internet and social media by political groups and individual MEPs suffers from the same 'bubble' effect as the official communications of the EP. Twitter, in particular, is seen as an 'elite' tool directed to those with a particular interest in and knowledge of European affairs. This means that its potential to engage with broader audiences and increase the level of political participation is more limited than might have been expected (Larsson 2015; Lorenzo Rodríguez and Garmendia Madariaga 2016; Vesnic-Alujevic 2013).

Conclusion

Although often forgotten, MEPs would not be able to be as efficient and successful if it were not for the inputs received in their daily work. To this effect, they rely on a diffuse group of actors that mediate between the public and the EU institutions. Organised interest groups and the media facilitate the translation of inputs into outputs by raising new problems, shaping the agenda and contributing to the process of finding solutions. Their close link to the political system comes, however, with caveats – since the line between inside and outside is often blurry. The close links with interest and media representatives are raising concerns about transparency and accountability. This shows the symbiotic relationship between these actors, which cannot exist in complete independence, but also the risks it has for the EP's legitimacy and that of the EU system as a whole. In the end, if the EP wants to be seen as a democratic institution, it has to accept that citizens should be able to attribute responsibilities, so that, either in elections or through other channels of communication, they can praise or place blame where it is due.

Chapter 8

MEPs and Their Offices: Managing Frontstage and Backstage Roles

Introduction: exploring the micro level

As we have seen in the previous chapters, MEPs form a direct link between citizens and the EU's political system – they are the main transmission belt between their demands and the final outputs. However, how do MEPs aggregate these demands and what do they do when they receive conflicting inputs?

The activities of MEPs and their offices have received increasing attention, since it has become evident that members tend to adopt different roles and set different priorities according to the environment in which they perform. This observation resonates with older studies that examined US or UK parliamentarians and their attitudes as representatives (Davidson 1969; Fenno 1978). Although there have been many different definitions of roles, Searing (1991: 1248) understands them as 'the part one plays in an event or process'. This, of course, is a rather basic definition, but it encourages us to ask individual members how they think they should behave and why. Indeed, the increasing professionalisation and specialisation of the EP shows us that MEPs have different understandings of what part they should play as parliamentarians (Beauvallet and Michon 2010).

Of course, individual members do not act in a vacuum and are often constrained by long-standing institutional norms and rules. Once they start working in the EP, new members spend some time learning the formal and informal working methods of the institution (Lindstädt et al. 2012). This process of socialisation may happen at different levels – in the context of national party delegations, political groups, but also in committee work. New MEPs usually adapt to the worldviews and practices of their colleagues and we often see a distinct *esprit de corps* emerging inside committees (Neuhold 2007; see also Chapter 10). It is important to note, however, that this process of socialisation is not synonymous with 'Europeanisation' – MEPs do not necessarily 'go native' and become more pro-European during their mandate (Katz 1997; Scully 2005; Scully et al. 2012).

Despite this process of socialisation, one can observe significant variation in the way individual MEPs shape their behaviour and set their priorities. These differences are dependent on a variety of factors, such as individual role perceptions, previous career paths, the domestic electoral system or their conceptions of European integration. As a result, MEPs may have very different understandings of their functions: some of them may prefer to specialise in a policy field, while others will focus on strengthening the institutional influence of the EP or use the plenary as an arena to contest the EU (Bale and Taggart 2006; Navarro 2009; Scully and Farrell 2003). These different roles do not just affect their priorities or the way they behave, but also colour the way they vote (Meserve et al. 2009; Blomgren 2003; Scully 1997) and how they behave when they have to deliver frontstage performances (cf. Goffman 1959).

However, with the growing importance of the EP in the legislative arena, MEPs express difficulties to deal with the amount of technical work and information required to perform successfully and have some influence on the EU's policy outputs. MEPs often need to specialise and become experts if they want to play a role in the EP; therefore, their frontstage performance largely depends on how well they can prepare it backstage. There, MEPs' offices help to manage large amounts of information and an agenda characterised by time constraints and constant travel. Indeed, although MEPs are key actors in the life of the EP, their functions and roles would not be successful without the support of other actors who usually remain hidden behind the scenes. Therefore, the second half of this chapter concentrates on these less well-known figures and examines their role in aggregating, filtering and shaping demands.

A new European parliamentary elite?

Before we start looking into MEPs' roles and considering different ideal-types, we need to understand how one chooses this career path, since this is particularly critical in a parliament characterised by high levels of turnover.

In the 2014 elections, 52.73 per cent of the members were newly elected (see Table 8.1). Therefore, in comparison to national parliaments, the percentage of new members between two legislative terms is high and has remained relatively constant for the last 20 years. Certainly, it hides a high disparity across member states – with Greece having renewed *all* of its members in 2014, while Germany only changed 31 per cent of them (European Parliament 2014c: 36). These differences can be traced

Table 8.1 *Turnover in the 2014 European Parliament elections per member state*

Member state	Seats	Total number		Total percentage	
		Re-elected MEPs	New MEPs	Re-elected MEPs	New MEPs
Austria	18	10	8	56%	44%
Belgium	21	12	9	57%	43%
Bulgaria	17	6	11	35%	65%
Czech Republic	21	6	15	29%	71%
Croatia	11	7	4	64%	36%
Cyprus	6	2	4	33%	67%
Denmark	13	7	6	54%	46%
Estonia	6	2	4	33%	67%
Finland	13	6	7	46%	54%
France	74	37	37	50%	50%
Germany	96	66	30	69%	31%
Greece	21	0	21	0%	100%
Hungary	21	10	11	48%	52%
Ireland	11	5	6	45%	55%
Italy	73	18	55	25%	75%
Latvia	8	4	4	50%	50%
Lithuania	11	5	6	45%	55%
Luxembourg	6	4	2	67%	33%
Malta	6	3	3	50%	50%
Netherlands	26	12	14	46%	54%
Poland	51	22	29	43%	57%
Portugal	21	9	12	43%	57%
Romania	32	18	14	56%	44%
Slovakia	13	7	6	54%	46%
Slovenia	8	4	4	50%	50%
Spain	54	23	31	43%	57%
Sweden	20	10	10	50%	50%
United Kingdom	73	40	33	55%	45%
Total	751	355	396	47.27%	52.73%

Source: European Parliament (2014d: 36).

back to different selection systems at the national level or even their political system: MEPs coming from unitary countries like France have lower chances of being re-elected than those stemming from federal systems like Germany (Daniel 2015).

Despite its high level of turnover, the EP has become a more likely place to build a political career; nowadays, MEPs tend to stay longer and have a lengthier term of service in committees. In addition, the average age is now lower, which means that new members do not see the EP merely as a retirement home. It seems, thus, that with increasing legislative powers, the EP has become more professionalised and is now the home of a new European parliamentary elite (Norris 1999; Scarrow 1997; Whitaker 2014). Verzichelli and Edinger (2005) have drawn a typology of MEPs based on their competences and their career trajectories: apart from those who come to the EP to end their careers, the principal distinction is between those who use the EP as a 'stepping stone' – generally young MEPs who tend to focus on the local level – and those who aim to pursue a European career. They separate the latter into two groups, namely 'Euro-experts' who have already had a previous political career at the national level and 'Euro-politicians' elected directly to the EP. Salvati (2016) has examined the biographies of the 2009–2014 MEPs and found that 78.5 per cent of them had previous political experience, at either the European or the national level. This trend is particularly noticeable in the new member states. This means that national political parties are becoming increasingly reluctant to recruit amateurs and see the EP as an interesting path for national members to pursue their careers. Some have noted, however, that candidates are often recruited from the 'periphery' of national political fields; the EP serves thus as an alternative for those who do not fit the profile expected in national politics. This is often good for the EP, since it now welcomes parliamentarians with a higher educational and more international background and provides a better home for female candidates (Beauvallet-Haddad et al. 2016).

There is, thus, an increasing number of politicians who decide to swap a national for a European career and who then become more active than those who see the EP as a 'one-off' experience (Daniel 2015; van Geffen 2016). The investment in a European career allows MEPs to acquire the necessary 'internal political capital' – that is, the reputation that comes from making the institution work, fostering professional networks and learning the ropes of internal and inter-institutional games – to win 'prizes', such as rapporteurships and leadership positions (Beauvallet and Michon 2010). At the same time, once someone has invested time and efforts in climbing the leadership ladder inside the EP, it is less likely that they will leave the institution and change their career path (Navarro 2009: 219).

The multiple roles and functions of MEPs

What MEPs do with their careers inside Parliament is a very individual choice that might be determined by a wide range of factors, such as the electoral system, their previous career, their professional background or even their personal interests. In order to understand these different role orientations, this chapter focuses on a typology of MEPs' roles proposed by Bale and Taggart (2006) and complemented by Navarro (2009), and draws on their findings to help us understand how individual members set their priorities and behave in the EP. We can identify four ideal-types of mainstream MEPs: constituency representatives, policy advocates, European evangelists and institutionalists. It is important to keep in mind that these ideal-types are just that, ideal; therefore, it is unlikely that any MEP will fit the description one-to-one, while several roles might be performed by the same member when performing in different contexts.

Representing their constituency

Whether one can pursue a European career is largely determined by the second-order nature of the EP elections and other characteristics of the national electoral and party system (Whitaker 2014). MEPs depend largely on their electors to be re-elected and must speak for them, especially in those electoral systems where the link between parliamentarians and citizens is closest. As we have seen in Chapter 6, elections can be understood as 'geographical representation' (Farrell and Scully 2010: 38), that is, as a link between the domestic electorates and their elected members. In this sense, the domestic electoral systems may have an impact on how MEPs define their role once working in the EP (Bowler and Farrell 1993; Farrell and Scully 2010). For many, the role of 'constituency representative' is the most obvious one to adopt if they aim to be re-elected or if they wish to use their stint as MEPs as a springboard for a national political career.

However, the idea of 'constituency' can go beyond the geographical district where a member is elected. It can also represent a whole country, a region – especially in those areas with ethnic or other types of minorities – or a particular interest group. What is essential here is that the priorities will be set not by the MEP, but by this specific group. Therefore, constituency representatives see the EP as a way to deliver 'goods' to their constituents. They are more likely to come from countries with single-member districts or with a strong culture of constituency service, like the UK (Scholl 1986). Sozzi (2016) compared the use of written parliamentary questions by MEPs elected under open or closed ballot systems. He found that Italians elected under open ballot made more use of questions to cultivate a personal relationship with their electorate than French MEPs, elected through a closed-ballot system.

Constituency representatives may play an important role in the agricultural committee, not because they are particularly interested in crops and animal husbandry, but because their constituents come from a region that heavily depends on European farming subsidies. However, since it is difficult to use the EP to deliver 'pork-barrel policies' (that is, to influence policy outputs so as to provide their constituents with funding or other types of goods), they may choose to sit in committees where they can exert some sort of oversight – such as the Budgetary Control (CONT), Regional Development (REGI) or Petitions (PETI) committees. This type of MEP eschews positions of responsibility such as political coordinator or (vice-)chair, but might be interested in heading a national party delegation, so as to get their national view through when matters are discussed inside a political group. They may also become a member of an intergroup that deals with topics of local or regional interest such as minority languages or 'rural, mountainous and remote areas'. Therefore, the close links to their constituents might mean travelling back and forth between the EP and their country of origin more often than other MEPs (see Box 8.1).

Constituency representatives are usually supporters of the EU, but may prefer to limit its competences and often fight for a strict interpretation of the subsidiarity principle. They derive legitimacy from their role

---

Box 8.1 Two types of German 'constituency representative'

Until July 2017, Herbert Reul and Angelika Niebler shared the leadership of the CDU/CSU delegation. Reul was well known for keeping in contact with his grass roots in the Bergische Land (a region in North Rhine-Westphalia), he was a member of the Industry, Research and Energy (ITRE) committee and substitute at the Transport and Tourism committee, both dealing with issues where MEPs may be well placed to represent the interests of their region. In contrast, Angelika Niebler is better known for representing another type of constituency through her parallel job as a media, tech and privacy lawyer. She is a member of the ITRE and Women's Rights committees and sits as substitute on the Legal Affairs committee. Her professional activities, however, have raised criticisms and she has been accused of conflict of interests for representing groups that are not registered as lobbyists (The Parliament Magazine 2016a).

as representatives and see themselves as a solution to the EU's democratic deficit. Therefore, they will seek to reinforce Parliament, since they see it as a source of accountability and a way to ensure the 'checks and balances' of the EU's political system. As a result, they will insist on procedural issues – such as ensuring a way for citizens to raise their demands and have an input in the system.

Specialising in a policy field

Since the connection between MEPs and their voters is generally weak, European parliamentarians may choose to become policy specialists; gaining expertise in one particular issue may give them a bigger say in (legislative) negotiations, and, therefore, a better chance to frame demands and shape outputs (cf. Kreppel 2002: 23). 'Policy advocates' are more likely to be found in committees with a high legislative workload, especially those that work under co-decision and where the EP has more influence. It would, thus, be typical for such MEPs to work in the Environment (ENVI) or the Internal Market and Consumer Protection (IMCO) committees. Becoming a policy specialist is a good way to rapidly gain a reputation in the EP, especially if one is able to 'crack' difficult dossiers. That is why first-timers, especially young ones, choose this path to make a career and gain visibility. For instance, Jan Philipp Albrecht (German Green) took on the challenge of the Data Protection Reform Package in 2012 shortly after arriving in the EP, and was made committee vice-chair in the next legislature. Liberal Estonian Kaja Kallas has taken a similar path after arriving in the Parliament in 2014; her background as a competition lawyer put her in the ideal position to become rapporteur for the accident-prone Digital Single Market project.

The advantage of becoming a 'policy advocate' is that one can concentrate on a limited number of issues and become an expert, which is highly important in a parliament that depends on expertise to form cohesive positions. As Ringe (2010) has argued, experts are the principal providers of 'focal points', that is, their positions serve as a reference for those that do not know the issue well enough to form their own opinion. MEPs who can show proof of their expertise tend to be offered more reports – they become 'repeated' rapporteurs (Yoshinaka et al. 2010) – and often end up acting as political coordinators for their party group. Their status as experts may come as a result of their previous activities, the policy focus of their political party or as an acquired taste nurtured over the years. For instance, Sven Giegold (German Green) has become synonymous with left economic policies and transparency and is an active member of the ECON committee and the Special Committee on Tax Rulings (TAXE 2); his foci of interest are probably not surprising if one takes into account that he is a former member of the left-wing group

ATTAC. Julia Reda (also German Green) was the youngest MEP elected in the 2014 Parliament. She is a member of the 'Pirate Party', a one-issue party focusing on digital freedom and related issues such as privacy and patents, which explains her expertise on copyright issues (Politico 2017e). For an example of a 'policy advocate', who has gained expertise by focusing on the same type of reports, see Box 8.2.

These MEPs see their legitimacy stemming from their capacity to deliver policy outputs. Therefore, they aim to improve the efficiency of the system, so as to deliver better and quicker results for citizens. However, this might weaken their contact with their party back home, making it more difficult to change their careers or to go back to pursuing national careers. Their satisfaction comes from finding solutions to problems, even if it means that they spend hours searching for the right wording or deciding the position of a comma in a legislative text. For this type of MEP, the most important work is done in committees, which might lead them to dismiss the actions of other members who

---

Box 8.2 The 'data protection' champion

Sophie in 't Veld is well known in the EP for being a very vocal advocate for privacy and data protection – she has even dedicated part of her website to the topic (http://www.sophieintveld.eu/privacy/). A member of the LIBE committee since her arrival in the EP in 2004, she has become associated with epic battles such as the fight against a Passenger Name Record (PNR) Agreement with the US, for which she was rapporteur in 2007 and 2012. In this last episode, she decided to withdraw her name from the report when the EP decided not to back her recommendation to reject the agreement. She became particularly notorious when she brought the Council and the Commission to Court for not being sufficiently transparent in the negotiations of an EU–US bank data (SWIFT) Agreement (cases T-529/09 and T-301/10). As rapporteur for the EU–Canada PNR Agreement, she also recommended a referral to the CJEU to check its conformity with the Charter of Fundamental Rights (Opinion 1/15). In general, she has been highly critical of the use that law enforcement makes of personal data, underlining issues such as mass surveillance and profiling, and has repeatedly questioned the necessity and proportionality of measures that use data retention for security purposes. However, since she rose to vice-chair of the liberal group in 2014, she has had to check her words, since her opinions are often more left-wing than those of the majority of her group. She was, for example, little heard during negotiations on a PNR system for planes flying in and out of the EU, which eventually passed in 2016 (Directive 2016/681/EU).

focus on delivering speeches in plenary or on the deliberative side of the Parliament. Their position as experts helps them to exert influence throughout the policy cycle – that is, they will know how to shape the agenda and frame problems and solutions from an early stage and might also raise problems in the implementation phase. The EP is, thus, understood first and foremost as a decision-making body in charge of finding solutions – therefore, it should focus on those areas where the EU can deliver some added value, while offering an opportunity to those that have a stake in the outputs to intervene and give their opinion.

Making a career inside the EP

With the emergence of a European parliamentary elite, there is also a growing number of MEPs who decide to dedicate their efforts to expanding the powers of the EP and climb the internal steps to reach one of the leadership positions described in Chapter 3. The 'institutionalist' role might have different facets: some might decide to dedicate their efforts to improving the functioning of the Parliament and the situation of MEPs or their staff – many of those who choose the Constitutional Affairs (AFCO) committee are interested in the governance of the institution. Therefore, they generally become experts in the rules that constitute the core of the EP's empowerment and its relations with other EU institutions (see Box 8.3). Others might have leadership aspirations and,

---

Box 8.3   Pulling strings behind the scenes

Richard Corbett has been a British MEP since 1996 (with a break between 2009 and 2014) and a permanent fixture of the AFCO committee. He is probably one of the most knowledgeable members when it comes to the functioning of the EU institutions, having been behind many treaty and inter-institutional reforms. He was rapporteur during the drafting of the Treaty of Lisbon, master of numerous modifications to the EP's Rules of Procedure and one of the few who could deal with the reform of the expert committee system (comitology) in 2006. After his re-election, he was in charge of the 2016 Inter-institutional Agreement on Better Law-Making. In his words, that probably makes him 'the most boring person you can safely vote for' (http://www.richardcorbett.org.uk/about-me/). However, he has also repeatedly shown a more extroverted side and has put his knowledge at the service of the public by publishing various books on the EP and trying to dispel the most common myths about the EU on his personal website. His app, 'Doorstep EU', which offers analyses of media reports on the EU, can be downloaded there.

therefore, their 'institutionalist' career will be oriented towards their political group. As we have seen in Chapter 3, many of the EP Presidents started their career by working hard inside their groups, acting as political coordinators and chairs of the party group in order to gain enough reputation and support from their colleagues before becoming a candidate for the presidency.

Usually, 'institutionalists' are interested first and foremost in the big political issues. They look down on the policy specialists and their fascination for the legislative nitty-gritty and prefer to focus on the big ideas. Their preferences are often influenced by their previous careers: they tend to be older and have either spent more time in the institution or have had a long political trajectory back home. That gives them a taste for abstraction and high politics, which is reflected in a higher rate of participation in plenary debates and motions for resolution than in committee work or the submission of questions. They tend to see themselves as part of a political elite and derive satisfaction from fostering cooperation across political groups and participating in what they see as a unique historical opportunity to build a new parliament and develop its powers. Therefore, they consider that the legitimacy of the EP comes principally from its role as a 'talking shop' – a place for deliberation for people with very different backgrounds and interests. The role of the EP is to offer a space to debate and find a consensus on the future of the European integration process. It should thus be in a permanent dialogue with the Commission and the Council in order to reinforce the role of the EU and increase its weight at the international level.

Using the EP to promote or contest European integration

MEPs might also use the EP as a platform to either promote or contest the idea of European integration – a role that sets the Parliament apart from most national systems. Those who show a strong commitment towards the EU can be labelled 'European evangelists'; they are convinced Europeans, probably federalists, and they see their main task as promulgating the need for further European integration back home and abroad (see Box 8.4). Many of the MEPs who adopt this role have a clear European or international curriculum – they may have lived in different countries and speak several languages, which makes it easier for them to work with colleagues from other nationalities. For those that are interested in disseminating the idea of the EU outside its borders, a position like delegation chair, member of the Foreign Affairs (AFET) committee or especially the post of EP President might give them the perfect opportunity to travel and foster cooperation with external organisations. Indeed, the members of AFET have a high political profile; the committee counts about a dozen former foreign affairs

---

Box 8.4   An 'evangelist' and a 'public orator' react to Brexit

In the aftermath of the British referendum of 23 June 2016, pro- and anti-EU MEPs were quick to express their sentiments on an eventual Brexit. Among the French, two stood out for their diametrically opposed opinions: while Liberal Sylvie Goulard (2016) considered it 'a grave day' and that the UK should 'not hold other EU states to ransom', Marine Le Pen rejoiced and called it 'the most important moment since the fall of the Berlin Wall' (BBC 2016). Their reactions should not come as a surprise. Goulard – a former political advisor to Commission President Romano Prodi and short-lived French Defence Minister between May and June 2017 – has been an outspoken defender of European federalism and against the accession of Turkey. President of the French branch of the European Movement between 2006 and 2009, she is a habitual contributor in the French, British, German and Italian written press and has published numerous books, such as 'Europe for Dummies' or her latest work 'Goodbye Europe' on Brexit. In comparison, Le Pen rose as a frontrunner to the French presidency on clear nationalist and Eurosceptic stances. Despite declaring the EP 'democratic in appearance only, because it's based on a lie' (Le Pen 2016), she has used Parliament as a tribune. In comparison to her co-chair Marcel de Graaff, however, she was known to attend Parliament regularly and use her position as a political group leader to access information.

---

ministers or vice-ministers, half a dozen former ministers and a number of members with expertise in foreign or European affairs in a diverse number of roles – for instance, as ministerial advisors or chairs in their political parties. Others have had international or European careers in institutions such as NATO or the Council of Europe. An example of an MEP with a high profile and a role oriented towards the EU's external relations is Michèle Alliot-Marie, former French Minister for Foreign Affairs, Defence, Interior and Justice. Not only is she a member of AFET, but she also chairs the Delegation for relations with the Arab Peninsula.

However, not all those that take a strong position on European integration do it in a positive way. In the last years, there has been a rise in the number of Eurosceptic MEPs. As members of an assembly that represents an idea that is antithetic to their ideological positions, how do Eurosceptic MEPs behave and how do they understand their role? The most straightforward answer is: differently. There is not a single role orientation among those opposing the EU. Brack (2013, 2015) has identified four types of behaviour: the public orator, the absentee, the pragmatist and the participant. *Public orators* use the EP as a tribune – their activities concentrate on delivering speeches in plenary and advertising negative information about the EU either by asking questions or by using new technologies like Facebook or Twitter. They see themselves as the voice of those against further European integration and, as such, consider themselves the only proper opposition party in the EP. In this sense, they are not completely absent from the institution and do master their internal workings, although they do not participate actively in legislative work and focus more on disrupting its normal proceedings. The second type is that of the *absentee*, who, as the name indicates, is often missing from Parliament. Absentees are generally more visible in domestic politics as they put more emphasis on the national arena. Their absence can be due to their refusal to participate in the workings of the Parliament or just to indifference towards what they perceive to be an irrelevant institution. They do take advantage of the benefits offered by being an MEP, such as money and reputation, or the fact that in some countries it is easier for non-mainstream parties to win seats at the EP elections than in national polls – as is the case with Front National in France or UKIP in Britain. *Pragmatists*, in contrast, do want to be seen as efficient MEPs and, to achieve this, they tend to follow the rules and norms of the EP and engage with the system in an effort to change it from the inside. They become, thus, a form of 'constructive opposition', which can take the shape of institutional watchdogs. These kinds of MEP tend to use parliamentary questions to control the national government back home or to scrutinise EU policies, especially in those areas where it enjoys more competences. They can also act as constituency representatives and thus use their actions in the EP to deliver goods for their voters. Therefore, in contrast to the two previous types of Eurosceptic, pragmatists do participate in committees and may become rapporteurs if they see a chance to exert some influence on policy outputs. Finally, the *participants* can be found mostly among 'softer' Eurosceptics like those in the ECR group. They see themselves as normal legislators, not as part of the opposition. As a result, they act in perfect accordance with the rules and the practices of coalition-seeking; they 'play the game', even to the point where they compromise their ideological positions for the sake of finding an agreement. This type of MEP might reach relatively influential positions, like committee chair, and be an active rapporteur.

As mentioned above, roles are an ideal-type and real MEPs rarely fit one-to-one into them. For instance, Nigel Farage (British chair of the EFDD group) is probably the best example of a public orator (see also Box 8.4). He is well known for his irreverent speeches in plenary, which have contributed to his renown all over Europe. In 2010, he confronted former European Council President Herman Van Rompuy for having 'all the charisma of a damp rag and the appearance of a low-grade bank clerk' (in The *Guardian* 2010b) and he celebrated Brexit by telling other MEPs 'You're not laughing now' and accusing them of not having 'ever done a proper job in your lives, or worked in business, or worked in trade, or indeed ever created a job' (in The *Guardian* 2016c). At the same time, he holds the record for having the lowest level of participation in roll-call votes at around 40 per cent (votewatch.eu), which would fit better with the behaviour of an absentee. He has also been involved in various scandals that fit into the role of absentee, with repeated accusations of using expenses money to fund UKIP and pay for a constituency office that had been offered rent-free by a party supporter (The *Guardian* 2009, 2014b).

As for the other ideal-types, it is often difficult to associate Eurosceptic MEPs with the roles of pragmatist and participant. However, if one looks, for instance, at the activities and declarations of Morten Messerschmidt, a member of the Danish People's Party (since 2014 in the ECR group), one could identify him as a pragmatist. Although his campaign motto was 'More Denmark, Less EU', he is an engaged MEP, highly active in the Economic and Monetary Affairs committee. He has been critical of the role of the EU in dealing with the banking crisis, claiming that it interferes too much, and has attacked the EPP and the S&D for failing to advance negotiations in this area. As a member of the Constitutional Affairs committee, he also acts as a 'watchdog', participating in debates on the role of the Parliament in budgetary procedures or on financial matters. He has also promoted the idea of a 'Council of National Parliaments'. For an example of a participant Eurosceptic, there is Syed Kamall, co-chair of the ECR group and one of the British Conservatives in favour of Brexit. Despite his well-known Eurosceptic positions, as a chair of the third-biggest group in the EP, he needs to participate in the daily work of the EP and ensure that his party group is taken into consideration when building coalitions.

Following ideological lines? MEPs' voting behaviour

As we have seen with this overview of MEPs' roles, individual members may have different understandings of how their functions should be exerted. Their decision might depend on their personal motivations or other incentives like the electoral system in their member states. It shows, thus, that members can follow different interests and incentives when they decide how to behave and that might also play a role when they cast a vote. For instance, Eurosceptics – especially those that adopt the role of 'public orator' or 'absentee' – tend to vote against most decisions, regardless of whether they are actually against them or not; their behaviour aims to publicise their principled opposition to the EP and its activities (Brack 2015). What about mainstream MEPs? How do they vote in cases where the position of their national parties enters into conflict with that of their EP political group? The longitudinal study of roll-call votes has shown that, despite high levels of cohesion in EP groups, MEPs still tend to be more loyal to their national colleagues than their European ones: when a vote is highly salient at the domestic (or even local) level, especially when it affects the speed and depth of EU integration, MEPs tend to defect from their EP political group or abstain from the vote (Frantescu 2015; Hix et al. 2007; Meserve et al. 2017; Mühlböck and Yordanova 2017; M.K. Rasmussen 2008; see also Chapter 9).

This behaviour, however, is neither constant nor automatic: new members suffer more from competing demands, since they have not yet learned when they can disobey their national or European party. This is particularly visible among new MEPs from accession countries – they tend to show more loyalty towards their national parties than other newcomers from the older member states. However, with the experience gained by spending more time in the EP, both groups learn when to defect and who to defect from and display then similar behaviour to longer-serving MEPs (Lindstädt et al. 2012). The decision to defect can also depend on the career paths and levels of ambition displayed by MEPs. As seen at the beginning of this chapter, the EP has become a new home for young ambitious politicians willing to gain more experience and raise their profile. As a result, national parties are increasingly using the EP as a ground to test their young protégés with the idea of calling them back home after they have proved their worth. Therefore, young MEPs may have higher incentives to stick to their national party lines. Also, MEPs who seek a national career might become less loyal to their EP group when national elections come closer and they need to send a signal to their party back home (Meserve et al. 2009). This is particularly the case if the result of domestic elections is uncertain, in which case MEPs might prefer to signal their allegiance to national parties rather than to their EP political group (Meserve et al. 2017).

Finally, the conflict between national and European interests might be dealt with differently by MEPs whose national political party sits in government and those who are part of the opposition. Indeed, the former are under more pressure to vote along domestic lines when their eventual re-selection as candidates is in the hands of the national party leadership, especially if, in addition, it develops mechanisms to scrutinise and control how MEPs vote in the EP – that is, whether they stick to the governmental line or not (Finke 2014; Mühlböck 2012).

EP staff and MEPs' offices: expertise and the management of information

The EP has now around 6,000 officials (counting those working for political parties), which make up for 35 per cent of the EP's budget. This means that, if we include assistants, about 10,000 people work in the EP providing support to MEPs (Corbett et al. 2016: 253). These roles can be split into three groups. First, personal assistants are chosen directly by MEPs and fulfil both secretarial and political tasks, such as doing background research, drafting amendments, coordinating with other MEPs and advising on political decisions. Second, political advisors are part of political groups, and, therefore, in charge of steering negotiations according to their ideological lines, particularly when it comes to inter-institutional negotiations or determining voting positions. Finally, EP officials work in the Secretariat and hold the status of EU civil servants (although some work there with temporary contracts); they ensure the smooth running of the institution and provide a wide range of services, from security to translation and interpretation, although here we focus on the parliamentary work of administrators (cf. Pegan 2017). As can be seen, the tasks that these three groups fulfil often overlap and there is a high potential for competition and conflict between them. Indeed, there have been long-standing tensions between the EP Secretariat and the staff of political groups, who have repeatedly tried to take away any political tasks exerted by the Secretariat (Neunreither 2002).

Research into the behaviour and functions of these actors is growing fast and there are now two general approaches to investigating EP staff. The first one takes an organisational perspective and examines the profiles and backgrounds of those working in the EP in order to better understand their behaviour. These studies have shown that, although many of the people choosing to work in the EP share certain characteristics – they have generally had international experiences, speak several languages and have an academic background in European-related studies – their behaviour is more influenced by where they sit than where they come from. Therefore, their pre-socialisation (that is, characteristics such as nationality, gender or educational background) does not seem to matter once they start working in the EP; their behaviour can be better explained by looking into their job profiles: while assistants pay more attention to constituents' concerns, political advisors focus on ideology, whereas EP officials tend to stress issues that might affect the power or influence of the institution as a whole (Costa 2003; Egeberg et al. 2013, 2014; Michon 2004, 2008; Pegan 2017).

The second approach focuses on the growing importance of information and expertise for the EP. It questions the divide between political and technical issues and functions. The capacity of bureaucracies to exert influence on the policy process is not a unique phenomenon of the EP; indeed, one can identify four roles performed by bureaucrats. First, when they draft policy documents or draw agendas and minutes, they provide a *production* role, whereas their efforts to ensure that the institution runs smoothly and that people are aware of the procedural rules could be linked to a *maintenance* role. Bureaucrats can also provide a *service* role, for instance when they do background research on issues under discussion or offer advice on the implications of policy solutions. However, if this role goes further into *steering* the policy process, then bureaucrats have a chance to actually shape policy outputs and directly exert influence on the policy process (Neuhold and Dobbels 2015; Page and Jenkins 2005).

This section examines the different types of staff in order to understand both their organisational profile (that is, where they come from and how they behave) as well as the role they play in managing information in a parliament that has a direct impact on both technical and political decisions.

Assistants: acquiring and filtering information

Apart from the support offered by the EP's Secretariat and the staff of their own political group, MEPs can also employ personal assistants and trainees to support their day-to-day activities. Each member receives a 'parliamentary assistance allowance' as part of their budget – in 2016 the upper limit was set at a monthly sum of €23,392 per MEP. Each member has usually different types of assistant: at least a quarter of the allowance goes to those 'accredited' assistants who are directly employed by the EP and work in Brussels, Luxembourg or Strasbourg. They are the ones in charge of secretarial tasks, research and accompanying (or representing) the MEP in meetings. 'Local' assistants are based in the constituency, and, therefore, their contract follows national law. They help MEPs keep in contact with their electorate and organise visits, activities and party meetings when members are back home. Finally, members can also offer trainees (*stagiaires*) an opportunity to work for them, but their status will be regulated differently according to each political group or MEP.

In November 2015, the Parliament's Bureau decided to regulate the distribution of allowances across 'accredited' and 'local' assistants, since quite a few MEPs used the funds to finance a network of supporters back home who were often occupied in non-EP-related matters (Euractiv 2015). The working conditions of accredited assistants were made more stable with the adoption in 2009 of an Assistants' Statute (Regulation 160/2009), a long sought-after solution to the job insecurity and wide disparities in working conditions caused by the different national legislations that regulated their employment. Thanks to the Statute, assistants now receive similar benefits to other EU employees, especially when it comes to medical insurance and retirement benefits. MEPs have retained the right to choose freely their assistants, who are often selected among supporters of their national party or previous trainees, as well as their pay level. As a result, they are generally paid less than EP or political group staff and can be easily dismissed, which explains their lower status inside the EP and the higher rates of turnover (Corbett et al. 2016: 83–84).

Indeed, assistants are usually young and do not stay for long; for them, it is often a first step in their political career or an opportunity to build their networks and progress in their profession. Most assistants and *stagiaires* have a background in social sciences – mostly political science – and have often pursued programmes in European studies. They are highly mobile, with experiences abroad, and multilingual. Interestingly, those recruited via a political party are often those who display a weaker academic curriculum – there, getting a traineeship or an assistant post comes as a reward for their political activism (Michon 2004, 2008). Some assistants and *stagiaires* have gone on to pursue political careers, either as MEPs or at the national level. In some cases, the career path is reversed and former MEPs become assistants (Corbett et al. 2016: 82). Having some experience as an assistant or a political advisor can be helpful for new MEPs. For instance, Bulgarian MEP Eva Paunova remarked how 'as an assistant, I gained not only a unique understanding of every aspect of parliamentary and legislative work, but also managed to build valuable contacts and fruitful partnerships … These connections and experiences meant stepping into my new position as an MEP with higher expectations, allowing myself barely any time to adapt to my new role' (in The Parliament Magazine 2014a).

Assistants and MEPs' offices are essential in the process of gathering and filtering information. They are the interface between parliamentarians and citizens, interest groups and the media. Therefore, they yield considerable influence in managing the knowledge and information that reaches MEPs and who can access them directly. Their role has become increasingly important with the growing powers of the EP – MEPs now need to manage more files of a highly technical nature, while being held responsible for the potential implications of their legislative inputs. Therefore, in the words of a former assistant turned MEP, assistants need first and foremost 'knowledge, skills and networking' (Lenaers in The Parliament Magazine 2014b) to deal with the information overload and lack of time that characterises the life of a parliamentarian.

However, there is not just one type of assistant but a 'spectrum' that goes from 'being a personal slave to a chief executive policy adviser' (Lenaers in The Parliament Magazine 2014b). Indeed, the assistant spectrum covers many different types of task that have to be performed in an MEP's office. Secretarial tasks might comprise managing the diary, booking travel, sorting the email and phone calls and all other office jobs that make the daily life of an MEP easier. Legislative and research tasks might let assistants intervene in the policy process by writing speeches, doing background research, drafting amendments or own-initiative reports, offering political advice and any other activity that might facilitate the frontage performance of their MEP. Finally, assistants might also be in charge of public relations and organising events for external parties or their constituencies. Therefore, the spectrum covers roles that span from the purely secretarial to the political advisor – and it is perfectly possible for one person to cover the whole spectrum in a single day or over one parliamentary month (see Box 8.5). Multitasking is expected, but most offices also reveal a relatively hierarchical division of labour – where trainees are put in charge of photocopying or answering the phone, while more senior assistants are usually responsible

---

Box 8.5   The EP's calendar: Regimenting institutional life

One of the most common sights in the EP is its slightly vintage and very colourful calendar. The EP's life is compartmentalised in different weeks: committee week is pink, while the week dedicated to working with political groups is blue. Green weeks indicate constituency weeks, which means that MEPs will be travelling back home. In addition, red weeks or days indicate plenary sessions. The order of the weeks is not random – it follows a specific political cycle: legislative work is first prepared 'backstage' during committee week, followed up by any decisions on agreements and voting weeks that need to be made by each political group in group week. These decisions are then ratified during the plenary week in Strasbourg (or Brussels for the couple of mini-plenaries taking place there). MEPs then go back home during constituency weeks to disseminate the results of the votes.

This strict rhythm not only helps MEPs perform their different roles, it also allows EP staff to organise themselves and know when to expect the 'ebbs and flows'. It is also important for external actors – such as lobbyists and academics – to know the best time to have access to an MEP: no one wants to end up in Brussels and realise that everyone is in Strasbourg for the week! Therefore, the calendar is a reminder of the lack of time and constant travelling that MEPs have to accept, but it also facilitates forward planning and helps manage contacts with the external world (Busby 2013).

for following the work of the main committee where their MEP is a member – sometimes even replacing them (Busby and Belkacem 2013). Therefore, with most MEPs employing between two and three assistants and probably one trainee, 'the office of an MEP is like a small company' (Huitema in The Parliament Magazine 2014b). This means, however, that despite offering many opportunities to learn and advance in their professional careers, the job of assistant can also prove frustrating for highly educated graduates, since they are always in the shadow of their 'boss' (Michon 2008).

Busby and Belkacem (2013) identified three different functions that assistants might fulfil in their daily work. First, they act as gatekeepers, both physically and symbolically. As many researchers have experienced, assistants are the ones answering emails and phones and by so doing can facilitate or prevent access to the MEP. Second, they are also in charge of filtering communications, therefore they sort MEPs' inboxes so that they only receive information that is related to their priorities or that can help them be effective in their decision-making activities. They also act as their 'eyes and ears' to spot any important development. Finally, their most important task is that of tailoring information so as to shape the work of an MEP. That might imply doing research in their area of specialisation, but also acting as policy advisors. In this function, assistants might play an active role in the EP's policy process and might end up shaping policy outputs. For instance, in cases where MEPs prefer to concentrate on institutional matters rather than playing the role of policy specialists, it is not unheard of for an assistant to act as the actual rapporteur, attending meetings, writing the report and managing compromises with the other groups. This, of course, is not without risks – the MEP is ultimately responsible for the content of the report and losing control of it can also lead to awkward situations, as Louis Michel experienced in 2013, when it came to light that his office had proposed 150 amendments to the Data Protection Regulation redacted word-by-word by interest group representatives; he blamed his assistant, who immediately resigned, but it is still relevant to ask whether he really did not know about it, and if that is the case, what it says about his ability to manage his 'business' (Euobserver 2013a).

Political advisors

Parliamentarians also rely on advisors working for their political group to gain specific expertise on policy issues or institutional matters. Political advisors are often long-term figures in political groups and, therefore, are attuned to their preoccupations and biases. Indeed, part of the EP budget is dedicated to providing staff to support political groups: the 2016 budget foresaw €61 million to cover their various expenses, including staff, administrative costs and other information activities. This money cannot be used for electoral campaigns or to finance their national parties. The money was previously distributed according to the group's size and the number of languages used by its members, but in April 2015, the Bureau decided to change the rules. Since then, the non-attached members receive 60 per cent of the amount to which each MEP is entitled and the rest is then split among the political groups: 2.5 per cent of this remaining amount is given as a flat rate to each group and the remaining 97.5 per cent is allocated in proportion to their number of seats (PE 422.537/BUR). This complicated rule also reflects the way political advisors (that is, staff at the AD – administrator level) are distributed across political groups – 15 per cent of the positions are distributed equally across all groups, while additional advisors are then allocated in proportion to the group's size.

It is important to note that the number of staff allocated for political groups has increased steeply over the years – while in 1982 there were only 285 people working for the groups, in 2014 they came to just over 1,000 (including posts at the AST – assistant – level) (Corbett et al. 2016: 132). When it comes to those working at the AD level, numbers can change considerably depending on the group's size. In 2016, the EPP group had around 100 people working in its Secretariat, most of them doing parliamentary work, which involved following the activities of one or two committees or delegations. In comparison, the EFDD group had around 37 political advisors, which means that some of them needed to follow up on four committees at the same time. It is also interesting to see how different groups allocate posts – while the EPP had five political advisors following foreign affairs (AFET), the EFDD had only one and preferred to spend its resources on other committees like the ECON or LIBE committees. EP political groups have sought to further increase the number of staff; despite an agreement reached with the Council to reduce their number by 2019. In practice, by the end of 2016, the EP planned to add 76 new posts – meaning that some political groups like the EPP or the S&D would end up having a larger number of staff than of MEPs (Politico 2016f).

The selection of political advisors has become increasingly based on merit instead of political patronage, although holding the card of a political party does help (Corbett et al. 2016: 132; Egeberg et al. 2014). The position of political advisor is more stable than that of assistant and many spend their entire careers working for a political group. Some become MEPs or go on to pursue other political careers and it is not rare for them to become part of the EP Secretariat. Indeed, there are now rules that make it easier for political advisors who have been in the Parliament for over ten years to attempt an internal competition that allows them to become an EP official. Some of them have even been appointed to highly reputed positions; for instance, in 2016, the EPP pressured the EP to make one of its most influential policy advisors (Michael Speiser) head of the Directorate for Citizens' Rights and Constitutional Affairs, which coordinates the work of some of the most important EP committees like Civil Liberties, Constitutional and Legal Affairs, among others (Politico 2016d). Therefore, it is quite normal to see some staff members going back and forth between the political groups and the EP Secretariat, which has led to the emergence of a more politicised civil service and the development of a patronage system (Costa 2003).

How does the job of political advisor influence the behaviour of individual members of staff? Not surprisingly, people in these positions adopt more ideological views than other civil servants given that theirs is, after all, a political job. Their mandate is to 'sell' the political stances of their party group and advise their members on how to provide content to reports and amendments that will satisfy a majority of members in the group. Therefore, they tend to choose their contacts based on their political leanings and will listen to those interest groups that are closer to the concerns of their constituents. In addition, since they are working more closely with national delegations, they tend to pay more attention to national concerns (Egeberg et al. 2013, 2014; Winzen 2011).

EP staff

In contrast, EP staff provide technical support, particularly in very salient files or when specific expertise is required. Their intervention may prove essential in shaping outputs and choosing specific solutions during negotiations. Permanent EP staff are recruited through the *concours* system – an open competition to become a European civil servant. Members of the Secretariat are thus subjected to the general EU Staff Regulations, which explicitly indicate that civil servants need to 'carry out the duties assigned to [them] objectively, impartially and in keeping with [their] duty of loyalty to the Communities' (Article 11). This means that they cannot exert an openly political role and need to offer a service to MEPs of all ideologies. In addition, the EP also employs temporary and contractual agents, who are there for a limited period of time or to do a specific job, as well as *stagiaires* working under the Robert Schuman trainee scheme.

As mentioned above, staff are separated between administrators (AD), assistants (AST) and secretarial posts (AST/SC). The AD group is composed of translators and interpreters (who, due to the existence of 24 official languages in the EP, have become the largest group) and administrators, who are employed in a wide variety of tasks, such as human resources, research or committee work. They usually stay only between three and seven years in their position and are then forced to rotate jobs – either inside their own service or (more rarely) in a completely different DG. Finally, it is important to remark that, although the Secretariat has historically had its seat in Luxembourg, only a third remains there, while the majority of its staff sits now in Brussels, especially those who are in close contact with MEPs and help with parliamentary work (Corbett et al. 2016: 256–258, 271).

At the top of the Secretariat sits the Secretary-General, a political heavyweight acting mostly behind the scenes. As mentioned in Chapter 3, the Secretary-General is appointed by the Bureau (Rule 222); therefore, despite officially being civil servants, secretaries-general have often had a clear political profile and forged their careers working for political groups. For instance, Sir Julian Priestley, who served between 1997 and 2007, had acted as Secretary-General for the socialist Group (1989–1994) and became Klaus Hänsch's (German Socialist) *chef de cabinet* during his presidency between 1994 and 1997. Klaus Welle – appointed Secretary-General in 2009 – was Secretary-General of the EPP from 1994 until 2003. He was also *chef de cabinet* under Hans-Gert Pöttering (also a German Christian Democrat) between 2007 and 2009. Welle has become a controversial figure due to his institutional activism – largely inspired by the US Congress – which has led him to make substantial changes to the EP's structure. He was responsible for setting up a new European Parliament Research Service (EPRS) – an attempt to provide MEPs with an in-house think tank that helps to sever the EP's dependence on the Commission as a source of expertise and technical information (see Box 8.6).

Welle was also the mastermind behind the new Parlamentarium, the Parliament's visitor centre, which offers an overview of the Parliament's history and functioning but also other activities such as role-play games for groups. However, having a clear political profile does not always help: after 2012, tensions increased between Schulz and Welle. These were partly due to different visions of how the EP should grow – with Welle preferring more expertise and credibility and Schulz attempting to concentrate powers around the political groups and his role as EP President; it also reflected an ideological clash that hid power struggles over administrative decisions. The feud led Schulz to empty Welle's duties by giving more powers to the deputy Secretary-General and appointing his *chef de cabinet*, German Martin Winkler, to this position, thereby increasing Winkler's chances to succeed Welle in 2019 (Der Spiegel 2016; Politico 2015c). One could say that Welle was very happy to see the resignation of Martin Schulz in 2017 as he greeted the election of Tajani 'as a triumph of the institution over its personalities' (Politico 2017i).

Under the Secretary-General, the EP's Secretariat is organised into 12 DGs and the Legal Services. The role of the DGs is varied: some take

Box 8.6   The political life of information: Experimenting with the EP's research service

There is probably no other type of service that has seen as many structural changes as parliamentary research. Since the early days, the Secretariat realised the importance of providing information to support the parliamentary work of its members and complement other sources like the Commission or national governments. To this effect, DG Research (IV) provided in-depth studies and background research for specific reports, but only rarely worked directly with rapporteurs. Indeed, the need for independent advice has been the source of a steady increase in EP staff dedicated to providing research and expertise – made even more transparent with the establishment of a new European Parliament Research Service (EPRS).

However, the attempt to model the EP's research services on the US or German models is not new – already in the early 1990s there were proposals to change DG Research into a fully-fledged documentation centre. This idea was not successful and the DG was ultimately incorporated into the DGs Internal and External Policies in 2004 under the form of 'policy departments'. These five units provide a horizontal service and are not attached to specific committees. In 2016, they had just over €9 million to acquire external expertise, generally in the form of in-depth studies (Corbett et al. 2016: 262; Neunreither 2002).

This model did not prove as satisfactory as expected and the circle was closed when a new DG for Parliamentary Research Services (the EPRS) was re-established in November 2013. The EPRS presents itself as an in-house think tank that aims to 'to provide independent, objective and authoritative information' (https://epthinktank.eu/about/). It is organised around three directorates: the Members' Research Service, which provides tailored analysis to support MEPs' parliamentary work; the library, which includes the historical archives; and the Impact Assessment and European Added Value directorate. The last is probably the most innovative, since it monitors the entire policy cycle and aims to build enough independent expertise to compete with the Commission. For instance, it provides reports on the 'Cost of Non-Europe' and ex ante impact assessments to evaluate the need and potential repercussions of EU legislation. It also has units doing ex post impact assessments and assessing whether the European Council has delivered the commitments made during its meetings (see also Box 5.1). Finally, the EPRS also integrates the long-standing Scientific Foresight Unit, which analyses emerging issues identified by the Science and Technology Options Assessment (STOA) panel.

care of research, communication, translation, security or finances, while three of them – Presidency, Internal and External Policies – have a more political role, since they are heavily involved in the organisation of the EP's legislative work and its relations with external bodies. At the higher levels, there is an attempt to distribute positions across nationalities, although the larger member states tend to be better represented – for instance, in 2017, there were three Italian directors-general and two French. When it comes to gender balance, there is still work to be done, since at that point in time, only two out of 13 directors-general were female. Generally, the Secretariat has witnessed a steep increase in its numbers that corresponds to various factors: for one, the different enlargement waves brought more members and more languages; at the same time, this geographical widening was accompanied by the deepening of EU integration and an increase in the workload and influence of the EP. Its growing role as co-legislator created new demands for the Secretariat, like a new unit to deal with conciliation and co-decision negotiations and a gradual strengthening of the committees' secretariats.

The Secretariat occupies an ambiguous position in the EP's structure: unlike other bureaucracies, it is well provided with resources and staff but at the same time does not display the *esprit de corps* or independence of other civil services. This is due to its history and development: the structure of the Common Assembly needed an active Secretariat that would support parliamentarians who were not permanently there and often fulfilled a double mandate. As this is still the case, one of its functions is to keep the institution 'ticking over' while MEPs are travelling (Busby and Belkacem 2013: 8). At the same time, the multilingual and international character of its staff has made it more difficult to develop an institutional culture and common interests. The EP Secretariat is also, unlike many national ministries, a 'service administration': its role is to help and support the MEPs, not to impose their choices (Costa 2003). Therefore, it would be rare to see many Sir Humphrey Applebys (the infamous Cabinet Secretary in *Yes, Minister*) in the Parliament. Most agree that interpersonal relations are key to exerting influence in the EP: successful officials need to prove their expertise and gain the trust of MEPs, and, therefore, should avoid getting involved in political controversies which might affect their status as neutral players. This does not mean that, behind the scenes, officials do not take part in the political game – indeed, they are very sensitive to the political needs of MEPs and might shape reports or proposals differently depending on whether they draft them for the Greens or the ECR group. Therefore, the line between 'neutral' and 'politicised' technical advice is very thin and might require acting with some finesse and a high dose of intuition (Dobbels and Neuhold 2013; Winzen 2011).

Still, EP officials tend to emphasise sectoral and expert considerations over ideological ones and they hold the Commission as their privileged source of information (Egeberg et al. 2013). This is not surprising, since the EP Secretariat now acts mostly as a source of institutional memory and an expert in procedural and legal issues. In a parliament with a high turnover of MEPs and assistants, it becomes all the more important to have permanent staff that can provide a longer perspective on (inter-)institutional issues and specific policy proposals. Their position often helps to avoid overlaps, conflicts between different policy sectors and contradictions with past decisions. This experience turns EP officials into natural 'archives' of the institution that MEPs can consult and ask for advice. Apart from providing expertise, officials – especially those attached to committees – exert other (more banal) tasks that can also shape decision-making processes. Simple things like drafting an agenda, deciding on the timing of debates, helping table amendments and voting lists or choosing external experts for hearings can have major effects on allowing certain actors to participate in the process (or not) and pushing for specific policy solutions or compromises (Winzen 2011).

However, the chances for the EP Secretariat to exert direct influence seem to have decreased over time. For one, assistants and political advisors have become increasingly important and have taken over many of the more political functions exerted by officials in the past (Neunreither 2002; Pegan 2017). In addition, co-decision seems to have been a poisoned chalice for the Secretariat – although many of its officials fought relentlessly to increase Parliament's powers, their success has actually curtailed the chances for officials to play an active role – MEPs are now more active when it comes to drafting reports and taking a stance on legislative matters. As a result, co-decision has actually diminished the Secretariat's scope for intervention, especially when negotiations become more contentious and there is more need for coordination and compromise (Dobbels and Neuhold 2013). Some have noted, however, that committee secretariats have become more important actors in trilogue negotiations (see also Chapter 11). They often participate in the 'speed-dating' meetings organised at the start of Council Presidencies to set the legislative priorities of the co-legislators. EP staff might even replace chairs in trilogue meetings and negotiate on behalf of the committee. In addition, the EP Secretariat now provides a 'project support team' for each trilogue, which is there to offer legal support, research assistance and advice from the Conciliations and Co-decision Unit (Roederer-Rynning and Greenwood 2017: 743).

Indeed, it seems that there are certain conditions that make it easier for EP staff to play a role in policy-making. First, in cases where MEPs have had no experience with a specific procedure (for instance, if they are new to co-decision) and the file under discussion is not excessively salient or important, it will be more likely that officials will use their expertise to advise MEPs in procedural and technical matters. Also, when Parliament is very cohesive and there are no major ideological conflicts, it is easier for the Secretariat to steer the process and propose solutions. In contrast, if a file is seen as highly salient or in cases where there are major conflicts between political groups, then officials are likely to exercise only a production role. Even more interesting, it has been noted that the 'steering role EP officials adopt is linked to the preservation of the institutional prerogatives of the EP rather than to the provision of policy expertise' (Neuhold and Dobbels 2015: 591) and linked to its role 'as "guardian" of the rights of the institution claiming a bigger role in the policy-making process' (Dobbels and Neuhold 2013: 387). It seems, thus, that officials are particularly good at steering the process when it is seen to affect the institutional powers of the EP – that is, its 'institutional patriotism' (Priestley 2008). This, however, might become problematic, since the new generation of officials seems to be cut from a different cloth: in comparison to the 'old guard', they are less attached to this institutional idea and more concerned with fulfilling more administrative and technical roles (Costa 2003).

Conclusion

MEPs play an essential role in capturing the multiple demands coming from outside the EU's political system and translating them into (policy) outputs. However, these demands can enter into conflict and force individual members to choose. How MEPs set their priorities may depend on a range of factors, such as the salience of an issue back home, the position of their national or European party or the influence of specific interest groups. However, the process of filtering and ordering these priorities also hinges on how individual MEPs understand their role as parliamentarians. MEPs who see themselves as the voice of their constituents might be more prone to defect from their EP political group than those who seek to pursue a career inside Parliament. Therefore, from the moment they step into the EP, their role perception colours their choices – not only how they vote, but also which committee they try to get into, whether they try to climb the leadership ladder or become interested in the internal functioning of the institution. However, roles are ideal-types – there is probably not one single MEP who fits perfectly into one of the descriptions that have been given here – and they can be performed concurrently depending on the setting. For example, an institutionalist might suddenly become a policy advocate when interacting with specific interest groups or members of a legislative committee. Finally, although most of these roles are not exclusive to the EP and could be found in most other parliaments, the roles adopted by Eurosceptic MEPs are largely unique to the EP and show us the limitations of considering it a 'normal' Parliament. Not many other parliamentary systems welcome within their doors representatives that are there to contest the very existence of the institution and the political system it embodies.

MEPs choose the roles they believe are adequate to perform frontstage; however, this performance would not be successful without the intensive work going on backstage, mostly done by the staff hidden behind them. From *stagiaires* to the Secretary-General, staff in the EP is at the service of parliamentarians. This means that they have a wide margin of manoeuvre and, under certain circumstances, can steer the policy-making process and exert some degree of influence on policy outputs. They are, indeed, an additional filter provided by the EU's political system that serves to mediate and manage the link between inputs and outputs. However, EP staff are part of a service administration and that means that, effectively, they can steer and advise but never impose. Indeed, it is their position as filter and interface that allows them to manage the flows of information, a basic resource for any policy-making system. Therefore, the tasks of assistants, political advisors and EP officials often overlap, but we can see differences depending on their position. Therefore, where they sit does shape who they are and what they do. In any of these positions, their functions cover both a technical and a political dimension, which means that these two aspects are complementary rather than exclusive and dependent on the context in which each of these actors operates behind the scenes.

Chapter 9

Political Groups and National Party Delegations

Introduction: multi-level party politics

Parties are often considered essential elements of democratic systems (Schattschneider 1942) – they are the transmission belts that help to input demands into the political system while providing the necessary stability for this system to work. Parties aggregate individual members into a coherent whole and provide the necessary ideological orientation to help form coalitions and pass legislative proposals. As we have seen in Chapter 6, Article 10.4 TEU considers that '[p]olitical parties at European level contribute to forming European political awareness and to expressing the will of citizens of the Union'. At the same time, the nature of the EP elections, the lack of clear majorities and the absence of government/opposition dynamics suppose a challenge for those embarking on the study of the EU's party system. On the one hand, Chapter 6 has shown us how tenuous the link between electors and their MEPs is. Indeed, the second-order nature of the elections and the control of national parties over nominations even question the necessity of stable political parties. Why invest in formal parties if they cannot reward (or sanction) MEPs with votes (re-election) or offices (government)? On the other hand, the EP's party system has existed since the establishment of the Common Assembly and has managed to maintain a high degree of stability. This means that MEPs see in political groups an added value when trying to translate demands into outputs. Indeed, political groups show a high level of ideological coherence and an increasing level of internal cohesion. This chapter examines their role and how we can explain this efficiency despite lacking some of the core instruments of party control over their members.

Research on the EU's party system has greatly benefitted from the 'comparativist' turn that took place in EU studies in the mid-1990s. By leaving behind the understanding of the EU as a 'unique' case, comparative politics drew from a wider range of classical literature on national party politics (e.g. Sartori 1976). While it opened a new field of research, it also underlined the differences between the EU and more traditional political systems. Even comparisons with the US Congress need to be strongly nuanced and adapted to fit the particularities of political parties

in the EP (Lindberg et al. 2008). Therefore, we need to think about political parties in the Parliament as nested in a complex system of multi-level
party politics (Crum and Fossum 2009; Hix 2008a; Lord 2002; Mair
and Thomassen 2010; Moon and Bratberg 2010).

One of the difficulties in studying the complexity of party politics in
the EU is its terminology. The multiple levels of representation are often
confused and given similar names, which does not help in distinguishing
these different phenomena. To this effect, we use here the terminology given by Lindberg and his colleagues (2008), who differentiate
between the *transnational parties* that operate inside the EP (what we
have called 'EP political groups' but which are sometimes referred to
as 'Europarties'), the *European party federations* that operate outside
of the EU institutions and help to coordinate national parties in the
same political family (that is, extra-parliamentary organisations like
the Party of European Socialists), the *national party delegations* (NPDs)
that exist in each EP political group and serve to coordinate the work of
MEPs who belong to the same national party and, finally, the *national
parties* in charge of candidate nominations to the EP elections. These
four categories make up the main levels of governance in the European
party system, although we could add an additional regional level –
especially in member states with federal or federal-like political systems
(De Winter and Tursan 2003).

This chapter examines the role of political parties inside the EP in
order to understand why they have become highly institutionalised in a
system where it would not necessarily be expected. It also explains their
level of ideological coherence and voting cohesion in order to better
understand the patterns of coalition building in the framework of the
EU's multi-level governance system.

Political groups: aggregating demands and seeking cohesion

In the EP, MEPs sit with their political group, not with members of the
same country. Therefore, the presence of political groups is central to
the workings of the Parliament and enhances the supranational character of the institution (Gaffney 1996; Hix and Lord 1997; Kreppel
2002; Maurer et al. 2007). The composition of EP groups has remained
relatively stable in the last decades, with two large groups dominating
its political life. As Lord (2002: 42) noted, the EP provides a 'complete
parliamentary party system [and includes] all the party families to be
found in various member states'. The centre-right Christian Democrats –
now the EPP – are the largest group in the EP and are flanked on the

right by the conservative ECR, the Eurosceptic EFDD and the far-right ENF group (for more information on these groups, see Brack 2013; Jansen 1998; Wagner 2011). Parties on the right of the EPP have shown difficulties in maintaining a stable membership and a coherent profile (Abedi and Lundberg 2009; Startin 2010). On the left side of the political spectrum, the Socialists – now the S&D – represent the largest number of MEPs (cf. Külahci and Lightfoot 2014). They are joined on the left side of the spectrum by the Greens/EFA and the far-left GUE/NGL, which comprises mostly reformed communist parties (Dunphy and March 2013). Finally, ALDE occupies the middle ground and is, hence, often essential to build winning majorities (cf. Smith 2014).

This reduced number of EP political groups hides a high diversity in terms of individual national parties (Table 9.1). The steady increase in national parties in the EP can be attributed to various factors. The various enlargement waves have been a source of structural growth, since they have automatically led to a rise in the number of domestic parties being represented in the EP. They have also led to more ideological diversity, since each new member state has brought with it different concerns and political priorities. In particular, the enlargement to Central and Eastern Europe in 2004 and 2007 was seen as a major challenge, since the party system in post-Soviet countries was characterised by a different set of political cleavages, high volatility in the number and type of parties and a growing presence of Euroscepticism (Szczerbiak and Taggart 2008). However, Western Europe has also experienced deep changes to its party system, with a growing importance of groups focused on niche issues, such as the environment, regionalism and far-right nationalism (Ladrech 1996). There are, however, no clear differences in the number of parties in old and new member states: Malta has the lowest number of parties with a clear bipartisan system, while Spain shows a highly fractioned domestic party system – a reflection of its regionalist structure as well as the emergence of new parties like Podemos or Ciutadans/Ciudadanos.

Table 9.1 also shows that the same political group in the EP may house various national parties from the same country. Consequently, parties that might be used to competing against each other at the domestic level become partners in the EP. For instance, ALDE has two Dutch parties as members: the People's Party for Freedom and Democracy (Volkspartij voor Vrijheid en Democratie [VVD]), which is economically liberal but more conservative on social issues, and the Democrats 66 (Democraten 66 [D66]), a post-materialist party that is very liberal on social matters (Viola 2015: 8). This has led to regular splits within the Dutch national delegation on topics like counter-terrorism and data protection – which has clear repercussions for ALDE as a whole, since the Dutch delegation

Table 9.1 *Number of national parties in EP political groups (February 2017)*

Member state	EPP	S&D	ALDE	ECR	Greens/EFA	GUE/NGL	EFDD	ENF	Non-aligned	Total
Austria	1	1	1	0	1	0	0	1	0	5
Belgium	3	2	2	1	2	0	0	1	0	11
Bulgaria	2	1	1	2	0	0	0	0	0	6
Croatia	2	1	2	1	1	0	0	0	0	7
Cyprus	1	2	0	(1)	0	1	0	0	0	4(1)
Czech	3	1	1	1	0	1	1	0	0	8
Denmark	1	1	2	1(1)	1	1	0	0	0	7(1)
Estonia	1	1	2	0	1	0	0	0	0	5
Finland	1	1	2	1	1	1	0	0	0	7
France	1(1)	2	4	0	1	2	1	2	2[1]	14[1](1)
Germany	1	1	2	2	3	1(1)	1	1	2	14(1)
Greece	1	2	0	1	0	2(1)	0	0	2	8(1)
Hungary	2	2	0	0	2	0	0	0	1	7
Ireland	1	1	1	1	0	1(1)	0	0	0	5(1)
Italy	3	1(2)	0	1	1[2]	1(1)	1	1(1)	1[3]	8[2,3](4)
Latvia	1	1	1	1	1	0	0	0	0	5

Lithuania	1(1)	2	1	1	0	1	0	0	7(1)
Luxembourg	1	1	0	1	0	0	0	0	4
Malta	1	0	0	0	0	0	0	0	2
Netherlands	1	2	2	1	2	1	1	1	11
Poland	2	0	4(1)	0	0	1	1	1	12(1)
Portugal	2	1	0	0	2	0	0	0	6
Romania	3(1)	3	1	0	0	0	1	0	10(2)
Slovakia	3(1)	0	3	0	0	0	0	0	7(1)
Slovenia	3	1	0	1	0	0	0	0	6
Spain	1(1)	2	0	4	4	0	0	0	16(1)
Sweden	2	2	0	1	1	1	0	0	9
UK	0	1	2	3	1	1	1	2	12
Total	45(5)	39	27(3)	26²	21(4)	8	10(1)	10^{1,3}	223 (16)

[1] Two members of the French Front National decided to sit as non-aligned.

[2] One member of the Italian 5 Stelle party sat with the Greens instead of the EFDD.

[3] One member of the Italian Partito Democratico sat with the non-aligned.

Numbers in parentheses indicate MEPs standing as independents.

Source: European Parliament.

is one of its strongest components. In a few cases, MEPs from the same national party have decided (or been persuaded) to sit in a different EP political group, as is the case of Jean-Marie Le Pen, who was suspended from his own party for various racist utterings and forced to seek exile in the non-attached group.

Despite the potential for internal conflict and ideological disunity, political groups in the EP have managed to hold high levels of internal coherence and voting cohesion (Bressanelli 2013; Hix et al. 2003). They have been able to aggregate a wide range of interests and created a minimum amount of stability that ensures efficiency and influence in day-to-day legislative policy-making. What is all the more surprising is that EP political groups have managed to establish a durable party system based on a left-right ideological dimension without the instruments that national parties usually employ to control their members.

Aggregation: to what extent are EP political groups coherent?

As we have seen in the previous chapter, MEPs tend to vote according to their ideology rather than their nationality. However, that does not mean that the EP as a whole will automatically translate the positions of its members (and their constituents) into policy outputs that reflect coherent and stable ideological dimensions. We need, therefore, to examine whether EP party groups are organised along specific dimensions of politics and how this comes about.

Studies looking at the voting behaviour, electoral programmes and even tweeting activities of the EP groups confirm that the positions taken in the EP are not random, but organised along a bi-dimensional political space. Political groups can be situated along two main axes: a left-right ideological axis and a pro-/anti-EU one. It is important to note that they are orthogonal dimensions, that is, anti-EU groups can be situated both on the right and on the left of the political spectrum (Hix et al. 2006; McElroy and Benoit 2012; Raunio 1999).

The presence of these two dimensions means that, while EP groups show high levels of internal coherence, there are clear differences between them. Therefore, we can identify distinct 'party families' among the EP groups – for instance Socialists, Christian Democrats, post-material groups like the Greens, etc. Rose and Borz (2013) checked the similarities between national party programmes and the dominant position of their respective EP groups and found a high degree of correlation. Therefore, there is a match between the ideology of parties at the European level and their national members and this relationship has nothing to do with the size of the group – it applies to both larger and smaller political groups. This, of course, is relevant to assess the quality of representation: the more there is an ideological match between EP political groups and their national delegations, the better EU citizens will be represented at the European level. More importantly, the coherence of EP groups and the importance of an ideological dimension have not changed substantially after the 2004 and 2007 enlargements. Although many expected to see a big rupture in the EP's party system with the entrance of post-Soviet countries, various studies show that the left-right dimension has continued to structure inter-party cleavages. Therefore, we see a high level of coherence inside the groups, although some like ALDE have been more disrupted by the entrance of the Central and Eastern European countries, while others, like the EPP, have actually managed to increase their coherence (Bressanelli 2014; Schmitt and Thomassen 2009).

The remaining question is: why would political groups show high levels of internal coherence? Of course, as we have seen in Chapter 3, national parties have pragmatic incentives to join an EP group. On the one hand, the formal rules of procedure make it difficult to create new political groups since, at the time of writing, a minimum of 25 MEPs is needed from at least seven member states. Remaining as a non-attached party is also unattractive, since this status confers less speaking time, no voting rights in the Conference of Presidents, less funding, etc. Therefore, for national parties joining the EP for the first time, there are high incentives to become a member of an already existing group. It is the only way to access positions such as rapporteurs, committee chairs or other political offices – those that are at the source of political influence in the EP. Nevertheless, this explanation is not sufficient to understand why EP groups show such high levels of ideological coherence. If aggregation into political groups was only due to pragmatic reasons, one would rather expect the opposite to happen: national political parties would opt for 'marriages of convenience' that would hide wide ideological differences. Although that was the case with some post-Soviet parties, their choices were also determined by the legitimacy that affiliation to an EP group would give them vis-à-vis their national competitors (Bressanelli 2014).

Indeed, the main explanation for coherence resides in the search for political congruence between national and European parties, that is, their ideological compatibility (McElroy and Benoit 2012). Congruence appears almost in a functional manner: when deciding on which EP group to join, national parties examine the positions of EP groups and make sure that they represent the major values of their own party, which, in turn, leads to a very high degree of shared positions and ideology (Rose and Borz 2013). At the same time, EP political groups screen the ideology of candidate parties to ensure that their positions do not diverge too much and make internal decision-making too complicated.

Table 9.2   *Cohesion in the European Parliament*

	EPP-ED (EP6)/EPP	PES (EP6)/ S&D	ALDE	UEN
2004–2009	88%	91%	89%	76%
2009–2014	92.63%	91.54%	88.40%	–
2014–2016	93.71%	91.99%	88.69%	–

Source: Votewatch.eu.

Political congruence explains also why some national parties decide to switch groups or form a completely new political group: if the differences between the core values of the European and national groups grow, a split might be necessary to accommodate the ideological needs of both partners. For instance, when the UK Conservatives took a turn towards more Eurosceptic positions in 2005, their positions on the pro-/anti-EU integration dimension became increasingly difficult to accommodate within the Christian-democratic group. In the end, they decided to split and create the new Eurosceptic conservative ECR grouping (McElroy and Benoit 2010).

Voting cohesion: a necessary condition for policy influence

In national parties, there are two important reasons for party discipline and cohesiveness, namely building majorities that can ensure the support of a party's position in government and sanctioning rebel voters. These two mechanisms do not exist in the EP; European party groups lack the power to seek votes or promise governmental offices. As we have seen in Chapter 6, candidate selection is in the hands of national parties, and the European political groups or the extra-parliamentary federations cannot do anything about it. At the same time, after 2014, the appointment of the Commission might be more closely tied to the outcome of the EP's elections, but its members are still proposed by national governments. Therefore, EP political groups lack the essential sticks and carrots that help domestic parties achieve internal cohesion. And yet, cohesion is as crucial for the functioning of European political groups as it is for their national counterparts: it allows parties to translate inputs into their preferred outputs. If parties vote cohesively, it makes it easier to estimate

Greens/ EFA	*GUE/NGL*	*IND/DEM*	*ECR*	*EFD (EP7)/ EFDD*	*ENF*
91%	85%	47%	–		
94.68%	79.37%	–	86.65%	48.59%	–
95.62%	83.32%	–	79.27%	48.48%	69.89%

how many MEPs are likely to support a proposal, which is essential in forming stable coalitions and passing legislation.

In a transnational and highly diverse parliament, cohesion is deemed to be more difficult to achieve, since it needs to take more views into account (Raunio 1999: 192). It is, thus, surprising to see the high levels of cohesion that most EP political groups have achieved in the last legislatures (Table 9.2). Cohesion in the EP is now even higher than in the US Congress (Hix and Høyland 2013: 181). Indeed, various studies show that cohesion has remained high over time and across different policy areas. Generally, the Greens, the S&D and the EPP are the groups with the greatest cohesion, while the far-right and Eurosceptic groups show the greatest difficulties in voting together (Cherepnalkoski et al. 2016; Hix and Noury 2009).

The question is, therefore, how do EP groups manage to achieve such levels of cohesion? We can find three types of explanation based on preferences, institutions and processes. Preference-led explanations are grounded on a functional argument: if national parties base their choice of EP group on ideology, then it is not surprising that MEPs from the same group vote together. Their cohesion can be explained by ideological homogeneity: the party does not need to exert pressure or use sanctions, because their members hold very similar opinions and automatically follow the same voting behaviour (Kreppel 2002). This explanation seems to hold even after the last big enlargement: MEPs from the new member states show even more loyalty towards their political groups than those from old member states, which seems to indicate that cohesion is largely due to similar ideological preferences (Bressanelli 2014).

Models based on institutions look at the formal rules and organisational incentives that might facilitate or hinder cohesion. As seen above, the EP does not offer very auspicious conditions, since EP groups have to function without the sticks and carrots – that is, offices and votes – at the disposal of national parties. There are, however, some sanctions that can be used to ensure discipline. For instance, those who defy the voting position of a political group might be sidelined and have a more difficult time getting offices – notably committee chairmanships – or reports (Faas 2003; Yoshinaka et al. 2010). Indeed, as we have seen in previous chapters, political groups have undergone processes of power concentration. Political leaders – especially through the Conference of Presidents – have now much tighter control over final voting decisions and the allocation of key offices; their personality may also have a direct impact on the quality of cohesion in a group (Bailer et al. 2009). Hix (2008a) argues that this process can be largely accounted for by looking at the empowerment of the EP and the need to delegate certain competences and powers to the leadership in order to find a more efficient division of labour – although the reasons why national parties would accept losing power are not yet clear.

Finally, the third set of explanations looks at the policy-making process in order to understand how political groups reach their voting positions. The argument here is that cohesion in the EP can be largely explained by the need to find compromises inside each political party, across political parties and with the Council. Indeed, Bowler and McElroy (2015) point at the absence of contestation in plenary votes, which means that having high levels of cohesion does not matter much if all EP groups vote in the same direction. It indicates, rather, that conflicts have been settled before they reach the plenary and that the behaviour of EP groups is largely shaped by norms of consensus (see also Chapter 11). This mechanism has been explained by Ringe (2010), who proposed a model of 'perceived preference coherence', where expert MEPs inside each committee serve as focal points for other members of their national delegation or political group. Therefore, non-expert MEPs generally rely on the judgement of expert colleagues to cast their final vote. Cohesion here is largely explained by the process of policy specialisation that occurs in committees and the central role this plays in striking intra- and inter-institutional agreements (see Chapter 10). EP committees can be used to achieve specialisation and serve as a focus of orientation and learning for those MEPs and group leaders who are not as involved in particular decision-making processes as their members (Hix et al. 2009; McElroy 2001).

However, as we have seen in the previous chapter, these high levels of cohesion should not hide the tensions faced by MEPs on a daily basis – namely the need to accommodate the demands of their EP group with those of their national party. Certainly, on a day-to-day basis, MEPs may be able to ignore the shadow of re-election and the pressures from their national party, but when conflicts do arise, individual members tend to vote with their national party rather than their EP group (Coman 2009; Hix 2008a; Meserve et al. 2017; A. Rasmussen 2008a). This shows that, despite this gradual process of institutionalisation of EP political groups, national parties remain the main point of reference for many MEPs.

National party delegations: the link between Europe and home

National party delegations (NPDs) are the institutions that connect the different levels of governance in the European multi-level party system. Their influence in the European party system can be roughly estimated by comparing the differences in cohesion between the national party delegations and the transnational party as a whole (Table 9.3).

In most cases, NPDs are almost perfectly cohesive (Faas 2003), which means that, despite the growing institutionalisation of EP groups, individual MEPs consider their national party an even more important reference point. Therefore, they represent a source of anxiety for EP political groups, which have seen national parties increase their attempts to supervise and control their national delegations in the EP in the last couple of decades (Raunio 2000; Whitaker 2011).

Stealing power away from EP political groups

The emergence of national delegations inside EP political groups came as a response to the growing size of the Parliament and the need to find a better way to represent national particularities. Since the EP formally ignored geographical representation, EP political groups developed internal rules to ensure a fair distribution of key positions among their national delegations. In practice, this means that most positions (group bureau; committee and delegation chairs, vice-chairs and membership; political coordinators; working groups' chairs, etc.) are distributed following the D'Hondt principle among the NPDs and then allocated by the leaders of each national delegation. This makes it more difficult for EP group leaders to reward or punish their members and reinforces the power of the NPDs (Kreppel 2002: 203–204).

In addition, most groups are largely dependent on their largest delegations. Historically, there have been two dominant delegations inside the S&D – with the UK and Germany (sometimes joined by Italy) accounting for almost half of the group members – while in the

Table 9.3   *Cohesion in NPDs – Top three and bottom three national delegations per political group (July 2014–December 2016)*

	Country	National party	Loyalty to party group
EPP			
1.	Romania	Partidul Naţional Liberal	98.97%
2.	Lithuania	Tėvynės sąjunga-Lietuvos krikščionys demokratai	98.87%
3.	Bulgaria	Citizens for European Development of Bulgaria	98.67%
...	...	...	...
48.	Belgium	Christlich Soziale Partei	86.41%
49.	Belgium	Centre Démocrate Humaniste	80.90%
50.	Cyprus	Independent	75.84%
S&D			
1.	Portugal	Partido Socialista	99.53%
2.	Croatia	Socijaldemokratska partija Hrvatske	99.39%
3.	Lithuania	Lietuvos socialdemokratų partija	99.13%
...	...	...	...
37.	Denmark	Socialdemokratiet	90.57%
38.	Sweden	Arbetarepartiet-Socialdemokraterna	89.79%
39.	Sweden	Feministiskt initiativ	82.88%
ECR			
1.	Finland	Perussuomalaiset	96.86%
2.	Bulgaria	Internal Macedonian Revolutionary Organization (VMRO)	95.93%
3.	Italy	Conservatori e Riformisti	95.20%
...	...	...	...
26.	Germany	Alternative für Deutschland	74.53%

→

→

27.	Denmark	Independent	71.69%
28.	Greece	Independent	37.22%

ALDE

1.	Bulgaria	Movement for Rights and Freedoms	99.16%
2.	Estonia	Eesti Reformierakond	98.82%
3.	Lithuania	Lietuvos Respublikos liberalų sąjūdis	98.71%
...	...	...	...
37.	Ireland	Independent	76.00%
38.	Latvia	Zaļo un Zemnieku savienība	75.51%
39.	Italy	Independent	70.95%

GUE/NGL

1.	Germany	DIE LINKE	96.27%
2.	Italy	Lista Tsipras-L'Altra Europa	96.12%
3.	Portugal	Bloco de Esquerda	93.53%
...	...	...	...
20.	Denmark	Folkebevægelsen mod EU	83.83%
21.	Portugal	Partido Comunista Português	79.62%
22.	Netherlands	Socialistische Partij	75.58%

Greens/EFA

1.	Hungary	Együtt 2014 – Párbeszéd Magyarországért	99.25%
2.	Spain	Esquerra Republicana de Catalunya	99.12%
3.	Germany	Bündnis 90/Die Grünen	99.10%
...	...	...	...
24.	Spain	Iniciativa per Catalunya Verds	93.41%
25.	Latvia	Latvijas Krievu savienība	93.16%
26.	United Kingdom	Scottish National Party	92.77%

→

→

EFDD			
1.	United Kingdom	United Kingdom Independence Party	76.91%
2.	Czech Republic	Strana svobodných občanů	71.72%
3.	Sweden	Sverigedemokraterna	70.29%
4.	France	Sans étiquette	58.33%
5.	Italy	Movimento 5 Stelle	51.83%
6.	Lithuania	Partija Tvarka ir teisingumas	41.29%
ENF			
1.	France	Front national	78.19%
2.	France	Front national/ Rassemblement Bleu Marine	77.02%
3.	France	Rassemblement Bleu Marine	76.15%
…	…	…	…
6.	Italy	Lega Nord	48.45%
7.	Netherlands	Partij voor de Vrijheid	47.61%
8.	Austria	Freiheitliche Partei Österreichs	44.56%

Source: Votewatch.eu.

EPP, the German Christian Democratic Party/Christian Social Union (CDU/CSU) has tended to dominate (Kreppel 2002: 204–205). This is less the case in the 2014–2019 Parliament, where the Italian and German social-democratic delegations dominate, but to a lesser extent than in the past. In the EPP, influence has become even more widely spread, with the German delegation clearly in the lead, but followed by much smaller delegations (see Table 9.4).

In general, the larger NPDs have a disproportionate influence over EP groups and, if they manage to work together, they can sway the positions of the entire group. In addition, individual NPDs can develop alternative organisational structures, with their own officers – for instance chairs and treasurers – staff and financial resources that make it easier to function independently from the EP political group. Bigger delegations can participate in more committees and have

Table 9.4 *Size of the largest national delegations in the EPP and S&D groups (February 2017)*

	National party delegation	Number of MEPs	Percentage of total number of members
EPP	*49*	*217*	
Germany	Christlich Demokratische Union/Christlich-Soziale Union	34	15.67%
France	Les Républicains	19	8.75%
Poland	Platforma Obywatelska	19	8.75%
Spain	Partido Popular	16	7.37%
Italy	Forza Italia	13	5.99%
Hungary	Fidesz	11	5.07%
S&D	*38*	*188*	
Italy	Partito Democratico	29	15.34%
Germany	Sozialdemokratische Partei Deutschlands	27	14.29%
UK	Labour	20	10.58%
Spain	Partido Socialista Obrero Español	13	6.88%
France	Parti Socialiste	12	6.35%
Romania	Partidul Social Democrat	12	6.35%

Source: Votewatch.eu.

more resources to check reports and follow debates, which helps them to keep better informed about potential conflicts. These formal and informal resources put them at a clear advantage over smaller NPDs (Busby 2014; Corbett et al. 2016: 139; Kreppel 2002: 204; Raunio 1999: 190–191).

National party delegations as instruments of control

In addition, NPDs serve also as a direct link between the EP and national politics, and, therefore, are a potential mechanism for national parties to control the activities and loyalty of their members. As we have seen in Chapter 6, the ability of national parties to control their members is directly linked to the electoral system: MEPs elected via closed-list systems are more dependent on their national parties than those elected with open lists. This means that candidate (re-)selection may be a strong instrument to control individual members, especially in those cases where NPDs have a say on future electoral lists. There, NPD leaders might effectively use re-selection as a sanction for those individual members that do not stick to the party line (Kreppel 2002: 205; Mühlböck 2012).

Control can come from more informal sources, such as the capacity of national parties to keep informed about what goes on in the EP and to provide guidance or even instructions on how the NPD should vote in a given issue. Formal and informal links between NPDs and national parties have grown in the last decades. Most MEPs are involved in the work of their national party and participate in their executive organs, for instance as members of national party working groups dedicated to European affairs. When it comes to smaller parties that have difficulties getting elected to parliament back home, it is not uncommon that an MEP will serve as a national party leader. This has been the case with Caroline Lucas for the Greens in the UK and Bernd Lucke for the Alternative for Germany (AfD) until he was ousted in 2015 from the party's leadership. The links between NPD and national parties are stronger when the latter are in government, since they need to ensure better coordination and some consistency in their voting behaviour. A failure to do so might expose the national party to embarrassment in the media or cause difficulties for their colleagues in the Council, especially if they are in the minority or dealing with a particularly salient issue for their member state (Busby 2014; Corbett et al. 2016: 140; Costello and Thomson 2016: 781; Mühlböck 2012).

Lastly, as we have seen above, NPDs are in a better position to formally sanction their members, since they are in control of both carrots and sticks. It is an NPD prerogative to allocate benefits, such as committee membership or rapporteurships. Therefore, they can reward loyal members with positions that allow them to exert influence over the policy process. At the same time, they can also punish those that systematically defect from the party line or even go against its principles by asking their national party to suspend them from the party membership (Corbett et al. 2016: 142). Of course, it might not be surprising to hear that most cases of suspension or expulsion have affected far-right MEPs, although there are some examples in mainstream groups. For example, in 2015, UKIP suspended its EP party whip, Janice Atkinson, after she was accused of an expenses fraud, thus becoming the latest in a long list of problematic cases in the Eurosceptic party (see Corbett 2017). Accusations of vote rigging led the Estonian Reform Party (a member of ALDE) in 2013 to expel Kristiina Ojuland from the party.

Although fraud has been the most recurrent ground for suspension, other MEPs have been sanctioned for their racist or extreme behaviour. Jean-Marie Le Pen's expulsion from his own party after a series of racist interventions is probably the most infamous example. In other cases, parties have expelled MEPs for disloyalty. Brian Crowley, the only member of Fianna Fail elected to the EP in 2014, decided to move from ALDE to the ECR group – a decision that enraged his party and led to his expulsion. Therefore, although suspending or expelling members is an extreme sanction, it is not unheard of and can be actively used by an NPD to control their MEPs.

The importance of national party delegations in the everyday life of MEPs

One should not see NPDs only as an instrument of control. Their importance for the everyday life of the EP resides rather in their capacity to act as a framework that helps MEPs negotiate their multiple roles, especially when controversial issues between the national party and the EP group arise (see also Chapter 8). NPDs help MEPs to remain informed in the day-to-day life of the EP and help them negotiate the conflicts between their national and ideological roles (Busby 2014). This function is important in two different respects: first, it helps to coordinate and improve efficiency; second, it also promotes compromise and the formation of a cohesive party line.

NPDs function as the 'first port of call' for a majority of MEPs: members of the same national group are generally located in close proximity in the EP buildings (for instance, along the same corridor), which makes it easier to use NPDs as the first contact point when in need of information or advice. NPDs also play a crucial role in socialising new members and staff – helping them learn the routines and codes that inform such a complex institution as the EP. Finally, they help increase efficiency by organising regular meetings that function as clearing houses: members of the same NPD can inform the others about upcoming negotiations, potential conflicts and important decisions with the knowledge that they share not only ideological but also similar geographical concerns. Therefore, it is in these meetings (which take place in the committee, group and plenary weeks) where NPDs decide whether to vote with the EP group or whether they need to defect. Coordinating positions is important to increase leverage in the EP group, but also to be perceived as a reliable and serious delegation in those cases where it decides to defect. Indeed, voting against the EP group line is not such a big issue when the decision is known in advance and can be taken into consideration during the process of building coalitions (Busby 2013, 2014). As Ringe (2010) has shown, group cohesion basically depends on an endogenous process that consists in finding compromise at various levels of decision-making. NPDs are essential to this process. When facing a vote, most MEPs check whether a colleague from their national delegation sits on the committee in charge of the report. If that is the case, they generally follow their advice. If there is not a member of their NPD on that committee, they look for members of their EP group. Therefore, MEPs tend to 'triangulate' the information they receive from their EP group and their NPD representatives. If the positions diverge, a political group might face high uncertainty when the time to vote in the plenary comes, which means that most political groups try very hard to coordinate and negotiate their positions before they get to plenary voting.

Ringe's main point is, therefore, that we need to understand the relationship between NPDs and EP groups as fluid. Positions are not dictated from above (or from outside in the case of NPDs), but are negotiated endogenously. Therefore, it is crucial to understand who is perceived as an 'expert': for instance, when an NPD forms its position, rapporteurs, shadow rapporteurs or political coordinators might be seen as more authoritative and knowledgeable than the leader of an NPD and might exert more influence than the instructions received from their capitals. In the end, understanding how EP groups achieve cohesion is a matter not just of checking whether NPDs and political groups share the same position, but rather of looking at it as a process where the positions of political groups emerge after a long process of negotiating and building compromises among its different NPDs.

Coalition formation: an issue of size?

The process of finding a cohesive position within a group does not occur in a vacuum; political groups are under constant pressure to find compromises across their own national delegations *and* with other political groups. As we will see in Chapter 11, this process is all the more complicated by the need to build coalitions that make an agreement with the Council possible. Consensus is, therefore, a basic norm in this complex process of policy-making. That might explain why the EP has been dominated by a grand coalition dynamic – whereby the two largest groups (the EPP and the S&D) tend to vote together in the plenary.

The predominance of the grand coalition is due to a combination of ideological and structural factors.

Indeed, size and ideology have served as the two main factors to explain coalition-building in the EP. Size has become a crucial matter since the mid-1980s, when the EP introduced new rules that favoured larger groups and limited the independence of smaller political groups (Kreppel 2002). Size is, therefore, crucial to examine the weight and power of larger and smaller political groups during the process of coalition-building. That is why 'power indices' have often been used to calculate how many groups are necessary to reach a winning coalition and which groups might be pivotal to the process of building majorities (Hosli 1997). Size is, indeed, a key determinant for groups when they need to evaluate whether they have enough support for certain amendments or a political agreement with the Council. Therefore, 'the likelihood that a party will be pivotal or decisive is highly correlated with the size of the party group relative to the other parties' (Hix et al. 2005: 214). As we have seen in Chapter 4, the need to reach an absolute majority of EP members in the second reading of the co-decision procedure makes coalition-building a challenging enterprise. In the 2014–2019 legislative term, the only winning coalition that reached the absolute majority threshold (376) was a grand coalition of the EPP and the S&D (406 votes). A right-wing coalition of the EPP, the ECR and ALDE could ensure 359 votes (up to 373 if one added the radical and Eurosceptic groups EFDD and ENF). The left-wing coalition was even weaker, with 360 if one counted the S&D, the Greens, GUE/NGL and ALDE. Therefore, the rising number of Eurosceptic and radical MEPs at the wings of the EP has reinforced this trend, since it has reduced the size of mainstream political groups and made it more difficult to build coalitions along ideological lines (see Box 9.1). Therefore, it is not so surprising to see the two largest groups voting together more often, especially when issues are salient and the outcome of the vote is more uncertain (Kreppel and Hix 2003).

Indeed, in Figure 9.1, we can see that the EPP and the S&D are in almost 90 per cent of the votes part of the winning coalition. However, the figure also shows that ALDE is equally part of the majority in most occasions (see also Cherepnalkoski et al. 2016). Why would that be the case? If we think of coalition-building in terms of size, ALDE is not necessary to form stable coalitions, even when an absolute majority is required. This 'super grand coalition' has been a normal pattern in past legislative terms. Hix and Høyland (2013: 179) calculated that over 60 per cent of the winning coalitions in the sixth and seventh parliamentary terms were 'super grand coalitions' – while right-wing and left-wing coalitions each won in 15 per cent of the votes. The

Box 9.1   The election of Antonio Tajani and the end of the 'grand coalition'

On 17 January 2017, Italian EPP member Antonio Tajani secured a victory against his countryman Gianni Pittella (S&D), only after an 11th-hour deal struck between Guy Verhofstadt and Manfred Weber, leaders of ALDE and the EPP. Guy Verhofstadt played a rather curious role: he had initially been in the running for the post, which led him to seek an agreement with the Eurosceptic, populist 5-Star movement – a move ultimately rejected by his federalist-minded group. This impasse led him to withdraw his candidacy and switch his support to Tajani, while securing a backroom deal that ensured the end of the grand coalition between the EPP and the S&D. The existence of the grand coalition had been denied by both parties, until the S&D decided to nominate Pittella for the EP's presidency – at which point Weber revealed that the two parties had been in agreement since the contraction of a previous backroom deal formalised in 2014.

The mid-term reshuffle led to the formal demise of the grand coalition, which was replaced by a coalition agreement between the EPP and ALDE. However, given that this coalition only reached 259 votes, it opened new questions regarding its chances of survival and the position of other key players like the S&D and the ECR. Some saw the new coalition as a chance to end the status quo and allow for clear political choices between left and right, especially in light of the 2019 EP elections. The S&D called the end of the grand coalition a moment of 'liberation'. Indeed, this new balance of power offered the prospect of real adversarial politics, with the left-wing parties developing into proper opposition parties. However, given that the new coalition remained far away from an absolute majority, it might become more dependent on fringe groups like the ECR, which could potentially lead to a more politicised second half of the 2014–2019 legislature (Crombez 2017; Euobserver 2017b; Euractiv 2017a, 2017b; Politico 2017b). At the same time, the numerical majorities might lead to a de facto continuation of the grand coalition, with the EPP and the S&D continuing to vote together in a majority of files.

overwhelming presence of 'super grand' or oversized winning coalitions has been explained by looking at both institutional and ideological factors. On the one hand, there are institutional factors that incentivise the formation of oversized majorities. As we have seen previously, the formal rules of co-decision force political groups to seek wide support for a proposal, especially if they are afraid that they may not reach enough support in the first reading and need to go to a second reading

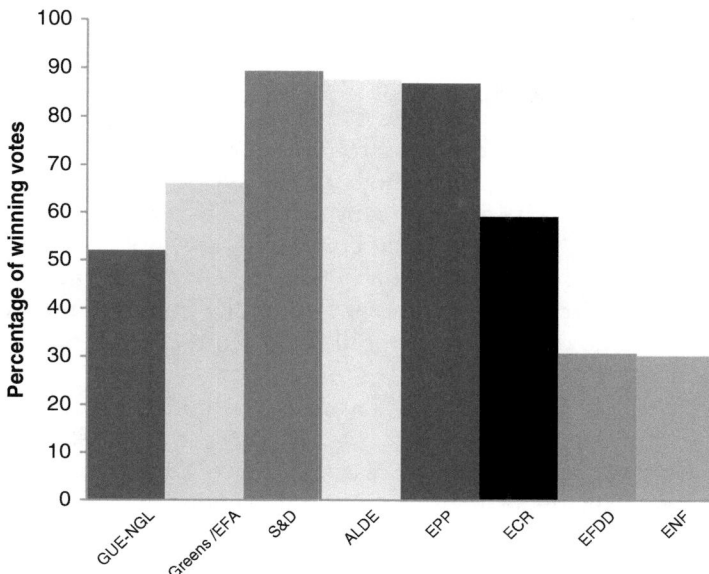

Figure 9.1   *Percentage of votes in which political groups are on the winning side (July 2014–December 2016)*

Source: Votewatch.eu.

– therefore, these kinds of majorities are more normal in co-decision than in consultation (Finke 2012). However, big coalitions can also serve another purpose, namely that of exerting pressure on the Council by showing a unified front and widespread support for an EP position (Kreppel and Hix 2003). Rose and Borz (2013) even speak of a 'black-red' cartel (that is, the S&D and the EPP) willing to sacrifice their ideological differences in order to secure collective benefits and maximise the influence of the EP in negotiations with the Council.

On the other hand, ideology might not be as absent as we might think in coalition-building. The ideological distance between the S&D, the EPP and ALDE is often smaller than one might imagine, especially when it comes to deciding on regulatory or technical matters or when decisions affect the internal organisation of the EP (Bressanelli 2014: 152). There are, certainly, some differences across policy areas, but they are minimal. In most cases, the 'super grand coalition' tends to vote together; for example, between July 2014 and December 2016, the EPP and the S&D formed a coalition and ALDE joined them in almost 94 per cent of cases (votewatch.eu). It is also not surprising that ALDE is often part of the winning coalitions, since 'on average the EU produces a particular set of policy outcomes that is close to the preferences of many European liberal parties and centrist voters' (Hix and Høyland 2013: 181). Even if in some policy areas policy outcomes are more left-wing (such as civil liberties or gender) or more right-wing (for instance international trade, internal market and industry or agriculture), the Liberals tend to then fluctuate with the majority, and move their position accordingly to the left or the right side of the political spectrum (Hix and Høyland 2013). Therefore, even if we see a high proportion of 'super grand coalitions', this does not mean that they are necessarily sacrificing their ideology. Given the importance of consensus in EU politics and the nature of the policies under discussion, winning coalitions are generally minimum-*connected*-coalitions (Hix et al. 2005).

Therefore, coalition-building is a matter of both size and ideology; these two requirements provoke clear tensions for the political groups, which often have to choose 'between forming a grand coalition and competing along political lines' (Hix and Høyland 2013: 179). This tension might also raise concerns regarding the degree of political representation and the capacity of political groups in the EP to communicate clear and distinct programmes to the electorate – a problem closely related to the perceived deficit in democracy and political competition in the EU's political system (Rose and Borz 2013).

European party federations

Despite the absence of a government and proper EU elections, embryonic forms of transnational political parties have emerged over time. European party federations have been central in managing the domestic and ideological tensions that naturally occur in such a multicultural and multilingual setting. There are now 17 'political parties at European level' that function as the extra-parliamentary counterparts to EP political groups (see Table 9.5). Their evolution has run parallel to the institutionalisation and emancipation of the Parliament and they have developed a wide-range of coordination and policy-making functions. The question remains, however, whether these transnational federations have the necessary autonomy to exert influence and have some impact on the EU's political system.

The evolution of European party federations

As can be seen in Table 9.5, there have been three main waves of party emergence – before the 1979 direct elections, between 1980 and 2003, and from 2004 onwards. These waves respond to three main drivers leading to the formation of new transnational parties.

First, the announcement of EP direct elections gave the necessary impetus to persuade the three main political groups to institutionalise transnational cooperation in the form of political federations. In 1973, the Confederation of the Socialist Parties – in 1992 transformed into the Party of European Socialists – paved the way and was followed in 1976 by the European People's Party and the Federation of European Liberals and Democrats (ELD) – which evolved into the Federation of European Liberal, Democrat and Reform Parties (ELDR) and in 2012 adopted the same name as its EP counterpart, namely, the Alliance of Liberals and Democrats for Europe (ALDE). Despite this initial enthusiasm, it quickly became clear that the formation of federations and the direct mandate for the EP elections did not translate into a 'Europe of the parties'. The role of these federations remained loose and weak, very dependent on the capabilities and ideological differences of their members; therefore, although they managed to issue manifestos for EP elections, these generally reflected the lowest common denominator among their members (Hix and Lord 1997; Pridham and Pridham 1981).

Despite these structural limitations, the 1980s saw the emergence of regionalist parties, which regrouped under the European Free Alliance in 1981, and some loose forms of cooperation among Green groups. It was, however, the ability of the main three groups to join forces in the eve of the Treaty of Maastricht that led to an important victory in the form of Article 138a TEU, which formally recognised the importance of political parties for the functioning of the EU's political system (now Article 10.4 TEU). This paved the way for a process of constitutionalisation, in which European federations looked for new forms of influence in EU politics beyond the Parliament. Most of the big federations aligned their party meetings to coincide with the major intergovernmental conferences – promoting new ways to advance partisan views across the EU institutions (Hix and Lord 1997). It was in this period (1993) that the European Federation of Green Parties emerged – converted into the European Green Party in 2004.

However, the major driver for expansion and emancipation of European party federations came with the decision to create a statute for European parties (Regulation 2004/2003/EC), which was expanded to European foundations by the amending Regulation 1524/2007/EC (see Box 9.2). These two regulations have been replaced with Regulation 1141/2014/EU, which consolidates two essential elements for the creation of genuine European parties: legal personality and funding. According to the 2014 regulation, a 'political party at the European level' should: (1) represent at least one-quarter of member states, MEPs or members of a national or a regional parliament or (2) have received at least 3 per cent of votes in at least one-quarter of member states in the last EP elections. (3) They have to show a past or future interest in

Table 9.5 *European party federations registered and financed by the European Parliament*

	Existence	Maximum funding for 2017 (in euros)	Links to EP political groups	Number of national party members (and individual members)	Number of MEPs
Alliance for Direct Democracy in Europe	2014–	1,102,643	EFDD	6(4)	22
Alliance of Conservatives and Reformists in Europe (formerly Alliance of European Conservatives and Reformists)	(2009)2016–	2,468,649	ECR	24(1)	56
Alliance of Liberals and Democrats for Europe Party (formerly European Liberal Democrat and Reform Party and European Liberals and Democrats)	(1976)(1986)2012–	2,468,649	ALDE	60	50
European Alliance for Freedom	2010–	419,639	ENF, EFDD, NI	individual membership	n/a
Alliance of European National Movements	2009[1]–	419,639	NI	n/a	n/a
Alliance for Peace and Freedom	2015–	419,639	NI	11	4
Coalition pour la Vie et la Famille	2016–	299,109	n/a	individual membership	8

Party	Period	Amount	Group		
Europeans United for Democracy (formerly EU Democrats)	(2005)2014–	419,639	GUE/NGL	11(7)	1
European Christian Political Movement	2002[2]–	499,993	ECR	15	3
European Democratic Party	2004–	552,500	ALDE	15(4)	11
European Free Alliance	1981–	781,229	Greens/EFA, GUE/NGL, ECR	38	12
European Green Party (formerly European Federation of Green Parties)	(1993)2004–	1,865,999	Greens/EFA	41	38
European People's Party	1976–	8,893,000	EPP	78	216
Movement for a Europe of Nations and Freedom	2014–	1,696,660	ENF	5	30
Party of European Socialists	1973(1992)–	6,941,145	S&D	33	191
Party of the European Left	2004–	1,624,939	GUE/NGL	34	28
Movement for a Europe of Liberties and Democracy	2011–	grants only between 2012 and 2015	ECR	8	4
Alliance for Europe of the Nations	2002–2009	grants only between 2004 and 2009			
Alliance of Independent Democrats in Europe	2005–2008	grants only between 2006 and 2008			
The Libertas Party Limited	2008–2010	grants only in 2009			

[1] Funding since 2012; [2] Funding since 2010.
Source: European Parliament.

Box 9.2   Political foundations at the European level

Political foundations function as support organisations of European party federations; they promote their goals and contribute to fostering political debates on European issues. In addition, political foundations organise events such as seminars or conferences and develop policy studies. Their funding is coupled to the same criteria that apply to federations and is also capped at 85 per cent, which is more problematic for them, since they might not have another source of income that provides the additional 15 per cent. The grants are supposed to be used for the programme activities of the foundations, such as meetings, research, administrative or travel costs, but not for campaigning or financing national parties. Most party families now have a political foundation (Table 9.6).

Table 9.6   *Political foundations registered and financed by the European Parliament*

Political foundation	European party federation	Maximum grant awarded for 2017 (in euros)
Larger political foundations		
Wilfried Martens Centre for European Studies	European People's Party	5,357,039
Foundation for European Progressive Studies	Party of European Socialists	4,536,250
European Liberal Forum	Alliance of Liberals and Democrats for Europe Party	1,487,768
New Direction-Foundation for European Reform	Alliance of Conservatives and Reformists in Europe	1,487,768
Green European Foundations	European Green Party	1,127,277
Foundation for a Europe of Liberties and Democracy	Movement for a Europe of Liberties and Democracy	1,010,392
Transform Europe	Party of the European Left	983,080

→

→

Smaller political foundations		
Initiative for Direct Democracy in Europe	Alliance for Direct Democracy in Europe	670,655
Centrum Maurits Coppieters	European Free Alliance	457,035
Institute for European Democrats	European Democratic Party	403,750
Christian Political Foundation of Europe	European Christian Political Movement	310,164
Europa Terra Nostra	Alliance for Peace and Freedom	262,098
Identités & Traditions Européennes	European Alliance of National Movements	262,098
European Foundation for Freedom	European Alliance for Freedom	261,250
Fondation Pegasus	Coalition Pour la Vie et la Famille	190,000
Organisation for European Interstate Cooperation	Europeans United for Democracy	Funded until 2016

Source: European Parliament.

Depending on their size, political foundations offer various benefits: while larger ones can contribute to the work of European party federations by drafting programmatic documents and developing scientific expertise, smaller ones might not have enough resources to play such extensive roles and focus on working with the members or act as a laboratory for new ideas. These differences also hide the existence of two different models among political foundations. 'Brussels-oriented' ones tend to make European party federations their main audience and contribute more actively in developing their political programmes, whereas 'Germany-type' foundations are more oriented towards member states and emphasise activities that foster civic education and democracy-building. In general, however, these foundations share a common weakness: they are largely ignored by national political parties, which do not engage much in their activities (Gagatek and van Hecke 2014).

participating in the EP elections and, (4) most importantly, 'observe ... the values on which the Union is founded, ... namely respect for human dignity, freedom, democracy, equality, the rule of law and respect for human rights, including the rights of persons belonging to minorities' (Article 3.1c). In addition, federations have to declare their incomes and expenditures, cannot accept donations over €18,000 per year per donor and can only claim up to 85 per cent of annual expenditures from the EU budget.

These rules are not unproblematic: when it comes to financing European party federations, the Regulation specifies that the money provided by the EU cannot be used to finance national parties or their candidates. While some have argued that this curtails the ability of transnational federations to participate in and influence the activities of national parties, especially during the period preceding the EP elections (van Hecke 2010), the bigger challenge is how to prevent fraud and recover misspent funds. In recent years, there have been various scandals, where mainly far-right and Eurosceptic federations such as the Alliance for Direct Democracy in Europe (linked to UKIP), the Movement for a Europe of Nations and Freedom (Marine Le Pen's party federation) and the Movement for a Europe of Liberties and Democracy (led by the Danish People's Party) have used EP money to pay for the activities of national parties and their members (Politico 2016a; The *Guardian* 2016b; The Parliament Magazine 2016b). These cases have led to an increasing malaise among mainstream EP groups, which have tried to find ways to stop or even ban funding for these parties. The attempts to do so have failed – either because the federations only exposed an anti-EU sentiment (which is not formally prohibited) or because it has been difficult to prove that some of the members committed offences *against* the EU values while acting in the name of the European party federation. Since 2016, the EP has tried to limit funding to some extremist parties by requiring bank guarantees (especially if they had been involved in funding scandals in the past) or, as in the case of the far-right Alliance for Peace and Freedom, setting up special committees to examine the activities of the federation and whether they conform with EU values (Euobserver 2016b, 2017a).

Therefore, while the introduction of the statute has led to a new wave of Europeanisation in the EU's party system, it has mainly facilitated the emergence of far-right and Eurosceptic groupings. The latter have been characterised by their instability and constant splits, which makes it very difficult to trace membership and linkages with EP political groups. In addition, we have also seen the emergence of party federations on the left of the political spectrum – notably the European Left, which reunites the post-communist (and more Europeanist) national parties.

At the centre, a new European Democratic Party aims to reassemble liberal parties to the right of ALDE and from the centre of the EPP group, while on the right, the soft Eurosceptic European Conservative and Reformists was created under the initiative of the British and Polish delegations, which wished to move away from the Christian-democratic tradition prevailing in the EPP.

Functions and influence of European party federations

Do European party federations actually matter? Do they have an impact on the EU's political system? Although these questions remain open for discussion, there is some agreement on the kind of functions that transnational parties play.

The major role that they fulfil is that of coordination. Some have called them 'co-ordination nuclei' (Delwit et al. 2004: 10) or 'co-ordinating nexus[es]' (Lightfoot 2005), since they provide a venue where members of the same party family can meet and share ideas and information. Party federations provide a vertical and horizontal connection between members: on the vertical level, it allows them to keep in touch with other national parties and follow any relevant policy developments or new practices; on the horizontal level, it facilitates contacts between members of the same ideological family sitting in different EU institutions, bringing together MEPs, Commissioners and national governments sitting in the two Councils. This function can be particularly important when decisions – notably the appointment of the Commission President – do not depend on one institution but require some inter-institutional linkage (Hix and Lord 1997; Poguntke et al. 2007; van Hecke 2010).

This coordination function has had socialisation effects among the national and European political elites. Socialisation has helped to Europeanise national parties by providing feedback and feeding them with best practices; it has also underlined the impact of EU politics on domestic affairs and the necessity for national parties to engage with the European level. At the same time, socialisation in European federations has necessitated a process of ideological dialogue and approximation. The act of coming together in transnational parties has often revealed deep ideological disagreements, but also helped to surmount these divisions and create a common party culture. While the PES had to find a 'common cause' between the more traditional socialists and the new social-democratic variants, the European Left and the European Greens faced rather a division between their Europeanist branches and their more sovereignist or decentralised members (Dietz 2000; Dunphy and March 2013; Hix and Lord 1997; Lightfoot 2005; Poguntke et al.

2007). Over time, European party federations have served to define the new party cleavages in the EU and acted as promoters of democratic norms and specific programmatic profiles in post-communist countries. European party federations have also helped aspiring members to gain legitimacy by separating the wheat from the chaff and determining who qualifies as a democratic and appropriate partner (Bressanelli 2014; Chryssogelos 2017).

Despite these different roles, the question of impact, especially policy-making impact, remains. Party federations have adapted their structures to make the most out of this function: since the early 1990s, they organise party summits before each European Council in order to align their positions and enhance information flows. Some federations like the EPP and the PES also convene before ordinary Council meetings, so that their ministers, group coordinators and Commissioners can be apprised of the most recent developments in each institution (Corbett et al. 2016: 146). Transnational federations are also responsible for drafting electoral manifestos, which should then guide the actions of Commissioners, EP groups and national parties. Whether these efforts at influencing policy-making yield any results is still an open question, but some have remarked that those EP groups that are represented in one single transnational federation show more cohesion than those like ALDE, the Greens/EFA or the ECR that are split into several European party federations (Thorlakson 2005).

Towards genuine transnational parties?

Transnational federations have become more emancipated, especially after the introduction of the political parties' statute. Since then, most parties have become more independent of their EP groups, setting separate secretariats and hiring their own staff (Corbett et al. 2016: 147), which has led to higher levels of institutionalisation and increasing similarities in their organisational structures. They have been remarkably skilful at dealing with diversity and change, managing to incorporate a rapidly growing number of national parties and building a common ideological core (van Hecke 2010). Certainly, diversity is still important inside these federations: the size and weight of national delegations can have a decisive impact on their direction and cohesion (Delwit et al. 2004; Pridham and Pridham 1981).

However, despite their success in promoting coherence among political elites, transnational party federations have failed to develop a similar link with citizens – their electoral connection remains extremely weak. This is not surprising, since European party federations remain highly dependent on both national parties and EP groups: their capacity to act is too restrained by their lack of say in decisions over office, votes or policies. European party federations may help to coordinate the appointment of important offices like the European Council or Commission Presidents, but the ultimate decisions rest on member states. Similarly, despite playing a growing role in the drafting of manifestos and the coordination of electoral campaigns (especially since the appointment of Spitzenkandidaten in 2014), they still have no say in the (re-)selection of individual candidates, which is in the hands of national parties. Finally, we have seen how limited their opportunities for guiding and influencing policy-making can be. These shortcomings make it difficult to characterise European party federations as genuine European parties. They remain, first and foremost, party networks, albeit with the institutional potential to become something more in the future (Delwit et al. 2004; Dunphy and March 2013).

Conclusion

Political parties are key components of the EU's political system: they help to input demands and translate them into outputs by providing ideological lenses to problems and solutions. However, although European parties have become central actors to the policy-making process, we should be careful in drawing comparisons with their national counterparts. European parties remain embedded in a multi-level system that constrains them and curtails their normal functions as instruments of aggregation and representation (Blomgren 2015). Certainly, there is now a left-right political system that covers the entire ideological spectrum; at the same time, the need for intra- and inter-institutional consensus often renders ideological cleavages moot (see also Chapter 11). The lack of a government/opposition dynamic, the absence of transnational parties that organise Europe-wide electoral campaigns and the inability of citizens to distinguish between different political programmes confirm some of the main arguments for the proponents of a 'democratic deficit' thesis.

It is, therefore, not surprising that parties have also been the main response to these arguments. Since its inception, the EP has been seen as a solution to the lack of democratic representation in the EU, and with it, the necessity to have a proper parliamentary system. Hix and his colleagues (2007) have repeatedly put forward the idea that giving more power to the parties might be the best solution to the representation gap that exists today in the EU. A clearer link between political programmes and the election of the Commission might make it easier for citizens to select between various projects of European integration and facilitate deeper policy change. However, as the Spitzenkandidaten model has shown, linking the choice of Commission President to the outcomes of the EP election is only a small step towards creating a proper parliamentary system. That would require major constitutional change and the willingness of member states to give up on their Commissioners – a step that might be far away and not necessarily the right one for the EU's political system (Fabbrini 2015).

Chapter 10

Sites of Translation: From Committees to the Plenary

Introduction: legislative politics inside the EP

The previous chapters examined the role of individual actors and their aggregation in ideological groups. Indeed, political groups serve as an instrument of aggregation that helps organise and translate demands into outputs. However, this process does not occur in an institutional vacuum; it develops in the framework of specialised committees. As we have seen in Chapter 3, standing committees occupy a central position in internal decision-making: policy outputs are formulated and agreed upon at committee level, with the EP plenary generally ratifying these decisions. Therefore, committees are the main site of translation and perform core functions of deliberation and negotiation. They are a 'microcosm' of the larger assembly; committees define 'a set of *privileged groups*, sub-groups of parliamentarians with specific powers, and a set of *procedures* that specifies the powers of these sub-groups with respect to the functions that legislatures perform' (Strøm 1998: 23).

EP committees are probably more similar to the US Congress than to many European parliamentary systems: the US's political system also separates the executive and the legislative branches of power, functions with two legislative chambers and shows weak control of political parties. The main differences rest on the party system – more complex in the EU – and the multilingual and multinational structure of the EP (McElroy 2007). A comparative analysis of committee systems showed that these characteristics (separated systems of government, multiparty systems and bicameralism) facilitate the emergence of strong committees, since the absence of a link between parliament and government makes it easier for parliamentarians to express independent opinions and gives them an opportunity to have a say on policy outputs. Since the EU does not have an executive elected directly by Parliament, MEPs do not have to ensure that the government has the necessary votes to pass legislation and they are not dependent on getting into the executive to have a say in formulating legislative acts (Mattson and Strøm 1995).

Given the importance of committees, two major questions have emerged: what are their functions and how representative are they of the EP as a whole? To answer these questions, most studies of EP

215

committees have turned to rational-choice institutionalist approaches developed in the framework of the US Congress to understand why committees specialise and what this means for the internal life of an assembly (cf. Asher 1974; Brenner 1974; Davidson 1974). In time, three main theoretical models have been put forward to explain the mechanisms and conditions that lie behind specialisation. *Distributive* theories look at the special interests of legislators and their ability to produce gains for their constituencies in order to secure votes for the next elections (Shepsle and Weingast 1987). *Informational* approaches focus rather on the need of parliaments to have trustworthy expertise that can give them an advantage vis-à-vis the other legislative chamber (Krehbiel 1991). Finally, *partisan* theories emphasise the role of political parties and their role in decision-making; committee members are first and foremost there to serve parties and help them build winning coalitions (Cox and McCubbins 2007). These perspectives have dominated explanations of EP committees and form the point of departure for this chapter. One should not forget that there is life beyond this literature; therefore, the chapter also incorporates sociological approaches looking into organisational cultures, norms and the emergence of collective identities in committees (Fenno 1973; cf. Powell and DiMaggio 1991).

This chapter looks at the crucial role that committees play in the EP as the main fora in which the process of translation takes place – looking at internal negotiations in committees and how agreements are shifted up to the plenary level. It aims to go beyond the emphasis put on voting behaviour in order to better understand how positions are formed and aggregated well before MEPs get to vote in the plenary and what this means for the representativeness and democratic standards of the EP as a whole.

Committees: the backbone of the institution

Westlake (1994: 191) considered EP committees the 'legislative backbone' of the institution reflecting the central role they play during the legislative process. Legislative proposals coming from the Commission are allocated to a responsible committee, which is then in charge of examining it and proposing amendments until an agreement is shifted up to the plenary. Therefore, although committees are not really in control of their agenda and timetable, and do not have the ability to initiate legislation, they are given wide room for manoeuvre when performing decision-making tasks. The fact that any proposal is discussed in committee before it goes to the plenary and that committees are the main source of legislative amendments give them a great deal of power and the ability to influence and shape policy outputs (Mamadouh and Raunio 2003).

Decision-making inside committees occurs in three main steps: once the EP President has determined the committee responsible for a proposal, an exchange of views ensues, with the aim of helping the rapporteur write the draft report. In this initial debate, the Commission is invited to present the main points of the text, so that committee members may raise questions and gather the necessary information to position themselves and their political group. While the rapporteur prepares amendments and the draft report, a series of informal meetings takes place inside the EP (for instance, among shadow rapporteurs or within political groups) and with the other EU institutions. It is an open process that allows for dialogue and ends with the main committee debate, where the rapporteur presents the amendments to the legislative proposal. It is at this stage that the main cleavages appear and a process of negotiation starts with the hope of finding a compromise. In the final stage, shadows draft their own amendments, which are often aggregated into 'compromise amendments' by the staff of the committee and the rapporteur and then vote on the final report. Despite being more flexible than those in the plenary, debates in committees are still restricted by tight schedules and the need for interpretation, which makes for rather stultified debates. Adding this to the fact that most negotiations happen outside of the committee in informal settings, the tasks of committee meetings seem to be almost as symbolic as those of the plenary (Roger 2016).

Functions

Given these limitations, why set up committees? What is the main rationale behind creating and empowering them? Although the key function of committees is that of specialisation, the purpose of specialising is very different in the three approaches to legislative organisation. Distributive models consider that members with particular interests will have high incentives to participate in committees where they can reap benefits. They can then trade these benefits with those of other committees at the plenary level. This model would then expect MEPs to choose a committee that is closer to the interests of their constituency (for instance, their region or their country of origin) or even those of a particular societal or economic group (such as an NGO or an interest group); by pleasing their constituency, they might have better chances to be re-elected. The main function of committees is hence that of securing votes. This model is, however, difficult to apply to the EP, since the links between MEPs and their constituencies remain tenuous and most policies do not have clear distributive implications (Bowler and Farrell 1995; Yordanova 2013).

In comparison, informational approaches consider that, in order to obtain balanced policy outputs in the absence of clear majorities,

Parliament needs to delegate policy-making to a smaller group of members that can specialise and provide unbiased expertise. Committees are thus seen as agents, or microcosms, of the bigger chamber and their main function is to provide the necessary information to obtain stable majorities and strengthen the EP's position in inter-institutional negotiations. Given that the EP's increasing workload is of a highly technical nature, it needs to specialise and seek expertise in order to be more effective when negotiating with the Council. Committees help then to fulfil policy-seeking functions (McElroy 2006; Ringe 2010; Yordanova 2013).

Finally, partisan models emphasise the role of political parties in setting up committees, considering that their main purpose is to represent those groups that are part of the winning majority. Therefore, political parties use committees to ensure a fair representation of their views, so as to facilitate coalition-building, but they are also used as instruments of control. Party leaders can improve cohesion by promising members of their group a seat in their preferred committee or offices like those of chair or rapporteur to those that are loyal and contribute to the collective reputation of the party (Yordanova 2013). In this approach, the main function of committees is a mixture of office-seeking (for individual members) and vote-seeking (from the political groups' perspective).

Are any of the three models adequate in explaining the nature of EP committees? The growing consensus seems to be that none of the three approaches can capture single-handedly the functions of these committees and that the relevance of these explanations depends largely on the type of committee we examine. Although everyone underlines the rising role of specialisation and expertise in EP committees, the mechanisms behind this process are largely determined by their jurisdictions and formal powers. Yordanova (2013) has encapsulated these differences by differentiating between committees that produce predominantly regulatory outputs with broad implications for EU citizens (uniform externalities), those driven by specific interests – that is, distributive committees producing targeted externalities (outputs where it is very easy to see who wins and who loses) and mixed committees. She also looks at their influence over legislative and budgetary decisions – leading to a typology of highly influential committees: Budgets, Transport, Internal Market and Consumer Protection as well as Legal Affairs are the most salient information-driven committees, whereas Employment used to be a typical distributive committee. It is highly likely that Agriculture and Fisheries will also join this category now that it works under co-decision. Among the mixed committees, Economic and Monetary Affairs, Environment, Civil Liberties and Industry are the most powerful. These are probably the committees with a higher probability of attracting the attention of political parties, since they concentrate most on legislative activities (cf. Whitaker 2011: 88). Therefore, the three explanations proposed by models of committee specialisation are present in the EP, although those proposed by the informational and partisan approaches seem to fit better. Indeed, specialisation in EP committees is generally driven by the need to acquire (better) information and build the Parliament's expertise; however, this process does not only occur in policy-seeking; but is also tightly coordinated by party leaders with the aim of maintaining cohesion and building winning majorities (Bowler and Farrell 1995).

Organisational cultures

Although the involvement of committees in legislative or budgetary activities might be a good indicator of their relative strength (see Table 10.1), reputation is not always connected to formal powers. For instance, if one compares the number of co-decision reports, it is clear that the Committee on Foreign Affairs (AFET) deals with a very low number of them. And still, AFET is one of the largest committees, and as we have seen in Chapter 8, an attractive one at that – many former heads of government or ministers choose to serve on this committee, despite its lack of legislative 'teeth' (Neuhold 2001). Power and prestige are, hence, related to a committee's jurisdiction, but it also entails the ability to build a corporate identity – an *esprit de corps* – that is recognised and valued by external actors (Neuhold 2007).

Reputations can be built on different bases: the development of collective behaviour that resonates with shared institutional norms or of a clear 'brand' is among the most usual. We have now various studies observing particular institutional cultures across EP committees, but we still lack a proper comparison of these patterns. One of the few comparative studies showed that some committees adopted more competitive positions, while some remained more consensual (Settembri and Neuhold 2009). This trend has been related to the decision-making procedures predominating in a committee: those working under consultation tend(ed) to show more confrontational attitudes than those working mostly under co-decision. We saw, for instance, a clear change in the behaviour of the Civil Liberties (LIBE) committee, which went from being very confrontational to adopting a more consensual behaviour when it shifted to co-decision in 2005. Under consultation, it tended to write opinions considered by the Council as 'wish lists' – a behaviour quickly abandoned under co-decision, where LIBE often showed its willingness to sacrifice some of its core demands in order to appear 'responsible' and ready to compromise for the sake of finding early agreements under co-decision (Ripoll Servent 2015). This change in behaviour has also been remarked in committee debates, which show a more moderate and consensual use of language focused on the interests of their political parties

Table 10.1 Types of procedure for committee reports (July 2014–December 2016)

Committee	Consent	Budgetary procedure	Co-decision 1st reading	Co-decision 2nd/3rd reading	Consultation procedure	Discharge procedure	Immunity	Inter-institutional Agreement	Own initiative	Rules of Procedure	Total
Agriculture and Rural Development (AGRI)	0	0	2	2	0	0	0	0	17	0	21
Civil Liberties, Justice and Home Affairs (LIBE)	2	0	7	6	6	0	0	0	25	0	46
Culture and Education (CULT)	0	0	0	0	0	0	0	0	20	0	20
Development (DEVE)	0	0	0	0	0	0	0	0	25	0	25
Economic and Monetary Affairs (ECON)	0	0	7	3	8	0	0	0	33	0	51
Employment and Social Affairs (EMPL)	1	0	1	0	2	0	0	0	40	0	44
Environment, Public Health and Food Safety (ENVI)	0	0	2	4	0	0	0	0	34	0	40
Fisheries (PECH)	0	0	2	3	0	0	0	0	14	0	19
Foreign Affairs (AFET)	0	0	0	0	0	0	0	0	66	0	66

Committee											Total
Human Rights (DROI, sub-committee)	0	0	0	0	0	0	0	0	0	0	0
Industry, Research and Energy (ITRE)	6	0	7	1	1	0	0	0	15	0	30
Internal Market and Consumer Protection (IMCO)	0	0	5	5	0	0	0	0	16	0	26
International Trade (INTA)	0	0	17	1	0	0	0	0	25	0	43
Regional Development (REGI)	0	0	2	0	1	0	0	0	26	0	29
Transport and Tourism (TRAN)	0	0	2	10	0	0	0	0	15	0	27
Budgets (BUDG)	2	83	2	0	0	0	0	0	5	0	92
Budgetary Control (CONT)	0	0	1	0	0	115	0	0	11	0	127
Constitutional Affairs (AFCO)	0	0	0	0	0	0	0	1	10	5	16
Legal Affairs (JURI)	0	0	23	5	2	0	34	0	24	1	89
Petitions (PETI)	0	0	0	0	0	0	0	0	9	0	9
Women's Rights and Gender Equality (FEMM)	0	0	0	0	0	0	0	0	31	0	31
Total	5	83	73	39	19	115	34	1	446	6	821

Source: European Parliament.

or constituents when it is seen to matter, whereas on those occasions that do not draw public attention, MEPs become more free to display the attitudes they want (Roger 2016).

In some cases, committees have been able to 'brand' themselves and link their organisational culture to the history of their policy area. As shown above, the LIBE committee used its confrontational tone to successfully build a reputation as a 'liberal' committee. The over-representation of left-wing and liberal MEPs helped the committee to unite behind policy positions in favour of civil and migrant rights – repeatedly challenging member states' policies and external forces like the US in highly visible cases like Passenger Name Records agreements. Interestingly, this reputation has survived even with the advent of co-decision and the shift in the committee's behaviour, which has become more inclined to accept the security-led demands of member states (Ripoll Servent 2015; Trauner and Ripoll Servent 2016). The committee for Environment (ENVI) has witnessed a similar process. Being one of the first committees to work under co-decision, its legislative weight helped to build its 'green' credentials (Burns and Carter 2010; Judge 1992; Judge and Earnshaw 1994). Although this reputation remains, many have noted a shift in the attitudes of the committee, which has become less radical (and less successful) in its defence of green positions. These changes are largely the product of a shift in its membership, particularly noticeable after the 2004 enlargement and the subsequent increase in the number of MEPs linked to industry (Burns et al. 2012, 2013; Smith 2008).

Roederer–Rynning (2003) looked at the AGRI committee and its use of informal measures to amplify and politicise European debates as a way to compensate for its lack of formal decision-making powers. She also showed the presence of a conservative culture with corporatist leanings among its membership – a bias that has remained in place even after the shift to co-decision in 2009 (Roederer-Rynning 2015: 216). The ability to play with formal and informal rules has also manifested itself in the Women's Rights and Gender Equality committee (FEMM). Its status as a 'neutralised' committee – where membership does not count – has made it easier to resist various attempts to eliminate it and to avoid conflicts with other committees. The members of FEMM have actually promoted it as a 'weaker' committee, which has made it simpler for them to network and mainstream the 'gender equality' norm across EP committees (Ahrens 2016).

Finally, if we come back to our initial example, AFET: why is the committee so highly valued despite not having as much legislative influence as some of the other committees? One reason is related to the subject matter: foreign policy has traditionally been seen as an area of high politics and is surrounded by an aura of importance and strength.

People might have the feeling of being involved in something relevant when working in this committee; indeed, information gathering and networking have been tasks where the AFET committee has excelled. It has also become more relevant as foreign policy has gradually been linked to more EU policies, such as enlargement or civil missions in the area of defence (see also Box 10.1).

Through these channels, it has been able to link debates to decisions taken either under the ordinary or budgetary procedures. In addition, the committee has been very successful at building a large base of expertise, both in terms of committee staff and in the shape of its two sub-committees on Human Rights (DROI) and Defence (SEDE) (Diedrichs 2004; Herranz Surrallés 2011). These explanations can be largely applied also to the Committee of Constitutional Affairs (AFCO), which has forged its reputation by building expertise on the internal functioning of the EP and using it to expand Parliament's formal and informal powers. The presence of a core group of members perceived as possessing long-term expertise in these issues has made it easier to gain the trust of non-committee members and given it the necessary legitimacy to act in the name of the EP and make crucial decisions for its development and weight in the EU's political system (Beauvallet et al. 2009).

Inter-committee cooperation and conflict

The emergence of specific organisational cultures has enhanced the chances for conflicts between committees. The relatively high number of standing committees increases the potential for overlaps and disagreements over who is responsible for a given issue (Bowler and Farrell 1995: 223). To this effect, the EP has developed various procedures to deal with potential conflicts of competence. Rule 201a determines that, in cases where there are questions about which committee should be named as 'lead' committee, the Conference of Committee Chairs (or if the Conference cannot agree, then its president) will submit a recommendation to the Conference of Presidents. In that case, a usual solution is to ask the other committees concerned to deliver an opinion, although Rule 201 specifies that, ideally, no more than three committees should be involved in a decision. Rule 53 determines that opinion-giving committees can propose amendments, but only in those areas that fall under their competence. The lead committee has to cast a vote on these amendments, but is not obliged to include them in the final report. If the amendments fail, the opinion-giving committee cannot reintroduce them at the plenary stage, except if it can obtain the support of a political group or at least 5 per cent of MEPs.

Box 10.1   The EP's symbolic role in foreign policy

Although some consider that the EP has more control over foreign policy than many national parliaments (Furness 2013: 113), its powers are limited to shaping the budget and ratifying international agreements. In an attempt to increase its involvement in foreign affairs, the EP has sought to informally widen its participation by strengthening various information channels and stressing the necessity of parliamentary involvement on the grounds of accountability and democratic legitimacy when dealing both with external policies that fall in the community domain – such as trade or development – and with those that remain in the intergovernmental realm of foreign security and defence (Barbé and Herranz Surrallés 2008; Diedrichs 2004). To this effect, the EP has reinforced the activities of the AFET committee by building a dialogue with key foreign policy actors and expressing its views through own-initiative reports (Thym 2006). Other (sub-)committees – on Human Rights (DROI), Security and Defence (SEDE), Development (DEVE) and International Trade (INTA) – also play a role in the EP's foreign policy. In addition, the EP attempts to improve its information and gain some advantage over the other EU institutions by developing direct linkages with third-country parliaments and parliamentary assemblies of international organisations. To this effect, it has created various inter-parliamentary delegations focused on a specific world region or country and it is also physically present with more than 40 delegations worldwide (see also Chapter 3). These efforts have not always proved successful; the Council and the High Representative have often remained impervious to the EP's attempts to participate in   →

These constraints on opinion-givers, made more noticeable under co-decision II, encouraged inter-committee conflict during the 1990s and early 2000s (Burns 2006). As a result, the EP developed a set of informal mechanisms to foster cooperation, notably the two procedures known as 'Gomes' and 'Hughes'; more recently, opinion-giving rapporteurs have been allowed to participate in meetings of the lead committee and even sit in trilogues under what is known as 'Rule 53+'. In 2009, the Conference of Presidents decided to adopt a package of reforms that institutionalised some of these informal mechanisms. The new rules allowed committees to organise joint meetings if they were to discuss complex issues that affected more than one area. Rule 54 now includes a 'procedure with associated committees', which makes it possible to share a report among two committees. In this case, rapporteurs should agree to a common time-table and strive to propose a common text to their respective committees. The procedure maintains a 'lead' committee, but associated committees

→ foreign policy. They have insisted on the intergovernmental character of this area, raising even alternative sources of funding when the EP has tried to block the budget dedicated to security and defence (Crum 2006; Thym 2006).

The Treaty of Lisbon did not substantially improve the role of the EP in foreign policy. Article 36 TEU only grants a consultative role, which means that the High Representative has to consult the EP when it makes essential choices and keep it informed on how foreign security and defence policies evolve. In turn, the EP holds a debate on the implementation of these policies twice a year and can always refer questions or comments to the High Representative or the Council. It also has a tangential influence on the selection of the High Representative, who, due to its role as vice-president of the Commission, must undergo a parliamentary hearing before entering into office. This is the same as for every other commissioner with a foreign policy portfolio such as trade, development or enlargement (Keukeleire and Delreux 2014: 86).

Indeed, through various institutional arrangements and concessions from the Commission and the Council, the EP has gradually achieved a slightly stronger position. For instance, it has pointed at the democratic gap in EU foreign policy-making to improve its access to confidential documents (Rosén 2015) and to participate more actively in setting up and controlling the budget of the EEAS. However, it remains outside the realm of decision-making and cannot participate in the nomination of high political positions such as heads of delegations (Keukeleire and Delreux 2014: 86–87; Sjursen 2011; Wisniewski 2013). Therefore, despite pushing the boundaries of many institutional rules, the main power left to the EP is to play a symbolic role in EU foreign policy.

can delimit an area of 'exclusive competence', which means that if the lead committee goes against their recommendations in this area, the associated committee can still try to present the amendments directly to the plenary for a vote. The 2009 reforms also introduced a 'joint committee procedure' (Rule 55), where in questions of major importance, two or three committees are supposed to produce a joint report and vote on it together. For instance, in September 2016, the Commission proposed a new European Fund for Sustainable Development (EFSD), which aimed to tackle the root causes of emigration in countries of origin. Given the transversal nature of the initiative, the EP decided to nominate three lead committees: the Development, Foreign Affairs and Budget committees, with Budgetary Control as the opinion-giving committee (2016/0281/ COD). Coordinating the work of two committees – or even three, like in this case – is not an easy task, but it has shown to produce very positive results (Corbett et al. 2016: 178–180).

Shifting up: the relationship between committees and the plenary

As we have seen, most political debates take place at the committee level: the lead committee is largely responsible for examining the details of the proposal and starting negotiations with the Council and the Commission. As a result, debates in the plenary rarely go into details. New amendments are hardly ever introduced at the plenary level, where committee reports are treated as 'take-it-or-leave-it' options (Hix 2005: 93; Neuhold 2001). Given that committees enjoy a high degree of autonomy, how representative are they of Parliament as a whole and what are the mechanisms connecting committee decision-making and plenary voting? If we look back at the three models of legislative organisation, they offer us very different expectations on their representativeness.

As we have seen above, distributive approaches assume that committee members serve particular interests, like their constituents or specific interest groups. Therefore, they expect that the decisions made by committees will not be representative of the median position in the plenary, but will rather try to maximise the benefits for their constituents. Committee members are thus self-selected and have more at stake in that particular area than non-committee members. For instance, we might expect parliamentarians coming from a rural area to be particularly interested in serving in the AGRI committee, so as to get more funds or policy outputs that benefit their regions. However, as we have seen, the formal rules regulating the distribution of committee seats make self-selection difficult, since membership allocation is guided by strict proportionality rules. Therefore, committee seats are distributed across political groups (and then internally across nationalities) following the D'Hondt method. However, there is always room for manoeuvre in deciding who is going to occupy the seat allocated to a political group and individual members can also indicate their priorities (Yordanova 2013).

Informational approaches, on the other hand, consider that committees act as agents of the plenary, and are therefore highly representative. In order to ensure that a report will be voted on in the plenary, committees have to reflect the same diversity of views. Knowing that committee members mirror the political balance of parliament as a whole helps those who do not sit in a committee to trust the decisions made by their members. As we have seen, the EP is pressed for information and does rely extensively on policy experts, since MEPs cannot follow each file voted on in the plenary (Ringe 2010; Yordanova 2013).

The informational perspective largely dismisses the role of political parties. To fill in this gap, the partisan model remarked that political groups provide the major link between committees and the plenary: committee members are selected by parties and do respond to their wishes. Therefore, committees should be representative of the majority forces in the plenary, since individual MEPs depend on them to keep their place, move to their preferred committee or have access to offices like chairmanships or rapporteurships. This partisan dimension might reflect national biases, since, as we have seen in Chapter 9, MEPs are also constrained by their national parties (Whitaker 2011; Yordanova 2013).

There have been contradictory reports on who drives the allocation of committee seats and how representative committees are (see Box 10.2 on the conciliation committee).

Box 10.2 Representativeness in the conciliation committee

The conciliation committee was established after the introduction of co-decision in the Treaty of Maastricht. It is an inter-institutional body convened when an agreement cannot be found in the second reading of the co-decision procedure. It combines both representatives of the EP and the Council whose aim is to settle on a joint text. The conciliation committee consists of 28 representatives of the Council and an equal number of MEPs, chosen individually for each negotiation, although the three vice-presidents in charge of conciliation are always part of the team. The remaining members are usually the rapporteur and the committee chair as well as other MEPs deemed to be experts in the field (for example, shadow rapporteurs, political coordinators or rapporteurs for opinion).

Compromises tabled in the conciliation committee can be either approved or rejected by the EP and the Council, but not amended. Therefore, since these committees work in an isolated setting, they may have more opportunities to shape the final compromise. At the same time, other members of the EP and the Council might feel under pressure to approve the committee's joint text if they do not want to see negotiations fail at the very last moment. Therefore, given the nature of delegation to conciliation committees, there was some expectation, in the early days of co-decision, that MEPs representing the Parliament might run away and just present a 'take-it-or-leave-it' decision to the plenary. There were also concerns that those chosen to represent the EP might have particular (national) interests in mind. However, studies into the composition of conciliation committees confirmed the assumptions of informational models and showed that they were generally representative of the EP. It seems, thus, that since EP delegations try to maintain the same balance of power that exists in the plenary, it proves difficult for particular MEPs to bias the final agreement and present an unexpected deal back to the plenary (Rasmussen 2005, 2008b).

When it comes to the first point – who drives the selection process – the answers are highly nuanced. One reason is the strong proportionality rules mentioned above, which make self-selection difficult: as much as some MEPs might want to sit in on a specific committee, they might not manage it because their political group and/or their national party delegation have not been assigned a seat. Personal interests, professional expertise and the relevance of the topic do drive the choices of individual MEPs and that often translates into some degree of self-selection: MEPs with special interests or previous expertise in a given topic have higher chances to sit on a committee that fits their knowledge (Bowler and Farrell 1995; Yordanova 2013). Therefore, although committees are, in general, highly representative of the EP as a whole (McElroy 2006), recent studies have shown that there are differences between them. MEPs with previous expertise in a policy area tend to be assigned to those committees that deal mostly with regulatory (and thus highly technical) matters like Environment, Economic Affairs or Trade, while those who show particular interests have higher chances of working in interest-driven committees, such as Agriculture, Regional Policy or Fisheries. It seems, thus, that the mechanisms defined by the distributive and informational models exist in parallel and may apply to different types of committee (Whitaker 2011; Yordanova 2013).

Despite these differences, committees seem to be generally representative of the EP's partisan composition. The same cannot be said of its national components, which is not surprising given what we have seen in Chapter 9: national party delegations control the allocation of important offices, including the allocation of committee seats – especially in larger political groups. Therefore, NPDs do try to influence the selection of individual members, so that the most qualified are appointed to committees that are of particular interest for the national party. Indeed, there seems to be some over- or under-representation of specific countries in some committees. For instance, Italy is over-represented in the Industry, Legal Affairs and LIBE committees, but under-represented in the AFET committee (Bendjallah 2009; Whitaker 2011; Yordanova 2013). This disproportional representation of national delegations is also clearly seen in the allocation of reports (Mamadouh and Raunio 2003) and in the selection of committee chairs (Box 10.3).

These different findings do not tell us much about the role of parties. That might have to do with the fact that many of those who have examined this question have tied it to the question of loyalty. On that point, some have suggested that political groups (and national delegations) use offices such as committee seats, chairmanships and rapporteurships as a reward for loyal members (Mamadouh and Raunio 2003; McElroy

Box 10.3   Over- and under-representation of nationalities in committee chairmanships

Although chairs are distributed according to the D'Hondt system, there is always a certain leeway, especially when it comes to balancing nationalities and allocating other leadership positions like vice-presidencies. The need to keep a partisan balance means that there is not much room for meritocracy or specialisation: chairs tend to stay in their positions for a relatively short time – many for only two and a half years and very few over ten years. Therefore, there is little danger that they will gain too much autonomy vis-à-vis the plenary or their political groups. On the contrary, chairmanships are usually trophies to be used as a reward for members loyal to the national party delegation (Whitaker 2011).

When chairs were distributed after the 2014 elections, larger NPDs in large political groups were seen as the main winners: 17 out of 20 chairs came from the six largest member states (Piedrafita 2014). The mid-term reshuffle in early 2017 was influenced by the agreement reached between ALDE and the EPP in the days before Antonio Tajani was elected as EP President. The deal explains why Cecilia Wikström (ALDE) became the new President of the Conference of Committee Chairs, replacing Jerzy Buzek (EPP). Although committee chairs remained in the hands of the same political groups, there were significant changes in the balance between nationalities with Maltese, Lithuanians, Czechs, Swedes and Italians winning the most and Croatians, Finns, Slovenians and Estonians being the biggest losers (Votewatch 2017). For example, Adina-Ioana Vălean (EPP, Romania) took over for Giovanni La Via (EPP, Italy) in the Environment committee (ENVI), whereas Vilija Blinkevičiūtė (S&D, Lithuania) took over for Iratxe García Pérez (S&D, Spain) in the Women's Rights committee (FEMM). Some of the changes were not expected: Karima Delli (Greens/EFA, France) became the youngest chair and broke the unofficial rule of only appointing 'white male' MEPs as chairs of the Transport committee (Politico 2017h).

Despite some voices claiming that 'British MEPs [should] keep their mouths shut and their heads down as the UK heads to the EU exit' (Politico 2017c), they were allowed to stay in their offices, with key actors like Claude Moraes (S&D) and Linda McAvan (S&D) remaining chairs of the LIBE and DEVE committees respectively. This decision was particularly surprising in the case of Conservative Vicky Ford (ECR), who was allowed to remain as chair of the IMCO committee until she left the EP in June 2017, probably also a result of the deal that brought Tajani into office (Politico 2017c).

2001), while others have not seen any evidence of it, giving support to the informational rather than the partisan approach (Whitaker 2011; Yordanova 2013). However, the role played by political parties is probably difficult to measure in such terms. In a sense, they are the essential interface between committees and the plenary, since no decision made by a committee can go through without a vote from the plenary. The plenary can also be a last resort for political groups or individual MEPs that were not successful in passing their amendments in committees. Therefore, even if decision-making in committees is steered by highly specialised MEPs, political balances cannot be ignored. Majorities still have to be formed and political groups have an incentive to do so as early as possible in the process. Therefore, the fact that committee reports are rarely overthrown in the plenary has very much to do with the shadow that majorities and coalitions cast over committee decisions. Rapporteurs and shadow rapporteurs deliberate and negotiate inside their committee, but they also hold periodic meetings with their political groups and receive the support of other relais actors like political coordinators and political advisors. Their ability to report back and forth between political groups and committees prevents major conflicts in the plenary and reinforces the reputation of their political groups and that of the EP as a whole (Bendjallah 2009; Roger 2016; Roger and Winzen 2015).

Trust is a key element here: in order to ensure support from non-committee members, expert MEPs have to be aware of what might be problematic for the plenary as a whole. The process of building coalitions is based to a large extent on this element of representativeness and trust: those who do not know about the content of a proposal need to count on those who do. However, as Ringe (2010) showed, trust is highly mediated by partisan (and national) considerations – non-committee members will trust expert members, especially if they are from the same national party or, at least, from the same political group. Trust may, however, also be linked to the reputation of a committee. As we have seen above, certain committees have built a particular *esprit de corps*, which has increased their standing in the eyes of external actors and made it easier to receive the support of the plenary. However, trust can be lost easily if the behaviour of a committee is not consistent. As we have seen above, the ENVI committee was generally considered an 'environmental champion', but started to acquire a more sympathetic stance towards pro-industry positions, which led it to abandon some of its traditional green standards. This shift in its positions had an immediate effect on its relationship with the plenary, which stopped displaying the same level of deference towards the committee as in the past (Burns 2005; Burns and Carter 2010; Smith 2008). Therefore, the links between committee and plenary are delicate and the support of non-committee members cannot be taken for granted. The latest reform of the Rules of Procedure introduced a new option (Rule 69c), whereby the committee has to announce the start of first-reading negotiations with the Council in the plenary; if the plenary is concerned about the content of the legislative report, it can force a vote and change the direction of negotiations. This means that, whether they are representative of the EP as a whole or not, committees cannot just act autonomously from the plenary, but need to coordinate intensively with political groups and external members so as not to lose sight of potential conflicts once a decision reaches a plenary vote.

The symbolic power of the plenary

Plenary is now an arena largely reserved for voting and holding ceremonial debates. As we have seen, most of the action occurs before decisions are put to the plenary for ratification. That does not mean that MEPs are completely devoid of powers when sitting in the plenary; indeed, it is often the last resort for cases gone wrong and it may also provide members with an arena to communicate their positions and raise the attention of the outside world.

The plenary as an instrument of last resort

What are the opportunities left to those not happy with the decision made by a committee? There are various strategies that can be used by political groups or a group of over 5 per cent of MEPs. The most obvious is the possibility to table amendments to be considered directly in the plenary. Indeed, groups left in the minority position in a committee can use the plenary stage to reintroduce amendments that were not included in the report (cf. Yordanova 2013: 20). Amendments can be used to add to, change or delete any part of the text, but cannot propose to delete the report or replace it in its entirety. Although usually there are deadlines for submission, so that amendments can be translated into all official languages, the President may admit last-minute compromise amendments, especially if they are proposed by political groups representing the majority of the EP (Rules 169 and 170). As we have seen, the plenary generally accepts the amendments proposed by the committee responsible, but on some rare occasions, EP groups have used the plenary to propose alternative agreements – as was the case with the Returns Directive (Ripoll Servent 2013; see also Chapter 11) – or even bypass the rapporteur. For instance, in the Advanced Therapies Regulation (1394/2007/EC), the rapporteur from the EPP-ED decided to include two amendments concerning the ethics of stem-cell research in medicine that had been hotly disputed by the other political groups and the Council. This led a coalition of the PES (now the S&D), ALDE and the GUE/NGL to propose a 'counter-report' in the plenary, which out-voted and replaced the committee report (Judge and Earnshaw 2011). Therefore, tabling amendments in plenary can be used as a last resort in highly conflictual situations.

There are other, rarer instruments that can also be activated to delay or avoid a decision. Rule 188 provides for the possibility to ask the plenary to refer an issue back to committee. It can again be requested by political groups or a group of individual MEPs, although it is often demanded by the lead committee itself when disagreements or techni-cal issues arise. In some cases, it might be used by certain groups to block a report seen as controversial or highly biased. For instance, in September 2013, the FEMM committee approved a non-legislative report on sexual and reproductive rights for women (Estrela Report, 2013/2040/INI), which was not to the taste of right-wing groups. The latter sent it back to the committee for re-consideration. After only minimal changes, in December 2013, the report was put again to a vote in the plenary, where it was eventually voted down (Euobserver 2013b). In other occasions, political groups ask to adjourn a debate or a vote. In some cases, this decision may be based on technical con-cerns, as was the case in the vote on an EP recommendation on TTIP, postponed due to the high number of amendments tabled (2014/2228/INI). In other cases, it might be a very useful technique to take cer-tain issues off the agenda, as we saw in Chapter 7 with the proposal on transparency and lobbying prepared by Sven Giegold. Finally, in very exceptional circumstances, MEPs may request the President to check whether there is a quorum of one-third of MEPs (Rule 168). This technique can be used to delay the vote until the next session, but not to block the adoption of the agenda or the scheduled debates (Corbett et al. 2016: 238–239).

Voting time as a ritualised performance

When proposals reach the voting stage, there is usually a debate, but unlike in many national parliaments, it is not followed immediately by a vote. Votes are grouped together in what is sometimes referred to as a 'voting marathon', which takes place around noon during the plenary week. This arrangement makes for a highly ritualised procedure that can be confusing for external observers, especially given that the pro-cess of voting is extremely fast paced. The voting sequence adds to the confusion, since it can prove difficult to follow the order of precedence and how voting in favour of some amendments causes others to fall (Rule 174). In addition, the EP allows for requests to separate votes on a particular paragraph from the rest of the text or to split votes on parts of an amendment or a paragraph, which makes the procedure even more unclear. The 2016 change to the Rules of Procedure tried to clarify the sequencing when voting on legislation, starting with a vote to reject the proposal. If the plenary decides not to reject, it considers then the committee report as a whole – except if a political group or at least 40 MEPs prefer to vote on the amendments separately. Finally, the EP votes on the draft legislative act for adoption (or rejection). With this change, the perplexing habit of voting first on a draft legislative act and then a legislative resolution to confirm that vote has been put to an end (Rule 59).

As a general rule, MEPs vote by show of hands, except if the President cannot clearly see who has won, in which case the vote is repeated electronically (Rule 178). The exceptions to this rule are single or final votes on a report, where electronic votes are used as a norm (Rule 179). Political groups or a minimum of 5 per cent of members can also request an electronic roll-call vote (RCV), although Rule 180 now specifies that each political group can only request a maximum of 100 RCVs per part-session. As seen in Chapter 9, RCVs are often used by political groups as a mechanism to control their MEPs, since they can check who has followed the party line and who has defected (see Box 10.4). They can also be used to display high levels of cohesion in specific decisions – or shame other groups by showing that they could not hold the group together or that they voted in an unexpected direction (Thiem 2006).

In some special cases, MEPs are asked to vote by secret ballot – particularly when appointing the President, Vice-Presidents and Quaestors as well as the ombudsman and the Commission President. This voting mode can also be requested by at least 20 per cent of MEPs, although the high threshold dissuades members and groups from doing so and it remains until now a rare occurrence. It was, for instance, used in 2004 to decide on the opening of accession negotiations with Turkey (P6_TA(2004)0096), but when it was proposed for the vote on the 2014–2020 MFF, the idea did not bear any fruits (Crowe 2016; Euractiv 2004).

Voting has indeed become a ritualised hour characterised by speed and a highly technical character. Despite being one of the few times that the chamber is full, it is not an attractive time for observers looking out for debates or controversies. In general, voting is uneventful, except in exceptional cases where there are accusations of voting fraud, such as in an episode involving the then two ENF leaders. On 28 October 2015, Marcel de Graaff seemed to forget that votes in the EP are non-transferrable (proxies are not allowed) and decided to use Marine Le Pen's voting card when she was absent from the chamber. In the end, 'clumsy' de Graaff was penalised with a reduction of €1,530 off his daily allowances (Euobserver 2015a).

Box 10.4 Using roll-call votes to study the EP: A biased exercise?

The vote by roll-call is one of three types of voting mechanism in the EP. It is the only type where the full information of voting behaviour is made publicly accessible. That is why RCVs have been the preferred method to study voting behaviour in the Parliament (cf. Hix and Høyland 2013). However, some experts have voiced concerns, suggesting that studies of RCVs suffer from behavioural and selection biases, which render them unsuitable for making reliable assumptions about the general voting behaviour of MEPs (Carrubba et al. 2006). One of the main sources of potential bias derives from the intentionality behind RCVs. Generally, political groups call the roll when they expect many national party delegations to defect and vote against the position of their EP political group; calling the roll may help to boost cohesion levels (Trumm 2015), although some consider it more likely that it helps national parties control their MEPs (Finke 2015). These effects may now be better controlled by the change in the Rules of Procedure for the seventh EP term (2009–2014), which required using RCVs for all final reports. A comparison between the sixth and seventh legislatures showed that, indeed, MEPs seemed to feel the need to stick to the voting line if a political group called the roll and that previous studies had underestimated the effect of RCVs on cohesion (Hug 2016; Yordanova and Mühlböck 2015). Similar comparisons can also be done now with RCVs in committee: since 2014, committees have been asked to call the roll for final votes. RCVs may also be used for reasons unrelated to internal party discipline, for instance, in cases where political groups want to take a stance against a decision made at the committee stage (Thierse 2016). Finally, one should take into account that, sometimes, studying RCVs might hide conflicts that concentrated on specific amendments, rather than on the text as a whole (Corbett et al. 2016: 234). Therefore, RCVs might need to be complemented with more in-depth (qualitative) analyses of particular decisions (cf. M.K. Rasmussen 2008).

Signalling and justifying positions in plenary debates

If one is looking for fora in which parliamentarians can deliberate and offer justifications for their positions, plenary debates might be a better place to go. Indeed, speaking time is a highly coveted resource in the EP plenary. It is distributed according to various criteria: a first portion is divided equally among political groups and then a second portion is allocated in proportion to the size of each group, which also determines the speaking order. Therefore, debates usually start with a priority slot given to the Commission and the Council followed by rapporteurs and then by representatives of each political group in descending order – that is, usually the political coordinator of the EPP starts, followed by the S&D, then the ECR, and so on until those not aligned with a political group have spoken. In addition, MEPs may raise a blue card to ask a short direct question to a speaker, which offers an opportunity to exchange views in a more dynamic way (Rule 162). At the end of a debate, there is usually some time reserved for a short open debate where members try to 'catch the eye' of the President to inform him or her of their wish to speak. It becomes quickly clear that debates are extremely regulated and do not facilitate an open exchange of views. The debates are made even more unexciting by the tendency of MEPs to read off of a script and the time lags caused by interpretation (Corbett et al. 2016: 232).

MEPs can express their own political opinions in different types of debate. Until 2002, the EP held three-hour-long debates in every part-session, touching upon topical and urgent matters. In 2002, these general debates were substituted by two different procedures: a regular debate on 'human rights, democracy and the rule of law' and 'extraordinary' debates to deal with urgent political matters. Although both are one-hour-long debates, there are small differences between them. Debates on human rights, democracy and the rule of law can be requested in writing by a committee, an inter-parliamentary delegation, a political group or a group of at least 5 per cent of MEPs. The one-hour-long debate is limited to a maximum of three items and takes place on Thursday afternoon, followed by a vote on a resolution (Rule 135 and Annex III). These debates can cover a wide range of issues, from very personal problems to large-scale human rights concerns. In comparison, extraordinary debates occur less frequently and can only be requested by a political group or more than 5 per cent of MEPs. The one-hour debate is limited to one single item and there is no vote on a resolution to conclude the discussion (Rule 153). As an example, the session of 30 April 2015 witnessed both an extraordinary debate on the use of the death penalty in Indonesia (where eight prisoners had been executed two days earlier) and a debate on human rights dealing with the imprisonment of Ukrainian Lieutenant Nadiya Savchenko by Russian forces, the situation of the Yarmouk refugee camp in Syria and the imprisonment of human and workers' rights activists in Algeria.

The 2016 reform of the Rules of Procedure added a new 'topical debate' inspired by the German Bundestag's 'Aktuelle Stunde' (current hour), in which political groups can propose a one-hour debate on a matter of major interest to EU policy. This new format complements the Question Time and question hour with the Commission, the High Representative and the Council (see Chapter 5). The Conference of Presidents should ensure a fair distribution of topics across political groups, but reserves itself the right to veto a proposed subject if a majority representing four-fifths of MEPs do not agree with it (Rule 153a). Finally, the plenary is also the site of formal sittings when the EP receives visits from heads of state or religious representatives. In this case, a debate is organised during the part-session in Strasbourg. Most EU heads of state have addressed the EP; for instance, on 14 February 2017, the EP received the new Austrian President Alexander Van der Bellen. Some visits have not been exempted of controversy: the invitation of the EP to the Dalai Lama in September 2016 led to China threatening with countermeasures for ignoring their 'strong opposition' to the visit (The *Guardian* 2016a). Formally, heads of government and foreign ministers do not have the right to address the plenary, but the EP has developed informal rules so that they can address either the AFET committee together with other relevant delegations (known as the Shevardnadze procedure) or a meeting of the Conference of Presidents open to all members. This modality was chosen in May 2010 when US Foreign Minister Joe Biden visited Parliament in the midst of negotiations on the SWIFT Agreement (Corbett et al. 2016: 227; Ripoll Servent 2014).

Apart from these debates, which are focused on a few pre-selected topics, the 2002 reform of the Rules of Procedure introduced a more diverse type of debate in which MEPs could raise questions or comment on any issue of personal (or constituency) concern for a maximum of one minute. This type of debate is now known as 'one-minute speeches' and takes place for half an hour during the EP's part-session on Monday afternoon (Rule 163). Although not every MEP that requests to speak can do so, in general there are around 24 to 30 interventions. In addition, members can give an explanation of their vote after the voting session is over – although this has been limited to three oral explanations per part-session (Rule 183). This is due to the high amount of time that was usually dedicated to justifying one's position in the votes.

Table 10.2 shows the duration of sittings per type of debate. As expected, most of the time is spent on legislative and non-legislative debates (around 35 per cent in the seventh legislature); however, some of the other activities also take a large proportion of the EP's working time in the plenary, notably statements (29.7 per cent in the seventh term) and explanations of vote (almost 10 per cent). In comparison, debates on human rights and democracy occupied only over 3 per cent of time, while extraordinary debates and formal sittings accounted only for 0.1 and 0.7 per cent respectively. Given this distribution of plenary time, it seems that MEPs use this forum to offer justifications and to signal their position to national parties, constituents or interest groups. Indeed, the quality of discourses is very high in the EP – with people showing great respect for others and spelling out arguments for their positions, but rarely demanding accounts from others (Lord and Tamvaki 2013).

Table 10.2   *Distribution of time in plenary sessions*

	2009–2014	*2014–2016*
Elections	6h 17	5h 23
Legislative debates	367h 37	102h 04
Non-legislative debates	374h 21	186h 35
Oral questions	205h 60	105h 46
Other (extraordinary) debates	2h 09	7h 43
Statements	638h 51	485h 52
Debate on human rights, democracy and the rule of law	69h 40	37h 48
Formal sittings	14h 58	8h 19
One-minute speeches	42h 12	24h 36
Question Time	61h 47	–
Votes	119h 25	56h 41
Explanation of votes	213h 49	96h 36
Others	34h 31	16h 55
Total	2,151h 38	1,134h 18

Sources: European Parliament (2014c, 2016b).

Therefore, it seems that speeches in the plenary are not used to seek accountability, but rather to portray oneself towards external audiences. For instance, MEPs will use debates in the plenary to either explain why they have defected from their political group's position or signal allegiance to their national political party. Given the tenuous link between debates and European citizens, EP political groups do not seem as concerned about letting their dissident members speak as some political parties at the national level. Therefore, debates in plenary are characterised by a stronger 'national' dimension than votes (Proksch and Slapin 2010; Slapin and Proksch 2010).

Keeping order in the chamber

Although plenary proceedings are highly structured and do not offer many chances for spontaneous behaviour, disruptions in the chamber (or outside it) are not unheard of. In some cases, members use the Parliament's rules to obstruct its functioning, for instance, by including bogus items in the points of order or requesting too many separate or split votes (Corbett et al. 2016: 238). The 2016 reform of the Rules of Procedure has empowered the President by offering the possibility to put an end to these requests when it is manifest that the aim is to obstruct the smooth running of the EP (Rule 164a). In addition, the President has also been given more powers to counteract disturbances in Parliament – including unfurling banners with defamatory, racist or xenophobic language (Rule 11.3). This reflects the increase in anti-democratic language and actions displayed by Eurosceptic and far-right MEPs, although it has been criticised by smaller left-wing groups, which have seen their rights equally curtailed (Politico 2016g).

As we have seen in Chapter 8, those adopting the role of public orator often make use of plenary debates to capture the attention of outsiders – and often, there is no better way to attract media coverage than by being extremely polemical (Brack 2015). Nigel Farage is probably the best known among those adopting this type of role, but there have been other infamous incidents, like the time in November 2010 when Godfrey Bloom (UKIP) parroted Nazi logos to hackle Martin Schulz; his expulsion from the chamber led 20 other far-right MEPs to accompany him in solidarity. In March 2016, Golden Dawn member Eleftherios Synadinos was expelled from the chamber when he made extremely crude racist remarks against Turks during a summit between EU and Turkish leaders (Politico 2016b; The *Guardian* 2010a). Apart from expelling members – or even interrupting the session – the President can also decide to apply several types of sanctions, ranging from a mere reprimand to suspending daily allowances and participation in Parliament's activities (except voting) for up to 30 days. These sanctions might also be accompanied with a decision to remove the member from any offices (like committee chair) and bar them from representing the EP in inter-parliamentary conferences or delegations (Rule 168). A very exceptional case is that of Mike Hookem, who allegedly punched his UKIP colleague Steven Woolfe in the middle of the EP's building in Strasbourg. The statements regarding the incident were so contradictory that Martin Schulz preferred to leave the case to the French police authorities (The *Guardian* 2016d).

Conclusion

This chapter aimed to go beyond the focus on voting behaviour that often prevails in our understanding of how the EP works. The aim was to better appreciate the fact that positions are formed and aggregated well before MEPs get to vote in the plenary in a complex process that involves specialised committees, expert members and their respective political groups. This holistic view of policy-making in the EP is important, since it allows us to appreciate the links between micro- and macro-processes: individual MEPs may exert a large influence on the policy outputs of the EP, but they cannot act in complete independence of colleagues in their committee and the shadow exerted by political group leaders – especially in legislative negotiations. MEPs can, therefore, play with the various parliamentary fora to exercise different dimensions of their representative role: they can prioritise policy-making activities when they act as members of a committee, while exerting more constituency-oriented functions in plenary debates. This leads, of course, to a complex understanding of democracy and representativeness in the EP, since it is not always clear who and what is being represented and how accountable individual MEPs and committees are towards EU citizens and domestic audiences.

Clearly, policy-making is not a stable and settled process, but a changing one that makes it difficult to assess who is in charge of translating demands into outputs. The growing importance of co-decision has raised new challenges for committees and their role in the legislative process. Notably, the shift towards more informal arenas of policy-making questions the functions and authority of committees as they are becoming smaller versions of the plenary – used to signal positions to constituents and legitimise decisions that have already been made elsewhere (Roger 2016).

Chapter 11

The EP as a Co-Decider: Key Negotiating Roles and the Power of Consensus

Introduction: institutionalist approaches to EU decision-making

The capacity of the EP to successfully participate in and exert influence on the EU's political system is intimately linked to its role as co-legislator. Since 2009, the procedure by which the EP and the Council jointly decide on EU policies has been known as the 'ordinary legislative procedure' and is now in use for 85 policy areas – which cover around 95 per cent of EU legislation. Over the years, co-decision has grown in importance, to the point that it has managed to displace other legislative procedures, in particular the consultation procedure, which was considered as 'ordinary' in the past (see Chapter 4). Therefore, the change in the designation of the procedure is full of symbolic power and shows that co-decision has become a commonplace feature in the daily life of the EU institutions (Huber and Shackleton 2013). That is why, in order to understand the nature and functions of the EP, we need to understand its role in co-decision: how it negotiates, whose views are prioritised and how this affects the way inputs are translated into outputs.

Since the Single European Act introduced the cooperation procedure in the mid-1980s, there have been numerous attempts to measure to what extent the EP can have influence over the content of legislative outputs under different decision-making rules. This literature is largely influenced by US legislative studies and shows a preference for rational-choice institutionalism and game theory, which explains the widespread use of formal modelling (Crombez and Vangerven 2014; Dowding 2000). These models assume that the EP is a unitary actor that strives to maximise its preferences when negotiating with the other EU institutions (especially the Council and the Commission). These preferences are formed exogenously (outside the EU's political system) and remain stable until the game is over. The models try to understand how different players adapt their strategies under changing institutional conditions. Institutions are thus understood as the rules of the game that allow actors to calculate the costs and benefits of potential outcomes; they supply the stability and information necessary to make rational decisions (Elster 1986; Knight 1992; Shepsle 1989).

Given these assumptions, formal models have been mostly interested in evaluating the opportunities that different procedures offer to the EU decision-makers and how preferences are formed and bargained. Procedural models were the first to be developed and tried to ascertain which institution enjoyed the most influence in decision-making (see Box 11.1). Bargaining models widened the scope and attempted to evaluate whether the influence of EU institutions varies in accordance with

---

Box 11.1   A balancing act: The institutional triangle over time

With the introduction of the cooperation and the co-decision procedure in the late 1980s and early 1990s, a new area of research opened in studies of EU decision-making. Most authors used different procedural models to see whether and to what extent the EP had gained power compared to its role in consultation. Deep disagreements arose between those who considered that the EP had only gained very limited powers under the cooperation procedure and those who saw it as a new 'conditional agenda-setter', considering that it had become easier for the Council to accept rather than reject the EP's amendments – especially if the Commission agreed with them (Crombez 1996; Moser 1996; Tsebelis 1994).

The same debate surrounded co-decision I (Maastricht version), with Garrett and Tsebelis arguing that the EP had lost its role as a 'conditional agenda-setter' and was, therefore, less influential than under cooperation. Scully and Crombez questioned these findings and showed how the EP's amendments were more successful under co-decision I (Crombez et al. 2000; Garrett 1995; Scully 1997; Tsebelis and Garrett 1996). The changes introduced in co-decision II (Amsterdam version) ended this debate and those using procedural models now agree that the EU is moving towards a bicameral system, with the EP playing the role of a true co-legislator, which weakens the Commission's power (Crombez and Vangerven 2014; Tsebelis and Garrett 2000).

The debates have moved instead towards comparing the validity of procedural and bargaining models (Hörl et al. 2005; Thomson et al. 2006; Thomson 2011). Bargaining models underline that, despite the formal veto power of the EP, the Council still enjoys a certain advantage in bargaining processes (Costello and Thomson 2013; Napel and Widgrén 2006). Bargaining models, however, have been criticised for using methodologies that tend to underestimate the role of the Commission and the EP (Slapin 2014). There is, thus, still room for debate, especially when it comes to the role of the Commission and the extent to which it has lost power now that the EP and the Council have developed much closer ties under co-decision (Burns 2014; Crombez and Hix 2011; Nugent and Rhinard 2015).

policy issues or types of decision (e.g. Schneider et al. 2010; Thomson 2011). The focus on bargaining underlined the importance of informality; it showed how the process of finding a majority inside each co-legislator and between them occurred outside formal spaces of deliberation. Agreements were a product of informal talks in halls and corridors among a small number of actors rather than the result of formal negotiations (Farrell and Héritier 2003a; Reh et al. 2013). The importance of informal politics also led proponents of bargaining models to examine the role of actors and practices inside the EU institutions, which pointed at the emergence of new gatekeepers as well as shared institutional norms (Farrell and Héritier 2004; Shackleton 2000; Shackleton and Raunio 2003).

These new dynamics have opened a window for alternative understandings based on constructivist institutionalism. Constructivism assumes that actors do not use strategies to maximise their preferences, but choose rather the actions or roles that are considered most adequate for a given context (Hay 2010; Kauppi and Madsen 2008). Contrary to rational choice, which focuses on rules and procedures, constructivism understands institutions as 'symbol systems, cognitive scripts, and moral templates that provide the "frames of meaning" guiding human action' (Hall and Taylor 1996: 947). In this way, actors' beliefs and ideas can be influenced by an institutional setting, but at the same time, these same actors are also responsible for the inception and change of institutions (Kauppi 2010; Saurugger 2013). The broader understanding of institutions has led constructivist institutionalists to underline the importance of norms and practices as well as the effects of socialisation and learning on actors. This has led to questioning the implications of certain practices of co-decision (such as the informality of negotiations or the normalisation of consensus) on the quality of policy outputs and the legitimacy of the EU's political system (Lord 2013; Neuhold 2007; Reh et al. 2013; Ripoll Servent 2012).

This chapter draws on these different theoretical approaches to understand the role of the EP in co-decision and how this affects inter- and intra-institutional practices. The boxes on the Returns Directive (2008/115/EC) offer an illustration of the processes explained in each section of the chapter.

Early agreements and trilogues: looking for an efficient compromise

As seen in Chapter 4, co-decision has evolved into a procedure where *both* the EP and the Council enjoy the right to veto legislative outcomes. The empowerment of the EP has been at the source of some of the most far-reaching changes in the EU's political system. The necessity to find a compromise between the two co-legislators worked as a driver for the development of new fora for debate and negotiation. At the outset, the introduction of a new legislative body and a longer legislative procedure made many fear that co-decision would turn out to be a slow-moving procedure prone to failure. Since the EP and the Council were not used to working together, it was generally expected that many decisions would end in gridlock. This called for a radical change in the culture of both EU institutions and the development of new instruments that would foster dialogue and prevent stalemate. It resulted in a new institution called 'trilogue' (or 'trialogue') – a series of informal meetings that gather a reduced number of actors from the Council, the Commission and the EP. The Treaty of Amsterdam included the possibility to fast-track legislation, which means that a legislative act can be concluded either after the first reading before the Council decides on its common position or at an early second reading. It did not, however, formally regulate early second readings and the process leading to early agreements (de Ruiter and Neuhold 2012: 538, 541), which turned out to be one of the most 'unexpected informal institutional innovation[s]' of the Treaty of Amsterdam (Farrell and Héritier 2007a: 296). Indeed, early agreements, which started as a mechanism to avoid the time-consuming and unfruitful conciliation procedure, have reached the status of normal behaviour under co-decision (Burns and Carter 2010; Shackleton and Raunio 2003) and their use has steeply increased in recent terms (see Figure 4.4).

Many different reasons have been advanced to explain the rapid increase in early agreements. The EP offers a long list of arguments:

> The cultural 'rapprochement' of the institutions, their increasing familiarity with the codecision procedure, better interinstitutional cooperation at the strategic and agenda-setting levels, the willingness to work quickly, the more flexible procedural arrangements at first reading (where there are no time limits and Parliament votes by simple majority), the 'Coreper-isation' of the procedure in the Council, or the rotating Council Presidency 'scoreboard' mentality (European Parliament 2014a: 44).

Despite their apparent complexity, the majority of these arguments make reference either to the formal aspects of co-decision or to the bicameral nature of EU decision-making.

Formal rules

As seen in Chapter 4, co-decision is composed of three readings, each defined by a particular voting procedure, which offers a partial explanation as to why co-decision fosters early agreements (cf. de Ruiter and

Neuhold 2012). First, the voting majorities make it easier to pass a text in the first reading or early second reading (that is, after the Council reaches a common position) than if it reaches the 'full' second reading. In the first two cases, a simple majority of votes is sufficient to approve the amendments introduced to the Commission's proposal (first reading) or to accept the Council's common position (early second reading). In a 'normal' second reading, the EP requires an absolute majority of MEPs, which is often difficult to find in a chamber without a stable political majority. In addition, the EP's Rules of Procedure also limit the type of amendments that are admissible in the second reading to those that seek to reintroduce part of the EP's first-reading position, amend new elements introduced by the Council in its common position, take into account a new situation or to reach a compromise between the EP and the Council (Rule 69). Thus, these conditions constrain the EP's room for manoeuvre and add pressure to reach a compromise in the first reading. Finally, it should not be forgotten that the time limits for each reading also vary (see Chapter 4). While there is no time limit for the first-reading vote, both the EP and the Council have to cast a second-reading vote within a period of three months (with the possibility to extend it another month). Counter-intuitively, this lack of time constraints has proved especially valuable during difficult or sensitive negotiations (Shackleton 2000: 331). It gives time and space to negotiators from each institution to work informally and vote only when they can gather enough support inside both institutions. Taken together, these three formal elements add serious constraints to the use of a 'full' second reading and can explain why the EP and the Council have found ways to reach compromise as early as possible.

Bicameralism

As mentioned above, apart from formal reasons, there are other dynamics that contribute to early agreements, namely the emergence of a bicameral logic and a shared norm of consensus. The extension of co-decision has turned the EU's political system into something similar to a classic bicameral system. These systems are usually composed of one chamber representing territorial interests (the Council) and the other representing citizens (the Parliament). Under co-decision, the logic of bicameralism leads to a search for inter- and intra-institutional compromise: for instance, the EP has to ensure that it finds support inside the institution so that it can reach the required majority, while *at the same time* proposing amendments that can be backed by a majority in the Council (Costello 2011; Hagemann and Høyland 2010). This bicameral logic puts pressure on both co-legislators to find more efficient ways to work together. Rasmussen (2011) showed how the increased workload that the EP experienced under co-decision, the greater political salience of the files under negotiation (which leads to more political conflict and thus more complicated negotiations) and the need to maintain a good working relationship with the Council had led to a steep increase in the number of early agreements. Although some have remarked that salience and greater distance between the two co-legislators can explain why early agreements do not happen (Hansen 2014), most research coincides with Rasmussen and shows that 'fast-track' deals generally occur when the number of participants and the legislative workload increase, when the file is deemed to be complex and/or urgent, and when it is a political priority for either the EP or the Council (de Ruiter and Neuhold 2012; Reh et al. 2013). Box 11.2 shows how, despite their name, 'fast-track' deals should not be confused with faster legislation.

Box 11.2 A matter of time: How long does it take to reach a decision under co-decision?

Indeed, 'fast-track' legislation does not automatically lead to faster decision-making. As Table 11.1 shows, the increase in early agreements has not been accompanied by a reduction in the average length to find an agreement.

Table 11.1 *Average length for co-decision files*

	1st reading	2nd reading	3rd reading	Total average length
1999–2004	11 months	24 months	31 months	22 months
2004–2009	16 months	29 months	43 months	21 months
2009–2014	17 months	32 months	29 months	19 months
2014–2016	16 months	37 months	–	22 months

Source: European Parliament (2017: 12).

Rasmussen and Toshkov (2011, 2012) have shown that the EP dedicates more time where it enjoys greater formal influence – therefore, co-decision files tend to take longer than negotiations under consultation. In addition, when the EP and the Council hold very different positions on an issue and consider it salient, first-reading deals may take longer than less controversial files that go on to the second or third reading. Therefore, early agreements may hide longer negotiations than second- or third-reading agreements.

The search for more efficient procedures has had two connected consequences. First, early agreements have contributed to the emergence of a culture of consensus in the EU's political system (Reh et al. 2013; Shackleton 2000). This has led to a shift in the Council's behaviour, which has had to incorporate the EP into its legislative practices (Corbett et al. 2007: 226). The Commission has also learnt to involve the EP early during the agenda-setting stage (Kohler 2014). As for internal EP politics, the importance of consensus means that the level of left-right competition remains low – especially during the early stages of negotiations (Settembri and Neuhold 2009). In a way, the Council's long-standing culture of compromise and secrecy (Hayes-Renshaw and Wallace 2006) has made its way into the EP and affected the quality of political debates and the openness of negotiations (Huber and Shackleton 2013; Kohler 2014; Lord 2013; Reh 2014). As a result, many consider that policy outcomes have been affected by the culture of consensus, since only solutions situated at the centre of the political spectrum have a chance at success. It has also reinforced the importance of larger political groups and 'grand coalitions' (de Ruiter and Neuhold 2012; Ripoll Servent 2015).

Trilogues

This trend has been reinforced by the use of 'trilogues'. Shackleton (2000) carefully traced the creation and mainstreaming of trilogues in the legislative arena after co-decision was introduced in the Treaty of Maastricht. Trilogues were already in use for budgetary procedures (Huber and Shackleton 2013: 1043) and in 1993 an Inter-institutional Agreement included the first provisions for a conciliation procedure in the framework of budget negotiations (European Parliament et al. 1993). However, for co-decision, Article 189B (now article 294 TFEU) did not stipulate any provisions for the time preceding the conciliation procedure. This loophole gave way to meetings with more than 100 participants, where finding compromises was close to impossible. When conciliation led to the failure of some difficult files, such as the Biotechnology Directive in 1995 (eventually passed in Directive 98/44/EC), trilogues were introduced to reduce the number of interlocutors and overcome the distrust that had characterised EP–Council relations. This new instrument mirrored the Council's secluded decision-making methods and, therefore, contributed to 'confidence-building' between the two co-legislators (Benedetto 2005: 70; Farrell and Héritier 2007a: 294). In time, trilogues became an accepted institution of conciliation and were rapidly 'so self-evident that no one contested them' (Shackleton 2000: 334). The success of trilogues in the conciliation procedure was such that the Council soon asked for their extension to first- and second-reading negotiations – especially after the introduction of fast-track legislation in the Treaty of Amsterdam. The 'Joint Declaration on Practical Arrangements for the New Co-Decision Procedure' of 1999 identified the positive effects of trilogues and the necessity to extend them beyond conciliation to cover all stages of the co-decision procedure (European Parliament et al. 1999: 1). However, the use of trilogues in earlier stages of the procedure did not come without contestation, especially from some sectors of the EP, which were wary of shifting the debates to a secluded forum reuniting only a very small number of actors (Shackleton and Raunio 2003).

Trilogues are very difficult to study and categorise: they vary in size, frequency, membership and level of discussions. For instance, when the Joint Declaration was revised in 2007 (European Parliament 2007a, Annex B), it emphasised that the 'vitality and flexibility' of trilogues enhanced the chances of first- and second-reading agreements (point 7), but it left the composition and working arrangements relatively vague. Point 9 stated:

> Such trilogues are usually conducted in an informal framework. They may be held at all stages of the procedure and at different levels of representation, depending on the nature of the expected discussion. Each institution, in accordance with its own rules of procedure, will designate its participants for each meeting, define its mandate for the negotiations and inform the other institutions of arrangements for the meetings in good time.

Originally, the EP was represented only by the committee chair and the rapporteur, but this raised concerns about transparency and made it difficult to form coalitions among political groups. Although the early 2000s saw an increase in the size of the EP's delegations and their formalisation into 'negotiating teams', Rule 69f only indicates that these teams 'shall be led by the rapporteur and shall be presided over by the Chair of the committee responsible or by a Vice-Chair designated by the Chair' and that it 'comprise at least the shadow rapporteurs from each political group that wishes to participate'.

Roederer-Rynning and Greenwood (2015) have proposed a multi-layered typology of trilogues. The core of the structure is formed of 'political' trilogue meetings, which correspond to what we classically consider as 'trilogues'. There, the EP is usually represented by a 'negotiating team' of around eight people (one MEP per political group and the committee chair). Sometimes it sends an enlarged delegation that includes MEPs' assistants, political advisors or members of the EP Secretariat. The Council is usually represented by the Presidency and a member of the Council's Secretariat and the Commission by one official of the DG in charge of the dossier. Political trilogues can see ministers as representatives of the Presidency and higher officials, such as heads of unit or

Commissioners negotiating for the Council and the Commission respectively. They usually start after the EP's negotiating team has received a mandate from its committee and end when a compromise is reached.

'Technical' trilogues often precede full political trilogues, and since they often avoid political issues, MEPs may decide to send members of staff instead of attending themselves. The Commission and the Council also tend to send officials and diplomats lower in the hierarchy. Surrounding these two types of trilogue, there are also 'informal (bilateral) contacts', especially between the EP and a new Council Presidency. These contacts may take the form of 'speed-dating' meetings, which allow the Presidency's permanent representatives or the chairs of the relevant Council working group to meet with the respective EP committee chairs, so that they can agree on which files should be given priority and which ones should be closed by the end of the Presidency's six-month term. These informal contacts serve to adjust the agendas of the two co-legislators and may also offer an opportunity for the Presidency to approach shadow rapporteurs before an *esprit de corps* forms among the members of the EP's negotiating team. It is, therefore, very difficult to determine how many trilogues are necessary to reach an agreement. Many informal contacts take place well in advance, even before a member state is officially holding the Council Presidency (Roederer-Rynning and Greenwood 2015). However, the salience or difficulty of the dossier is usually indicative of the frequency and total number of trilogues; longer proposals, trilogues with a higher number of shadows, politicisation in the Council and opposition to the rapporteur's position (which implies a larger number of EP amendments) can all contribute to increasing the number of formal trilogues (Brandsma 2015). There are also variations across policy issues and EP committees, which may be related to the number and salience of dossiers they negotiate or the committee's culture when it comes to trilogues and early agreements. Table 11.2 offers an overview of the variation in the number of trilogues held by each EP committee – although in some cases files might be shared by two committees.

As can be seen in Table 11.2, four committees – ECON, ENVI, LIBE and AGRI – comprise half of the trilogue meetings. In some cases, this can be explained by their large share of co-decision files. For instance, the ENVI committee dealt with 14 per cent of co-decisions between 2009 and 2014, while the ECON committee took up 11 per cent of the share and the LIBE committee 10 per cent. However, International Trade (INTA), which also had 10 per cent of co-decision files, accounts only for fewer than 5 per cent of trilogues (European Parliament 2014a: 7). The percentages can also hide extreme variations in the number of trilogues held for every file. Normal negotiations require between one and four formal trilogues, preceded probably by around ten 'technical' trilogues (Roederer-Rynning and Greenwood 2015). However, some

Table 11.2 *Trilogues per committee during the 7th parliamentary term (2009–2014)*

Committee	Number of trilogues	Number of trilogues (%)
ECON	331	21.66
ENVI	172	11.26
LIBE	155	10.14
AGRI	105	6.87
REGI	96	6.28
EMPL	95	6.22
TRAN	89	5.82
ITRE	86	5.63
IMCO	71	4.65
INTA	67	4.38
JURI	66	4.32
AFET	41	2.68
PECH	34	2.23
BUDG	22	1.44
DEVE	20	1.31
BUDG/CONT	20	1.31
CULT	16	1.05
CONT	15	0.98
AFCO	9	0.59
ITRE/TRAN	9	0.59
LIBE/FEMM	6	0.39
FEMM	2	0.13
JURI/FEMM	1	0.07
Total	1,528	100.00

Source: European Parliament (2014a: 20).

cases need many more (political) trilogues to find an agreement. For instance, the Common Provisions Regulation (1303/2013/EU) needed 54 trilogues to be concluded (European Parliament 2014a: 19). This means that out of the 96 trilogues held by the REGI committee, 54 were dedicated to only one file. The remaining 42 would situate it in a similar league to the AFET committee.

Early agreements and trilogues have become a normal part of co-decision, although the ease with which they have seemingly been internalised into the practices of the EU's decision-making process hides wider dynamics of inclusion and exclusion (Farrell and Héritier 2004; Farrell and Héritier 2007a). As seen above, the bicameral logic driving co-decision has led to a smaller number of possible winning coalitions, usually situated at the centre of the political spectrum. This contributes to enhancing the coherence of coalitions, but it also creates clearer winners and losers during negotiations (Costello 2011). So, while the EPP and the S&D have become the main players of co-decision, smaller political groups have often suffered under it and have had to become accustomed to the 'tyranny of the majority' (de Ruiter and Neuhold 2012; Farrell and Héritier 2003a; Hausemer 2006; see also Chapter 8). Box 11.3 shows us the importance of trilogues in the course of specific

---

Box 11.3   The Returns Directive: The long shadow of a second-reading vote

The negotiations on common standards to return irregularly-staying migrants are considered to be the first 'normal' co-decision file in the Area of Freedom, Security and Justice. The directive (2008/115/EC) was finalised as a first-reading agreement in December 2008, more than three years after it had been proposed by the Commission. Negotiations spanned over six different Council Presidencies; some, like the German, almost managed to block the proposal while others, like the Portuguese and Slovenian Presidencies, were essential in securing a deal. Inside the EP, it was also very difficult to know where political groups stood, especially since there was an unusually long gap of around nine months between the committee and the plenary votes. During this period, there were both technical and political trilogues, in which the content of the proposal varied widely (and wildly).

It was a very salient and contested file, but the EP justified the early agreement by using both procedural and normative arguments. On the one hand, the EP was afraid that the Council would refuse to negotiate beyond the first-reading stage, since member states did not actually want common EU standards. There was also some uncertainty on whether the agreement would receive enough support to achieve the higher second-reading voting majorities, especially since some political groups were internally divided on the issue. Therefore, the EPP-ED and ALDE groups preferred to secure a deal at first reading than risk going further into a second reading. On the other hand, some political groups were particularly willing to show that they were 'responsible' and 'mature' partners for the Council and that they could be relied upon in further co-decision negotiations (Ripoll Servent 2015).

negotiations and how political actors justified the decision to stop after the EP's first-reading vote.

The growing importance of rapporteurs

If there is a category of actors that has increased in importance under co-decision, it is rapporteurs. As seen in Chapters 3 and 8, rapporteurs are key actors in decision-making. Those MEPs selected to lead negotiations and write a report are in a privileged position to select the demands that will be translated into outputs. The possibility to act as a rapporteur gives individual parliamentarians more scope for influence over specific files than in most national parliaments. It is, therefore, essential to understand how they are selected, their responsibilities and effectiveness and their leeway in inter-institutional negotiations.

The selection of rapporteurs

Despite the important role of rapporteurs, their appointment is largely informal and varies from committee to committee. The Rules of Procedure only establish that, for legislative reports, 'the committee shall appoint a rapporteur on the proposal for a legislative act from among its members or permanent substitutes' (Rule 49.2). Rapporteurships may be assigned at two different moments in time: the EP may allocate a rapporteur to particular proposals that have already been planned in the Commission's annual or multiannual Work Programme (see Box 5.2), so that rapporteurs can follow this file during the agenda-setting phase. Otherwise, rapporteurs are nominated when the EP has formally received a Commission proposal and appointed a lead committee to take care of that particular file. Either way, political coordinators are responsible for 'acquiring' and distributing rapporteurships among their members. This procedure is guided by complex and highly informal rules, which set up a points system similar to an auction. Political groups receive a number of points proportional to their members in Parliament or a particular committee. When a rapporteur needs to be assigned, political coordinators bid points depending on the importance they attach to the file. If more than one group bids the same number of points, the report should go to the group that has spent fewer points from the original quota; however, groups usually try to find an agreement, often in the form of a package deal. The system is relatively flexible – for instance, if a group has expired its points, more points are 'topped up' to the quota of each political group; at the same time, if a group proposes an MEP that is considered an expert in a specific topic early in the process, the file will most probably go to the group for few (or no) points. The system becomes more rigid and politicised for files that are seen as particularly sensitive, which may end up in a co-rapporteurship of two political groups (Benedetto 2005: 71; Corbett et al. 2016: 184–185). Once allocated to a specific group, the nomination of a specific MEP is an internal matter, with groups often seeking to balance the size of national delegations, expertise and constituency interests (Clark and Priestley 2012: 243).

Due to the informal nature of the system and the distribution of points, many have wondered whether the selection of rapporteurs is representative of the overall EP composition. Yordanova (2011) showed how, formally, the points system is more favourable to larger political groups, since they have more points to allocate and have better chances to obtain 'bigger' files. Smaller political groups are particularly disadvantaged in the allocation of co-decision reports, since these are usually more expensive. If a group tries to save points for a more important file by failing to bid for a report, it is often penalised and loses some points. Therefore, smaller political groups have to opt often for 'cheaper' reports; otherwise they can attempt to heighten the stakes of reports that are of particular interest for some of the larger political groups, so that they have to pay more for them (Corbett et al. 2016: 184–185; Yordanova 2011: 101).

In addition to formal sources of bias, there are other elements that can explain the 'world of disproportionality' in the allocation of reports (Kaeding 2005). At the level of individual MEPs, bias can be the result of self-selection: those parliamentarians with a clear interest or particular expertise on a topic will tend to put themselves forward. Therefore, it is normal that the rapporteur has more marked positions on a given policy issue than non-expert MEPs (Benedetto 2005; Kaeding 2004; Yoshinaka et al. 2010). At the same time, a disproportional distribution of reports can also be due to the fact that some parliamentarians are more active than others or that more senior and highly educated MEPs are believed to have more expertise, and thus get more reports. Clearly, the ideological distance between rapporteurs and their political groups matters: 'mainstream' MEPs have more chances to be selected than more extreme members. The allocation of reports is, thus, a strong mechanism to maintain the ideological cohesion of political groups (see also Chapter 9). Finally, it is interesting to note that Eurosceptic MEPs tend to be allocated fewer reports, even accounting for their absenteeism, which clearly reinforces the EP's pro-integration bias (Daniel 2013; Yordanova 2011; Yoshinaka et al. 2010).

At the level of political groups, disproportionality is generally linked to an unequal distribution of reports across groups and national party delegations. There are different explanations for this type of bias. First, it is perfectly possible that some political groups or nationalities (for example new member states) are more active than others, or that those with fewer resources (smaller groups or NPDs) concentrate on a limited number of issues or committees (Benedetto 2005; Hurka and Kaeding 2011; Kaeding 2005). Second, larger national delegations tend to be over-represented in the EPP and S&D groups, probably due to the fact that members from these countries can act as gatekeepers and ensure that reports go to colleagues from their country (Mamadouh and Raunio 2003). Finally, there are also sources of bias at the system level. Høyland (2006) has pointed out that the unequal distribution of reports could be explained by looking at the links between the Council and the EP. MEPs from national parties in government (and thus sitting in the Council) tend to get more rapporteurships. However, the same effect is visible when there is a clear ideological majority in the Council; in those cases, rapporteurs coming from the same party family are also more likely to get reports (even if their national party does not sit in the Council). Therefore, it seems that those MEPs who can more easily contribute to inter-institutional consensus are rewarded with more rapporteurships. Inside the EP, a similar logic explains why, during the sixth parliamentary term (2004–2009), members of the EPP-ED and ALDE were over-represented in the allocation of reports. Yordanova (2011) argues that the EPP-ED made it easier for members of the ALDE group to get rapporteurships, because they believed that offering them these positions would contribute to building coalitions large enough to secure a simple majority. As a consequence, ALDE got a disproportionate number of reports, especially when compared to the size of the socialist group. There are, thus, several dimensions that explain why the allocation of co-decision reports does not exactly mirror the composition of the EP's plenary: personal characteristics and interests, internal group dynamics, as well as an attempt to build successful coalitions inside the EP and with the Council. What is clear, however, is that the selection process does not contribute to improving the transparency and the democratic standards of the EP (Reh 2014).

Responsibilities and effectiveness

The work of the rapporteur is to gather any amendments to the Commission's proposal and add a short justification for their inclusion; draft a legislative resolution (a statement stating whether the EP approves, rejects or proposes amendments to the Commission's proposal as well as any procedural demands) and write an explanatory statement to clarify the changes and establish their financial implications (Rules 49). The rapporteur is also in charge of negotiations with the Council (as leader of the EP's negotiating team), although this is often shared with the committee chair, who is formally in charge of reporting back and explaining any amendments that have been tabled after discussions with the Council. Rapporteurs can try to smooth the process by proposing compromise amendments that gather the views of various political groups (Rule 170). In the event of a conciliation meeting, the rapporteur has to be a member of the EP's delegation (Rule 71). Finally, they are also in charge of presenting the report to the plenary and explaining the amendments introduced to a proposal before the vote takes place (Rules 162 and 171).

Therefore, by being in control of the entire procedure, rapporteurs can effectively leave their imprint on policy outputs (Benedetto 2005; Yordanova 2011; Yoshinaka et al. 2010). This means that acting as a rapporteur can make or break a political career and this is often difficult to predict at the outset of negotiations (Clark and Priestley 2012: 243). Since rapporteurs are in charge of writing the report and justifying amendments, they have a 'first-mover' advantage. It becomes more difficult for other MEPs to overturn amendments once they have been written down in a draft report. Therefore, rapporteurs can benefit from having better access to information and could even, theoretically, block or slow down legislative negotiations (Yoshinaka et al. 2010). Costello and Thomson (2010) have shown that rapporteurs are able to set the agenda and shape policy outcomes under co-decision since they are better informed about the content of the dossier (due to their expertise) and about the position of member states in the Council. This advantage is particularly important when legislation is decided in an early agreement, since it gives fewer opportunities to scrutinise legislation to other members (see also Farrell and Héritier 2004). Surprisingly, Costello and Thomson also noticed that the nationality of rapporteurs was a better indicator of personal biases than their partisan ideology. This unexpected outcome is easier to understand if rapporteurships are seen as occasions when MEPs enjoy greater autonomy and leadership and are thus more ready to listen to other sources of influence such as domestic actors or national governments. Indeed, the leeway of particular members is much greater in a system where the executive power is diluted and does not depend on the support of a legislative majority (Yoshinaka et al. 2010).

The influence of rapporteurs in co-decision negotiations

The question is thus, how much freedom do rapporteurs enjoy and how much can they bias the output of legislation? Actually, much less than what could be expected. As seen above, the selection of MEPs already prevents bias to a large extent. First, the majority of rapporteurs are 'median MEPs', who hold mainstream positions and rarely act in an extreme or 'irresponsible' manner (Costello and Thomson 2011; Rasmussen 2011). Most rapporteurs share certain institutional norms that define their role as that of a 'loyal agent'. In consequence, political coordinators tend to reward those rapporteurs that are seen to have been loyal to the EP's general interest, especially if they hold positions that are considered to foster internal and inter-institutional compromises (Costello and Thomson 2011; Hausemer 2006; Rasmussen and Reh 2013; Yordanova 2011).

There is, however, another aspect that limits the influence of rapporteurs. The bicameral nature of co-decision asks for consensus, which turns rapporteurs into 'Jekyll-and-Hyde' figures: they have to find a difficult balance between pushing for their personal or partisan interests and making sure that there is enough consensus among all the parties involved (Yoshinaka et al. 2010: 462). In practice, this means that rapporteurs have no space for radicalism (Finke 2012; Kreppel and Tsebelis 1999), especially once co-decision has gone beyond the early stages and compromises need to have the backing of an absolute majority (Benedetto 2005). The bicameral logic raises the chances of MEPs from centre-right and larger political groups to be appointed to rapporteurships – since they are at the core of most EP coalitions (Yordanova 2011). This also means that the largest groups enjoy the 'tyranny of the majority', since rapporteurs from smaller groups need to find the support of the EPP or the S&D to form a coalition that can ensure enough support at the plenary level (Hausemer 2006: 513). Box 11.4 shows that rapporteurs have a wide leeway, but the structural characteristics of the political system serve as checks on their initiatives and limit their actions leading to more moderate outcomes that reflect the balance of power among EP groups and with the Council.

Shaping the negotiations: shadow rapporteurs, committee chairs and 'relais' actors

The influence of rapporteurs has been gradually reduced through the participation of other 'relais' actors – that is, gatekeepers that can steer the internal and external organisation of the institution and exert some control over negotiations (Farrell and Héritier 2004; Judge and Earnshaw 2011). This group of actors is relatively diffuse, but it usually refers to the key actors that have been examined in Chapter 3, namely, committee chairs, political coordinators, leaders of national

---

Box 11.4   The Returns Directive: Biased by a more conservative rapporteur?

The choice of rapporteur was essential for the success of the Returns Directive. In fact, it seems that the report should have gone to the GUE/NGL group, but the EPP-ED fought to have a Christian Democrat appointed as rapporteur. Ultimately, the political coordinators in LIBE agreed to give the report to Manfred Weber, a German EPP-ED member (and now leader of the EPP group). The rapporteurship gave a clear advantage to the Christian Democrats, who could insert many of their positions into the final compromise. In order to ensure the support of the other political groups, Weber backed issues that were considered of high importance by the EPP-ED. For instance, smaller groups like the Greens had a keen interest in the protection of underage migrants. This did not stop him from introducing amendments (such as a longer period of detention for those migrants that are going to be sent back) that were convenient for both his country and his political group. Therefore, while the rapporteur had to take into consideration the position of other EP groups, he still had a strong impact on the final outcome. At the same time, it is fair to say that the choice of a (German) Christian Democrat made a political agreement much more likely than if a member of the radical left had been responsible for the file (Ripoll Servent 2015).

---

delegations and shadow rapporteurs. In one way or another, they all have the capacity to control the actions of rapporteurs and prevent negotiations from going too far away from a position that can be supported by a majority of MEPs. Their role has been enhanced with the formalisation of 'negotiating teams' and the obligation to report and follow the mandate of committees and/or plenary (see also Chapter 10).

The practice of an EP 'negotiating team' has led to more complex inter-personal dynamics, since the relationship between key players can make or break the outcome of a file. This is particularly true for shadow rapporteurs, that is, MEPs from other political groups that oversee the work of the rapporteur and usually participate in trilogues with the Council and the Commission. With the rise of informal politics, their role and the relationship they form with the rapporteur have become essential in determining their capacity to influence policy outcomes. Good working relationships between the shadows and the rapporteur can make the EP's position stronger in trilogues, while personal or partisan disputes can weaken the EP and offer opportunities to bypass the rapporteur and negotiate directly with shadow rapporteurs (Judge and Earnshaw 2011).

Leaders of national delegations and political coordinators are also in a privileged position vis-à-vis the members of their group (Whitaker 2011). Political coordinators have become central to the decision-making process, since they are responsible for allocating reports and ensuring the cohesion of their political group in a given issue area. By acting as agents of the political group's leadership, coordinators can reward or punish loyal MEPs and control committee business – especially in the presence of weak committee chairs (Whitaker 2001; Yordanova 2011). The Conference of Presidents also underlined in its 'Guidelines for First and Second Reading Agreements' that coordinators should be in charge of deciding the composition of the EP's negotiating team. Coordinators were thus identified as the main 'relais' between members of the trilogue and specific political groups (European Parliament 2004: 9).

There has long been some controversy on the role of committee chairs and their capacity to steer co-decision negotiations. Some consider that committee chairs have lost their influence on rapporteurs and group coordinators, who are in a better position thanks to their direct access to information (Farrell and Héritier 2004; Yordanova 2009a). Others remark that their influence is closely related to their personality and political capital, but that when they are 'active' chairs, their presence in the negotiation team and their formal role in committees offers them an excellent opportunity to check the rapporteur, steer debates and set the agenda (Clark and Priestley 2012: 198; Neuhold 2001; Rasmussen and Reh 2013: 1019; Whitaker 2001). Roederer-Rynning and Greenwood (2017) have explored the role of committee chairs in trilogues and come to the conclusion that there are important variations across committees and chairs. The default approach is that of a division of labour between technical and political trilogues, with the chair attending principally the latter. However, this approach varies in practice, with some chairs using more dramaturgical performances to enforce collective strategies and force the Council to send high-ranking representatives (what they call the 'gladiatorial' approach), whereas others prefer to adopt a problem-solving attitude, which means that they act in a neutral and businesslike manner. Finally, some chairs decide to keep trilogues at arm's length, so that when they decide to attend, everybody knows that things are getting serious. Roederer-Rynning and Greenwood have also showed that different committees understand the role of the chair in trilogues differently. In some cases, chairs concentrate on presiding over meetings, leaving the task of negotiating to the rapporteur. In other occasions, chairs are micro-managers that end up acting as de facto negotiators, whereas in some committees, chairs have been so erratic that the Secretariat has had to step in and behave as the EP negotiator.

Indeed, one should not forget that the EP's negotiating team receives technical and political support from a large number of actors that often remain hidden behind the scenes. As seen in Chapter 8, the negotiating team receives support from the EP's Secretariat and, in trilogue meetings, individual MEPs are often accompanied (or even represented) by their assistants or political advisors from their political groups (Benedetto 2005: 69). This means that information may flow through more channels than originally imagined and that the negotiating team may have a more diverse membership than what was formally foreseen in the Rules of Procedure.

Box 11.5 shows how important internal (and personal) dynamics are for determining the success and shape of policy outputs.

Box 11.5   The Returns Directive: The traps of non-representative shadows

The internal dynamics of the EP's negotiating team are decisive to explain the outcome of negotiations. On the left side of the political spectrum, the GUE/NGL simply refused to participate in trilogues because they did not agree with the idea that migrants should be returned. In comparison, the shadow rapporteur for the Greens (Jean Lambert, UK) learnt to be more moderate and deemed any outcome negotiated by the EP to be better than the status quo. The position of the Socialists was largely influenced by the two French shadow rapporteurs, who held more 'maximalist' and pro-migrant positions than was usual for the group. In the middle stood the liberal group, whose rapporteur (Jeanine Hennis-Plasschaert, NL) was more to the right and closer to the EPP-ED and the Council than other sections of her group. It was therefore relatively natural for the rapporteur to find in the ALDE shadow an ally, especially when the first socialist shadow rapporteur (Adeline Hazan) left and Martine Roure replaced her and took a more combative position, questioning most of the issues that had already been agreed upon with the Council. In addition, the LIBE committee was, at that time, chaired by a Belgian liberal MEP (Gérard Deprez), who followed the negotiations closely and tried to ensure that the rapporteur stuck to the committee's mandate. His position was, thus, more institutionally oriented and he considered that the priority was to deliver a compromise with the Council so that more co-decision would come their way (Ripoll Servent 2015).

Reversing political developments?

Despite the growing importance of relais actors, the increase in early agreements, followed by the normalisation of trilogues and the formalisation of a negotiating team, has led to new dynamics of inclusion and exclusion inside the EP (Farrell and Héritier 2003b; Héritier and Reh 2012). Those who do not take part in trilogues have increasingly felt that they were losing control over the content of agreements. As a result, the Parliament has witnessed a long process of institutional change started under the aegis of a 'Working Party for Parliamentary Reform' set up in 2007. The outcomes of the Working Party led to the introduction of a new 'Code of Conduct for Negotiating Codecision Files' in May 2009. Although the Code of Conduct did not clarify when it is appropriate to use the fast-track procedure (de Ruiter and Neuhold 2012: 542), it did address the question of control and oversight through two key arrangements. First, it introduced an 'orientation vote' that preceded the first-reading vote in a committee and led to a mandate for the negotiating team (point 4). In a way, this instrument added an informal half-reading before the first-reading vote – which compensates for the fact that co-decision has slowly become a single-reading procedure (Roederer-Rynning and Greenwood 2015: 1148). Second, the Code of Conduct also insisted on the necessity to report back to the responsible committee after each trilogue. It was an attempt to keep other members informed of the proceedings and offer them an opportunity to reel negotiations back in or update the mandate (point 6). After the Conference of Presidents requested a more thorough investigation on the EP's internal working methods in March 2011, the Committee on Constitutional Affairs produced a report that led to further changes in the EP's Rules of Procedure in late 2012 (2011/2298/REG). Rule 73 (now 69b) formalised the necessity to inform and receive a mandate from the committee responsible, while Rule 74 (now deleted) allowed the plenary to be informed if negotiations were started before a report was adopted in committee (European Parliament 2014a: 20–21). Despite these changes, trilogues have continued to raise criticism and have even become the object of an investigation by the ombudsman. Her inquiry led to the conclusion that, even with the efforts made by EU institutions to improve the transparency, for outsiders, 'it is difficult to find out when trilogues are taking place, what is being discussed and by whom without a great deal of time and effort' (European Ombudsman 2016). In order to limit some of these negative externalities, the EP, the Council and the Commission signed in May 2015 an Inter-institutional Agreement on Better Law-Making, which established that 'the three Institutions will ensure the transparency of legislative procedures ... including an appropriate handling of trilateral negotiations. The three Institutions will improve communication to the public during the whole legislative cycle' (point 38). To this effect, the 2016 reform of the EP's Rules of Procedure introduced a new section dedicated to 'Interinstitutional Negotiations during the Ordinary Legislative Procedure', which aimed to provide more guidance as regards the use of trilogues. The new rules contemplate the possibility that the plenary votes on the decision of a committee to start inter-institutional negotiations before the first-reading vote (Rule 69c).

We see, thus, how the fear of losing control over the content of agreements has led the EP to develop new mechanisms that offer a better oversight and reduce the informality of early agreements (see Box 11.6). These new instruments give more control to actors external to negotiations, which is particularly important in files which are highly politicised inside both the EP and the Council (Rasmussen and Reh 2013). Therefore, we have witnessed a process of gradual change that attempts to reverse some of the early informal developments that had led to many questioning the transparency and democracy of trilogues (Roederer-Rynning and Greenwood 2017).

Box 11.6   The Returns Directive: Leaving with a horse and coming back with a camel

Negotiated between 2006 and 2008, the Returns Directive is a good example of early-style trilogues and why they raised the hackles on those members who are not part of the negotiating team. As we have seen in Box 11.3, trilogue negotiations were extremely complex, to the point that the LIBE committee lost track of what was happening between the EP and the Council. The fact that the report had already been voted in committee meant that the other LIBE members had no formal way to control the activities of their negotiators. The latter were so desperate to get a deal out of an extremely reticent Council that they deviated widely from the content of the draft report. In the end, the political agreement was presented to the plenary as a 'take-it-or-leave-it' deal and submitted as an EPP-ED amendment for the plenary vote of 18 June 2008. The legislative resolution was eventually adopted with a relatively narrow majority of 369 votes in favour, 201 against and 106 abstentions. The Returns Directive left many LIBE members with a bad taste in their mouths, which led them to introduce a new 'orientation vote' that should act as a mandate for the committee's negotiating team (Ripoll Servent 2015).

Inter-institutional relations: policy-making and the weight of institutional interests

The introduction of co-decision has substantially changed the shape of the EU's policy process, both formally and informally. The increase in early readings and the consolidation of a culture of consensus has had a direct impact on the shape of policies and the internal politics of the EP. There are two main factors that explain why policy outputs are now more moderate and tend to represent positions at the centre of the political spectrum. First, as seen above, the formal structure of co-decision favours decisions made at an early stage. As a consequence, the EP often adopts a behaviour known as 'anticipatory compliance'. This means that the EP's negotiating team uses trilogues and informal negotiations to predict which amendments might have a better chance to succeed. Consequently, those amendments and proposals that are deemed too radical are not even included in the EP's (draft) report (Burns and Carter 2010). Given that this kind of behaviour can also be observed in the Council, and especially the Commission (Burns 2004), it is not surprising that the individual positions of the different EU institutions tend to look very similar. In most cases, negotiators do not have to make a choice between radically different solutions; rather, they merely calibrate and adjust their respective positions. It is, therefore, not surprising that most legislation negotiated under co-decision is characterised for its very temperate solutions and limited opportunities to change the core of specific policies (Costello 2011; Trauner and Ripoll Servent 2016).

In addition, co-decision has led to a new culture of consensus and inter-institutional loyalty. As a co-legislator, the EP has increasingly felt the weight of responsibility, towards both the other policy-makers and EP voters. An important consequence of this has been a marked decline in political conflict among parliamentarians, who have become more self-aware of the crucial role they play in shaping EU policies. As seen in Chapter 2, the EP had been perceived for a long time as a mere 'talking shop'; it could bark but not bite, and therefore, it tended to adopt relatively extreme or 'maximalist' positions (Huber and Shackleton 2013: 1041–1042). Once it gained the capacity to co-decide, many looked at the EP with suspicion – wondering whether it would be able to function as a 'responsible' legislator. The feeling of being under probation led MEPs to change their behaviour and show that they could become more 'mature' and adopt the 'realism' deemed necessary for reaching compromises (Huber and Shackleton 2013; Maurer 2007; Priestley 2008; Ripoll Servent 2015). For instance, it is quite telling that the EP sought from an early stage to learn the working methods of the

Council – which led to the emergence and normalisation of trilogues, as examined above. By doing so, the EP increased its reputation in front of a Council often dubious of Parliament's capacity to cooperate and be constructive (Shackleton 2000: 329). Equally telling is the central role that the liberal group has acquired for the success of EP coalitions – its median role, between Socialists and the centre-right, places it in a perfect position to offer support for more moderate and centrist policy solutions (Costello 2011: 137). More than 20 years after the introduction of co-decision, there has been an unerring willingness by the Parliament to show that it can be a full and trusted partner in co-decision, which has led to more moderate outputs as well as a recurrence of 'grand coalitions' in EP politics (Hix and Høyland 2013).

What has been the impact of co-decision for the overall balance of power? Not surprisingly, the EP is now seen as an equal partner with the Council, sharing responsibility (and blame) over legislative outcomes (see also Box 11.7). This is at least the formal part of the story; informally, the Council still enjoys a more predominant position in inter-institutional relations. There are two reasons that explain the Council's greater role in decision-making. The first one has to do with the formal structure of co-decision. If we look at the second-reading stage, it is easier for the EP to just accept the Council's common

---

Box 11.7   Conditions of EP success and failure under co-decision

When does the EP have better chances to influence policy outputs and when does it tend to fail? This is a question that still occupies researchers interested in EU policy-making; when taken in all its complexity, the legislative process can provide an extremely high number of conditions that help to explain the success or failure of the EP. Therefore, the conditions presented here are the most commonly cited, but offer only a partial picture. Farrell and Héritier (2007b) identified four conditions that may have an impact on the EP's influence. First, veto powers refer to the chances to block or delay legislation and are closely linked to factors like the shadow of an absolute majority in second reading. Second, time horizons consider the level of impatience of each co-legislator: the longer the EP can wait, the higher the chances of success. At the same time, if the outcome of a bargain casts a shadow over future or ongoing negotiations, this might make the EP more reluctant to push its luck and lead it to accept a sub-optimal solution. Third, the EP is often more sensitive to failure because of its pro-integrationist stances, which means that it prefers some limited change rather than going

→

position, since it needs only a simple majority. By contrast, if it wants to amend or reject it, the EP has to gather an absolute majority of its members, which is often a difficult task. Hagemann and Høyland (2010: 830) have shown how the Council enjoys a formal advantage over the EP, since

> while the qualified majority requirement in the Council is for making a proposal, the absolute majority requirement in the Parliament is for amending the proposal made by the Council. If the Council fails to meet the qualified majority requirement, the status quo continues. If the Parliament fails to meet the absolute majority requirement, the proposal from the Council is adopted.

The other reason why the bicameral system is biased towards the Council is the past and present role of member states in the EU's policy process. Member states were the sole legislative power until the late 1980s, when the SEA introduced the cooperation procedure. In some cases, this privileged position lasted until 2009, with the entry into force of the Treaty of Lisbon. In practice, this meant that many EU policies were decided by the Council alone. Therefore, the status quo is usually closer to the Council's position than to the EP's, in that if there is no

→

back to the status quo. Finally, the 'justiciability' of matters might help the EP to push for policy changes, since it can 'threaten' to refer conflicts to the CJEU.

Apart from these formal aspects, there are other 'softer' conditions that may affect the chances of the EP under co-decision. For instance, if the EP is able to show a unified front or frame its positions in a way that cannot be normatively contested (e.g. by alluding to international norms such as human rights), then it will prove more difficult for the Council to 'divide and conquer'. However, as mentioned above, the chances of success sometimes depend on conditions that are difficult to control, such as the Council Presidency leading the negotiations or the internal dynamics among the EP negotiating team (Judge and Earnshaw 2011; Kreppel and Hix 2003; Rose and Borz 2013; Trauner and Ripoll Servent 2016). Attention should also be paid to the changing nature of EU policy-making, especially in a setting where various crises have underscored the preference of member states for intergovernmental solutions and the capacity to use the European Council to bypass 'ordinary' forms of decision-making (e.g. Fabbrini and Puetter 2016). Therefore, if the EU's political system transforms itself radically, we may need more research to understand how this affects Parliament's position in the system and its capacity to influence outputs.

agreement between the two co-legislators, member states are usually less affected by keeping things as they are than the EP, which is often the one looking for changes in specific policies. Member states are usually in a better negotiating position than the EP, especially if the latter fails to adopt a united front and the Council can use the EP's internal divisions to 'divide and conquer' (Costello and Thomson 2013; Roederer-Rynning and Greenwood 2015; Trauner and Ripoll Servent 2016).

The informal advantage enjoyed by the Council under co-decision explains to a large extent why the EP still portrays a taste for big inter-institutional battles. As seen in Chapter 2, past imbalances in the balance of power have led the EP to be particularly self-conscious when it comes to asserting its influence (Priestley 2008). This tendency has manifested itself in two ways. In some cases, the EP has pushed its institutional interests almost to the point of blocking the EU's political process. Even after the Treaty of Lisbon, the EP has sought to expand or reaffirm its role in certain areas by proposing new interpretations of the formal rules. As we have seen in Chapter 4, in the area of international agreements, the EP blocked the first occasion in which it could consent on an agreement with the US in order to make sure that it would be fully involved in negotiations from the earliest possible stage (Ripoll Servent 2014). Similarly, negotiations on the budget and the Multiannual Financial Framework were blocked in 2013 when the EP felt that its voice was not getting through to the member states (Clark and Priestley 2012: 298–304). As Box 11.8 shows, the attempts to enlarge the EP's powers might sometimes have unexpected (and unwelcome) effects.

The primacy of institutional interests may have unintended consequences, especially when policy outputs are sacrificed at the expense of compromise. It is becoming apparent that early agreements and the culture of consensus affect the quality and effectiveness of the EU's policy process and deliver suboptimal results. There is indeed a feeling that the EP is often not getting as much out of co-decision as it could for fear of violating the shared institutional norm of consensus and 'responsibility' (Andlovic and Lehmann 2014; de Ruiter and Neuhold 2012; Ripoll Servent 2015). Box 11.9 shows a practical case in which the EP's attempts to assert its powers went against its potential use of co-decision to substantially change a very sensitive policy area.

Conclusion

Co-decision has revolutionised the way the EP works and its place in the EU's political system. The acquisition of full veto power over policy outcomes means that the EP is now a 'full' or 'mature' parliament

Box 11.8 The battle over delegated and implementing acts

The EU's political system has long been characterised by the high number of decisions delegated to the Commission. As the EEC developed, member states feared that the Commission would become too independent when adopting executive acts so, in order to control its autonomy, developed a complex system of committees formed of member states' representatives, known as 'comitology' that was only formalised with the Single European Act. In turn, the central role played by national officials and representatives raised concerns on the EP's side, since it suspected that member states and the Commission were using comitology to introduce changes to EU legislation that should have involved the EP, especially since the introduction of co-decision. Therefore, over the years, the EP tried to restrict the scope of comitology, while at the same time claiming that the power to co-decide should be matched with a similar power to participate in the control of executive acts. These wishes seemed to be fulfilled in the Treaty of Lisbon, which replaced the old comitology system with two new articles; Article 290 TFEU gave both the Council and the EP control over delegated acts, while Article 291 TFEU reserved control over implementing acts to member states (Brandsma and Blom-Hansen 2012; Héritier 2012; Héritier and Moury 2011).

However, what looked likely to be one of the most important victories for the EP has proved rather short-lived. The implementation of the two treaty articles has led to unexpected outcomes. First, through informal arrangements, many of the former comitology structures have been reinstated. Second, the interpretation that member states have made of the two articles has allowed the Council to 'claw back' powers from the EP. It seems, thus, that the EP was successful in influencing treaty negotiations, but that a lack of interest and expertise has affected its capacity to maintain its powers during the implementation of the treaties. The EP has paid more attention to securing its formal rights in delegated acts than overseeing the use of implementing acts. The irony is that the EP's power in delegating acts may turn out to be a 'nuclear' weapon that works better in theory than in practice, while implementing acts are now completely outside its control (Brandsma and Blom-Hansen 2012; Christiansen and Dobbels 2012, 2013a, 2013b).

with highly complex practices that allow for an efficient translation of inputs into outputs. In this sense, the EP has shown great ability to adapt its internal structures and find very imaginative solutions to the challenges brought by co-decision. Notably, early agreements have grown so quickly that they are now the expected outcome of any

---

Box 11.9   The Returns Directive: Legitimising security for the sake of institutional maturity

The Returns Directive is a classic example of policy interests being trumped by institutional concerns. Despite gaining the right to introduce substantial changes to the EU's immigration policies, the outcome of negotiations was generally criticised for being too close to the Council's interests. It was particularly disappointing for NGOs and human rights advocates, who saw how the EP went from being one of the most outspoken supporters of human rights and civil liberties to endorsing extremely contested principles, notably the possibility to detain migrants before they are returned to a country of transit or origin. We see, thus, how the wish to be taken seriously in co-decision and the internalisation of compromise-seeking practices were favourable for some actors who had been generally marginalised in the past (notably centre-right MEPs), but forced others (ALDE and the socialist group) to make very difficult choices between what they considered to be a good policy and what they thought best to ensure their long-term influence in co-decision negotiations (Ripoll Servent 2015).

---

inter-institutional negotiation. Even the criticisms that emerged after trilogues were extended beyond the conciliation procedure were taken care of with relative speed and ease.

It seems then that the culture of consensus that prevailed in the Council has now been successfully exported and internalised into the practices of the EP. The formalisation of a 'negotiating team' and the introduction of new procedures to improve the oversight of early readings have gone a long way to appease critical voices. They have also legitimised those instruments that contribute towards finding internal and inter-institutional compromise. As a result, the old institutional battles seem to be diminishing. Does this mean that the EP has become a mainstream institution mostly concerned with 'business as usual'? It certainly does seem that what started as a form of institutional experimentation has now been largely formalised and routinised. This leaves less room for conflict and new interpretations of how the game should be played. It also affects the very nature of the EP as a representative institution and a forum for debate and divergent voices. Therefore, it is not impossible to imagine that the reduction of conflict and the drift towards the political centre remain in place only until new critical voices and challengers of the status quo emerge and create new demands for a different kind of parliament.

Chapter 12

Conclusion

Introduction

From an unelected organ with almost no powers, the European Parliament has grown into a fully-fledged legislature. This answers the main question of the book: the EP does *actually* matter. It matters when the EU passes legislation, when it decides on how to allocate the budget, when it ratifies international agreements and when it seeks to use its normative power abroad. The days of 'talking shop' are well and truly over. The EP is now an indispensable component of the EU's political system, since it provides the legitimacy and accountability of a directly elected institution.

As part of the EP's increased powers, the EU has become a genuine bicameral political system: the Council acts as an upper-house in charge of representing territorial interests, while Parliament is the chamber representing the popular vote and its main ideological cleavages. The EP has thus become a central interface (along with the Council), where inputs are translated into outputs: it provides an additional channel of representation and another form of translation. Citizens, civil society and interest representatives have found in the EP a partner willing to listen to their demands. These demands are then filtered through ideological lenses and, although national characteristics are still relevant to understand individual members, aggregation functions first and foremost through a left-right divide.

Given that the EU has evolved into a bicameral political system, we need to examine the EP as part of a bigger whole. Parliament's complex rules and obscure working methods can sometimes be mystifying, but they become easier to understand if we consider that individuals inside it need to navigate its multi-partisan, multinational and multilingual nature and reconcile it with the external pressures coming from the Councils, the Commission, interest groups, civil society and national parties, among others. The European Union has always been a system characterised by its pluralism, which has transformed it into a highly consensual polity. Therefore, we need to study the EP in this institutional environment, which rewards inclusiveness and the ability to reach compromise. This might help us to understand why, unlike many national parliaments, left and right are more willing to work together in the EP and find solutions that can strike a middle ground.

267

Major themes

These general trends, which have led the EU to become a truly bicameral system, help us reflect on the place of the EP in the current political system of the EU and what it means for its empowered position, for its role as representative of EU citizens and for its claims of now being a 'normal' parliament.

Empowerment

That the Parliament has been greatly empowered since its origins is without doubt. It now enjoys significant powers in more areas of EU involvement, notably legislative and budgetary decision-making. How does more power translate into everyday political life? Well, in many respects, not as well as expected; despite its role as a co-legislator, the EP is still the lesser partner in bicameral politics. This status is the result of various formal and informal dynamics. On the formal side, we have seen how, in some crucial aspects, the EP still enjoys fewer powers than the member states. For instance, although co-decision has instated the EP as a co-legislator, Chapter 11 showed that the procedure still offers some structural advantages to the Council, which can more easily block or modify a Commission proposal than can the Parliament. Some disadvantages have come from unexpected quarters; for instance, despite claims of having won more budgetary powers in the Treaty of Lisbon, the EP quickly realised that the powers acquired in the annual budgetary procedure were relatively worthless if the long-term programming is set by austerity-minded governments with which it disagrees.

Member states have also maintained their stronger position in more informal ways. For one, the European Council does not limit itself to guiding policy-making and setting the political priorities of the EU any longer. In many cases, it has become an informal decision-maker – elaborating strategies and guidelines so tightly as to leave little room for interpretation. As a result, the Commission has become a proper executive power – translating the wishes of the European Council into technical proposals – while the EP has often been left with only a right to sanction member states' wishes. In the example of the 2014–2020 MFF, the European Council did not just elaborate a strict seven-year plan, but also tried to decide on specific spending programmes, encroaching on the Parliament's co-decision rights. A similar tool was used in the EU–Turkey statement dealing with refugee flows. The European Council suddenly came up with a press release that promised visa liberalisation to Turkey in exchange for re-admission of migrants who had crossed the border to Greece irregularly. The European Council left the (delicate) practical arrangements to be sorted out by the Commission, leaving the

Parliament to face an awkward decision with regard to visa liberalisation. These examples show a trend towards solving common problems with purely intergovernmentalist decision-making procedures that some have termed 'integration without supranationalisation' (Fabbrini and Puetter 2016). It certainly puts into question the actual empowerment of the EP and how much it can change in practice if the key decisions have already been made by national governments.

Representation

Representation is an important facet of the EP; as the only directly elected EU institution, it considers itself responsible for policy outputs and how these will affect EU citizens. However, the book has shown that representation in the EP is more complex than just translating external demands into policy outputs. One of the main tasks of MEPs is to navigate their different roles as representatives. As we have seen, parliamentarians adopt various roles depending on the environment in which they act and the functions they fulfil. Rapporteurs working in a committee might see their role as representing the European common good, but a little later they might ask questions in plenary that focus on particular problems of their constituencies. Representation is, therefore, a complex and flexible phenomenon that can be often adapted at will and used to justify (sometimes contradictory) positions. An MEP can, therefore, need to negotiate tensions among different publics: voters, EU citizens, particular interest groups, their national party and their EP political group. It is, therefore, difficult to draw general conclusions about loyalties – they might fluctuate in different contexts and at different moments in time. What we have seen, however, is that EP loyalties are still constrained by the dependency of MEPs on their national parties. As much as they want to act as independent members, the fact that re-selection and re-election are still decided at the national level casts a long shadow over the functioning of the EP and its relations with other EU institutions. MEPs remain *national* MEPs, and that is still patent when it comes to their voting behaviour, their loyalty to EP groups and the influence that Council members may exert on EP actors during negotiations.

The weight of representation is closely linked with the empowerment of the EP: more power means more responsibility. The growth in legislative powers has brought a marked change of behaviour in MEPs. The feeling that what the EP does actually matters and has consequences for EU citizens has led many MEPs to be more careful when writing amendments and proposing changes. This understanding of responsibility often contravenes the classical notions of representation, which see parliamentarians as the voice of particular constituents. As a result, it is now not uncommon for particular MEPs to vote against their partisan or territorial interests in order to show that they are capable of behaving responsibly. This notion of responsibility reveals the frictions between representing the whole and the parts and is closely linked to the tensions between consensus and ideology mentioned above.

The complexity of representation in a consensual political system lies also behind the growing tension between efficiency and transparency in co-decision negotiations. With the growing number of actors involved in decision-making, institutional actors felt the need to make the process more efficient in order to get better and quicker decisions for the benefit of EU citizens. This logic has resulted in a growing use of early agreements and a shift to informal decision-making fora, notably trilogues. One cannot deny that trilogues have proved extremely successful in avoiding deadlock and finding complex compromises between EP political groups and member states in the Council. At the same time, they have resulted in new dynamics of inclusion and exclusion inside and outside the EP. Paradoxically, an instrument designed to strengthen the EP's legitimacy in decision-making has ended up damaging it and stirring an increasing number of voices that question its democratic standards. Therefore, we see how the EP, for the sake of responsibility and efficiency, has developed technical solutions that strengthen compromise, which have unexpectedly harmed its status as a forum for democratic deliberation that fosters the representation of diverse groups and ideologies.

Normality

Are these tensions any different from those of national legislatures? In some respects, the answer is no. We know from other parliaments that members are often faced with choices and need to adapt their role and performance to their environment. We also know that parliaments where committees are strong tend to specialise; that means that members will become experts on specific issues. This gap between expertise and democracy has been noted in other legislatures – specialised committees tend to prioritise technical over political matters and they may become less aware of what matters to non-specialists. In short, specialisation may harm representation. In these respects, the EP is confronted with many of the challenges faced by other national parliaments, particularly the US Congress. We should perhaps try to draw wider comparisons with the formal and informal politics of national parliaments and examine how they tackle these challenges and in what respect these processes are similar or different from those experienced in the EP.

There are, however, other tensions that are particular to the EP and that question its 'normality'. A major particularity of the EP is that, despite having gained considerable powers in the last few decades, it does not seem to have internalised this sudden growth. If we were speaking about a person, we would talk about a 'complex of inferiority'. This is due to several reasons: its long absence from the legislative field turned it into an outsider that had to learn the rules of the game before being allowed to have a full say. In areas where the EP shifted from consultation to co-decision, member state actors often spoke of an 'immature' parliament that could not be trusted to do the right thing. Therefore, the EP had to show its willingness to compromise in order to be accepted in the club. A second reason why the EP is often seen as a lesser member of the club has very much to do with its position in the EU's political system. Despite now being a co-legislator – and hence being weighted with more responsibility – the EP is only involved in decision-making at the EU level. It is not in charge of agenda-setting, nor of implementation. As we have seen above, these functions have been increasingly captured (or even clawed back) by member states, which gives them an informal advantage during negotiations; ultimately, national governments may always claim that they know best about the problems affecting the EU. It is, therefore, not unusual for member states to force compromises on the EP using their legitimacy as implementers (and cheque-payers). With the growth of co-decision, we have seen an increasing number of compromises that often came at the expense of long-held legislative positions; in a sense, co-decision has 'tamed' the EP. We have seen it in the area of environmental policies, where its 'green credentials' have been put into question, and in the area of internal security and migration, where the EP cannot be categorically labelled as 'liberal' anymore.

This difficulty in exacting change out of EU negotiations is exacerbated by the composition of the EP in the 2014–2019 legislative term. The rise in the number of fringe parties has put the Parliament under increasing pressure. Extreme ideologies and Euroscepticism have become stronger over the years and this supposes a challenge not only for the day-to-day running of the chamber, but also for its ability to trigger change. On the one hand, it affects the running of daily business, since Eurosceptic MEPs are often not interested in participating normally in the functioning of the legislature. They have used the Parliament as a source of income and publicity, helping them to advertise their ideas back home. The direct consequence of their actions has been a transformation of the EP's internal organisation – turning it into a well-oiled machine where improvisation and spontaneity are not welcome. By obstructing plenary sessions and transgressing basic norms of behaviour, Eurosceptic MEPs have contributed to reinforcing many prejudices about the EP. They have also forced the leadership of the EP to curtail those rights or practices that could be abused – notably speaking time, declarations and questions – which has also affected other smaller groups. These changes have raised concerns about the legitimacy of the Parliament as a space for deliberation and exchange; in a way, fringe parties have been very successful at de-politicising the EP and rendering it more technocratic in the eyes of the public.

Finally, the EP remains very much attached to its institutional 'patriotism'. With the changes introduced by the Treaty of Lisbon, the EP's position has become stronger and it might seem that it has reached a level of institutional maturity that calls for normal relationships with the other EU organs. That is not yet the case; the EP has kept its taste for big inter-institutional battles and there is a certain automatism in its culture that makes it prone to look for new ways to enhance its powers and influence. Some have commented that this might slowly fade into the past – after all, many of those that helped build the EP and instigated these battles are gradually leaving the Parliament or will do so in the years to come. Whether this institutional 'patriotism' is inherited by the new generations of members and officials working in the Parliament will depend on whether they have been successfully socialised into this particular norm. Perhaps they will prefer to rebel against their elders and consider these battles as things of the past, developing hence a more 'normalised' understanding of the Parliament.

Concluding remarks: towards a parliamentary political system?

There is nothing that questions the normality of the EP more than the recurring debates on its powers and functions in the EU's political system. The idea of a 'parliamentary Europe' has existed since the inception of the ECSC Assembly (Rittberger 2005); however, in the last two decades, the idea that a parliamentarisation of the EU would solve many of the ills affecting it has taken hold. In a certain fashion, these claims have been backed by the constitutional evolution of the Union, which has seen closer links between the Parliament and the Commission emerge. The EP has also promoted this paradigm with new institutional devices like the 'Spitzenkandidaten'. After 2014, the fact that the European Council accepted to nominate Jean-Claude Juncker, candidate of the political party with more seats in the EP election, has helped him inject the Commission with a more political vision. He has also nurtured the formal and informal links with the EP in order to ensure its support.

Therefore, the signs of an incipient parliamentarisation of the European Union are there and seem likely to become stronger in the near future. In a sense, this is not surprising, given that parliamentary systems are the norm in Europe. They are the main points of reference and source of inspiration when looking for solutions to problems like the low turnout at elections or the difficulty in attributing responsibility for good or bad policy outputs. The idea advocated in many quarters is, thus, to push the Spitzenkandidaten model a step further by linking the choice of the Commission as a whole to the majority elected in Parliament. These would then lead to clear right- or left-wing 'governments' (or coalition governments), which would make it easier for EU citizens to choose among different political programmes. This model is certainly alluring, since it would make the EU more political – with dynamics of government and opposition that are familiar to most citizens and a break from the culture of consensus that now rules the EU's political system (Hix et al. 2007: 219–220).

The step towards nominating party-appointed candidates for Commission President seems to go in the direction of a fully-fledged parliamentarisation – although such a radical change in the EU's political system is difficult to contemplate in the near future, especially since it would require major constitutional reforms. Would national governments accept a more political Commission that is dependent on the EP for its election and survival? Paradoxically, the main question is whether a parliamentary system would actually be good for the EP. Certainly, it would control the Commission and appoint its members, which would probably contribute to the formation of stable majorities in the Parliament. At the same time, this would reduce the freedom of MEPs, since they would need to fall in line and ensure that their 'government' had enough support to pass legislative proposals. For a Parliament where members enjoy a high degree of individual influence and can make a difference in policy outputs, this change might not be as welcome as expected. Therefore, transforming the EU into a parliamentary system might come at the expense of the EP as a policy-*making* legislature and transform it into a policy-*reacting* one, with only a power to reject, but not really to amend legislative proposals coming from the Commission (Fabbrini 2013, 2015).

Although often linked together, this debate is not the same as that of a *partisan* Europe. Political parties have become central actors in EU politics generally, but especially in the EP. It seems, however, that they have now reached a structural glass ceiling that does not allow them to develop further. We have seen how European party federations have become more independent from EP political groups and gained in independence, but they are not yet proper political parties. They do not have the power to influence votes, offices or policies, since they are not responsible for electing candidates, selecting key positions such as the various presidents of the EU institutions, nor can they offer more than unambitious political programmes. This is certainly a field where more work can be done – decoupling EP elections from national elections and fostering real EU-wide parties that are involved in the selection of candidates and the development of common electoral programmes may raise the interest of citizens and soften the second-order character of the elections. It would also suppose a radical change for MEPs, who would not be dependent on national parties for re-selection and re-election anymore. This would suppose a small revolution when it comes to their voting behaviour, the definition of their parliamentary roles and a shift in loyalties towards their EP groups. Although the EP is well aware of the opportunities that a wide-reaching reform of the electoral system could suppose for its internal functioning and its position in the inter-institutional triangle, its realisation seems again unlikely in the foreseeable future. Member states are also conscious of the implications of such a reform and are not willing to give it the go-ahead.

This shows how the EP sits at a crossroad between supranationalism and intergovernmentalism – between the popular and the national dimensions that make up the EU's political system. Its efforts to gain more powers have certainly borne fruit and put it in a more central position. It has also made it more difficult to classify the EU's political system. For while key elements like the separation between executive and legislative or the presence of two co-legislators is typical of a separation-of-powers model, the appointment of the Commission and the creation of Spitzenkandidaten have brought it closer to a parliamentary system. The ambiguous place that the EP occupies reflects the ambiguity of the EU as this 'non-identified object' that has not yet reached the stability necessary for mature political systems. This, of course, leaves a door open for future changes – which, as things stand now, can go in very different directions.

What is certain is that, whatever comes, it will make for exciting times and that is something that has never lacked in the history of the Parliament. We now face new challenges in a world that presents us with bewildering developments. The EP will need to react to this shifting environment and find ways to adapt itself.

References

Abedi, A. and Lundberg, T.C. (2009) 'Doomed to Failure? UKIP and the Organisational Challenges Facing Right-Wing Populist Anti-Political Establishment Parties', *Parliamentary Affairs* 62(1): 72–87.

Adam, S., Maier, M., de Vreese, C.H., Schuck, A.R.T., Stetka, V., Jalali, C., Seeber, G.U.H., Negrine, R., Raycheva, L., Berganza, R., Róka, J., Dobek-Ostrowska, B., Nord, L., Balzer, M. and Baumli, M. (2013) 'Campaigning against Europe? The Role of Euroskeptic Fringe and Mainstream Parties in the 2009 European Parliament Election', *Journal of Political Marketing* 12(1): 77–99.

Ahrens, P. (2016) 'The Committee on Women's Rights and Gender Equality in the European Parliament: Taking Advantage of Institutional Power Play', *Parliamentary Affairs* 69(4): 778–793.

Anderson, P.J. and McLeod, A. (2004) 'The Great Non-Communicator? The Mass Communication Deficit of the European Parliament and Its Press Directorate', *Journal of Common Market Studies* 42(5): 897–917.

Andlovic, M. and Lehmann, W. (2014) 'Interest Group Influence and Interinstitutional Power Allocation in Early Second-Reading Agreements: A Re-Examination of Aviation Emissions Trading', *Journal of European Public Policy* 21(6): 802–821.

Arter, D. (2015) 'Why Do MPs Want to Be MEPs? Candidate Incentives and Party Nomination Strategies in European Parliament Elections in Finland', *European Politics and Society* 16(4): 540–555.

Asher, H.B. (1974) 'Committees and the Norm of Specialization', *Annals of the American Academy of Political and Social Science* 411: 63–74.

Auel, K. and Christiansen, T. (2015) 'After Lisbon: National Parliaments in the European Union', *West European Politics* 38(2): 261–281.

Bailer, S., Schulz, T. and Selb, P. (2009) 'What Role for the Party Group Leader? A Latent Variable Approach to Leadership Effects on Party Group Cohesion in the European Parliament', *The Journal of Legislative Studies* 15(4): 355–378.

Bale, T. and Taggart, P. (2006) 'First-Timers Yes, Virgins No: The Roles and Backgrounds of New Members of the European Parliament', *SEI Working Papers* 89, available at http://www.sussex.ac.uk/sei/documents/sei-working-paper-no-89.pdf (accessed July 2011).

Barbé, E. and Herranz, A. (2008) 'The Power and Practice of the European Parliament in Security Policies', in D. Peters, W. Wagner and N. Deitelhoff (eds) *The Parliamentary Control of European Security Policy*. Oslo: Arena, pp. 77–107.

Bartkowska, M. and Tiemann, G. (2015) 'The Impact of Economic Perceptions on Voting Behaviour in European Parliamentary Elections', *Journal of Common Market Studies* 53(2): 201–217.

BBC (2016) *Brexit 'most important moment since Berlin Wall': Le Pen*, 28 June 2016, BBC News, available at http://www.bbc.com/news/uk-politics-eu-referendum-36653381 (accessed August 2016).

Beach, D. (2007) 'The European Parliament in the 2000 IGC and the Constitutional Treaty Negotiations: From Loser to Winner', *Journal of European Public Policy* 14(8): 1271–1292.

Beauvallet, W., Godmer, L., Marrel, G. and Michon, S. (2009) 'La Production de la Légitimité Institutionnelle au Parlement Européen: Le Cas de la Commission des Affaires Constitutionnelles', *Politique européenne* 28(2): 73–102.

Beauvallet, W. and Michon, S. (2010) 'Professionalization and Socialization of the Members of the European Parliament', *French Politics* 8(2): 145–165.

Beauvallet-Haddad, W., Michon, S., Lepaux, V. and Monicolle, C. (2016) 'The Changing Composition of the European Parliament: MEPs from 1979 to 2014', *French Politics* 14(1): 101–125.

Bellamy, R. (2013) '"An Ever Closer Union among the Peoples of Europe": Republican Intergovernmentalism and Demoicratic Representation within the EU', *Journal of European Integration* 35(5): 499–516.

Bellamy, R. and Castiglione, D. (2013) 'Three Models of Democracy, Political Community and Representation in the EU', *Journal of European Public Policy* 20(2): 206–223.

Bendjallah, S. (2009) 'Politisation du Parlement Européen et Commissions Parlementaires', *Politique européenne* 28(2): 103–127.

Benedetto, G. (2005) 'Rapporteurs as Legislative Entrepreneurs: The Dynamics of the Codecision Procedure in Europe's Parliament', *Journal of European Public Policy* 12(1): 67–88.

Benedetto, G. (2013) 'The EU Budget after Lisbon: Rigidity and Reduced Spending?', *Journal of Public Policy* 33(3): 345–369.

Benedetto, G. (2017) 'Power, Money and Reversion Points: The European Union's Annual Budgets since 2010', *Journal of European Public Policy* 24(5): 633–652.

Benedetto, G. and Høyland, B. (2007) 'The EU Annual Budgetary Procedure: The Existing Rules and Proposed Reforms of the Convention and Intergovernmental Conference 2002–04', *Journal of Common Market Studies* 45(3): 565–587.

Beukers, T. (2006) 'The Barroso Drama: Enhancing Parliamentary Control over the European Commission and the Member States', *European Constitutional Law Review* 2(1): 21–53.

Beyers, J. (2004) 'Voice and Access Political Practices of European Interest Associations', *European Union Politics* 5(2): 211–240.

Binderkrantz, A.S., Pedersen, H.H. and Beyers, J. (2017) 'What Is Access? A Discussion of the Definition and Measurement of Interest Group Access', *European Political Science* 16(3): 306–321.

Blomgren, M. (2003) *Cross-Pressure and Political Representation in Europe: A Comparative Study of MEPs and the Intra-Party Arena*. Umeå: Department of Political Science, Umeå University.

Blomgren, M. (2015) 'Political Parties and the European Union', in K. Lynggaard, I. Manners and K. Löfgren (eds) *Research Methods in European Union Studies*. Houndmills: Palgrave Macmillan, pp. 266–280.

Blondel, J., Sinnott, R. and Svensson, P. (1997) 'Representation and Voter Participation', *European Journal of Political Research* 32(2): 243–272.

Blondel, J., Sinnott, R. and Svensson, P. (1998) *People and Parliament in the European Union: Participation, Democracy, and Legitimacy.* Oxford: Oxford University Press.

Boomgaarden, H.G., Johann, D. and Kritzinger, S. (2016) 'Voting at National versus European Elections: An Individual Level Test of the Second Order Paradigm for the 2014 European Parliament Elections', *Politics and Governance* 4(1): 130–144.

Bouwen, P. (2003) 'A Theoretical and Empirical Study of Corporate Lobbying in the European Parliament', *European Integration online Papers* 7(11), available at http://www.eiop.or.at/eiop/texte/2003-011.htm#3.5 (accessed August 2016).

Bouwen, P. (2004a) 'Exchanging Access Goods for Access: A Comparative Study of Business Lobbying in the European Union Institutions', *European Journal of Political Research* 43(3): 337–369.

Bouwen, P. (2004b) 'The Logic of Access to the European Parliament: Business Lobbying in the Committee on Economic and Monetary Affairs', *Journal of Common Market Studies* 42(3): 473–495.

Bowler, S. and Farrell, D.M. (1993) 'Legislator Shirking and Voter Monitoring: Impacts of European Parliament Electoral Systems upon Legislator-Voter Relationships', *Journal of Common Market Studies* 31(1): 45–70.

Bowler, S. and Farrell, D.M. (1995) 'The Organizing of the European Parliament: Committees, Specialization and Co-Ordination', *British Journal of Political Science* 25(2): 219–243.

Bowler, S. and Farrell, D.M. (2011) 'Electoral Institutions and Campaigning in Comparative Perspective: Electioneering in European Parliament Elections', *European Journal of Political Research* 50(5): 668–688.

Bowler, S. and McElroy, G. (2015) 'Political Group Cohesion and "Hurrah" Voting in the European Parliament', *Journal of European Public Policy* 22(9): 1355–1365.

Boyron, S. (1996) 'Maastricht and the Codecision Procedure: A Success Story', *International & Comparative Law Quarterly* 45(2): 293–318.

Brack, N. (2013) 'Euroscepticism at the Supranational Level: The Case of the "Untidy Right" in the European Parliament', *Journal of Common Market Studies* 51(1): 85–104.

Brack, N. (2015) 'The Roles of Eurosceptic Members of the European Parliament and Their Implications for the EU', *International Political Science Review* 36(3): 337–350.

Braghiroli, S. (2010) 'Politicians Online! MEP Communication Strategies in the Internet Era', *EPIN Working Paper* (29), available at https://www.ceps.eu/publications/politicians-online-mep-communication-strategies-internet-era (accessed December 2016).

Brandsma, G.J. (2015) 'Co-Decision after Lisbon: the Politics of Informal Trilogues in European Union Lawmaking', *European Union Politics* 16(2): 300–319.

Brandsma, G.J. and Blom-Hansen, J. (2012) 'Negotiating the Post-Lisbon Comitology System: Institutional Battles over Delegated Decision-Making', *Journal of Common Market Studies* 50(6): 939–957.

Braun, D., Hutter, S. and Kerscher, A. (2016) 'What Type of Europe? The Salience of Polity and Policy Issues in European Parliament Elections', *European Union Politics* 17(4): 570–592.

Brenner, P. (1974) 'Committee Conflict in the Congressional Arena', *Annals of the American Academy of Political and Social Science* 411: 87–101.

Bressanelli, E. (2013) 'Competitive and Coherent? Profiling the Europarties in the 2009 European Parliament Elections', *Journal of European Integration* 35(6): 653–668.

Bressanelli, E. (2014) *Europarties after Enlargement: Organization, Ideology and Competition*. Houndmills: Palgrave Macmillan.

Bressanelli, E. and Chelotti, N. (2016) 'The Shadow of the European Council. Understanding Legislation on Economic Governance', *Journal of European Integration* 38(5): 511–525.

Buonanno, L. and Nugent, N. (2013) *Policies and Policy Processes of the European Union*. Houndmills: Palgrave Macmillan.

Burns, C. (2004) 'Codecision and the European Commission: A Study of Declining Influence?', *Journal of European Public Policy* 11(1): 1–18.

Burns, C. (2005) 'Who Pays? Who Gains? How Do Costs and Benefits Shape the Policy Influence of the European Parliament?', *Journal of Common Market Studies* 43(3): 485–505.

Burns, C. (2006) 'Co-Decision and Inter-Committee Conflict in the European Parliament Post-Amsterdam', *Government and Opposition* 41(2): 230–248.

Burns, C. (2014) 'The European Commission as a Policy Actor under the Ordinary Legislative Procedure', in *7th Pan-European Conference on the European Union, ECPR Standing Group on the EU*, The Hague, The Netherlands.

Burns, C. and Carter, N. (2010) 'Is Co-decision Good for the Environment? An Analysis of the European Parliament's Green Credentials', *Political Studies* 58(1): 123–142.

Burns, C., Carter, N., Davies, G.A.M. and Worsfold, N. (2013) 'Still Saving the Earth? The European Parliament's Environmental Record', *Environmental Politics* 22(6): 935–954.

Burns, C., Carter, N. and Worsfold, N. (2012) 'Enlargement and the Environment: The Changing Behaviour of the European Parliament', *Journal of Common Market Studies* 50(1): 54–70.

Busby, A. (2013) '"Normal Parliament": Exploring the Organisation of Everyday Political Life in an MEP's Office', *Journal of Contemporary European Research* 9(1): 94–115.

Busby, A. (2014) *The Everyday Practice and Performance of European Politics: An Ethnography of the European Parliament*. Doctoral Thesis. University of Sussex, available at http://sro.sussex.ac.uk/48830/ (accessed July 2016).

Busby, A. and Belkacem, K. (2013) '"Coping with the Information Overload": An Exploration of Assistants' Backstage Role in the Everyday Practice of European Parliament Politics', *European Integration online Papers (EIoP)* 17(2): 1–28.

Carroll, B.J. and Rasmussen, A. (2017) 'Cultural Capital and the Density of Organised Interests Lobbying the European Parliament', *West European Politics* 40(5): 1132–1152.

Carrubba, C., Gabel, M., Murrah, L., Clough, R., Montgomery, E. and Schambach, R. (2006) 'Off the Record: Unrecorded Legislative Votes, Selection Bias and Roll-Call Vote Analysis', *British Journal of Political Science* 36(4): 691–704.

Carrubba, C. and Timpone, R.J. (2005) 'Explaining Vote Switching Across First- and Second-Order Elections Evidence from Europe', *Comparative Political Studies* 38(3): 260–281.

Cheneval, F., Lavenex, S. and Schimmelfennig, F. (2015) 'Demoi-cracy in the European Union: Principles, Institutions, Policies', *Journal of European Public Policy* 22(1): 1–18.

Cherepnalkoski, D., Karpf, A., Mozetič, I. and Grčar, M. (2016) 'Cohesion and Coalition Formation in the European Parliament: Roll-Call Votes and Twitter Activities', *PLoS ONE* 11(11): e0166586.

Chiva, C. (2014) 'Gender, European Integration and Candidate Recruitment: The European Parliament Elections in the New EU Member States', *Parliamentary Affairs* 67(2): 458–494.

Christiansen, T. and Dobbels, M. (2012) 'Comitology and Delegated Acts after Lisbon: How the European Parliament Lost the Implementation Game', *European Integration online Papers (EIoP)* 16(13): 1–23.

Christiansen, T. and Dobbels, M. (2013a) 'Delegated Powers and Inter-Institutional Relations in the EU after Lisbon: A Normative Assessment', *West European Politics* 36(6): 1159–1177.

Christiansen, T. and Dobbels, M. (2013b) 'Non-Legislative Rule Making after the Lisbon Treaty: Implementing the New System of Comitology and Delegated Acts', *European Law Journal* 19(1): 42–56.

Chryssogelos, A.-S. (2017) 'Transnational European Party Federations as EU Foreign Policy Actors: The Activities of Europarties in Eastern Partnership States', *Journal of Common Market Studies* 55(2): 257–274.

Clark, N. (2014) 'Explaining Low Turnout in European Elections: The Role of Issue Salience and Institutional Perceptions in Elections to the European Parliament', *Journal of European Integration* 36(4): 339–356.

Clark, N. (2015) 'The Federalist Perspective in Elections to the European Parliament', *Journal of Common Market Studies* 53(3): 524–541.

Clark, S. and Priestley, J. (2012) *Europe's Parliament: People, Places, Politics.* London: John Harper Publishing.

Coen, D. (2007) 'Empirical and Theoretical Studies in EU Lobbying', *Journal of European Public Policy* 14(3): 333–345.

Coman, E.E. (2009) 'Reassessing the Influence of Party Groups on Individual Members of the European Parliament', *West European Politics* 32(6): 1099–1117.

Corbett, R. (1999) 'The European Parliament and the Idea of European Representative Government', in J. Pinder (ed.) *Foundations of Democracy in the European Union: From the Genesis of Parliamentary Democracy to the European Parliament.* Houndmills: Palgrave Macmillan, pp. 87–106.

Corbett, R. (2014) 'MEPs Keeping the Commission in Line', *The Parliament Magazine*, 20 October, available at https://www.theparliamentmagazine.eu/articles/opinion/meps-keeping-commission-line (accessed May 2015).

Corbett, R. (2017) 'Defected, Arrested, Suspended, Convicted – Keeping Tabs on UKIP MEPs Who Meet Unsavoury Ends', available at http://www.richardcorbett.org.uk/defected-arrested-suspended-convicted/ (accessed February 2017).

Corbett, R., Jacobs, F. and Neville, D. (2016) *The European Parliament*, 9th ed. London: John Harper Publishing.

Corbett, R., Jacobs, F. and Shackleton, M. (2007) *The European Parliament*, 7th ed. London: John Harper.

Costa, O. (2003) 'Administrer le Parlement Européen: Les Paradoxes d'un Secrétariat Général Incontournable, mais Faible', *Politique européenne* 11(3): 143–161.

Costello, R. (2011) 'Does Bicameralism Promote Stability? Inter-institutional Relations and Coalition Formation in the European Parliament', *West European Politics* 34(1): 122–144.

Costello, R. and Thomson, R. (2010) 'The Policy Impact of Leadership in Committees: Rapporteurs' Influence on the European Parliament's Opinions', *European Union Politics* 11(2): 219–240.

Costello, R. and Thomson, R. (2011) 'The Nexus of Bicameralism: Rapporteurs' Impact on Decision Outcomes in the European Union', *European Union Politics* 12(3): 337–357.

Costello, R. and Thomson, R. (2013) 'The Distribution of Power among EU Institutions: Who Wins under Codecision and Why?', *Journal of European Public Policy* 20(7): 1025–1039.

Costello, R. and Thomson, R. (2016) 'Bicameralism, Nationality and Party Cohesion in the European Parliament', *Party Politics* 22(6): 773–783.

Cox, G.W. and McCubbins, M.D. (2007) *Legislative Leviathan: Party Government in the House*, 2nd ed. Cambridge: Cambridge University Press.

Crombez, C. (1996) 'Legislative Procedures in the European Community', *British Journal of Political Science* 26(02): 199–228.

Crombez, C. (1997) 'The Co-Decision Procedure in the European Union', *Legislative Studies Quarterly* 22(1): 97–119.

Crombez, C. (2017) 'The Election of Antonio Tajani as EP President: A Backroom Deal that Creates Clarity', *EUROPP*, available at http://blogs.lse.ac.uk/europpblog/2017/01/26/antonio-tajani-ep-president-backroom-deal/ (accessed February 2017).

Crombez, C. and Hix, S. (2011) 'Treaty Reform and the Commission's Appointment and Policy-Making Role in the European Union', *European Union Politics* 12(3): 291–314.

Crombez, C. and Høyland, B. (2015) 'The Budgetary Procedure in the European Union and the Implications of the Treaty of Lisbon', *European Union Politics* 16(1): 67–89.

Crombez, C., Steunenberg, B. and Corbett, R. (2000) 'Understanding the EU Legislative Process: Political Scientists' and Practitioners' Perspectives', *European Union Politics* 1(3): 363–381.

Crombez, C. and Vangerven, P. (2014) 'Procedural Models of European Union Politics: Contributions and Suggestions for Improvement', *European Union Politics* 15(2): 289–308.

Crowe, R. (2016) 'The European Council and the Multiannual Financial Framework', *Cambridge Yearbook of European Legal Studies* 18: 69–92.

Crum, B. (2006) 'Parliamentarization of the CFSP through Informal Institution-Making? The Fifth European Parliament and the EU High Representative', *Journal of European Public Policy* 13(3): 383–401.

Crum, B. and Fossum, J.E. (2009) 'The Multilevel Parliamentary Field: A Framework for Theorizing Representative Democracy in the EU', *European Political Science Review* 1(2): 249–271.

Daniel, W.T. (2013) 'When the Agent Knows Better than the Principal: The Effect of Education and Seniority on European Parliament Rapporteur Assignment', *Journal of Common Market Studies* 51(5): 832–848.

Daniel, W.T. (2015) *Career Behaviour and the European Parliament: All Roads Lead through Brussels?* Oxford: Oxford University Press.

Daniel, W.T. (2016) 'First-Order Contests for Second-Order Parties? Differentiated Candidate Nomination Strategies in European Parliament Elections', *Journal of European Integration* 38(7): 807–822.

Davidson, R.H. (1969) *The Role of the Congressman*, New York: Pegasus.

Davidson, R.H. (1974) 'Representation and Congressional Committees', *Annals of the American Academy of Political and Social Science* 411: 48–62.

de Ruiter, R. and Neuhold, C. (2012) 'Why Is Fast Track the Way to Go? Justifications for Early Agreement in the Co-Decision Procedure and Their Effects', *European Law Journal* 18(4): 536–554.

de Vreese, C.H., Banducci, S.A., Semetko, H.A. and Boomgaarden, H.G. (2006) 'The News Coverage of the 2004 European Parliamentary Election Campaign in 25 Countries', *European Union Politics* 7(4): 477–504.

de Vries, C.E., van der Brug, W., van Egmond, M.H. and van der Eijk, C. (2011) 'Individual and Contextual Variation in EU Issue Voting: The Role of Political Information', *Electoral Studies* 30(1): 16–28.

De Winter, L. and Tursan, H. (2003) *Regionalist Parties in Western Europe.* London: Routledge.

Delreux, T. (2008) 'The EU as a Negotiator in Multilateral Chemicals Negotiations: Multiple Principals, Different Agents', *Journal of European Public Policy* 15(7): 1069–1086.

Delwit, P., Külahci, E. and Van de Walle, C. (2004) *The Europarties: Organisation and Influence.* Brussels: CEVIPOL, Centre d'étude de la vie politique, Free University of Brussels.

Der Spiegel (2013) *'Mister Euro': Merkel Will Juncker auf EU-Spitzenposten Verhindern,* 29 December, available at http://www.spiegel.de/politik/ausland/merkel-will-juncker-auf-eu-spitzenposten-verhindern-a-941102.html (accessed May 2015).

Der Spiegel (2016) *Spitzenposten im Europäischen Parlament: Man spricht deutsch,* 6 July, available at http://www.spiegel.de/politik/ausland/eu-parlament-martin-schulz-versorgt-mitarbeiter-mit-spitzenposten-a-1096279.html (accessed August 2016).

Diedrichs, U. (2004) 'The European Parliament in CFSP: More than a Marginal Player?', *The International Spectator: Italian Journal of International Affairs* 39(2): 31–46.

Dietz, T.M. (2000) 'Similar but Different? The European Greens Compared to Other Transnational Party Federations in Europe', *Party Politics* 6(2): 199–210.

Dinan, D. (2004) 'Governance and Institutions: The Convention and the Intergovernmental Conference', *Journal of Common Market Studies* 42(s1): 27–42.

Dinan, D. (2005) 'Governance and Institutions: A New Constitution and a New Commission', *Journal of Common Market Studies* 43(s1): 37–54.

Dinan, D. (2008) 'Governance and Institutional Developments: Ending the Constitutional Impasse', *Journal of Common Market Studies* 46(s1): 71–90.

Dinan, D. (2009) 'Institutions and Governance: Saving the Lisbon Treaty – An Irish Solution to a European Problem', *Journal of Common Market Studies* 47(s1): 113–132.

Dinan, D. (2010) 'Institutions and Governance: A New Treaty, a Newly Elected Parliament and a New Commission', *Journal of Common Market Studies* 48(s1): 95–118.

Dinan, D. (2013) 'EU Governance and Institutions: Stresses Above and Below the Waterline', *Journal of Common Market Studies* 51(s1): 89–102.

Dinan, D. (2014) *Europe Recast: A History of European Union*, 2nd ed. Houndmills: Palgrave Macmillan.

Dionigi, M.K. (2017) *Lobbying in the European Parliament: The Battle for Influence*. Houndmills: Palgrave Macmillan.

Dionigi, M.K. and Martens, H. (2016) 'The EU Transparency Register: On the Right Path, but Not Quite There Yet', *European Policy Centre*, available at http://www.epc.eu/pub_details?cat_id=17&pub_id=7298 (accessed February 2017).

Dobbels, M. and Neuhold, C. (2013) '"The Roles Bureaucrats Play": The Input of European Parliament (EP) Administrators into the Ordinary Legislative Procedure: A Case Study Approach', *Journal of European Integration* 35(4): 375–390.

Dowding, K. (2000) 'Institutionalist Research on the European Union: A Critical Review', *European Union Politics* 1(1): 125–144.

Duff, A. (2006) *Plan B: How to Rescue the European Constitution*, available at http://www.delorsinstitute.eu/011-968-Plan-B-How-to-Rescue-the-European-Constitution.html (accessed July 2016).

Duff, A. (2012) 'Why Do MEPs Fear Electoral Reform?', *Euobserver* 14 March, available at https://euobserver.com/opinion/115596 (accessed April 2016).

Duff, A., Pukelsheim, F. and Oelbermann, K.-F. (2015) *The Electoral Reform of the European Parliament: Composition, Procedure and Legitimacy*, available at http://www.europarl.europa.eu/RegData/etudes/IDAN/2015/510002/IPOL_IDA(2015)510002_EN.pdf (accessed April 2016).

Dunphy, R. and March, L. (2013) 'Seven Year Itch? The European Left Party: Struggling to Transform the EU', *Perspectives on European Politics and Society* 14(4): 520–537.

Dür, A. (2008) 'Interest Groups in the European Union: How Powerful Are They?', *West European Politics* 31(6): 1212–1230.

Dür, A., Bernhagen, P. and Marshall, D. (2015) 'Interest Group Success in the European Union When (and Why) Does Business Lose?', *Comparative Political Studies* 48(8): 951–983.

Dutoit, L. (2016) 'The International Role of the European Parliament's Intergroups', *The Hague Journal of Diplomacy* 11(2–3): 182–195.

Earnshaw, D. and Judge, D. (1993) 'The European Parliament and the Sweeteners Directive: From Footnote to Inter-Institutional Conflict', *Journal of Common Market Studies* 31(1): 103–116.

Earnshaw, D. and Judge, D. (1995) 'Early Days: The European Parliament, Co-Decision and the European Union Legislative Process Post-Maastricht', *Journal of European Public Policy* 2(4): 624–649.

Easton, D. (1957) 'An Approach to the Analysis of Political Systems', *World Politics* 9(03): 383–400.

Egeberg, M., Gornitzka, Å. and Trondal, J. (2014) 'People Who Run the European Parliament: Staff Demography and Its Implications', *Journal of European Integration* 36(7): 659–675.

Egeberg, M., Gornitzka, Å., Trondal, J. and Johannessen, M. (2013) 'Parliament Staff: Unpacking the Behaviour of Officials in the European Parliament', *Journal of European Public Policy* 20(4): 495–514.

Eising, R. (2007) 'The Access of Business Interests to EU Institutions: Towards Élite Pluralism?', *Journal of European Public Policy* 14(3): 384–403.

Elsig, M. and Dupont, C. (2012) 'European Union Meets South Korea: Bureaucratic Interests, Exporter Discrimination and the Negotiations of Trade Agreements', *Journal of Common Market Studies* 50(3): 492–507.

Elster, J. (ed.) (1986) *Rational Choice*. Oxford: Basil Blackwell.

Euobserver (2013a) *Belgian MEP Blames Assistant for Industry-Scripted Amendments*, 22 November, available at https://euobserver.com/institutional/122205 (accessed August 2016).

Euobserver (2013b) *Parliament Fails to Pass Report on Women's Reproductive Rights*, 12 October, available at https://euobserver.com/social/122418 (accessed February 2017).

Euobserver (2014a) *Centre-Right to Strike Deal with Centre-Left on Juncker, Schulz*, 23 June, available at https://euobserver.com/eu-elections/124688 (accessed May 2015).

Euobserver (2014b) *Populist MEPs Lead Twitter Ranking*, 15 May, available at https://euobserver.com/eu-elections/124095 (accessed December 2016).

Euobserver (2015a) *Dutch MEP to Lose €1,530 in Le Pen Voting Penalty*, 17 December, available at https://euobserver.com/institutional/131571 (accessed February 2017).

Euobserver (2015b) *European Parliament Mulls Lobby Ban for Big Companies*, 20 July, available at https://euobserver.com/institutional/129702 (accessed November 2016).

Euobserver (2016a) *Danish Far-right MEP Ordered to Return €400,000*, 5 October, available at https://euobserver.com/institutional/133377 (accessed August 2016).

Euobserver (2016b) *MEPs Crack Down on Funding for Far Right*, 13 December, available at https://euobserver.com/institutional/136254 (accessed February 2017).

Euobserver (2017a) *MEPs Look for Ways to Defund Far-Right Party*, 2 October, available at https://euobserver.com/institutional/136858 (accessed February 2017).

Euobserver (2017b) *Socialist MEPs Seek New Role after Grand Coalition*, 17 February, available at https://euobserver.com/news/136933 (accessed February 2017).

Euractiv (2004) *Parliament Calls on EU to Open Turkey Talks*, 16 December, available at https://www.euractiv.com/section/central-europe/news/parliament-calls-on-eu-to-open-turkey-talks/ (accessed February 2017).

Euractiv (2006) *Duff's Plan B to Rescue Constitution*, 20 October 2006, available at https://www.euractiv.com/section/future-eu/news/duff-s-plan-b-to-rescue-constitution/ (accessed July 2016).

Euractiv (2012) *US Lobbying Waters Down EU Data Protection Reform*, 21 February, available at http://www.euractiv.com/section/digital/news/us-lobbying-waters-down-eu-data-protection-reform/ (accessed October 2016).

Euractiv (2014a) *Bratušek's Poor Showing Adds to Juncker's Worries*, 6 October, available at http://www.euractiv.com/sections/eu-elections-2014/bratuseks-poor-showing-adds-junckers-worries-308953 (accessed May 2015).

Euractiv (2014b) *Bulc Walks on Fire … and Survives*, 21 October, available at www.euractiv.com/sections/eu-elections-2014/bulc-walks-fire-and-survives-309344 (accessed May 2015).

Euractiv (2014c) *Court of Auditors Warns of Multi-Billion EU Budget Gap*, 25 November, available at http://www.euractiv.com/sections/eu-priorities-2020/court-auditors-warns-multi-billion-eu-budget-gap-310310 (accessed February 2015).

Euractiv (2014d) *Parliament Rejects Hungary's Navracsics as Education and Culture Commissioner*, 7 October, available at http://www.euractiv.com/video/parliament-rejects-hungarys-navracsics-education-and-culture-commissioner-308981 (accessed May 2015).

Euractiv (2014e) *Socialist Leaders Back Juncker, Want Other Top Jobs*, 23 June, available at http://www.euractiv.com/sections/eu-elections-2014/socialist-leaders-back-juncker-want-other-top-jobs-302977 (accessed May 2015).

Euractiv (2014f) *Socialists Set to Trade Cañete for Moscovici*, 8 October, available at http://www.euractiv.com/sections/eu-priorities-2020/socialists-set-trade-canete-moscovici-309033 (accessed May 2015).

Euractiv (2015) *European Parliament Questions Overabundance of MEP Assistants*, 2 April, available at https://www.euractiv.com/section/eu-priorities-2020/news/european-parliament-questions-overabundance-of-mep-assistants/ (accessed August 2016).

Euractiv (2016a) *European Parliament Demands EU Budget Reform*, 17 October, available at http://www.euractiv.com/section/euro-finance/news/european-parliament-demands-eu-budget-reform/ (accessed February 2017).

Euractiv (2016b) *European Parliament Quietly Scuppers Lobbying Reform*, 15 September, available at https://www.euractiv.com/section/public-affairs/

news/european-parliament-quietly-scuppers-lobbying-reform/ (accessed November 2016).

Euractiv (2016c) 'Parliament Approves Privacy Rules after Record Number of Amendments', *EurActiv.com*, 14 April, available at http://www.euractiv. com/section/digital/news/parliament-approves-privacy-rules-after-record-number-of-amendments/ (accessed May 2016).

Euractiv (2017a) *Guy Verhofstadt's Flagrant Opportunism in the Name of Europe*, 18 January, available at http://www.euractiv.com/section/elections/news/guy-verhofstadt-flagrant-opportunism-in-the-name-of-europe/ (accessed February 2017).

Euractiv (2017b) *Schulz's Departure Paves Way for Leftist Alliance in EU Parliament*, 19 January, available at https://www.euractiv.com/section/elections/news/schulzs-departure-paves-way-for-leftist-alliance-in-eu-parliament/ (accessed February 2017).

European Commission (2016) *Transparency Register – Statistics for Register*, 13 October 2016, available at http://ec.europa.eu/transparencyregister/public/consultation/statistics.do?locale=en&action=prepareView (accessed October 2016).

European Ombudsman (2016) *Ombudsman Calls for More Trilogues Transparency*, available at http://www.ombudsman.europa.eu/en/press/release.faces/en/69214/html.bookmark (accessed March 2017).

European Parliament (2004) *Conciliations and Codecision: A Guide to How the Parliament Co-legislates*, DV/547830EN.doc.

European Parliament (2007a) *Conciliations and Codecision: A Guide to How the Parliament Co-legislates*, available at http://www.europarl.europa.eu/RegistreWeb/search/resultDetail.htm?language=EN&reference=CCPE_MAN(2007)684001&lg=EN (accessed April 2011).

European Parliament (2007b) *Towards a Single Parliament: The Influence of the ECSC Common Assembly on the Treaties of Rome*, available at http://www.epgencms.europarl.europa.eu/cmsdata/upload/c1e97159-b23b-4008-ab0d-f0908b0ec3ed/plmt_50ans_en.pdf (accessed August 2016).

European Parliament (2008) *Working Party on Parliamentary Reform – Part B: Deliberations and Conclusions*, PE 406.309/CPG/GT PARTIE B.

European Parliament (2012) *Inside the European Parliament: A Guide to Its Parliamentary and Administrative Structures*, available at http://bookshop.europa.eu/en/inside-the-european-parliament-pbBB3013578/ (accessed August 2016).

European Parliament (2013) *Parliament's Legislative Initiative*, Library of the European Parliament, 130619REV2.

European Parliament (2014a) *Activity Report on Codecision and Conciliation 14 July 2009–30 June 2014*, available at http://www.europarl.europa.eu/code/default_en.htm (accessed October 2014).

European Parliament (2014b) *Duration of Sitting per Debate Type – 7th Parliamentary Term*, available at http://www.europarl.europa.eu/sed/doc/news/previoustermstatistic/7LEG_distrib%20par%20type%20de%20debat_en.pdf (accessed February 2017).

European Parliament (2014c) *European and National Elections Figured Out*, available at www.europarl.europa.eu/pdf/elections_results/review.pdf (accessed November 2016).

European Parliament (2014d) *European Parliament Delegation Completes Fact-Finding Mission on Palestinian Prisoners Despite Israeli Refusal to Co-Operate – Statement from European Parliament Ad Hoc Delegation*, available at http://www.europarl.europa.eu/meetdocs/2009_2014/documents/dplc/dv/adhocstatement/adhocstatementen.pdf (accessed February 2017).

European Parliament (2014e) *Motion of Censure against the Commission Rejected by a Large Majority*, 27 November 2014, available at http://www.europarl.europa.eu/news/en/news-room/content/20141121IPR79864 (accessed June 2015).

European Parliament (2014f) *Strategic Planning for the Secretariat-General of the European Parliament*, available at http://www.europarl.europa.eu/the-secretary-general/en/activities/documents/docs-2014/docs-2014-october/documents-2014-october-1.html (accessed May 2015).

European Parliament (2016a) *Agenda*, June 2016, European Parliament/The President, available at http://www.europarl.europa.eu/the-president/en/agenda/year_2016/html/agenda-week-25-2016 (accessed August 2016).

European Parliament (2016b) *Duration of Sitting per Debate Type – 8th Parliamentary Term*, available at http://www.europarl.europa.eu/sed/doc/news/currenttermstatistic/8LEG_distrib_par_type_de_debat_en.pdf (accessed February 2017).

European Parliament (2016c) *Multilingualism*, available at http://www.europarl.europa.eu/aboutparliament/en/20150201PVL00013/Multilingualism (accessed July 2016).

European Parliament (2016d) *Parliament Launches Investigation into Compliance by Alliance for Peace and Freedom with EU Founding Principles*, 5 December 2016, available at http://www.europarl.europa.eu/news/de/news-room/20160512IPR27173/EP-to-check-Alliance-for-Peace-and-Freedom%E2%80%99s-compliance-with-EU-basic-principles (accessed August 2016).

European Parliament (2016e) *Twitteropolis – A Map to the European Parliament on Twitter*, 19 May 2016, available at http://www.europarl.europa.eu/external/html/twitteropolis/index_en.htm (accessed December 2016).

European Parliament (2017) *Activity Report on the Ordinary Legislative Procedure: 4 July 2014–31 December 2016*, PE 595.931.

European Parliament, Council of the European Union and European Commission (1993). *Interinstitutional Agreement of 29 October 1993 on Budgetary Discipline and Improvement of the Budgetary Procedure* (Official Journal C 331/1).

European Parliament, Council of the European Union and European Commission (1999) *Joint Declaration on Practical Arrangements for the New Co-Decision Procedure (Article 251 of the Treaty Establishing the European Community)* (Official Journal C 148/1).

European Parliamentary Research Service (2014a) *2014 European Elections: National Rules*, 140762REV3, available at http://epthinktank.

eu/2013/11/14/2014-european-elections-national-rules-2/ (accessed November 2015).

European Parliamentary Research Service (2014b) *Discharge to the Council and European Council*, PE 538.960, available at http://www.europarl.europa.eu/RegData/etudes/ATAG/2014/538960/EPRS_ATA(2014)538960_REV1_EN.pdf (accessed February 2015).

European Parliamentary Research Service (2015a) *2014 European Elections: Profile of Voters and Non-voters*, available at http://www.europarl.europa.eu/thinktank/en/document.html?reference=EPRS_STU(2015)558344 (accessed February 2017).

European Parliamentary Research Service (2015b) *How Does Ex-Ante Impact Assessment Work in the EU?*, available at http://www.europarl.europa.eu/RegData/etudes/BRIE/2015/528809/EPRS_BRI(2015)528809_EN.pdf (accessed February 2017).

European Parliamentary Research Service (2015c) *Reform of European Electoral Law*, available at http://www.europarl.europa.eu/RegData/etudes/ATAG/2015/569025/EPRS_ATA(2015)569025_EN.pdf (accessed April 2016).

European Parliamentary Research Service (2015d) *Review of European and National Election Results*, available at http://www.europarl.europa.eu/thinktank/en/document.html?reference=EPRS_STU(2015)558343 (accessed February 2017).

European Parliamentary Research Service (2016a) *European Parliament Work in the Fields of Impact Assessment and European Added Value – Activity Report for July 2014–December 2015*, PE 558.790, available at http://www.europarl.europa.eu/EPRS/IA-EAV-Activity_Report-July_2014-December_2015.pdf (accessed February 2017).

European Parliamentary Research Service (2016b) *Evaluation and Ex-Post Impact Assessment at EU Level*, available at http://www.europarl.europa.eu/RegData/etudes/BRIE/2016/581415/EPRS_BRI(2016)581415_EN.pdf (accessed February 2017).

European Parliamentary Research Service (2016c) *Parliament's Committees of Inquiry and Special Committees*, available at http://www.europarl.europa.eu/thinktank/en/document.html?reference=EPRS_IDA(2016)582007 (accessed July 2016).

European Parliamentary Research Service (2017) *European Commission Follow-up to European Parliament Requests*, available at http://www.europarl.europa.eu/thinktank/en/document.html?reference=EPRS_STU(2017)593781 (accessed February 2017).

European Voice (2014a) *Gianni Pittella – Avuncular Doctor*, 18 June, available at http://www.politico.eu/article/gianni-pittella-avuncular-doctor/ (accessed August 2016).

European Voice (2014b) *Jean Arthuis – Veteran Debutant*, 11 December, available at http://www.politico.eu/article/jean-arthuis-veteran-debutant/ (accessed August 2016).

Evans, C.L. (1999) 'Legislative Structure: Rules, Precedents, and Jurisdictions', *Legislative Studies Quarterly* 24(4): 605–642.

Faas, T. (2003) 'To Defect or Not to Defect? National, Institutional and Party Group Pressures on MEPs and Their Consequences for Party Group Cohesion in the European Parliament', *European Journal of Political Research* 42(6): 841–866.

Fabbrini, S. (2013) *The Parliamentary Election of the Commission President: Constraints on the Parliamentarization of the European Union.* LUISS School of Government, available at http://sog.luiss.it/sites/sog.luiss.it/files/SOG%20Working%20Papers%20WP9-2013%20Fabbrini.pdf (accessed February 2017).

Fabbrini, S. (2015) *Which European Union? Europe after the Euro Crisis.* Cambridge: Cambridge University Press.

Fabbrini, S. and Puetter, U. (2016) 'Integration without Supranationalisation: Studying the Lead Roles of the European Council and the Council in Post-Lisbon EU Politics', *Journal of European Integration* 38(5): 481–495.

Farrell, D.M. (2011) *Electoral Systems: A Comparative Introduction.* Houndmills: Palgrave Macmillan.

Farrell, D.M. and Scully, R. (2005) 'Electing the European Parliament: How Uniform are "Uniform" Electoral Systems?', *Journal of Common Market Studies* 43(5): 969–984.

Farrell, D.M. and Scully, R. (2010) 'The European Parliament: One Parliament, Several Modes of Political Representation on the Ground?', *Journal of European Public Policy* 17(1): 36–54.

Farrell, H. and Héritier, A. (2003a) 'Formal and Informal Institutions under Codecision: Continuous Constitution-Building in Europe', *Governance* 16(4): 577–600.

Farrell, H. and Héritier, A. (2003b) 'The Invisible Transformation of Codecision: Problems of Democratic Legitimacy', *Sieps Report* (7), available at http://www.sieps.se/sites/default/files/9-20037.pdf (accessed February 2017).

Farrell, H. and Héritier, A. (2004) 'Interorganizational Negotiation and Intraorganizational Power in Shared Decision Making: Early Agreements under Codecision and Their Impact on the European Parliament and Council', *Comparative Political Studies* 37(10): 1184–1212.

Farrell, H. and Héritier, A. (2007a) 'Codecision and Institutional Change', *West European Politics* 30(2): 285–300.

Farrell, H. and Héritier, A. (2007b) 'Introduction: Contested Competences in the European Union', *West European Politics* 30(2): 227–243.

Fasone, C. (2014) 'European Economic Governance and Parliamentary Representation: What Place for the European Parliament?', *European Law Journal* 20(2): 164–185.

Fauvelle-Aymar, C. and Stegmaier, M. (2008) 'Economic and Political Effects on European Parliamentary Electoral Turnout in Post-Communist Europe', *Electoral Studies* 27(4): 661–672.

Featherstone, K. (1994) 'Jean Monnet and the "Democratic Deficit" in the European Union', *Journal of Common Market Studies* 32(2): 149–170.

Fenno, R.F. (1973) *Congressmen in Committees.* Boston: Little, Brown.

Fenno, R.F. (1978) *Home Style: House Members in Their Districts.* Boston: Little, Brown.

Ferrara, F. and Weishaupt, J.T. (2004) 'Get Your Act Together: Party Performance in European Parliament Elections', *European Union Politics* 5(3): 283–306.

Financial Times (2014) *Merkel Swaps Back to Supporting Juncker*, 30 May, available at http://www.ft.com/cms/s/0/539b1c68-e7d3-11e3-9af8-00144 feabdc0.html (accessed May 2015).

Finke, D. (2012) 'Proposal Stage Coalition-Building in the European Parliament', *European Union Politics* 13(4): 487–512.

Finke, D. (2014) 'Domestic-Level Parliamentary Scrutiny and Voting Behaviour in the European Parliament', *Government and Opposition* 49(02): 207–231.

Finke, D. (2015) 'Why Do European Political Groups Call the Roll?', *Party Politics* 21(5): 750–762.

Fitzmaurice, J. (1988) 'An Analysis of the European Community's Co-operation Procedure', *Journal of Common Market Studies* 26(4): 389–400.

Fleischman Hillard (2011) *European Parliament Digital Trends Survey Shows MEPs' Rocketing Use of Social Networks but Decline in Blogging*, available at https://fleishmanhillard.eu/2011/01/european-parliament-digital-trends-survey-shows-meps-rocketing-use-of-social-networks-but-decline-in-blogging/ (accessed December 2016).

Fleischman Hillard (2015) *EP Digital Trends Survey 2015*, available at http://www.epdigitaltrends.eu/ (accessed November 2016).

Flickinger, R.S. and Studlar, D.T. (2007) 'One Europe, Many Electorates? Models of Turnout in European Parliament Elections after 2004', *Comparative Political Studies* 40(4): 383–404.

Font, N. and Pérez Durán, I. (2016) 'The European Parliament Oversight of EU Agencies through Written Questions', *Journal of European Public Policy* 23(9): 1349–1366.

Fortin-Rittberger, J. and Rittberger, B. (2014) 'Do Electoral Rules Matter? Explaining National Differences in Women's Representation in the European Parliament', *European Union Politics* 15(4): 496–520.

Fortin-Rittberger, J. and Rittberger, B. (2015) 'Nominating Women for Europe: Exploring the Role of Political Parties' Recruitment Procedures for European Parliament Elections', *European Journal of Political Research* 54(4): 767–783.

Franklin, M.N. (2001) 'How Structural Factors Cause Turnout Variations at European Parliament Elections', *European Union Politics* 2(3): 309–328.

Franklin, M.N. (2014) 'Why Vote at an Election with No Apparent Purpose? Voter Turnout at Elections to the European Parliament', *European Policy Analysis* (4), available at http://www.sieps.se/en/publications/european-policy-analysis/why-vote-at-an-election-with-no-apparent-purpose-voter-turnout (accessed April 2016).

Franklin, M.N. and Hobolt, S.B. (2011) 'The Legacy of Lethargy: How Elections to the European Parliament Depress Turnout', *Electoral Studies* 30(1): 67–76.

Frantescu, D.P. (2015) 'Values Topple Nationality in the European Parliament', *European View* 14(1): 101–110.

Frantescu, D.P. (2016) 'Who Is For and Against Free Trade in the European Parliament', *VoteWatch*, available at http://www.votewatch.eu/blog/

who-is-for-and-against-free-trade-in-the-european-parliament/, http://www.votewatch.eu/blog/who-is-for-and-against-free-trade-in-the-european-parliament/ (accessed February 2017).

Frech, E. (2016) 'Re-Electing MEPs: The Factors Determining Re-Election Probabilities', *European Union Politics* 17(1): 69–90.

Furness, M. (2013) 'Who Controls the European External Action Service? Agent Autonomy in EU External Policy', *European Foreign Affairs Review* 18(1): 103–125.

Gaffney, J. (ed.) (1996) *Political Parties and the European Union*. London: Routledge.

Gagatek, W. and van Hecke, S. (2014) 'The Development of European Political Foundations and Their Role in Strengthening Europarties', *Acta Politica* 49(1): 86–104.

Garrett, G. (1995) 'From the Luxembourg Compromise to Codecision: Decision Making in the European Union', *Electoral Studies* 14(3): 289–308.

Gattermann, K. (2013) 'News about the European Parliament: Patterns and External Drivers of Broadsheet Coverage', *European Union Politics* 14(3): 436–457.

Gattermann, K. and Vasilopoulou, S. (2015) 'Absent yet Popular? Explaining News Visibility of Members of the European Parliament', *European Journal of Political Research* 54(1): 121–140.

Gherghina, S. and Chiru, M. (2010) 'Practice and Payment: Determinants of Candidate List Position in European Parliament Elections', *European Union Politics* 11(4): 533–552.

Goffman, E. (1959) *The Presentation of Self in Everyday Life*, New York: Anchor.

Goulard, S. (2016) 'Britain Must Not Hold Other EU States to Ransom', *Financial Times,* 25 June, available at http://www.ft.com/cms/s/0/0d9dc2a0-39cb-11e6-a780-b48ed7b6126f.html#axzz4GvDnpLKt (accessed August 2016).

Gray, M. and Stubb, A. (2001) 'Keynote Article: The Treaty of Nice – Negotiating a Poisoned Chalice?', *Journal of Common Market Studies* 39(s1): 5–23.

Greenwood, J. (2011) *Interest Representation in the European Union*. Houndmills: Palgrave Macmillan.

Greilsammer, I. (1991) 'The Non-Ratification of the EEC-Israel Protocols by the European Parliament (1988)', *Middle Eastern Studies* 27(2): 303–321.

Guerrieri, S. (2008) 'The Start of European Integration and the Parliamentary Dimension: The Common Assembly of the ECSC (1952–1958)', *Parliaments, Estates and Representation* 28(1): 183–193.

Haddadi, S. (2002) 'Two Cheers for Whom? The European Union and Democratization in Morocco', *Democratization* 9(1): 149–169.

Häge, F.M. (2011) 'The European Union Policy-Making Dataset', *European Union Politics* 12(3): 455–477.

Hagemann, S. and Høyland, B. (2010) 'Bicameral Politics in the European Union', *Journal of Common Market Studies* 48(4): 811–833.

Hall, P.A. and Taylor, R.C.R. (1996) 'Political Science and the Three New Institutionalisms', *Political Studies* 44(5): 936–957.

Hansen, V.W. (2014) 'Incomplete Information and Bargaining in the EU: An Explanation of First-Reading Non-Agreements', *European Union Politics* 15(4): 472–495.

Hausemer, P. (2006) 'Participation and Political Competition in Committee Report Allocation: Under What Conditions Do MEPs Represent Their Constituents?', *European Union Politics* 7(4): 505–530.

Hay, C. (2010) 'Ideas and the Construction of Interests', in D. Béland and R.H. Cox (eds) *Ideas and Politics in Social Science Research*. Oxford: Oxford University Press, pp. 65–82.

Hayes-Renshaw, F. and Wallace, H. (2006) *The Council of Ministers*, 2nd ed. Houndmills: Palgrave Macmillan.

Héritier, A. (2012) 'Institutional Change in Europe: Co-decision and Comitology Transformed', *Journal of Common Market Studies* 50(s1): 38–54.

Héritier, A. and Moury, C. (2011) 'Contested Delegation: The Impact of Co-decision on Comitology', *West European Politics* 34(1): 145–166.

Héritier, A. and Reh, C. (2012) 'Codecision and Its Discontents: Intra-Organisational Politics and Institutional Reform in the European Parliament', *West European Politics* 35(5): 1134–1157.

Hernández, E. and Kriesi, H. (2016) 'Turning Your Back on the EU. The Role of Eurosceptic Parties in the 2014 European Parliament Elections', *Electoral Studies* 44: 515–524.

Herranz Surrallés, A. (2011) 'The Contested "Parliamentarisation" of EU Foreign and Security Policy: The Role of the European Parliament following the Introduction of the Treaty of Lisbon', *Working Paper 104*, Frankfurt am Main: Hessische Stiftung Friedens-und Konfliktforschung, available at http://nbn-resolving.de/urn:nbn:de:0168-ssoar-320498 (accessed February 2017).

Herzog, A. and Rasmussen, M.K. (2015) *Parliamentary Own-Initiative Reports: Simply Theater of Engagement?*, unpublished manuscript.

High Level Group on Own Resources (2016) *Final Report and Recommendations*, available at http://ec.europa.eu/budget/mff/hlgor/library/reports-communication/hlgor-report_20170104.pdf (accessed February 2017).

Hix, S. (2002) 'Constitutional Agenda-Setting through Discretion in Rule Interpretation: Why the European Parliament Won at Amsterdam', *British Journal of Political Science* 32(2): 259–280.

Hix, S. (2004) 'Electoral Institutions and Legislative Behavior: Explaining Voting Defection in the European Parliament', *World Politics* 56(2): 194–223.

Hix, S. (2005) *The Political System of the European Union*. 2nd ed. Houndmills: Palgrave Macmillan.

Hix, S. (2008a) 'Towards a Partisan Theory of EU Politics', *Journal of European Public Policy* 15(8): 1254–1265.

Hix, S. (2008b) *What's Wrong with the European Union and How to Fix It*. Cambridge: Polity.

Hix, S. and Bartolini, S. (2006) *Politics: The Right or the Wrong Sort of Medicine for the EU?*, 2006, Notre Europe, Policy paper Number 19, available at http://www.epin.org/new/files/Policypaper19-en.pdf (accessed July 2011).

Hix, S. and Hagemann, S. (2009) 'Could Changing the Electoral Rules Fix European Parliament Elections?', *Politique européenne* 28(2): 37–52.

Hix, S. and Høyland, B. (2011) *The Political System of the European Union*, 3rd ed. Houndmills: Palgrave Macmillan.

Hix, S. and Høyland, B. (2013) 'Empowerment of the European Parliament', *Annual Review of Political Science* 16(1): 171–189.

Hix, S., Kreppel, A. and Noury, A. (2003) 'The Party System in the European Parliament: Collusive or Competitive?', *Journal of Common Market Studies* 41(2): 309–331.

Hix, S. and Lord, C. (1997) *Political Parties in the European Union*. Houndmills: Palgrave Macmillan.

Hix, S. and Marsh, M. (2007) 'Punishment or Protest? Understanding European Parliament Elections', *The Journal of Politics* 69(2): 495–510.

Hix, S. and Marsh, M. (2011) 'Second-Order Effects plus Pan-European Political Swings: An Analysis of European Parliament Elections across Time', *Electoral Studies* 30(1): 4–15.

Hix, S. and Noury, A. (2009) 'After Enlargement: Voting Patterns in the Sixth European Parliament', *Legislative Studies Quarterly* 34(2): 159–174.

Hix, S., Noury, A. and Roland, G. (2005) 'Power to the Parties: Cohesion and Competition in the European Parliament, 1979–2001', *British Journal of Political Science* 35(2): 209–234.

Hix, S., Noury, A. and Roland, G. (2006) 'Dimensions of Politics in the European Parliament', *American Journal of Political Science* 50(2): 494–520.

Hix, S., Noury, A. and Roland, G. (2007) *Democratic Politics in the European Parliament*. Cambridge: Cambridge University Press.

Hix, S., Noury, A. and Roland, G. (2009) 'Voting Patterns and Alliance Formation in the European Parliament', *Philosophical Transactions of the Royal Society* 364(1518): 821–831.

Hobolt, S.B. (2014) 'A Vote for the President? The Role of Spitzenkandidaten in the 2014 European Parliament Elections', *Journal of European Public Policy* 21(10): 1528–1540.

Hobolt, S.B. (2015) 'The 2014 European Parliament Elections: Divided in Unity?', *Journal of Common Market Studies* 53(s1): 6–21.

Hobolt, S.B. and Spoon, J.-J. (2012) 'Motivating the European Voter: Parties, Issues and Campaigns in European Parliament Elections', *European Journal of Political Research* 51(6): 701–727.

Hobolt, S.B., Spoon, J.-J. and Tilley, J. (2009) 'A Vote Against Europe? Explaining Defection at the 1999 and 2004 European Parliament Elections', *British Journal of Political Science* 39(01): 93–115.

Hobolt, S.B. and Wittrock, J. (2011) 'The Second-Order Election Model Revisited: An Experimental Test of Vote Choices in European Parliament Elections', *Electoral Studies* 30(1): 29–40.

Hoff, A., Lelieveldt, H. and van der Does, R. (2016) 'A Biased Rapporteur or Politics as Usual? Reassessing the Balance of Interests in the EU Food Information Labelling Case', *Journal of European Public Policy* 23(2): 296–313.

Hoffmeister, F. (2014) 'The EU as an International Trade Negotiator', in J. Koops and G. Macaj (eds) *The European Union as a Diplomatic Actor*. Houndmills: Palgrave Macmillan, pp. 138–154.

Holman, C. and Luneburg, W. (2012) 'Lobbying and Transparency: A Comparative Analysis of Regulatory Reform', *Interest Groups & Advocacy* 1(1): 75–104.

Hong, G. (2015) 'Explaining Vote Switching to Niche Parties in the 2009 European Parliament Elections', *European Union Politics* 16(4): 514–535.

Hörl, B., Warntjen, A. and Wonka, A. (2005) 'Built on Quicksand? A Decade of Procedural Spatial Models on EU Legislative Decision-Making', *Journal of European Public Policy* 12(3): 592–606.

Hosli, M.O. (1997) 'Voting Strength in the European Parliament: The Influence of National and of Partisan Actors', *European Journal of Political Research* 31(3): 351–366.

Høyland, B. (2006) 'Allocation of Codecision Reports in the Fifth European Parliament', *European Union Politics* 7(1): 30–50.

Huber, K. and Shackleton, M. (2013) 'Codecision: A Practitioners' View from Inside the Parliament', *Journal of European Public Policy* 20(7): 1040–1055.

Hug, S. (2016) 'Party Pressure in the European Parliament', *European Union Politics* 17(2): 201–218.

Hurka, S. and Kaeding, M. (2011) 'Report Allocation in the European Parliament after Eastern Enlargement', *Journal of European Public Policy* 19(4): 512–529.

Hurka, S., Obholzer, L. and Daniel, W.T. (2017) 'When Time Is Money: Sideline Jobs, Ancillary Income and Legislative Effort', *Journal of European Public Policy*. DOI: 10.1080/13501763.2017.1285341.

Hurrelmann, A. (2015) 'Demoi-cratic Citizenship in Europe: An Impossible Ideal?', *Journal of European Public Policy* 22(1): 19–36.

Jansen, T. (1998) *The European People's Party: Origins and Development*. Houndmills: MacMillan.

Jensen, C.B., Proksch, S.-O. and Slapin, J.B. (2013) 'Parliamentary Questions, Oversight, and National Opposition Status in the European Parliament', *Legislative Studies Quarterly* 38(2): 259–282.

Jiménez Lobeira, P.C. (2012) 'EU Citizenship and Political Identity: The Demos and Telos Problems', *European Law Journal* 18(4): 504–517.

Judge, D. (1992) '"Predestined to Save the Earth": The Environment Committee of the European Parliament', *Environmental Politics* 1(4): 186–212.

Judge, D. and Earnshaw, D. (1994) 'Weak European Parliament Influence? A Study of the Environment Committee of the European Parliament', *Government and Opposition* 29(2): 262–276.

Judge, D. and Earnshaw, D. (2002) 'The European Parliament and the Commission Crisis: A New Assertiveness?', *Governance* 15(3): 345–374.

Judge, D. and Earnshaw, D. (2008) *The European Parliament*, 2nd ed. Houndmills: Palgrave Macmillan.

Judge, D. and Earnshaw, D. (2011) '"Relais Actors" and Co-Decision First Reading Agreements in the European Parliament: The Case of the Advanced Therapies Regulation', *Journal of European Public Policy* 18(1): 53–71.

Jupille, J. (2004) *Procedural Politics: Issues, Influence, and Institutional Choice in the European Union*. Cambridge: Cambridge University Press.

Kaeding, M. (2004) 'Rapporteurship Allocation in the European Parliament: Information or Distribution?', *European Union Politics* 5(3): 353–371.

Kaeding, M. (2005) 'The World of Committee Reports: Rapporteurship Assignment in the European Parliament', *The Journal of Legislative Studies* 11(1): 82–104.

Kaeding, M. and Obholzer, L. (2012) 'Pulling the Strings: Party Group Coordinators in the European Parliament', *EIPAScope* 2012(1): 13–18.

Kaniovski, S. and Mueller, D.C. (2011) 'How Representative Is the European Union Parliament?', *European Journal of Political Economy* 27(1): 61–74.

Kardasheva, R. (2009) 'The Power to Delay: The European Parliament's Influence in the Consultation Procedure', *Journal of Common Market Studies* 47(2): 385–409.

Katz, R.S. (1997) 'Representational Roles', *European Journal of Political Research* 32(2): 211–226.

Kaufmann, B. (2006) 'One Million Reasons for More Democracy in Europe', *Euobserver* 21 September, available at https://euobserver.com/opinion/22468 (accessed July 2016).

Kaunert, C., Léonard, S. and MacKenzie, A. (2012) 'The Social Construction of an EU Interest in Counter-Terrorism: US Influence and Internal Struggles in the Cases of PNR and SWIFT', *European Security* 21(4): 474–496.

Kauppi, N. (2010) 'The Political Ontology of European Integration', *Comparative European Politics* 8(1): 19–36.

Kauppi, N. and Madsen, M.R. (2008) 'Institutions et Acteurs: Rationalité, Réflexivité et Analyse de l'UE', *Politique Européenne* 25(2): 87–113.

Keukeleire, S. and Delreux, T. (2014) *The Foreign Policy of the European Union.* Houndmills: Palgrave Macmillan.

Klüver, H. (2013) *Lobbying in the European Union: Interest Groups, Lobbying Coalitions, and Policy Change.* Oxford: Oxford University Press.

Knight, J. (1992) *Institutions and Social Conflict.* Cambridge: Cambridge University Press.

Koepke, J.R. and Ringe, N. (2006) 'The Second-Order Election Model in an Enlarged Europe', *European Union Politics* 7(3): 321–346.

Kohler, M. (2014) 'European Governance and the European Parliament: From Talking Shop to Legislative Powerhouse', *Journal of Common Market Studies* 52(3): 600–615.

Kohler-Koch, B. (1997) 'Organized Interests in the EC and the European Parliament', *European Integration online Papers (EIoP)* 1(9), available at http://www.eiop.or.at/eiop/texte/1997-009a.htm (accessed October 2016).

Kostadinova, T. (2003) 'Voter Turnout Dynamics in Post-Communist Europe', *European Journal of Political Research* 42(6): 741–759.

Kousser, T. (2004) 'Retrospective Voting and Strategic Behavior in European Parliament Elections', *Electoral Studies* 23(1): 1–21.

Krauss, S. (2000) 'The European Parliament in EU External Relations: The Customs Union with Turkey', *European Foreign Affairs Review* 5(2): 215–237.

Krehbiel, K. (1991) *Information and Legislative Organization.* Ann Arbor: University of Michigan Press.

Kreppel, A. (2002) *The European Parliament and Supranational Party System: A Study in Institutional Development.* Cambridge: Cambridge University Press.

Kreppel, A. and Hix, S. (2003) 'From "Grand Coalition" To Left-Right Confrontation: Explaining the Shifting Structure of Party Competition in the European Parliament', *Comparative Political Studies* 36(1–2): 75–96.

Kreppel, A. and Tsebelis, G. (1999) 'Coalition Formation in the European Parliament', *Comparative Political Studies* 32(8): 933–966.

Kroh, C. (2014) 'Stability Amid Change: Impact of the 2014 European Parliament Elections at the European Level', *Electoral Studies* 36: 204–209.

Külahci, E. and Lightfoot, S. (2014) 'Governance, Europarties and the Challenge of Democratic Representation in the EU: A Case Study of the Party of European Socialists', *Acta Politica* 49(1): 71–85.

Kurzer, P. and Cooper, A. (2013) 'Biased or Not? Organized Interests and the Case of EU Food Information Labeling', *Journal of European Public Policy* 20(5): 722–740.

Ladrech, R. (1996) 'Political Parties in the European Parliament', in J. Gaffney (ed.) *Political Parties and the European Union.* London: Routledge, pp. 291–307.

Laffan, B. (2003) 'Auditing and Accountability in the European Union', *Journal of European Public Policy* 10(5): 762–777.

Laffan, B. and Lindner, J. (2015) 'The Budget: Who Gets, What, When and How?', in H. Wallace, M.A. Pollack and A.R. Young (eds) *Policy-Making in the European Union.* Oxford: Oxford University Press, pp. 220–242.

Larsson, A.O. (2015) 'The EU Parliament on Twitter – Assessing the Permanent Online Practices of Parliamentarians', *Journal of Information Technology & Politics* 12(2): 149–166.

Laursen, B. and Valentini, C. (2015) 'Mediatization and Government Communication Press Work in the European Parliament', *The International Journal of Press/Politics* 20(1): 26–44.

Le Pen, M. (2016) 'Marine Le Pen: After Brexit, the People's Spring Is Inevitable', *The New York Times*, 28 June, available at http://www.nytimes.com/2016/06/28/opinion/marine-le-pen-after-brexit-the-peoples-spring-is-inevitable.html (accessed August 2016).

Lefkofridi, Z. and Katsanidou, A. (2014) 'Multilevel Representation in the European Parliament', *European Union Politics* 15(1): 108–131.

Lehmann, W. (2014) *The European Elections: EU Legislation, National Provisions and Civic Participation*, available at http://www.europarl.europa.eu/activities/committees/studies/download.do?language=en&file=19431 (accessed November 2015).

Leston-Bandeira, C. (2014) 'The Pursuit of Legitimacy as a Key Driver for Public Engagement: The European Parliament Case', *Parliamentary Affairs* 67(2): 415–436.

Lightfoot, S. (2005) *Europeanizing Social Democracy? The Rise of the Party of European Socialists.* London: Routledge.

Lilleker, D.G. and Koc-Michalska, K. (2013) 'Online Political Communication Strategies: MEPs, E-Representation, and Self-Representation', *Journal of Information Technology & Politics* 10(2): 190–207.

Lindberg, B., Rasmussen, A. and Warntjen, A. (2008) 'Party Politics as Usual? The Role of Political Parties in EU Legislative Decision-Making', *Journal of European Public Policy* 15(8): 1107–1126.

Lindstädt, R., Slapin, J.B. and Vander Wielen, R.J. (2012) 'Adaptive Behaviour in the European Parliament: Learning to Balance Competing Demands', *European Union Politics* 13(4): 465–486.

LobbyFacts (2016) *Statistics*, LobbyFacts Database, available at https://lobbyfacts.eu/reports/lobby-costs/all (accessed October 2016).

Lodge, J. (1984) 'European Union and the First Elected European Parliament: The Spinelli Initiative', *Journal of Common Market Studies* 22(4): 377–402.

Lord, C. (2002) 'What Role for Parties in EU Politics?', *Journal of European Integration* 24(1): 39–52.

Lord, C. (2011) 'The European Parliament and the Legitimation of Agencification', *Journal of European Public Policy* 18(6): 909–925.

Lord, C. (2013) 'The Democratic Legitimacy of Codecision', *Journal of European Public Policy* 20(7): 1056–1073.

Lord, C. and Tamvaki, D. (2013) 'The Politics of Justification? Applying the "Discourse Quality Index" to the Study of the European Parliament', *European Political Science Review* 5(1): 27–54.

Lorenzo Rodríguez, J. and Garmendia Madariaga, A. (2016) 'Going Public Against Institutional Constraints? Analyzing the Online Presence Intensity of 2014 European Parliament Election Candidates', *European Union Politics* 17(2): 303–323.

Lühiste, M. and Kenny, M. (2016) 'Pathways to Power: Women's Representation in the 2014 European Parliament Elections', *European Journal of Political Research* 55(3): 626–641.

Magnette, P. and Nicolaïdis, K. (2004) 'The European Convention: Bargaining in the Shadow of Rhetoric', *West European Politics* 27(3): 381–404.

Magnette, P. and Papadopoulos, Y. (2008) *On the Politicization of the European Consociation: A Middle Way between Hix and Bartolini*, European Governance Papers (EUROGOV), Number C-08-01, available at http://www.mzes.uni-mannheim.de/projekte/typo3/site/fileadmin/wp/pdf/egp-connex-C-08-01.pdf (accessed June 2014).

Maier, M., Strömbäck, J. and Kaid, L.L. (2011) *Political Communication in European Parliamentary Elections*. Farnham: Ashgate Publishing.

Mair, P. and Thomassen, J.J.A. (2010) 'Political Representation and Government in the European Union', *Journal of European Public Policy* 17(1): 20–35.

Mamadouh, V. and Raunio, T. (2003) 'The Committee System: Powers, Appointments and Report Allocation', *Journal of Common Market Studies* 41(2): 333–351.

Marsh, M. (2009) 'Vote Switching in European Parliament Elections: Evidence from June 2004', *Journal of European Integration* 31(5): 627–644.

Marsh, M. and Norris, P. (1997) 'Political Representation in the European Parliament', *European Journal of Political Research* 32(2): 153–164.

Marshall, D. (2010) 'Who to Lobby and When: Institutional Determinants of Interest Group Strategies in European Parliament Committees', *European Union Politics* 11(4): 553–575.

Marshall, D. (2012) 'Do Rapporteurs Receive Independent Expert Policy Advice? Indirect Lobbying Via the European Parliament's Committee Secretariat', *Journal of European Public Policy* 19(9): 1377–1395.

Marshall, D. (2015) 'Explaining Interest Group Interactions with Party Group Members in the European Parliament: Dominant Party Groups and Coalition Formation', *Journal of Common Market Studies* 53(2): 311–329.

Matthews, D. and Žikovská, P. (2013) 'The Rise and Fall of the Anti-Counterfeiting Trade Agreement (ACTA): Lessons for the European Union', *IIC – International Review of Intellectual Property and Competition Law* 44(6): 626–655.

Mattila, M. (2003) 'Why Bother? Determinants of Turnout in the European Elections', *Electoral Studies* 22(3): 449–468.

Mattila, M. and Raunio, T. (2012) 'Drifting Further Apart: National Parties and Their Electorates on the EU Dimension', *West European Politics* 35(3): 589–606.

Mattson, I. and Strøm, K. (1995) 'Parliamentary Committees', in H. Döring (ed.) *Parliaments and Majority Rule in Western Europe*. Frankfurt: Campus Verlag, pp. 249–307.

Maurer, A. (2007) 'The European Parliament Post-1993: Explaining Macroscopic Trends of Inter- and Intrainstitutional Developments', in *European Union Studies Association (EUSA), Biennial Conference 2007*, available at http://aei.pitt.edu/7968 (accessed February 2017).

Maurer, A., Parkes, R. and Wagner, M. (2007) 'The European Parliament in the Enlarged EU: Explaining Group Membership in the European Parliament', in *European Union Studies Association (EUSA), Biennial Conference 2007*, available at http://aei.pitt.edu/7969/ (accessed February 2017).

McCown, M. (2003) 'The European Parliament before the Bench: ECJ Precedent and EP Litigation Strategies', *Journal of European Public Policy* 10(6): 974–995.

McElroy, G. (2001) 'Committees and Party Cohesion in the European Parliament', *EPRG Working Papers* 8, available at http://www2.lse.ac.uk/government/research/resgroups/EPRG/pdf/workingPaper8.pdf (accessed June 2011).

McElroy, G. (2006) 'Committee Representation in the European Parliament', *European Union Politics* 7(1): 5–29.

McElroy, G. (2007) 'Legislative Politics as Normal? Voting Behaviour and Beyond in the European Parliament', *European Union Politics* 8(3): 433–448.

McElroy, G. and Benoit, K. (2010) 'Party Policy and Group Affiliation in the European Parliament', *British Journal of Political Science* 40(02): 377–398.

McElroy, G. and Benoit, K. (2012) 'Policy Positioning in the European Parliament', *European Union Politics* 13(1): 150–167.

McEvoy, C. (2012) 'Unequal Representation in the EU: A Multi-Level Analysis of Voter–Party Congruence in EP Elections', *Representation* 48(1): 83–99.

Meserve, S.A., Pemstein, D. and Bernhard, W.T. (2009) 'Political Ambition and Legislative Behavior in the European Parliament', *The Journal of Politics* 71(3): 1–18.

Meserve, S.A., Robbins, J. and Thames, F. (2017) 'Multiple Principals and Legislative Cohesion', *Legislative Studies Quarterly*. DOI: 10.1111/lsq.12165.

Meunier, S. and Nicolaïdis, K. (1999) 'Who Speaks for Europe? The Delegation of Trade Authority in the EU', *Journal of Common Market Studies* 37(3): 477–501.

Michon, S. (2004) 'Devenir Stagiaire au Parlement Européen: Une Entrée dans l'Espace Politique Européen', *Regards Sociologiques* (27–28): 85–95.

Michon, S. (2008) 'Assistant Parlementaire au Parlement Européen: Un Tremplin pour une Carrière Européenne', *Sociologie du Travail* 50(2): 169–183.

Moon, D.S. and Bratberg, Ø. (2010) 'Conceptualising the Multi-Level Party: Two Complementary Approaches', *Politics* 30(1): 52–60.

Moravcsik, A. (2000a) 'De Gaulle between Grain and Grandeur: The Political Economy of French EC Policy, 1958–1970 (Part 1)', *Journal of Cold War Studies* 2(2): 3–43.

Moravcsik, A. (2000b) 'De Gaulle between Grain and Grandeur: The Political Economy of French EC Policy, 1958–1970 (Part 2)', *Journal of Cold War Studies* 2(3): 4–68.

Moravcsik, A. and Nicolaïdis, K. (1999) 'Explaining the Treaty of Amsterdam: Interests, Influence, Institutions', *Journal of Common Market Studies* 37(1): 59–85.

Moser, P. (1996) 'The European Parliament as a Conditional Agenda Setter: What Are the Conditions? A Critique of Tsebelis (1994)', *The American Political Science Review* 90(4): 834–838.

Moser, P. (1997) 'A Theory of the Conditional Influence of the European Parliament in the Cooperation Procedure', *Public Choice* 91(3–4): 333–350.

Mühlböck, M. (2012) 'National versus European: Party Control over Members of the European Parliament', *West European Politics* 35(3): 607–631.

Mühlböck, M. and Yordanova, N. (2017) 'When Legislators Choose Not to Decide: Abstentions in the European Parliament', *European Union Politics* 18(2): 323–336.

Napel, S. and Widgrén, M. (2006) 'The Inter-Institutional Distribution of Power in EU Codecision', *Social Choice and Welfare* 27(1): 129–154.

Navarro, J. (2009) *Les Députés Européens et Leur Rôle: Sociologie Interprétative des Pratiques Parlementaires*. Brussels: Éditions de l'Université de Bruxelles.

Nedergaard, P. and Jensen, M.D. (2014) 'The Anatomy of Intergroups – Network Governance in the Political Engine Room of the European Parliament', *Policy Studies* 35(2): 192–209.

Neuhold, C. (2001) 'The "Legislative Backbone" Keeping the Institution Upright? The Role of European Parliament Committees in the EU Policy-Making Process', *European Integration online Papers (EIoP)* 5(10), available at http://eiop.or.at/eiop/pdf/2001-010.pdf (accessed June 2014).

Neuhold, C. (2007) ' "We are the Employment Team": Socialisation in European Parliament Committees and Possible Effects on Policy-Making', in *European Union Studies Association (EUSA), Biennial Conference 2007*, available at http://aei.pitt.edu/7983/01/neuhold-c-11b.pdf (accessed March 2009).

Neuhold, C. and Dobbels, M. (2015) 'Paper Keepers or Policy Shapers? The Conditions under which EP Officials Impact on the EU Policy Process', *Comparative European Politics* 13(5): 577–595.

Neuhold, C., Rozenberg, O., Smith, J. and Hefftler, C. (eds) (2015) *The Palgrave Handbook of National Parliaments and the European Union*. Houndmills: Palgrave Macmillan.

Neunreither, K. (2002) 'Elected Legislators and Their Unelected Assistants in the European Parliament', *The Journal of Legislative Studies* 8(4): 40–60.

Nicolaïdis, K. (2013) 'European Demoicracy and Its Crisis', *Journal of Common Market Studies* 51(2): 351–369.

Nicoll, S.W. (1994) 'The European Parliament's Post-Maastricht Rules of Procedures', *Journal of Common Market Studies* 32(3): 403–410.

Norris, P. (1999) 'Recruitment into the European Parliament', in R.S. Katz and B. Wessels (eds) *The European Parliament, the National Parliaments, and European Integration*. Oxford: Oxford University Press, pp. 86–102.

Nugent, N. and Rhinard, M. (2015) *The European Commission*, 2nd ed. Houndmills: Palgrave Macmillan.

Nulty, P., Theocharis, Y., Popa, S.A., Parnet, O. and Benoit, K. (2016) 'Social Media and Political Communication in the 2014 Elections to the European Parliament', *Electoral Studies* 44: 429–444.

Núñez Ferrer, J. and Katarivas, M. (2014) 'What Are the Effects of the EU Budget: Driving Force or Drop in the Ocean?', *CEPS Special Report* (86), available at http://www.ceps.be/book/what-are-effects-eu-budget-driving-force-or-drop-ocean (accessed February 2015).

Pacek, A.C. and Radcliff, B. (2003) 'Voter Participation and Party-Group Fortunes in European Parliament Elections, 1979–1999: A Cross-National Analysis', *Political Research Quarterly* 56(1): 91–95.

Page, E.C. and Jenkins, W.I. (2005) *Policy Bureaucracy: Government with a Cast of Thousands*. Oxford: Oxford University Press.

Pegan, A. (2017) 'The Role of Personal Parliamentary Assistants in the European Parliament', *West European Politics* 40(2): 295–315.

Pemstein, D., Meserve, S.A. and Bernhard, W.T. (2015) 'Brussels Bound: Policy Experience and Candidate Selection in European Elections', *Comparative Political Studies* 48(11): 1421–1453.

Piedrafita, S. (2014) *Who Calls the Shots in the Committees of the New European Parliament?*, CEPS Special Report 97, available at https://www.ceps.eu/publications/who-calls-shots-committees-new-european-parliament (accessed January 2016).

Pilet, J.-B., van Haute, E. and Kelbel, C. (2015) *The Electoral Reform of the European Parliament: Composition, Procedure and Legitimacy*, available at http://www.europarl.europa.eu/RegData/etudes/STUD/2015/519206/IPOL_STU(2015)519206_EN.pdf (accessed April 2016).

Poguntke, T., Aylott, N., Ladrech, R. and Luther, K.R. (2007) 'The Europeanisation of National Party Organisations: A Conceptual Analysis', *European Journal of Political Research* 46(6): 747–771.

Politico (2014) *EFDD Loses Out as Groups Share the Spoils*, 7 July, available at http://www.politico.eu/article/members-of-parliaments-committees-choose-their-leaders/ (accessed August 2016).

Politico (2015a) *Do MEPs Ask Too Many Questions? Do They?*, 8 September, available at http://www.politico.eu/article/meps-ask-too-many-questions-parliament-brussels-eu/ (accessed February 2017).

Politico (2015b) *EU Forces through Refugee Deal*, 21 September, available at http://www.politico.eu/article/eu-tries-to-unblock-refugee-migrants-relocation-deal-crisis/ (accessed July 2016).

Politico (2015c) *Parliament's Heavyweight Bout: Schulz vs Welle*, 11 June, available at http://www.politico.eu/article/parliament-power-martin-schulz-klaus-welle/ (accessed August 2016).

Politico (2015d) *The Ambitions of Martin Schulz*, 29 October, available at http://www.politico.eu/article/schulz-wants-showtime-parliament-president-lisbon-power/ (accessed August 2016).

Politico (2015e) *The Most Exclusive Dining Club in Brussels*, 18 June, available at http://www.politico.eu/article/g5-brussels-most-exclusive-dining-club/ (accessed August 2016).

Politico (2016a) *Far-right Groups Ordered to Pay European Parliament €800,000*, 13 September, available at http://www.politico.eu/article/national-front-marine-le-pen-far-right-groups-ordered-to-pay-european-parliament-e800000/ (accessed February 2017).

Politico (2016b) *Greek MEP Booted Out for Calling Turks 'Wild Dogs'*, 9 March, available at http://www.politico.eu/article/greek-mep-booted-calling-turks-barbaric-wild-dogs-european-parliament-golden-dawn-racism/ (accessed February 2017).

Politico (2016c) *Maltese Lawmaker Fails EU Test, but Carries on Regardless*, 13 September, available at http://www.politico.eu/article/maltese-lawmaker-fails-eu-test-but-carries-on-regardless/ (accessed February 2017).

Politico (2016d) *Martin Schulz's Staff Shuffle Riles Parliament*, 25 May, available at http://www.politico.eu/article/european-parliament-president-martin-schulzs-latest-power-grab-winkler/ (accessed August 2016).

Politico (2016e) *MEPs Crafting Netflix Legislation Sit on Board of German Public Broadcaster*, 13 June, available at http://www.politico.eu/article/meps-crafting-netflix-legislation-sit-on-board-of-german-public-broadcaster/ (accessed November 2016).

Politico (2016f) *New Growth and Jobs Plan ... for Parliament Staff*, 21 September, available at http://www.politico.eu/article/new-growth-and-jobs-plan-for-european-parliament-staff-contradicts-reducing-budget-spread-across-groups/ (accessed February 2017).

Politico (2016g) *Parliament's Small Parties Buck Overhaul*, 26 January, available at http://www.politico.eu/article/parliaments-small-parties-resist-reform-proposals-europe-legistation-euroskeptic/ (accessed February 2017).

Politico (2017a) *5 Stars to Remain in Nigel Farage's Group*, 10 January, available at http://www.politico.eu/article/5stars-to-remain-in-nigel-farages-group-beppe-grillo-efdd/ (accessed February 2017).

Politico (2017b) *And the Winner Is ... a Backroom Deal (and Antonio Tajani)*, 17 January, available at http://www.politico.eu/article/european-parliament-presidency-vote-election-and-the-winner-is-a-backroom-deal-and-antonio-tajani-epp/ (accessed February 2017).

Politico (2017c) *British MEPs Cling to Top Jobs*, 27 January, available at http://www.politico.eu/article/brexit-british-meps-cling-to-top-jobs/ (accessed February 2017).

Politico (2017d) *Digital Disruptors Take on Brussels Consultants*, 22 February, available at http://www.politico.eu/article/lobbying-in-the-age-of-populism/ (accessed February 2017).

Politico (2017e) *Europe's Last Internet Pirate*, 16 February, available at http://www.politico.eu/article/the-last-pirate-copyright-reform-european-commission/ (accessed February 2017).

Politico (2017f) *Germany's Weber Wants a 'G6' to Push Out the Populists*, 14 February, available at http://www.politico.eu/article/manfred-weber-wants-a-g6-to-push-out-populists-european-parliament/ (accessed February 2017).

Politico (2017g) *New Lobbying Rules Face Uncertain Future*, 16 February, available at http://www.politico.eu/article/new-lobbying-rules-face-uncertain-future-europe-transparency/ (accessed February 2017).

Politico (2017h) *Parliament's New Transport Committee Star*, 25 January, available at http://www.politico.eu/blogs/playbook-plus/2017/01/parliaments-new-transport-committee-star-karima-delli/ (accessed February 2017).

Politico (2017i) *Schulz's Departure Liberates Parliament's 'Dark Prince'*, 27 January, available at http://www.politico.eu/article/martin-schulz-departure-liberates-klaus-welle-dark-prince-of-parliament/ (accessed February 2017).

Polsby, N.W. (1968) 'The Institutionalization of the U.S. House of Representatives', *American Political Science Review* 62(01): 144–168.

Powell, W.W. and DiMaggio, P.J. (eds) (1991) *The New Institutionalism in Organizational Analysis*. Chicago: University of Chicago Press.

Pridham, G. and Pridham, P. (1981) *Transnational Party Co-operation and European Integration: The Process Towards Direct Elections*. London: Allen & Unwin.

Priestley, J. (2008) *Six Battles that Shaped Europe's Parliament*. London: John Harper.

Proksch, S.-O. and Slapin, J.B. (2010) 'Position Taking in European Parliament Speeches', *British Journal of Political Science* 40(3): 587–611.

Proksch, S.-O. and Slapin, J.B. (2011) 'Parliamentary Questions and Oversight in the European Union', *European Journal of Political Research* 50(1): 53–79.

Prosser, C. (2016) 'Second Order Electoral Rules and National Party Systems: The Duvergerian Effects of European Parliament Elections', *European Union Politics* 17(3): 366–386.

Rasmussen, A. (2005) 'EU Conciliation Delegates: Responsible or Runaway Agents?', *West European Politics* 28(5): 1015–1034.

Rasmussen, A. (2008a) 'Party Soldiers in a Non-Partisan Community? Party Linkage in the European Parliament', *Journal of European Public Policy* 15(8): 1164–1183.

Rasmussen, A. (2008b) 'The EU Conciliation Committee: One or Several Principals?', *European Union Politics* 9(1): 87–113.

Rasmussen, A. (2011) 'Early Conclusion in Bicameral Bargaining: Evidence from the Co-decision Legislative Procedure of the European Union', *European Union Politics* 12(1): 41–64.

Rasmussen, A. and Reh, C. (2013) 'The Consequences of Concluding Codecision Early: Trilogues and Intra-Institutional Bargaining Success', *Journal of European Public Policy* 20(7): 1006–1024.

Rasmussen, A. and Toshkov, D. (2011) 'The Inter-institutional Division of Power and Time Allocation in the European Parliament', *West European Politics* 34(1): 71–96.

Rasmussen, M.K. (2008) 'Another Side of the Story: A Qualitative Case Study of Voting Behaviour in the European Parliament', *Politics* 28(1): 11–18.

Rasmussen, M.K. (2015) 'The Battle for Influence: The Politics of Business Lobbying in the European Parliament', *Journal of Common Market Studies* 53(2): 365–382.

Raunio, T. (1996) 'Parliamentary Questions in the European Parliament: Representation, Information and Control', *The Journal of Legislative Studies* 2(4): 356–382.

Raunio, T. (1999) 'The Challenge of Diversity: Party Cohesion in the European Parliament', in S. Bowler, D.M. Farrell and R.S. Katz (eds) *Party Discipline and Parliamentary Government*. Columbus: Ohio State University Press, pp. 189–207.

Raunio, T. (2000) 'Losing Independence or Finally Gaining Recognition? Contacts between MEPs and National Parties', *Party Politics* 6(2): 211–223.

Reh, C. (2014) 'Is Informal Politics Undemocratic? Trilogues, Early Agreements and the Selection Model of Representation', *Journal of European Public Policy* 21(6): 822–841.

Reh, C., Héritier, A., Bressanelli, E. and Koop, C. (2013) 'The Informal Politics of Legislation Explaining Secluded Decision Making in the European Union', *Comparative Political Studies* 46(9): 1112–1142.

Reif, K. and Schmitt, H. (1980) 'Nine Second-Order National Elections – A Conceptual Framework for the Analysis of European Election Results', *European Journal of Political Research* 8(1): 3–44.

Reuters (2016) *EU Promises Protesting Farmers More Help, No New Money*, 14 March, available at http://uk.reuters.com/article/uk-france-eu-agriculture-idUKKCN0WG20Y (accessed October 2016).

Ringe, N. (2010) *Who Decides, and How? Preferences, Uncertainty, and Policy Choice in the European Parliament*. Oxford: Oxford University Press.

Ripoll Servent, A. (2012) 'Playing the Co-Decision Game? Rules' Changes and Institutional Adaptation at the LIBE Committee', *Journal of European Integration* 34(1): 55–73.

Ripoll Servent, A. (2013) 'Holding the European Parliament Responsible: Policy Shift in the Data Retention Directive from Consultation to Codecision', *Journal of European Public Policy* 20(7): 972–987.

Ripoll Servent, A. (2014) 'The Role of the European Parliament in International Negotiations after Lisbon', *Journal of European Public Policy* 21(4): 568–586.

Ripoll Servent, A. (2015) *Institutional and Policy Change in the European Parliament: Deciding on Freedom, Security and Justice*. Houndmills: Palgrave Macmillan.

Ripoll Servent, A. and MacKenzie, A. (2012) 'The European Parliament as a "Norm Taker"? EU-US Relations after the SWIFT Agreement', *European Foreign Affairs Review* 17(Special Issue 2/1): 71–86.

Rittberger, B. (2003) 'The Creation and Empowerment of the European Parliament', *Journal of Common Market Studies* 41(2): 203–225.

Rittberger, B. (2005) *Building Europe's Parliament*. Oxford: Oxford University Press.

Rittberger, B. (2009) 'The Historical Origins of the EU's System of Representation', *Journal of European Public Policy* 16(1): 43–61.

Rittberger, B. (2012) 'Institutionalizing Representative Democracy in the European Union: The Case of the European Parliament', *Journal of Common Market Studies* 50(s1): 18–37.

Rittberger, B. (2014) 'Integration without Representation? The European Parliament and the Reform of Economic Governance in the EU', *Journal of Common Market Studies* 52(6): 1174–1183.

Roederer-Rynning, C. (2003) 'From "Talking Shop" to "Working Parliament"? The European Parliament and Agricultural Change', *Journal of Common Market Studies* 41(1): 13–35.

Roederer-Rynning, C. (2015) 'The Common Agricultural Policy: The Fortress Challenged', in H. Wallace, M.A. Pollack and A.R. Young (eds) *Policy-Making in the European Union*. Oxford: Oxford University Press, pp. 196–219.

Roederer-Rynning, C. and Greenwood, J. (2015) 'The Culture of Trilogues', *Journal of European Public Policy* 22(8): 1148–1165.

Roederer-Rynning, C. and Greenwood, J. (2017) 'The European Parliament as a Developing Legislature: Coming of Age in Trilogues?', *Journal of European Public Policy* 24(5): 735–754.

Roger, L. (2016) *Voice(s) in the European Parliament*, Baden-Baden: Nomos.

Roger, L. and Winzen, T. (2015) 'Party Groups and Committee Negotiations in the European Parliament: Outside Attention and the Anticipation of Plenary Conflict', *Journal of European Public Policy* 22(3): 391–408.

Rose, R. and Borz, G. (2013) 'Aggregation and Representation in European Parliament Party Groups', *West European Politics* 36(3): 474–497.

Rosén, G. (2015) 'EU Confidential: The European Parliament's Involvement in EU Security and Defence Policy', *Journal of Common Market Studies* 53(2): 383–398.

Rozenberg, O. (2009) 'L'Influence du Parlement Européen et l'Indifférence de ses Electeurs: Une Corrélation Fallacieuse?', *Politique européenne* 28(2): 7–36.

Salvati, E. (2016) 'Towards an European Parliamentary Class? A Proposal for a Typology of the MEPs', *Journal of Comparative Politics* 9(1): 59–74.

Sapala, M. (2013) 'The European Union Multiannual Financial Framework 2014–2020: How to Do More for Less?', *Policy Brief, Institute for European Studies, Vrije Universiteit Brussel* (05), available at http://www.ies.be/node/1525 (accessed February 2015).

Sartori, G. (1976) *Parties and Party Systems: A Framework for Analysis*. Cambridge: Cambridge University Press.

Saurugger, S. (2013) 'Constructivism and Public Policy Approaches in the EU: From Ideas to Power Games', *Journal of European Public Policy* 20(6): 888–906.

Scarrow, S.E. (1997) 'Political Career Paths and the European Parliament', *Legislative Studies Quarterly* 22(2): 253–263.

Schattschneider, E.E. (1942) *Party Government*, New York: Holt, Rinehart and Winston.

Scherpereel, J.A., Wohlgemuth, J. and Schmelzinger, M. (2017) 'The Adoption and Use of Twitter as a Representational Tool among Members of the European Parliament', *European Politics and Society* 18(2): 111–127.

Schmitt, H. (2005) 'The European Parliament Elections of June 2004: Still Second-Order?', *West European Politics* 28(3): 650–679.

Schmitt, H., Hobolt, S. and Popa, S.A. (2015) 'Does Personalization Increase Turnout? Spitzenkandidaten in the 2014 European Parliament Elections', *European Union Politics* 16(3): 347–368.

Schmitt, H. and Teperoglou, E. (2015) 'The 2014 European Parliament Elections in Southern Europe: Second-Order or Critical Elections?', *South European Society and Politics* 20(3): 287–309.

Schmitt, H. and Thomassen, J.J.A. (2009) 'The EU-Party System after Eastern Enlargement', *Journal of European Integration* 31(5): 569–587.

Schmitt, H. and Toygür, I. (2016) 'European Parliament Elections of May 2014: Driven by National Politics or EU Policy Making?', *Politics and Governance* 4(1): 167–181.

Schneider, G., Finke, D. and Bailer, S. (2010) 'Bargaining Power in the European Union: An Evaluation of Competing Game-Theoretic Models', *Political Studies* 58(1): 85–103.

Scholl, E.L. (1986) 'The Electoral System and Constituency-Oriented Activity in the European Parliament', *International Studies Quarterly* 30(3): 315–332.

Scully, R. (1997) 'Policy Influence and Participation in the European Parliament', *Legislative Studies Quarterly* 22(2): 233–252.

Scully, R. (2005) *Becoming Europeans? Attitudes, Roles and Socialisation in the European Parliament*. Oxford: Oxford University Press.

Scully, R. and Farrell, D.M. (2003) 'MEPs as Representatives: Individual and Institutional Roles', *Journal of Common Market Studies* 41(2): 269–288.

Scully, R., Hix, S. and Farrell, D.M. (2012) 'National or European Parliamentarians? Evidence from a New Survey of the Members of the European Parliament', *Journal of Common Market Studies* 50(4): 670–683.

Searing, D.D. (1991) 'Roles, Rules, and Rationality in the New Institutionalism', *The American Political Science Review* 85(4): 1239–1260.

Semetko, H.A., de Vreese, C.H. and Peter, J. (2000) 'Europeanised Politics – Europeanised Media? European Integration and Political Communication', *West European Politics* 23(4): 121–141.

Settembri, P. and Neuhold, C. (2009) 'Achieving Consensus through Committees: Does the European Parliament Manage?', *Journal of Common Market Studies* 47(1): 127–151.

Shackleton, M. (1998) 'The European Parliament's New Committees of Inquiry: Tiger or Paper Tiger?', *Journal of Common Market Studies* 36(1): 115–130.

Shackleton, M. (2000) 'The Politics of Codecision', *Journal of Common Market Studies* 38(2): 325–342.

Shackleton, M. and Raunio, T. (2003) 'Codecision since Amsterdam: a Laboratory for Institutional Innovation and Change', *Journal of European Public Policy* 10(2): 171–188.

Shaw, J. (2001) 'The Treaty of Nice: Legal and Constitutional Implications', *European Public Law* 7(2): 195–215.

Shepsle, K.A. (1989) 'Studying Institutions: Some Lessons from the Rational Choice Approach', *Journal of Theoretical Politics* 1(2): 131–147.

Shepsle, K.A. and Weingast, B.R. (1987) 'The Institutional Foundations of Committee Power', *The American Political Science Review* 81(1): 85–104.

Sigalas, E. (2011) 'When Quantity Matters: Activity Levels and Re-Election Prospects of Members of the European Parliament', *RECON Online Working Paper* 2011/17, available at http://www.reconproject.eu/projectweb/portalproject/AbstractRECONwp1117.html (accessed April 2016).

Sjursen, H. (2011) 'Not So Intergovernmental after All? On Democracy and Integration in European Foreign and Security Policy', *Journal of European Public Policy* 18(8): 1078–1095.

Slapin, J.B. (2014) 'Measurement, Model Testing, and Legislative Influence in the European Union', *European Union Politics* 15(1): 24–42.

Slapin, J.B. and Proksch, S.-O. (2010) 'Look Who's Talking: Parliamentary Debate in the European Union', *European Union Politics* 11(3): 333–357.

Smith, J. (1999) *Europe's Elected Parliament*. Sheffield: Sheffield Academic Press.

Smith, J. (2014) 'Between Ideology and Pragmatism: Liberal Party Politics at the European level', *Acta Politica* 49(1): 105–121.

Smith, M.P. (2008) 'All Access Points Are Not Created Equal: Explaining the Fate of Diffuse Interests in the EU', *British Journal of Politics & International Relations* 10(1): 64–83.

Socialists & Democrats (2013) *Joint Declaration by the EPP Group, S&D Group and ALDE Group on the Multi-annual Financial Framework*, 9 October, available at http://www.socialistsanddemocrats.eu/newsroom/joint-declaration-epp-group-sd-group-and-alde-group-multi-annual-financial-framework (accessed June 2014).

Sozzi, F. (2016) 'Asking Territories: The Constituency Orientation of Italian and French Members of the European Parliament', *Italian Political Science Review/Rivista Italiana di Scienza Politica* 46(Special Issue 02): 199–217.

Staat, C. and Kuehnhanss, C.R. (2017) 'Outside Earnings, Electoral Systems and Legislative Effort in the European Parliament', *Journal of Common Market Studies* 55(2): 368–386.

Startin, N. (2010) 'Where to for the Radical Right in the European Parliament? The Rise and Fall of Transnational Political Cooperation', *Perspectives on European Politics and Society* 11(4): 429–449.

Stavridis, S. and Irrera, D. (2015) *The European Parliament and Its International Relations*. London: Routledge.

Steunenberg, B. (1994) 'Decision Making under Different Institutional Arrangements: Legislation by the European Community', *Journal of Institutional and Theoretical Economics (JITE)/Zeitschrift für die gesamte Staatswissenschaft* 150(4): 642–669.

Stockemer, D. (2012) 'Citizens' Support for the European Union and Participation in European Parliament Elections', *European Union Politics* 13(1): 26–46.

Strøm, K. (1998) 'Parliamentary Committees in European Democracies', *The Journal of Legislative Studies* 4(1): 21–59.

Szczerbiak, A. and Taggart, P. (eds) (2008) *Opposing Europe?: The Comparative Party Politics of Euroscepticism: Volume 2: Comparative and Theoretical Perspectives.* Oxford: Oxford University Press.

Teasdale, A. (2012) 'Conference of Presidents', *The Penguin Companion to European Union,* available at http://penguincompaniontoeu.com/additional_entries/conference-of-presidents/ (accessed August 2016).

The Guardian (2003) *MEPs' fury at Berlusconi's Nazi jibe,* 2 July, available at https://www.theguardian.com/world/2003/jul/02/italy.eu (accessed August 2016).

The Guardian (2009) *Ukip Leader Nigel Farage Boasts of His £2m in Expenses,* 24 May, available at http://www.theguardian.com/politics/2009/may/24/mps-expenses-ukip-nigel-farage (accessed August 2016).

The Guardian (2010a) *Ukip MEP ejected for 'Ein Volk, ein Reich, ein Führer' jibe,* 24 November, available at https://www.theguardian.com/world/2010/nov/24/ukip-mep-ejected-godfrey-bloom (accessed February 2017).

The Guardian (2010b) *Ukip's Nigel Farage Tells Van Rompuy: You Have the Charisma of a Damp Rag,* 25 February, available at https://www.theguardian.com/world/2010/feb/25/nigel-farage-herman-van-rompuy-damp-rag (accessed August 2016).

The Guardian (2012) *Acta Down, but Not Out, as Europe Votes against Controversial Treaty,* 4 July, available at http://www.guardian.co.uk/technology/2012/jul/04/acta-european-parliament-votes-against (accessed August 2012).

The Guardian (2014a) *European Parliament Has 24 Official Languages, but MEPs Prefer English,* 21 May, available at https://www.theguardian.com/education/datablog/2014/may/21/european-parliament-english-language-official-debates-data (accessed July 2016).

The Guardian (2014b) *Nigel Farage Faces New Questions Over European Expenses,* 12 June, available at http://www.theguardian.com/politics/2014/jun/12/nigel-farage-europe-expenses-ukip (accessed August 2016).

The Guardian (2016a) *Dalai Lama Visit to Strasbourg Provokes Threats from China,* 19 September, available at https://www.theguardian.com/world/2016/sep/19/dalai-lama-visit-to-strasbourg-european-parliament-provokes-threats-from-china (accessed February 2017).

The Guardian (2016b) *EU Set to Ask Ukip Group to Repay almost £150,000 in 'Misspent Funds',* 17 November, available at https://www.theguardian.com/politics/2016/nov/17/eu-set-to-ask-ukip-group-to-repay-almost-150000-in-misspent-funds (accessed February 2017).

The Guardian (2016c) *Is Nigel Farage Right to Say MEPs Have Not Done 'Proper Jobs'?,* 28 June, available at http://www.theguardian.com/politics/2016/jun/28/is-nigel-farage-right-meps-have-not-done-proper-jobs (accessed August 2016).

The Guardian (2016d) *Ukip Scuffle: MEPs Steven Woolfe and Mike Hookem Reported to French Police,* 26 October, available at https://www.theguardian.com/politics/2016/oct/26/ukip-meps-steven-woolfe-and-mike-hookem-reported-to-french-police (accessed February 2017).

The Guardian, D. (2017) *European Parliament Passes EU-Canada Free Trade Deal Amid Protests,* 15 February, available at https://www.theguardian.

com/business/2017/feb/15/ceta-trade-deal-canada-eu-passed-european-parliament (accessed February 2017).

The Parliament Magazine (2014a) *From Assistant to MEP in Five Years*, 12 September, available at https://www.theparliamentmagazine.eu/articles/feature/assistant-mep-five-years (accessed August 2016).

The Parliament Magazine (2014b) *Parliament Magazine Briefing Puts Spotlight on MEP Assistants*, 24 July, available at https://www.theparliamentmagazine.eu/articles/news/parliament-magazine-briefing-puts-spotlight-mep-assistants (accessed August 2016).

The Parliament Magazine (2016a) *EU Parliament Urged to Investigate Possible Conflict of Interest Case Involving MEP*, 29 June, available at https://www.theparliamentmagazine.eu/articles/news/eu-parliament-urged-investigate-possible-conflict-interest-case-involving-mep (accessed August 2016).

The Parliament Magazine (2016b) *Fresh Allegations of Fraud Against MEP Morten Messerschmidt*, 21 October, available at https://www.theparliamentmagazine.eu/articles/news/fresh-allegations-fraud-against-mep-morten-messerschmidt (accessed February 2017).

The Sunday Times (2011) *Insight: Euro MPs Exposed in 'Cash-for-Laws' Scandal*, 20 March, available at http://www.thesundaytimes.co.uk/sto/news/insight/article582604.ece (accessed November 2016).

Thiem, J. (2006) 'Explaining Roll Call Vote Request in the European Parliament', *Arbeitspapiere - Mannheimer Zentrum für Europäische Sozialforschung*, 90, available at http://www.mzes.uni-mannheim.de/publications/wp/wp-90.pdf (accessed July 2011).

Thierse, S. (2016) 'Going on Record: Revisiting the Logic of Roll-Call Vote Requests in the European Parliament', *European Union Politics* 17(2): 219–241.

Thomson, R. (2011) *Resolving Controversy in the European Union: Legislative Decision-Making Before and After Enlargement*. Cambridge: Cambridge University Press.

Thomson, R., Stokman, F.N., Achen, C.H. and König, T. (eds) (2006) *The European Union Decides*. Cambridge: Cambridge University Press.

Thorlakson, L. (2005) 'Federalism and the European Party System', *Journal of European Public Policy* 12(3): 468–487.

Thym, D. (2006) 'Beyond Parliament's Reach? The Role of the European Parliament in the CFSP', *European Foreign Affairs Review* 11(1): 109–127.

Tilley, J., Garry, J. and Bold, T. (2008) 'Perceptions and Reality: Economic Voting at the 2004 European Parliament Elections', *European Journal of Political Research* 47(5): 665–686.

Tillman, E.R. (2004) 'The European Union at the Ballot Box? European Integration and Voting Behavior in the New Member States', *Comparative Political Studies* 37(5): 590–610.

Toshkov, D. and Rasmussen, A. (2012) 'Time to Decide: The Effect of Early Agreements on Legislative Duration in the EU', *European Integration online Papers (EIoP)* 16(1), available at http://eiop.or.at/eiop/index.php/eiop/article/view/2012_011a/228 (accessed May 2012).

Transparency International (2016) *How Many Lobbyists Are There in Brussels?*, available at http://www.transparencyinternational.eu/2016/09/how-many-lobbyists-are-there-in-brussels/ (accessed October 2016).

Transparency International (2017) *Access All Areas – When EU Politicians Become Lobbyists*, available at http://transparency.eu/access-all-areas (accessed February 2017).

Trauner, F. (2012) 'The European Parliament and Agency Control in the Area of Freedom, Security and Justice', *West European Politics* 35(4): 784–802.

Trauner, F. and Ripoll Servent, A. (2016) 'The Communitarization of the Area of Freedom, Security and Justice: Why Institutional Change Does Not Translate into Policy Change', *Journal of Common Market Studies* 54(6): 1417–1432.

Treib, O. (2014) 'The Voter Says No, but Nobody Listens: Causes and Consequences of the Eurosceptic Vote in the 2014 European Elections', *Journal of European Public Policy* 21(10): 1541–1554.

Trenz, H.-J. (2004) 'Media Coverage on European Governance Exploring the European Public Sphere in National Quality Newspapers', *European Journal of Communication* 19(3): 291–319.

Trumm, S. (2015) 'Voting Procedures and Parliamentary Representation in the European Parliament', *Journal of Common Market Studies* 53(5): 1126–1142.

Tsebelis, G. (1994) 'The Power of the European Parliament as a Conditional Agenda Setter', *The American Political Science Review* 88(1): 128–142.

Tsebelis, G. (1995) 'Conditional Agenda-Setting and Decision-Making Inside the European Parliament', *The Journal of Legislative Studies* 1(1): 65–93.

Tsebelis, G. and Garrett, G. (1996) 'Agenda Setting Power, Power Indices, and Decision Making in the European Union', *International Review of Law and Economics* 16(3): 345–361.

Tsebelis, G. and Garrett, G. (2000) 'Legislative Politics in the European Union', *European Union Politics* 1(1): 9–36.

Van den Putte, L., De Ville, F. and Orbie, J. (2014) 'The European Parliament's New Role in Trade Policy: Turning Power into Impact', *CEPS Special Reports* 89, available at http://www.ceps.eu/book/european-parliament%E2%80%99s-new-role-trade-policy-turning-power-impact (accessed February 2015).

van der Brug, W., Franklin, M.N. and Tóka, G. (2008) 'One Electorate or Many? Differences in Party Preference Formation between New and Established European Democracies', *Electoral Studies* 27(4): 589–600.

van der Eijk, C. and van Egmond, M. (2007) 'Political Effects of Low Turnout in National and European Elections', *Electoral Studies* 26(3): 561–573.

van der Eijk, C. and Franklin, M.N. (1996) *Choosing Europe? The European Electorate and National Politics in the Face of Union*. Ann Arbor: University of Michigan Press.

van der Eijk, C., Franklin, M.N. and Marsh, M. (1996) 'What Voters Teach Us about Europe-Wide Elections: What Europe-Wide Elections Teach Us about Voters', *Electoral Studies* 15(2): 149–166.

van Geffen, R. (2016) 'Impact of Career Paths on MEPs' Activities', *Journal of Common Market Studies* 54(4): 1017–1032.

van Hecke, S. (2010) 'Do Transnational Party Federations Matter? (… and Why Should We Care?)', *Journal of Contemporary European Research* 6(3): 395–411.

van Noije, L. (2010) 'The European Paradox: A Communication Deficit as Long as European Integration Steals the Headlines', *European Journal of Communication* 25(3): 259–272.

van Spanje, J. and de Vreese, C. (2011) 'So What's Wrong with the EU? Motivations Underlying the Eurosceptic Vote in the 2009 European Elections', *European Union Politics* 12(3): 405–29.

van Thomme, J., Ringe, N. and Victor, J.N. (2015) 'Explaining Reelection in the European Elections 2014', in M. Kaeding and N. Switek (eds) *Die Europawahl 2014*. Wiesbaden: Springer, pp. 335–344.

Varela, D. (2009) 'Just a Lobbyist?: The European Parliament and the Consultation Procedure', *European Union Politics* 10(1): 7–34.

Versluis, E., van Keulen, M. and Stephenson, P. (2010) *Analyzing the European Union Policy Process*. Houndmills: Palgrave Macmillan.

Verzichelli, L. and Edinger, M. (2005) 'A Critical Juncture? The 2004 European Elections and the Making of a Supranational Elite', *Journal of Legislative Studies* 11(2): 254–274.

Vesnic-Alujevic, L. (2013) 'Members of the European Parliament Online: The Use of Social Media in Political Marketing', *Centre for European Studies*, available at http://www.martenscentre.eu/publications/political-marketing-use-of-social-media (accessed December 2016).

Viola, D.M. (ed.) (2015) *Routledge Handbook of European Elections*. London: Routledge.

Votewatch (2014a) *End of Term Scorecard: The Activity Records of MEPs Analysed by Member State*, available at http://60811b39eee4e42e277a-72b421883bb5b133f34e068afdd7cb11.r29.cf3.rackcdn.com/2014/05/votewatch-europe-special-policy-brief-meps-activities-final-6-may.pdf (accessed February 2017).

Votewatch (2014b) *Super Grand Coalition EPP-S&D-ALDE Approves the New European Commission*, available at http://www.votewatch.eu/blog/super-grand-coalition-epp-sd-alde-approves-the-new-european-commission/ (accessed May 2015).

Votewatch (2015a) *Spitzenkandidaten, EU-Wide Constituency and 'Europeanisations' of Elections Rules for 2019, MEPs Asked*, available at http://www.votewatch.eu/blog/spitzenkandidaten-eu-wide-constituency-and-europenisations-of-elections-rules-for-2019-meps-asked/ (accessed April 2016).

Votewatch (2015b) *Who Holds the Power in the New European Parliament? And Why?*, available at http://www.votewatch.eu/blog/press-release-who-holds-the-power-in-the-new-european-parliament-and-why/, http://www.votewatch.eu/blog/press-release-who-holds-the-power-in-the-new-european-parliament-and-why/ (accessed February 2017).

Votewatch (2017) *Who are the Winners and Losers of the European Parliament's Reshuffle?*, available at http://www.votewatch.eu/blog/who-are-the-winners-and-losers-of-the-european-parliaments-reshuffle/, http://www.votewatch.eu/blog/who-are-the-winners-and-losers-of-the-european-parliaments-reshuffle/ (accessed February 2017).

Wagner, M. (2011) 'The Right in the European Parliament Since 1979', *Perspectives on European Politics and Society* 12(1): 52–67.

Walczak, A. and van der Brug, W. (2013) 'Representation in the European Parliament: Factors Affecting the Attitude Congruence of Voters and Candidates in the EP Elections', *European Union Politics* 14(1): 3–22.

Weber, T. (2007) 'Campaign Effects and Second-Order Cycles: A Top-Down Approach to European Parliament Elections', *European Union Politics* 8(4): 509–536.

Weber, T. (2009) 'When the Cat Is Away the Mice will Play: Why Elections to the European Parliament Are about Europe after All', *Politique européenne* 28(2): 53–71.

Weiler, J.H.H. (1995) 'Does Europe Need a Constitution? Demos, Telos and the German Maastricht Decision', *European Law Journal* 1(3): 219–258.

Weiler, J.H.H. (1999) *The Constitution of Europe: 'Do the New Clothes Have an Emperor?' and Other Essays on European Integration.* Cambridge: Cambridge University Press.

Wessels, B. and Franklin, M.N. (2009) 'Turning Out or Turning Off: Do Mobilization and Attitudes Account for Turnout Differences between New and Established Member States at the 2004 EP Elections?', *Journal of European Integration* 31(5): 609–626.

Westlake, M. (1994) *A Modern Guide to the European Parliament.* London: Pinter.

Whitaker, R. (2001) 'Party Control in a Committee-Based Legislature? The Case of the European Parliament', *Journal of Legislative Studies* 7(4): 63–88.

Whitaker, R. (2011) *The European Parliament's Committees: National Party Influence and Legislative Empowerment.* London: Routledge.

Whitaker, R. (2014) 'Tenure, Turnover and Careers in the European Parliament: MEPs as Policy-Seekers', *Journal of European Public Policy* 21(10): 1509–1527.

Wille, A. (2010) 'Political–Bureaucratic Accountability in the EU Commission: Modernising the Executive', *West European Politics* 33(5): 1093–1116.

Wille, A. (2012) 'The Politicization of the EU Commission: Democratic Control and the Dynamics of Executive Selection', *International Review of Administrative Sciences* 78(3): 383–402.

Wille, A. (2013) *The Normalization of the European Commission: Politics and Bureaucracy in the EU Executive.* Oxford: Oxford University Press.

Williams, C. and Spoon, J.-J. (2015) 'Differentiated Party Response: The Effect of Euroskeptic Public Opinion on Party Positions', *European Union Politics* 16(2): 176–193.

Wilson, S.L., Ringe, N. and van Thomme, J. (2016) 'Policy Leadership and Re-Election in the European Parliament', *Journal of European Public Policy* 23(8): 1158–1179.

Winzen, T. (2011) 'Technical or Political? An Exploration of the Work of Officials in the Committees of the European Parliament', *The Journal of Legislative Studies* 17(1): 27–44.

Winzen, T., Roederer-Rynning, C. and Schimmelfennig, F. (2015) 'Parliamentary Co-Evolution: National Parliamentary Reactions to the Empowerment of the European Parliament', *Journal of European Public Policy* 22(1): 75–93.

Wisniewski, E. (2013) 'The Influence of the European Parliament on the European External Action Service', *European Foreign Affairs Review* 18(1): 81–101.

Wüst, A.M. (2009) 'Parties in European Parliament Elections: Issues, Framing, the EU, and the Question of Supply and Demand', *German Politics* 18(3): 426–440.

Yordanova, N. (2009a) 'Legislative Power of the European Parliament Committees: Plenary Adoption of Committee Reports', in *European Union Studies Association (EUSA), Biennial Conference 2009*, available at http://www.unc.edu/euce/eusa2009/papers/yordanova_09D.pdf (accessed January 2015).

Yordanova, N. (2009b) 'The Effect of Inter-institutional Rules on the Division of Power in the European Parliament: Allocation of Consultation versus Codecision Reports', in *European Union Studies Association (EUSA), Biennial Conference 2009*, available at http://www.unc.edu/euce/eusa2009/papers/yordanova_10A.pdf (accessed January 2015).

Yordanova, N. (2011) 'Inter-institutional Rules and Division of Power in the European Parliament: Allocation of Consultation and Co-decision Reports', *West European Politics* 34(1): 97–121.

Yordanova, N. (2013) *Organising the European Parliament: The Role of Committees and Their Legislative Influence*. Colchester: ECPR Press.

Yordanova, N. and Mühlböck, M. (2015) 'Tracing the Selection Bias in Roll Call Votes: Party Group Cohesion in the European Parliament', *European Political Science Review* 7(03): 373–399.

Yoshinaka, A., McElroy, G. and Bowler, S. (2010) 'The Appointment of Rapporteurs in the European Parliament', *Legislative Studies Quarterly* 35(4): 457–486.

Index

Key: **bold** = extended discussion; b = box; f = figure; n = note; t = table

Name Index